THE CHURCHES AND SOCIAL ORDER IN
NINETEENTH- AND TWENTIETH-CENTURY CANADA

MCGILL-QUEEN'S STUDIES IN THE HISTORY OF RELIGION

Volumes in this series have been supported by the Jackman Foundation of Toronto.

SERIES TWO   In memory of George Rawlyk
Donald Harman Akenson, Editor

The Churches and Social Order in Nineteenth- and Twentieth-Century Canada

Edited by
Michael Gauvreau and
Ollivier Hubert

McGill-Queen's University Press
Montreal & Kingston · London · Ithaca

ISBN-13: 978-0-7735-3057-7   ISBN-10: 0-7735-3057-6 (cloth)
ISBN-13: 978-0-7734-3098-0   ISBN-10: 0-7735-3098-3 (paper)

Legal deposit third quarter 2006
Bibliothèque nationale du Québec

Printed in Canada on acid-free paper.

This book has been published with the help of a grant from the Canadian
Federation for the Humanities and Social Sciences, through the Aid
to Scholarly Publications Programme, using funds provided by
the Social Sciences and Humanities Research Council of Canada.

McGill-Queen's University Press acknowledges the support of the Canada
Council for the Arts for our publishing program. We also acknowledge
the financial support of the Government of Canada through the Book
Publishing Industry Development Program (BPIDP) for our publishing
activities.

Library and Archives Canada Cataloguing in Publication

The churches and social order in nineteeth and twentieth-century Canada/
edited by Michael Gauvreau and Ollivier Hubert.

(McGill-Queen's studies in the history of religion. Series two; 45)
Includes bibliographical references.
ISBN-13: 978-0-7735-3057-7   ISBN-10: 0-7735-3057-6 (bnd)
ISBN-13: 978-0-7734-3098-0   ISBN-10: 0-7735-3098-3 (pbk)

1. Christian sociology – Canada – History – 19th century. 2. Christian
sociology – Canada – History – 20th century. 3. Canada – Church history –
19th century. 4. Canada – Church history – 20th century. I. Gauvreau,
Michael, 1956– II. Hubert, Ollivier, 1968– III. Series.

BR570.C495 2006   277.1′081   C2006-901445-0

This book was typeset by Interscript in 10/13 Sabon.

Contents

Acknowledgments

This comparative conversation between specialists in English Canada and Quebec around the suggested theme of the interface of religious institutions and practices and the social order has incurred a number of debts. Nancy Christie launched our thinking in this direction during a stimulating evening of conversation in Montreal by suggesting the theme of "religion and social order" around which Protestant and Catholic historiographies might converge. As the project unfolded, participants had the opportunity to meet and discuss preliminary results of their research during a two-day symposium organized by Ollivier Hubert, "The Social Role of the Churches/Le rôle social des Églises," held at the Université de Montréal on 8-9 November 2002. The editors are grateful to the Social Sciences and Humanities Research Council's Aid to Occasional Conferences and International Congresses in Canada Programme, whose funds assisted both the organization of the symposium and the publication of this volume, to the Département d'histoire, Université de Montréal, and to Isabel Ménard, who ably took charge of organizational matters during the conference. Yvonne M. Klein skillfully and efficiently translated the French-language contributions into English.

We especially appreciate the keen interest and sound advice of Don Akenson, senior editor at McGill-Queen's University Press. From the inception of this project, Don urged us to consider ways in which to bring these findings to an international scholarly audience, and thus enhance the comparative dimension of the volume. Kyla Madden, editor at McGill-Queen's University Press, was always available to patiently answer our questions and to provide good advice while the manuscript was evaluated. We have had the benefit, during the course of many publication projects, of the skills and commitment of Joan McGilvray, the coordinating editor at the McGill office of the Press. Once again, we are extremely appreciative of her efforts to secure the highest standard of presentation. At the copyediting stage, Claude Lalumière brought a keen eye and sense of readable prose to the text, which has greatly improved the style of the manuscript.

Finally, we owe thanks to the anonymous readers, who offered the benefits of their insights into both Canadian and international social history of religion. However, this collective work would not have been possible without the enthusiasm, energy, and intellectual rigour of the contributors to this volume. We are profoundly grateful to them and to their willingness to explore a new pathway in Canadian religious history.

THE CHURCHES AND SOCIAL ORDER IN
NINETEENTH- AND TWENTIETH-CENTURY CANADA

Beyond Church History: Recent Developments in the History of Religion in Canada

MICHAEL GAUVREAU AND OLLIVIER HUBERT

"Monseigneur l'Évêque," declared the prominent Montreal Catholic layman George Edward Clerk in 1849, "preached an excellent sermon on the authority of the church."[1] Bishop Ignace Bourget's message insisted that Catholicism's claim to superiority over Protestantism's confusing welter of sects was founded upon a doctrinal and ritual integrity that had survived unaltered from a remote antiquity. However, Clerk's Catholic and Protestant contemporaries would have experienced the impact of the institutional church not simply through the oral medium of preaching, by which doctrinal imperatives were relayed to the audience, but through several overlapping systems of authority: church ritual and ceremonial, voluntary societies of philanthropy and moral reform, initiatives of popular education, and the print culture of public discourse. Particularly in Quebec, the Roman Catholic Church was massively engaged in the development of social services and both public and private education.[2] Despite Bourget's evocation of a church institution based upon a set of timeless truths and rituals, recent historical scholarship has insisted upon the recent nature and innovative quality of some of these modes of authority and social practice. The very claim to remote antiquity expressed by the sermons, elaborate ceremonies, and ritual performances was not a description of reality but a strategy designed to enhance and project the Church's authority in a civic order characterized by religious and ethnic pluralism and by religious conviction founded on voluntary choice.[3]

The existence of these differing institutional strategies in the Canadian churches, and the fact that both Protestant and Catholic clergy were constantly engaged in crafting an elaborate discourse setting forth the authority of the institutional church, raise the central questions around which the essays in this book revolve. What was the nature of the relationship between the Catholic and Protestant churches and the systems of social order that prevailed in Canada after 1800? Did the ways in which the institution presented and exercised its authority change over time, and did these transformations have a dynamic relationship to wider processes of change in the Canadian civic order during the nineteenth and twentieth centuries? Why did some modes of institutional authority fall into disuse, while newer strategies were introduced? To what degree were ordinary Catholics and Protestants able to appropriate church institutions to reinforce or alter their social aspirations or patterns of sociability, and how did these choices diverge from, or accord with, the social and cultural strategies outlined by the clergy? What new social and cultural dynamics, encompassing both consent and resistance, resulted from attempts made by institutional churches at particular historical junctures to modernize their structures and strategies of authority? Did these efforts produce overlapping systems of authority that caused stresses and tensions within the churches?

In addressing these questions, this volume, the fruit of sustained research and reflection by scholars in English Canada and Quebec, asserts a conviction that is fundamental to this line of inquiry: the necessity of a continued conversation and an ongoing elaboration of thematic comparisons between Protestantism and Catholicism.[4] It should be acknowledged at the outset that there have been historically significant theological, doctrinal, and liturgical differences between these two branches of Christianity, which have induced scholars to treat them in separate denominational compartments or to privilege the study of clerical ideologies that emphasize theological difference, taking this to be coextensive with the authority of the institution. However, a key consideration that emerges from the essays in this volume is that historical analysis of the strategies by which Catholic and Protestant churches elaborated and exercised authority and the ways in which believers participated in these systems of authority reveal a number of important similarities around which fruitful comparative research can be organized. The essays in this volume collectively demonstrate that by shifting the terrain of historical inquiry from intellectual history, which privileges theology and ideology, to the realm of the sociocultural, with its emphasis upon appropriation, meaning, and practice, the lineaments of the similar historical trajectories experienced by Catholics and Protestants are brought into the foreground. Indeed, by bringing together aspects of the historical experience of English Canada and Quebec, this project takes up the challenge posed by the eminent French religious historian Michel Lagrée, who urged religious historians to move beyond segmented geographical or national studies to explore more fully the "intra-Christian" dimensions of their sub-discipline.[5] For Canadians, who live in a society in which the historical enterprise is organized into linguistically separate "national" compartments that privilege exceptionalism, efforts at historical comparison serve the valuable purpose of providing both empirical evidence and methodological pathways that will contribute to the softening of deeply engrained cultural dissonances through shared scholarly endeavour.

Why do we need a historical treatment of the institutional churches, when both English Canada and Quebec already possess a substantial historiography that has positioned religion firmly within the trajectory of social history? In answering this question, two key considerations emerge. The first is the historical truism that, although religious belief and practice is not coterminous with religious organizations, the fact remains that in Canada, as in the rest of North America and in Western Europe during the nineteenth and twentieth centuries, the way in which people experienced and expressed their religious beliefs and values was dominated by continuous organizations such as churches, chapels, and voluntary associations linked to these bodies.[6] Although an important current of recent religious scholarship has insisted on the necessity of studying "lived religion" and directed attention to the need to examine the human agency implicit in the "extra-ecclesial" manifestations of religious belief and practice that occurred outside clerical "traditions" or denominational expressions, one of its leading practitioners, the US historian Robert Orsi, has cautioned historians against reading into this a dualistic model with an "elite" religion expressed in church institutions and a largely separate "popular" religion practiced outside institutional contexts. "[I]t would be unfortunate," concludes Orsi, "if the turn to lived religion meant simply changing the valence of the familiar dualities while preserving them, just substituting religious practices in the streets and workplaces for what goes on in the churches."[7] These considerations recapitulate the positions of an older historical debate that, in France,[8] emerged from the first attempts to use the concept of "popular religion." In Quebec, scholars have resolved this debate through studies that have, in essence, determined that religious practice and belief, at least before the mid-twentieth century, possessed no autonomy vis-à-vis the institutional church.[9] This scholarly consensus regarding the close fit between "popular" and institutional definitions of religion was accompanied in Quebec by a reorientation of research that, in a number of ways, has sought to understand, in all its complexity, the role of the institutional Catholic Church in the history of Quebec. The key corollary of this new trajectory in religious history is the question of regulation, which implies a relationship of social and cultural power between laypeople and church institution, or what David Hall has termed the "politics of religious practice," which revalidates the necessity of studying institutional strategies and their exercise in historical context.[10]

A second, and equally compelling, reason for a volume centred more precisely upon the institutional churches as entities, rather than upon the broader but more nebulous terrain of "religion," is that the social history of both English Canada and Quebec has experienced enormous difficulty – and evinced considerable resistance – at integrating the institutional expressions of Protestantism and Catholicism into its guiding interpretive or methodological frameworks. In the case of English Canada, there has been much recent criticism directed at the "fragmenting" nature of a type of social history based on the study of the limited identities of class, gender, ethnicity, and region.[11] These interpretive directions arose initially as a protest against the inattention to human agency and social conflict inherent in older models of "national" history that were driven by a political-economy calculus that privileged the centralizing projects of political and business elites and identified these with the Canadian nation itself. Despite the considerable animosity that this debate has generated, the critics of social history have by and large failed to appreciate that the study of the variables of class, ethnicity, gender, and region are in fact undergirded by a coherent view of the past and a precise set of historical assumptions shared by these scholars.[12] These assumptions rest, in their basic form, on a view of modernization driven by economic transformation as the primary motor of social change, which attempts to explain the social and cultural impact of the transition experienced by ordinary Canadians as they journeyed from a world of rural, pre-industrial social relations to an urban, industrial social environment. These socioeconomic categories are then presumed to drive cultural change by offering an irrefutable description of the passage from "tradition" to "modernity." At the same time in Quebec, historians coined the term "normal society" to affirm their society's confident and enthusiastic participation in the same process of socioeconomic, political, and even ideological transformation and, more programmatically, as a way of distancing themselves from earlier historical models centred on Quebec's religiocultural exceptionalism.[13]

In both societies, one great obstacle stands in the way of a dynamic and creative application of social history frameworks and methods to the institutional church. Both dominant historiographic paradigms, the "social history" and "normal society" approaches, rely implicitly and unquestioningly upon a master narrative of historical change supplied by the classic secularization theory, positing that modernization, generally defined as industrialization, urbanization, and the expansion of the capitalist market economy, necessarily diminishes the social significance of religion – if not giving rise to outright unbelief – by producing new forms of social differentiation, an individualist ethos, and cultural pluralism.[14] In this historical schema, secularization is both the religious flipside and the ineluctable outcome of modernization, which is viewed as a linear, irreversible process driven by economic causes. For this conventional interpretive framework of "modernization as secularization," churches and religious institutions are essentialized as passive entities acted upon, or belatedly responding to, larger processes of social change that are in the final analysis economic in character. First and foremost, social history posits religious institutions as typical of the close-knit, face-to-face communitarian social relations of premodern and pre-industrial people. In a period of rapid economic and social transformation, such as experienced by English Canada and Quebec especially after the 1880s, the churches become, in the orthodox secularization model, the repository of unchanging "tradition," buttresses of older communal social relations and remain mired in an idealized, utopian past. Because these relations are destined to rupture and disappear, the churches, out of step with new urban modes of social organization and industrial relations of production, are ultimately marginal to the course of history. In Quebec, the extra-religious role of the church (education, health, social assistance) was too important to be simply obliterated, and it thus posed problems because it could not be easily incorporated into the narrative structure of the "normal society." The Church was, to quote Louise Bienvenue, the basis of a "guilty conscience" for modernist Quebec historians.[15] Quebec's past, heavily imprinted by Catholicism, was, in the first instance, demonized, and then systematically attenuated, so that much of it still remains to be understood. However, Quebec historiography is now characterized by a postrevisionist current that seeks to escape the ideological paradigm of modernity and to come to terms with the obvious importance of religion and the Catholic Church in the history of Quebec.[16]

The linear historical trajectory of the classic secularization thesis has been recently refurbished in the context of the warfare in Canada between proponents of the new social history and the older nationalist school. A new organizing principle for Canadian history has been suggested by Ian McKay, who has proffered Foucauldian notions of "governmentality" to resolve acrimony between social history and the older nationalist paradigm. Canada, McKay asserts, can best be understood as a "liberal order," and he defines Canadian history as an ongoing application of liberalism as a "politico-economic logic." This involved the attempt by promoters of the liberal order – whom McKay dubs "insiders" – to extend "a belief in the epistemological and primacy of the category 'liberal'" across time and space. However, the liberal project was also, to some degree, resisted or reshaped by more or less marginal "outsiders."[17] In this key respect, McKay's positing of economic individualism as the motor of sociocultural change subscribes to the view of modernization that lies at the heart of the orthodox secularization thesis. However, if the intent of the "liberal order" paradigm is to provide a new, pan-Canadian standpoint that transcends the discourse of nationalist politics and from which to bring together and compare the histories of English Canada and Quebec, one of its consequences is to once again legitimize a perception of Quebec as a foil to English Canada that, because of the prominence of Catholic religious institutions, is rooted in ancient tradition and is thus ineluctably antimodern, standing outside and thus marginal to the Canadian liberal historical logic. Such a perspective would simply revitalize older tendencies in Quebec historical writing, which sought to minimize the place of religion in Quebec history in order to make it more "normal" – that is, a history that conforms to the dominant Canadian liberal myth.

For social historians who follow a more empirical agenda directed to exploring the process of class formation, churches likewise serve as antimodernist pillars of social hierarchy. According to this historical trajectory, churches are institutions in which middle-class dominance is assumed *a priori*. Religious institutions incarnate a "hegemony" of respectable values that they seek to impose on working-class or other "marginal" people; religious institutions are thus designated as a site of conflictual social relations between capitalists and workers or, in another version of the story, between the conflicting gender aspirations of men and women.[18] This type of interpretive strategy clearly essentializes the church as expressing at all times the values of social elites and the middle class and posits its essential function as a conservative pole in a social dynamic in which questions of power and inequality are treated as the expressions of an oscillation between imposition and resistance. Here, religion is but a superstructure of the economic and political order.

Another take on the story of "modernization as secularization" has been particularly attractive to a group of English Canadian religious historians who have sought to explain what they interpret as a period of extraordinary early-twentieth-century intellectual ferment and social activism in the Protestant churches. Rejecting the idea that the churches can simply be consigned to the realm of an inflexible social and cultural conservatism, they argue that, in fact, church institutions in Canada did seek to respond to the new liberal capitalist order by modernizing institutional values and practices. However, this "modernization" ultimately led to "secularization," because these cultural and intellectual accommodations were transitory and inherently unstable. Using a standard of theological orthodoxy that celebrates immobility as the touchstone of "true" religion – thus implicitly validating the view that churches can only be "traditional" institutions – they posit changing institutional structures and strategies as symptoms of inevitable decline, arguing that, in surrendering their distinctive theologies, Canada's Protestant churches ultimately weakened their own social and cultural power, as their heightened social initiatives did not compensate for the loss of a secure religious identity.[19] In both cases, although social historians concede that churches may retain considerable authority at certain moments during this process of social transformation, this social and cultural power is in the final analysis compromised and illegitimate. In the "modernization as secularization" story, the church has only two roles: either it acts as a conservative bulwark of elite hegemony and "traditional" social values that stands as an obstacle to the socially progressive, secular aspirations of an industrial working class; or it is a kind of unstable liberal consciousness destined to melt away under a corrosive individualism or to be recuperated by an expansive modern state. Because, in this type of narrative, church institutions can only be diminished by urban and industrial modernity, characterized by individualism, impersonal relations of production, the growth of class conflict, and the rise of bureaucratic state structures – concepts that form the metastructure of social history praxis – they are marginal and irrelevant, present in historical narrative only as a backdrop acted upon by larger social forces, rather than dynamic entities worthy of further study.

The central difficulty with the "modernization as secularization" pillar that undergirds the structure of Canadian social history is that it has largely lost any concrete point of reference in actual historical contexts or events, to become, in the words of the British historian Jeffrey Cox, a kind of free-floating, grand "master narrative" or "invocatory theory" that serves a kind of explanatory rhetorical purpose, operating in the background to "fill in the gaps in the historian's narrative, and to provide implicit explanation where explicit ones cannot be found."[20] Cox suggests that the central reason why this linear historical account that relates economic transformation, social history, and religious decline has enjoyed such power has little to do with whether it can be verified or falsified but that so many social scientists take secularization for granted and find the master narrative useful. Thus,

Cox urges historians to undertake a more modest enterprise when it comes
to relating churches to the dynamic of social history: rather than advancing
alternative master narratives, they should write persuasive critiques of the
"modernization as secularization" story that contest and unmask the master
narrative and, in so doing, suggest the possibility that there are other accounts of the human past[21] in which church institutions occupy different,
more dynamic social and cultural roles.

In particular, recent studies of religious change that focus on the experience of nineteenth-century Western Europe, generally viewed by historians
as the high age of social transformation, have seriously undermined the
necessary causal connection between economic modernization, urbanization, industrialization, and religious decline. Two main trajectories have
contributed to directing this new approach, both of which lead historians
ultimately to revise conventional notions that church institutions simply encapsulated the "traditional," unchanging, residual elements destined to be
displaced by the forces of urbanization and industrialization.

The first, building upon local community studies in a number of regions
of Western Europe, has adduced strong evidence for considerable religious
dynamism in industrial society, particularly during the nineteenth century.
This has had the effect of eroding the orthodox view of secularization as a
linear process and has implicitly urged historians to rethink the way in
which they have related church institutions to the analytical frameworks of
social history. Callum Brown, one of the most effective critics of the orthodox model of secularization, has shifted the axis of religious change from
urban to rural, contending that earlier accounts of the social history of religion had invested far too much in assuming a simple dichotomy between
rural/pre-industrial and urban/industrial capitalism. Rather than being the
repositories of immobile traditional social relations, rural areas in Europe
after 1750 were the crucibles of new, dynamic religious cultures whose institutional expressions promoted greater individualism, the linking of religious dissent to emerging class identities, and a separation of religion and
the work system – all values identified by social historians as synonymous
with a rising capitalist society.[22] Recently, French historiography has generated a number of syntheses organized around the theme of religion and culture in nineteenth-century Europe. These works, written as texts for a
university competition on the theme, allow us to appreciate, apart from the
still rather rudimentary integration of comparative insights by francophone
scholarship, the scope of the historiographic reversal that has occurred in
European studies of religion.[23] Secularization is no longer the unifying paradigm, and the imperative is now to explore the crises and adaptations that

have occurred in the religious sphere. More significantly, there is a common insistence among these scholars that historical chronologies of religious change are complex and non-linear, with wide national and regional variations, and that these differ also according to gender, class, ethnicity, and other social variables. Thus, beneath the dominant antimodernist discourse of the Catholic Church, we find a religious culture in step with new developments in technology[24] and mass culture.[25]

By describing rural societies as socially and culturally dynamic in terms of large-scale social change, Brown makes a strong case for considering the cultural continuities in the values and experiences rural migrants brought to large cities, stating that when these people saw urban churches divided by social class, and perceived the churchgoers and non-churchgoers also divided by level of wealth, he or she was not in essence seeing something new. He/she was not being confronted with a new agenda of issues upon which to make his/her own decisions about religious affiliation. The rural environment he/she had just left not only replicated those divisions, but had in essence created them. Pluralization of denominations started in the countryside and then spread to cities, not vice versa.[26]

If, in fact, the story of modernization begins in the countryside, this radical shift in religious ecology also entails considerable revision to the orthodox categorization and chronology that social history has assigned to the churches. One of the central tenets of the "modernization as secularization" master narrative that has dominated social history practice is the assumption that secularization's relationship to the rise of urbanization and industrial capitalism can be summed up in the alienation of the working class from the churches during the course of the nineteenth century. In the highly industrialized society of Great Britain, not only were there important continuities in popular culture and religious life at least until the 1870s, which sustained the growth of church institutions of all types, but the view that churches were the purview of the middle classes and either excluded or marginalized working-class people fails the empirical test of evidence. As Simon Green has succinctly concluded: "Religious commitment – total, partial, negligible – was not a function of social class."[27] Well into the mid-twentieth century, according to British social historians, working-class membership and participation in church institutions remained very high,[28] indicating that institutional definitions of religious identity and practice evoked considerable resonance, and not simply alienation, in working-class communities.

In a significant, more culturalist direction to the story of the relationship of the Churches to the working classes, a number of British historians have argued that this involvement cannot simply be summed up by statistical measures of official membership, attendance, or non-attendance at church services. Men and women of all social classes also encountered the institutional churches through the public discourses these bodies produced, a "discursive" religiosity in which ordinary people subscribed to, appropriated, selected, and altered official Christian prescriptions regarding personal identity and conduct.[29] Such studies, however, should not lead historians into the fallacy of dismissing working-class alienation from and outright ideological opposition to churches in the form of militant unbelief. Powerful currents and movements of alienation did exist, as a number of studies of France, Germany, and Spain reveal. These, however, had particular contingent causes other than simply the presence of cities and industrial capitalism: in France, governments after 1870 deliberately set out to construct a republican political citizenship anchored on an outright evisceration of Catholicism's institutional presence in the state; in Germany, a socialist subculture in a number of large cities offered working-class people an alternative, "secular" pole of identity[30]; and in Spain the Catholic Church was prevented by internal institutional considerations from expanding its parish structure into working-class neighbourhoods.[31] By contrast, during this period, industrialized societies like Britain, the Netherlands, and Belgium experienced high levels of both Protestant and Catholic church growth and a considerable expansion of the churches' presence in urban settings; these developments fostered a strong sense of religious adherence and identity among significant sections of the industrial working class in each of these countries.[32] In each of these cases, institutional logics, organizational alternatives, and the political relationship between church and state appear to have been decisive, and not the fact that there was a working class. From this literature emerges one forceful conclusion: working-class alienation from the institution simply cannot be taken as an inevitable axiom of social relations in urban industrial capitalism. Indeed, as Hugh McLeod concludes, some of the lowest levels of church participation in Western Europe could be found in rural sections of France and Germany.[33]

A second trajectory of revision to the conventional view of secularization takes a more cultural history direction, moving away from the emphasis in British and French historiography on statistical measurements of phenomena like church membership and the class character of churches to consider the question of what did religious institutions mean in particular historical contexts. One of the central problems facing social historians who write about religious institutions is a tendency to essentialize, to assume implicitly that churches represent the immobile and unchanging "traditional" elements of Western society and that key concepts like "church," "religiosity," "world," and "society" have undergone fundamentally no transformation in meaning since the seventeenth century. One particularly long-abiding historical fallacy is the idea that rural, premodern societies were characterized by nearly unanimous levels of religious conviction and commitment and that, consequently, "modernization" marks a declension of religion because people fell away from supposedly high levels of church participation and commitment. As stated by the German historian Lucian Hölscher, "Only a few historians realize that the relationship between religious and urban life was shaped not only by structural change in secular society but, equally, by a change in the understanding of 'religion.'"[34]

According to Hölscher, two key developments in the meaning of religious institutions characterized the passage from pre-industrial to modern, changes that cannot simply be ascribed to the impact of industrial capitalism. In most European countries in the early eighteenth century, spiritual and secular authority, religion and law, were completely intermeshed, and "spiritual authority concerned itself as much with people's lives as citizens as with their souls."[35] Sometime after 1750, in a gradual series of developments that characterized both Catholics and Protestants, the church came to be seen less as an official institution of authority and control than as a religious society of those sharing in a common faith, in which the strengthening and expansion of religion could not be left to the civil authorities but was a task that had to be undertaken by the faithful themselves. Here, the change cannot simply be attributed to economic causes: policies of religious toleration pursued by European monarchies and the intellectual and cultural impact of the Enlightenment, which more firmly located religious conviction in the individual conscience, powerfully contributed to this new understanding. What emerged after 1800 was a new concept of Christian piety more narrowly concentrated in the specifically religious sphere, which accented church life, rather than outward civic conformity, as its real religious content. Church practices became freed from civil tasks, an outlook evident in various forms of Protestant evangelicalism and equally in Catholic ultramontanism.[36] Ironically, some of the characteristic assumptions of social historians concerning religious change emerge from the particular religious mentality that arose at this time. European clergy construed the cities and the working classes as special "problems" from which irreligion would emerge and, against this, juxtaposed an idealized view of rural areas as bastions of solid religious values and patterns of adherence, notions that had less to do with social description than with particular rhetorical strategies. From the new religious values of this period came a fixation on church attendance – the question that drives so many approaches to the social history of religion – as the principal barometer of religiosity, an insistence that did not characterize premodern societies.[37]

A second key change in meaning identified by Hölscher was more evident after the 1840s: first in Catholicism, and followed by Protestants by the 1880s, the definition of religious mentality and loyalty to the church expanded outward from the confines of the congregation, a process that had little to do with formal measurements of church attendance and cannot be directly connected to higher rates of urbanization or changes in the nature of industrial capitalism. No longer was religious commitment understood merely as participation in church rites; increasingly, church life was taken up by "church organizations, and, on the periphery of the church, by religious associations, lectures, and evangelistic missions,"[38] a culture of lay religious voluntarism outside of formal church structures that significantly expanded the institutional presence of the churches and the meaning of religious conviction and commitment. Although similar to the British historiographical trajectory, this culturalist approach has not yet offered sufficient data regarding the social presence of the churches in the twentieth century. However, its distinctive contribution has been to alert historians to the possibility that the study of religious institutions can enter social history without being confined within the conventional subset of questions restricted to notions of urbanization and class formation, and one in which the churches need not be situated within a metanarrative fixated on secularization and decline. Thus, this approach works within a more nuanced historical framework that considers churches as a system of shifting meanings and practices and pays particular attention to specific intra- and inter-institutional dynamics.

Hugh McLeod has aptly summarized what he considers the new historical consensus on the subject of secularization, describing Western Europe in 1914 as characterized by a "fine balance" between the forces of religion and secularity that endured until the 1960s. The clearest evidence for secularization, he argues, can be seen in areas of individual religious belief and evidence of formal religious practice. Secularization was far more ambiguous on the terrain of interaction between religion and public institutions and much weaker when historians consider religious identities and popular culture.[39] McLeod's caveats, and the culturalist emphasis on contextualized meanings, implicitly urge social historians to consider more intensively the changes in institutional frameworks, organizational strategies, and the church-generated discourses by which the churches sought to secure greater public authority. Of equal significance, it was always within and in reference to institutions that people practiced their forms of Christianity and expressed their personal religious identities: there is no absolute dichotomy between an elite institution incarnating "official" religion and a "popular" religion existing outside, and in opposition to, institutional definitions.

What, then, are the implications of this revisionist historiography for social historians concerned with elucidating a relationship between religious transformation and social change? First, if secularization is to be retained as a concept that describes an ongoing interface between religion and society, it must be separated from an idea of linear causation that overprivileges economic transformation and identifies it as the simple outcome of the attainment of an urban, industrial capitalist society. Second, historians urgently require an alternative to the identification of churches purely with the static, the unchanging, the antimodern, and the impositional models of class hegemony, in which religious institutions serve as a sort of "foil" to "the social" characterized by the dynamisms of class and gender that are setting the pace of modernization. If, in a number of key historical contexts, the churches themselves were active mediators of social and cultural modernity, this realization bids historians to generate a language and set of conceptual tools that do not simply rely upon a monolithic model of capitalist transformation but appreciate that church institutions have their own social and cultural logics that are not necessarily dictated by economic change or that exist to encapsulate overly dichotomized notions of class oppression and resistance. More generally, the theory of secularization has been exposed as too Western-centred and elitist[40] and, further, has been unable to account for the evolution of the religious factor in human societies, an evolution that presents itself as an ongoing and complex recomposition of beliefs, practices, and institutions. This reversal of perspective will contribute to a new and lasting relationship between religious history and social history by recognizing religion as a social fact.[41]

To what extent can these new approaches to the history of religious institutions reshape the way in which Canadian historians have approached the relationship between the churches and social history? For all the cultural distances between English Canada and Quebec, the linear, economically driven model of secularization and its central corollary, the immobile church, has had considerable resonance in both historical communities. Among historians of Protestantism, the work of the sociologist S.D. Clark stands out particularly as having cast a very long shadow over the agenda and content of religious history. Written just after the Second World War, Clark's magisterial *Church and Sect in Canada* posited a "conflict between forces of order and separation" as fundamental to understanding Canadian social and religious development.[42] In tracing Canadian religious history from 1760 to 1940, he insisted upon the perpetual central tension between, on the one hand, formal, bureaucratic "churches" – which he considered a function of "capitalist forms of organization and of economic enterprise," incarnating the social aspirations of urban social elites and the middle classes, and which were increasingly run as capitalist business organizations devoted to evolving "techniques of control" – and, on the other, the "sect" – which expressed the social and cultural instability of the marginal inhabitants of frontier settler communities and which was evident in wildly irrational, enthusiastic forms of religion.[43] In Clark's historical narrative, the church had only one role: it was the institutional expression of the middle class and the emerging capitalist order, i.e., the product of new economic conditions.[44] The ultimate fate of church institutions in urbanizing society could, in Clark's story, be summed up as loss and decline: identification with the middle classes meant loss of spirituality in favour of rational discourses, approaches, and methods and a consequent alienation of workers and rural folk from this middle-class social and cultural hegemony. These social elements, much to the chagrin of Clark and like-minded academics, frequently chose membership in new sectarian religions, such as the Salvation Army, as a form of protest against the bureaucratized class dominance evident in the churches.[45]

Similarly, fear of the "masses" and critiques of rural, "folk" forms of Catholicism held sway among Catholic intellectuals in postwar Quebec. Powerfully influenced by currents of US social science, with its concept of static "folk society," and the French religious sociology of Gabriel LeBras, which introduced the idea of quantitative study of Catholic religious practice as a supposedly objective measurement of religious vitality or decline,[46] these social scientists highlighted two key concepts of the conventional secularization story: that urban growth and the working classes were agents of dechristianization; that there existed radically dichotomized "elite" and "popular" religions. These Catholic academics agonized over what they maintained was the inevitable decline of this type of "folk society" religion when confronted by the new "global society" characterized by metropolitan cities, mass media, and new, totalizing state institutions that redefined citizenship in completely secular terms.[47] These historiographical priorities crystallized around the problem of explaining why Quebec had supposedly, until the cultural and ideological ferment of the 1960s, been a monolithically, largely immobile Catholic society and was now experiencing a spiritually disorienting process of rapid secularization. The result was a series of colloquia held in the 1970s and early 1980s on the problem of "popular religion,"[48] which, according to its promoters, had been, until very recently among the francophone Catholics of North America, "medieval in its structures, in its forms and mentalities."[49] The fascination with this supposed popular religion[50] was due to the fact that historians reckoned that it was one of the crucial factors explaining why Quebec's cultural and ideological entry into the modern world had been so long delayed. They believed that this type of religion, a central feature of rural communities, had anchored an immobile Catholic Church institution that stood outside and opposed to the "modernizing" forces of industrialization and urbanization. Despite the endurance and institutional power of the Catholic Church – and here lay the central foundation of the antimodern exceptionalism that governed the historiographic agenda of this generation of Quebec historians – Catholicism's decline and dissolution was the fated outcome of the same universal processes of urban and industrial modernization.

In English Canada, two key historiographical developments refurbished and reinvigorated Clark's paradigm between the 1970s and the mid-1990s; despite growing interest in religious phenomena and identities among social historians, their combined influence contributed to the even further abstraction and virtual disappearance of church institutions as a historical problem. The first was the importation of US social science models that privileged religious revivals and awakenings as "exceptional" moments of cultural transformation. In and of themselves, the theories of the anthropologist Anthony Wallace and the historian William McLoughlin could have led to a more sensitive treatment of the historical negotiation between religious institutions and individual beliefs and practices. However, they took as their starting point a static, virtually ahistorical definition of institutions that posited that these stood for continuity, regularity, and normative order, and thus served as an immobile structure acted upon by more dynamic impulses in history and society. Indeed, it is difficult to escape the conclusion that religious institutions were simply a foil that repressed the creativity and spontaneity of individuals. For these interpreters of revivals, the motive impulses of history had their roots in the stress and loss of identity experienced at particular junctures in the past by individuals whose lives were lived within institutional constraints. The result of this encounter was a "crisis of legitimacy" in the institution, and thus began a cycle of protest, experimentation, and greater spontaneity, culminating finally in mass conversion to new religious movements and, ultimately, the elaboration of new institutional structures and practices – what Wallace termed the "mazeways" of society.[51] In the US context, the anti-institutional implications of this historical theory were eagerly seized upon by a number of religious historians who appropriated it as a fundamental explanation for the supposed post-Revolutionary novelty of US cultural life, characterized by radical individualism, a democratization of culture, an assault on older ideas of hierarchy and order in church and state, and the possibility of new charismatic leadership outside of the confines of institutions, which implicitly were devalued and viewed with suspicion as in some way opposed to the desirable elements of the US character.[52] Because these historians viewed revivals and awakenings as cyclical phenomena, the dynamic was always the same: a struggle between, on the on hand, conservatism and tradition – always represented by inflexible priorities of the organization and the institution – and, on the other, the spontaneity and desire for freedom of the individual.

What occurred when this US revivalist paradigm was applied to English Canada's non-revolutionary politico-religious culture? During the 1980s, the work of George Rawlyk and William Westfall followed the US trajectory in identifying religious revivals as defining moments of fundamental cultural change. While Rawlyk's work largely celebrated the highly individualist, anti-institutional character of enthusiastic religion and regarded the emergence of more structured religious organizations and practices after 1830 as a religious declension,[53] that of Westfall paid considerably more attention to the content of religious ideology and discourse. Unlike Rawlyk, Westfall acknowledged the more culturally dynamic role of "order" and "institutions" in shaping Canadian society, but he gave relatively little attention to describing or contextualizing how and why the practices, structures, and meanings of religious institutions changed. More tellingly, the centrality of the emergence of a "Protestant consensus" simply made more ironclad Clark's belief that the churches were simply hegemonic expressions of middle-class notions of social order.[54] In the 1990s, a second historiographic current, owing its inspiration to currents of cultural Marxism that influenced the wider climate of Canadian social history, was superimposed on the trajectory of English Canadian Protestantism. Lynne Marks's study of small-town Ontario in the 1880s rested on two central dialectical oppositions: the first was one in which mainstream churches, controlled by the middle classes and expressing hegemonic values and gender identities of middle-class respectability – Westfall's "Protestant consensus" with a much harder capitalist edge – were sources of alienation for the "marginal" members of society, the working class, women, and the young, who found their outlets in sectarian, revivalistic religions like the Salvation Army.[55] The second was revivalistic religion, which functioned in this narrative as the antithesis of the institution and was treated by Marks in a manner similar to that of the British Marxist E.P. Thompson. Thompson's relationship (and, by implication, the relationship of cultural Marxism) to enthusiastic, revivalistic religions like Methodism was complex and ambiguous. At one level, Thompson believed that these religious expressions limited and constrained the political consciousness of working-class people – and acted to this extent as a structure of "false" consciousness. However, they were important subjects of historical study because they played a role in shaping the identity of the common people, as they incarnated a set of practices and ideologies and a sense of community that were assumed to be opposed to the structured, bureaucratic religion of "elites" such as the clergy.[56]

For all its emphasis on collective identity and examination of working-class institutions, the application of cultural Marxism to Canadian religious history has not fundamentally altered the parameters established by the church-sect dichotomy and the US revivalist celebration of individualism and spontaneity. Indeed, the fundamental assumption remains that the progressive impulses in human society are anti-institutional and that in religious terms they are to be found in the spontaneous and enthusiastic movements that are assumed, rather than demonstrated, to be working class in character. Opposed to these is an "official" system of religious and social constraints, found in mainstream church institutions that, again, are cast as class expressions of conservatism and social immobility. The institution is essentialized, rather than problematized, because there is no sense that the whole concept of "church" itself may have been in the process of change during the 1880s, from an institution based on a structure of local congregations directed to securing "public order" to a more complex and diverse organization that was attempting to restate and reposition its authority in a more voluntaristic culture.[57] Despite much recent attention historians of both English Canada and Quebec have given to the emergence of a "liberal order," analytical treatments have remained tethered to a top-down, state-centred model and have, to date, largely neglected Jean-Marie Fecteau's call for a more finely textured analysis of the voluntaristic impulse that, of necessity, would centre upon the way in which church institutions responded both to government imperatives and the demands of local groups for new devotional styles and the urge for self-improvement.[58] What effects did the spread of a penumbra of Christian and often interdenominational voluntary associations associated with the churches producing a specialized discourse directed at age and gender categories have on older ideas of membership, commitment, methods of finance, and older discourses of social authority?[59] Can these institutional choices and often acrimonious negotiations that accompanied them simply be explained by constantly deploying hackneyed, free-floating concepts like "industrialization" and the "rise of the working classes," which reduce religious institutions to a simple function of changing economic relations? Because of the centrality of revivalism as the central hermeneutic for both cultural Marxist and neo-conservative historians of religion,[60] both accept the ironclad linear equation between religious change and decline.

With or without the class superstructure added to Clark's conflictual model of church and sect, the polarizing of revivalism/popular/dynamic versus institutional church/elite/immobility posits an antithesis that simply may not have been lived by people in the past. The few intensive examinations of Protestant institutions that we have reveal that, unlike historians, contemporaries rarely made a choice between spontaneous enthusiasm and institutional control. How, for example, are we to interpret the decision of mainstream church institutions in the early twentieth century to create organizational machinery on a national scale that would deploy *both* revivalism and new, more bureaucratic methods of social service to defining a new, more inclusive kind of "cultural" Christianity that de-emphasized older denominational identities and overtly sought to undermine structures of local religious authority?[61]

By contrast, in Quebec, the 1980s and 1990s witnessed not the disappearance of religious institutions from the historiographic terrain but their movement to the centre of historical debate. By 1982, the attempt to elucidate an autonomous "popular religion" had come to an end: as bluntly stated by Guy Laperrière, "in Quebec, popular religion exists only because of the clergy, whereas in Europe, it was the expression of pagan survivals that the clergy could not uproot."[62] Here was a clear message to historians to bring the institutional church back into the spotlight as the key reference point around which people articulated their religious identities and practices. However, cautioned Laperrière, historians must not fall back into the fallacy of refurbishing the pre-Quiet Revolution idea that Catholicism had been, from 1840 until 1960, a social and cultural monolith in which the clergy exerted a total hegemonic control over religious life. The urgent task, in his estimation, was that historians should problematize ultramontanism by introducing the history of theology and spirituality to interpret it as a system of religious practices and devotions that had succeeded earlier ones. By implication, this raised the possibility of institutional dynamism and change, in that the rise of ultramontanism may not have been simply imposed but had to be promoted through a variety of new institutions and strategies by particular groups of Catholics.[63]

Extending from the 1980s and into the 1990s, historians took up Laperrière's challenge, and one overriding question came to the fore among historians of Catholicism: what was the nature and meaning of the social and cultural transformation that occurred within Catholicism between 1840 and 1890? Two strands of interpretation, each marked by a particular reference point in international historical paradigms, became locked in debate. One trajectory, associated with Louis Rousseau, sought to explain ultramontanism within categories imported from the United States and Ireland, drawn from the "cultural revitalization" hypothesis of US Protestant historians and from Emmet Larkin's influential concept of a "devotional revolution" applied to the relationship between the Famine and the transformation of Irish Catholicism.[64] Based on clerically generated data concerning the adherence to the Church's prescription of Easter communion, Rousseau argued that, prior to the 1840s, Quebec Catholics were not a particularly believing or devout people, and in 1836 religious life was at a low ebb, the Church's institutions were characterized by spiritual lukewarmness, political conservatism and alliance with British colonial elites, and general pastoral inefficiency. As a result of the defeat of political nationalism during the Rebellions of 1837, Quebec experienced a "cultural crisis" at the levels of both collective and individual psychology. The outcome was a mass reawakening of individual religious fervour in the early 1840s, marked by a growing propensity to take Easter communion and a series of large-scale religious revivals, which prompted Catholic leaders to undertake a series of institutional innovations in training new clergy, initiatives of popular education, and the creation of devotional and voluntary associations.[65]

A second historiographical trajectory emerged from a series of criticisms leveled at Rousseau's work. Although Rousseau certainly subscribed to the notion that changing religious institutions were a key element in Quebec's religious revival and cultural transition to ultramontanism, they were assigned a secondary role to psychological seismic shifts within the culture, which were given pride of place as causal factors in Quebec's religious revolution. Rousseau's views on both the timing and nature of the rise of ultramontanism in Quebec were soon subjected to critical scrutiny by a group of historians operating out of the Université du Québec à Trois-Rivières. These scholars did not adopt the metahistorical categories of US or Irish historians; rather, they sought a more precise series of comparisons provided by data derived from a series of regional French monographs on nineteenth-century religious changes in a variety of dioceses.[66] René Hardy, for example, contended that Rousseau had overstated the suddenness of the religious transformation: very few cultures, he believed, ever experienced the kind of "revolution" that Rousseau described.[67] The process, which he described as an "acculturation" rather than an "awakening," began in fact within the precincts of the institutional Catholic Church in the 1820s and continued over the course of several decades. It was not until the late 1880s that the religious practices of the people had actually been brought into conformity with clerical prescription.[68] In this process, the key actor was the institutional church itself, rather than the impact of outside "crises" or the occasional interpositions of mass religious fervour. Religious change was the result of a gradual perfecting of an institutional apparatus of social control, evident in clerical training, a devotional culture that reinterpreted the place of sacraments like confession, the organization of parish life in voluntary associations, and the control of public education by the Catholic Church. Hardy's relationship between institutional change and cultural renewal was dynamic, because the implication was always present that the church's social control could be negotiated or contested. However, unlike the view that prevailed among many historians of English Canadian Protestantism, religious contestation was not primarily a function of class antagonism, although Hardy's analysis frequently noted the collaboration between the French Canadian bourgeoisie and the clergy. Conflicts often resulted from the presence in parishes of both lay and clerical elements who adhered to older models of spirituality and devotional practice and who, for religious reasons, were reluctant to adopt the innovations of the senior clergy and church hierarchy.

While the controversy over the origins of ultramontanism in Quebec has certainly brought religious institutions into greater relief, the basis of historical inquiry still remains narrow. The debate turns on the measurement of indices of Easter communion and confession, which takes in only a small range of how people actually experienced the institution. For example, while historians of English Canadian Catholicism have devoted considerable attention to changing views of charity and the nature of associational life,[69] these strategies of authority have received very little study from historians of ultramontanism in Quebec.[70] Further, despite Hardy's claim that the most important component in the Church's structure of authority was public education, there has been a dearth of scholarly work that actually contextualizes the nature and content of the Catholic Church's control of the school. More problematically, this historiography, like its English Protestant counterpart, falls too easily back on linear and economically determinist views of religious decline, particularly in attempting to describe what happened to Catholic Quebec in the twentieth century. Hardy, for example, concludes that the weakening and ultimate collapse of Catholicism was a function of "the capitalist logic of the urban environment,"[71] a falling back on a historical position already disproved for a number of highly industrialized societies, but an explanation attractive for historians who seek more remote causes for the rapid loss of Catholicism's political, cultural, and social authority in the 1960s. For historians of Quebec Catholicism, further advances in placing religious institutions into the mainstream of social history will hinge upon their ability to resist simply reading the Quiet Revolution backwards and positing it as the fated outcome of an encounter between an immobile, antimodern church and dynamic, nonreligious social forces that epitomize modernity.

In Quebec, historical research on religion has been strongly oriented to accounting for the apparent and unsettling exceptionalism defined by the weakness of the state and the correspondingly important social role of the Catholic Church and, more generally, the issue of the confessionalization of the social sphere. These studies have, however, adopted divergent emphases according to whether one seeks to explain the rise of this system (in the middle of the nineteenth century) or its progressive dismantling (after the mid-twentieth century). The conventional tendency of historians has been to show that events such as the establishment of the ultramontane hegemony or the "Quiet Revolution" had long chronological antecedents. Thus, René Hardy characterized the "Réveil" of the 1840s as but a stage in a long and conscious attempt by the Church to extend its authority. Ollivier Hubert has taken this argument further in situating the power of the clergy in the second half of the nineteenth century within a long process by which the Church, from its beginnings in colonial New France in the seventeenth century, sought to affirm and consolidate the Tridentine model.[72]

If, on the one hand, specialists in nineteenth- and twentieth-century religious history have been brought together by the common practice of seeking increasingly remote antecedents for the stereotypical moments of historical rupture, on the other, the way in which these two groups have treated the question of the social role of the Church has driven them apart. If we overlook the debates over timing and rival explanations as to the rising power of the Church, historians of the nineteenth century have usually described the assumption of social power by the clergy as a total and spectacular phenomenon and have, in a wider sense, attributed it to the failure of the republican project of 1837 and the subsequent incorporation of Lower Canada into a union with Upper Canada. At the other end of the chronological spectrum, twentieth-century historians have produced a multiplicity of specialized studies that have nuanced the older portrait of a hegemonic and ultra-conservative Church. Their work has demonstrated that, to a considerable extent, the Church and the social institutions under its control were, sooner or later, profoundly traversed by powerful modernizing currents that reflected, at least in part, a society undergoing change well before the second half of the twentieth century.[73] While, as a whole, there is at present no overarching consensus that characterizes this historiography, we should note that its essential direction lies in displacing paradigms that emphasize "rupture" with interpretations focusing on evolution. Thus, the development of the social role of the Catholic Church can be seen as a rising tide culminating in the final decades of the nineteenth century, followed by a gradual receding in the next century, a description reminiscent of the "ebb and flow" model proffered by the French historian Gérard Cholvy.[74] Religion in modern societies, far from undergoing an ineluctable linear declension, moves like a pendulum, swinging through continuing cycles of erosion and resurgence. It is the historian's task to discern acutely the inner logic of this movement.

A number of approaches could enrich this type of perspective both in Quebec and English Canada. The first would be to go beyond traditional syntheses and to place the churches within social history over a much longer time span. This would allow a much more precise articulation between those analyses that go against the grain and those studies that begin from the origin of the institution and follow it through time. The second approach would strive to transcend the segmented histories of health, education, and social assistance and consider the social role of the churches as a whole, in some ways inseparable from the history of the state. The question then becomes: how better to understand the apparent and relative exceptionalism of Quebec (with the supposed hypertrophying of the presence of the Catholic Church), without falling into the rather vague propensity of trying to determine whether or not this exceptionalism is the vector of a type of "modernity."[75] Such a perspective necessarily alters the parameters of the way in which the social sphere was managed and its history, and this within the framework of a society described as "normal," that is, one that in its main outlines conforms to the evolution of other Western societies. It must be underscored that, in all countries of Western Europe and North America, the churches played a determining role in education, taking charge of youth, and questions of public morality. As well, there was a general movement of social Catholicism and social Christianity in many countries. Given these considerations, how is the Quebec case special? There is a crying need and urgency for the development of a third way of historical enquiry: not only in furthering comparisons with other Catholic societies (the Irish case is frequently mentioned) but more necessarily in integrating Quebec Catholicism into a multiconfessional history of the social role of the churches that explores both Quebec and English Canada. From the standpoint of Quebec historians, the central problem should not be framed as a so-called late secularization (in reference to which other societies?), nor as a supposed monolithic ideological conservatism that ruled unchallenged in Quebec between 1850 and 1950.[76] Rather, the central problem becomes how to account for a relatively acute degree of confessionalization of large swathes of public life. To frame the question in this way opens us to the prospect of a more unbiased history, because it bids us study a terrain that both deeply structured social institutions and relations and leads us to the question of the degree to which this social presence of the churches is shared with other societies.

This book begins and ends with the problem of the relations of power and the internal mechanisms of regulation in the churches. Ollivier Hubert and Christine Hudon trace, over the course of a long time span extending from the seventeenth to the nineteenth century, the history of the way in which bishops acquired information regarding the people in their parishes. In order to do this, the episcopal authorities employed two administrative procedures: the visitation and the annual report. These devices produced sources of a serial nature, evidence that hitherto has been used by quantitative religious history. These records also give insight into a gradual process by which a practice of bureaucratic management and bookkeeping mentality emerged at the very heart of Quebec's Catholic religious culture. Uniformity of belief and practice, as well as the quantitative measure of the results, thus became the criteria by which to gauge religious vitality. Over time, bishops controlled their clergy with growing efficiency, developed more precise ways of knowing and managing their personnel, and calibrated instruments by which to measure faith. Here, we see in this apparent modernization of Catholicism's institutional apparatus, in addition to a desire to construct the Catholic population as a society of those who practice, a logic that resembles, if certain nuances are borne in mind, the history of the state. At the very least, the institution of this control highlights the fact that the quasi-state exercise of extra-institutional functions by the Catholic Church in Quebec was prepared by the episcopal pastoral management of its clergy and faithful. In addition, it shows the Church's fascination with numbers, a method that in the eyes of the clergy seemed to yield greater objectivity but also furnished evidence of religious progress and pastoral success. The sense that its priests were well managed and trained enabled the Catholic Church to provide, in a society characterized by denominational competition and within a framework of collective self-representations as a cultural minority whose future was fragile, a key structure of homogenization for francophone Catholic society. Further, these bureaucratic practices ensured that ultramontane religion became a method of constantly numbering the faithful, and thus, for individuals, it acted as a way to internalize the sense that they belonged to a threatened collectivity.

Nancy Christie's article provides concrete illustration of how modernity emerged through church institutions, how these institutions were spaces where they were themselves contested, and, paradoxically, how churches diffused liberal values in the larger society. The example of the evolution of the way in which people in Upper and Lower Canada used the Presbyterian church courts affords insight into how inherited and hierarchical practices of regulation were transformed by the experience of modernization and ended up functioning as sites in which newer moral codes could be both mediated and appropriated, before finally disappearing under the assaults of individualism. To be sure, these "courts" – which acted as a paralegal, or community infralegal, system – should and must be viewed as institutions of social control. However, at the same time, they were primary mechanisms of social integration, and thus served a fundamental purpose in an immigrant society. This foreshadows the process identified in Roberto Perin's article, which deals with mid-twentieth century Ontario. This apparatus of community control not only effectively punished deviant behaviours but also defined the contours of a more restricted "public" space defined by religious persuasion, in which individual identities could be affirmed, expressed, defended, and interiorized and where the claims of subordinate social groups, particularly women, could be heard. In a manner symbolic of wider sociocultural transformation, the church courts studied by Christie declined at the end of the nineteenth century under the double impact of the professionalization and bureaucratization of religious life and of the privatization of large swathes of social life. Significantly, however, this movement towards the private was negotiated within the very apparatus of the church courts. At the same time in Catholic Quebec, older practices of public penance disappeared in favour of the confessional, which, with a greater emphasis on self-control, represented a more individualized system of social behaviour.

However, Christie's contribution also indicates the outlines of a specifically Canadian type of modernity that is not constituted solely in the construction of a state apparatus but is equally shaped within the more limited cultural spaces defined by ethnoreligious social bonds. These acted at the same time as both the means of articulating and constructing a primary form of citizenship and as a way of diffusing liberal social values. This view of modernity is one of the striking and common elements that emerge from the comparative perspective that informs this book. As in premodern times, membership in a religious confession was the fundamental element of one's integration into society. However, after the early nineteenth century, it also served as a new cultural site in which people sought recognition and legitimation for new identities, and thus a way of affirming their positions within a society increasingly characterized by meritocratic understandings (which was central to notions of reputation). This phenomenon made religion the sphere in which a more limited form of citizenship could be defined and expressed, and it was especially used in this way by minority groups, a process explored not only in Perin's contribution to this volume but also evident on a larger scale with the example of francophone Catholicism. This eminently sociological function of church institutions moves us beyond a religious-centred idea of religious history and opens us to questions that more directly inform social history. Thus, the subject matter of religious history is no longer the reverse or the residue of modernization but becomes the way in which we can observe social transformations working within the very structures of religious life.

More and more, religious history has become a type of social microhistory. In the historiography of Catholicism, scholarly monographs organized around the diocese have been gradually displaced by those anchored on the parish. It is in the smaller local context that we find the most exciting possibilities for a comparative and integrated social history across denominational groups. In this volume, Hannah M. Lane has reconstructed the broader texture of social relationships through a precise comparative scrutiny of two small communities in nineteenth-century New Brunswick and Maine. In particular, her analysis shows how these Protestant churches, as a normative cultural apparatus, not only effectively constructed the social sphere but also managed the changing character of sociability through their day-to-day local operations. In a similar way, historians who have examined the Catholic parishes of pre-Confederation Quebec treat them increasingly as prisms through which to analyze social groups, strategies of hierarchy and status, and proto-democratic forms of social life.[77] Although this type of sociopolitical religious history is distant from older histories by scholars who shared the faith of the communities they described, written either to celebrate local faith communities, or the institutional church itself, it should be pursued, because it is permeated by the complexity of social relations that are elaborated through the structures of religion. As Lane effectively shows, the local level of religious life offers historians a window into how notions of class, gender, and age are constructed in specific socioreligious contexts. Far from adhering to the usual story in which local churches progressively came under the dominance of a local male bourgeoisie and consequently excluded the poorest members from religious life, Lane's work points to a set of far more complex processes at work. She draws attention to the high degree of variation in the methods of church finance, even though pew rents, as in Catholic parishes, remained the most frequent source of revenue. The constant struggle for money necessarily created distinctions of hierarchy within these local communities, but these divisions were far more complex, dynamic, and negotiable than those suggested by the conventional findings of macrosocial history. For example, we can discern a commercial culture vigorously penetrating local communities and subjecting church pews to the "rules" of a liberal market economy, driving older distinctions of social rank, gender, or long-time residency into the background. Certain local churches were more resistant than others to this "modernization" of their social and religious economy and still left considerable scope for the play of customary relations.

In Lane's analysis, religion is neither "for" nor "against" modernity but, rather, functions as a space in which modernity (as well as its contestation) takes concrete form as a historical phenomenon. Religion, for the historian, provides a privileged starting point for an understanding of how society evolves. In the Protestant context examined by Lane, once local religious communities acquire the means to provide for more clergy and build more places of worship, a state of real competition among the churches, which in turn engenders a form of social segregation, can then emerge. For example, to belong to the Congregational Church of Milltown, New Brunswick, was clearly a form of higher social status. However, it should be pointed out that while this kind of sociodenominational division certainly existed in rural and small-town communities, it was less clear-cut than in larger cities. In the rural Catholic society of Quebec, the configuration suggested by Lane was not possible. Although a free market in religion existed in theory, it was circumscribed in practice and rendered largely inoperable by the success of the ultramontane Church in making the choice to belong to another denomination next to impossible for a French Canadian. Thus, rural Catholics had only one parish church in which the many divisions of their society could be lived and expressed.

Kenneth L. Draper's contribution allows us to assess the degree of difference between the ways in which Protestants and Catholics thought about religious institutions. While the Catholic Church in Quebec followed the logic of an increasing administrative bureaucratization centred on the clergy, the Ontario Protestant churches studied by Draper were characterized by the rising power of laypeople at the parish level. If Catholic priests were subjected to the rigorous control of the institutional hierarchy, Protestant clergymen were increasingly the objects, not only of the attentive scrutiny of church members – and in this respect, their experience resembled that of the Catholic clergy, which was under the double surveillance of both the bishop and the faithful – but also of a direct and extremely vigilant administrative control by laypeople. These new mechanisms of Protestant lay control were evident in three instances of conflict between the pastor and the congregation, each of these terminating by the expulsion of the clergyman. These local stories of conflict, far from suggesting the decline of religious belief, as interpreted by the orthodox theory of secularization, provide counterevidence of people who felt challenged by the religious message and sought greater involvement in the life of the churches. Here is a type of secularization of religious life that does not signify decline or privatization. Within the context of a modernist view of social relationships, the clergyman was increasingly perceived as an expert, a purveyor of services accountable to his clients. This constituted a reversal of the old vectors of religious authority that, although to a lesser degree than in the Catholic Church, operated vertically in some Protestant denominations from the clerical hierarchy to the believer. However, far from indicating a weakening of religion in society, this manifested a clear desire on the part of extremely demanding local congregations to take charge of their religious lives. In a movement of democratization, laypeople now felt that they were legitimately entitled to exert religious authority, a power that they did not hesitate to use, even if it meant taking legal action against the clergy by resorting to the civil tribunals.

A comparative analysis of the way in which religion was deployed in the education of Protestant and Catholic children in Quebec from the end of the nineteenth century through to the 1950s allows further insight into the parallels and contrasts between the ways in which different Canadian churches permeated social life at the same time that general theories of modernization would have predicted their decline. If all the Christian churches in Quebec exerted a form of direct, institutionalized authority because the school system itself was profoundly confessionalized, the education and instruction of the young was accorded much greater weight by the Catholic Church. Catholicism participated in a common suspicion, expressed by both state and religious authorities, of the family's ability to carry out its educative mission and thus serve as the ideological foundation of society's future. In this respect, it is easy to understand why the school system in many countries became the bone of contention in intense political and institutional struggles. In the Catholic public schools, religious instruction was an invasive subject that tended to become the master discipline of education itself. The curriculum was thus directed to the formation, above all, of good Catholics and instruction was subordinated to the inculcation of a worldview and of daily comportment structured by religion. The public school became, for the Catholic Church in Quebec, the preferred means by which to exercise its great influence over society and to construct francophone Quebec as a Catholic society. In the Protestant sector, the existence of denominational pluralism precluded the elaboration of a school system powerfully imprinted by a single religious ideology. The reading of the Bible and occasional prayer was the most concrete evidence of the presence of religion in the school, which was very little when compared with the Catholic system. For Protestants, religion was neither the starting point nor the goal of education, and their school system allowed for the emergence of a public space that transcended religious particularism, although reference to a more general Christian heritage remained important. However, this did not affect Catholics. Apart from the specific methods and the intensity with which the different churches involved themselves in education, it is the high level of confessionalization of public schooling in Quebec, which was far more than a mere endorsement of Christian values, that arrests historical attention. Since no common educational project arose to transcend the cultural particularisms that were excessively and consciously reinforced by the lasting and powerful intervention of the churches, the confessional nature of public education was a fundamental characteristic that structured Quebec's history.

Because this question is of such urgent contemporary interest in Quebec, the article written by Jean-Marie Fecteau and Éric Vaillancourt takes as its starting point the confessionalization of public space in Quebec, rather than the idea of secularization. The authors elaborate their own position in this hotly contested debate in the following terms: how to explain why, in Quebec, the type of religious freedom underwritten by the liberal mode of regulating the political order in the nineteenth century resulted in "the crystallization of confessional division" and, more generally, in a place for the Catholic Church that was both unprecedented and unequalled in any Western society? Following the line of René Hardy's work, the authors suggest that the exceptional hold of the Church on wide aspects of public life in Quebec was rendered possible precisely under cover of liberalization of the religious sphere and the confessionalization of social life, within the framework of a well-scripted, active, and effective strategy that was furthered by the Church's historically favourable position. Fecteau and Vaillancourt identify two central explanatory factors: on the one hand, the weakness of the provincial state; on the other, the ability possessed by the Church to define the boundaries of a specific type of citizenship within a wider Canadian public culture, one whose primary criterion was being a Catholic. Here, we see again the broad outlines that complement Brigitte Caulier's analysis.

In addition, Fecteau and Vaillancourt's contribution illustrates, through the example of the St Vincent de Paul Society, how the Catholic Church was able to play a key role in the management of eminently modern social problems linked to urbanization, the precarious economic status of individuals, and social mobility. These latter three attributes of modernity have usually been read by historians as the conventional sources of working-class religious alienation, a key harbinger of secularism, in a historical dynamic in which church institutions have been identified with the middle classes. Michael Gauvreau's treatment of the expansion of Protestant congregations in Canada's working-class neighbourhoods at the turn of the century suggests the need to nuance this dynamic. What emerges from a particularly lively period of church extension and religious innovation, in response to migration from country to city and the arrival of large masses of British immigrants after 1890, is that church institutions, although becoming more centralized, were successful in mobilizing new local religious constituencies by promoting a more "populist" evangelical message and in extensively deploying the voluntary principle to meet a host of economic and social needs. From a comparative perspective, Gauvreau's article extends one of Jean-Marie Fecteau's key insights – namely, that the reconceptualizing of the church in relation to state and society in the 1850s as a free association of individuals was a key moment of transition to modernity[78] – to suggest that, by 1900, the inner meaning of the institutional church and denominational allegiance had itself been transformed by a literal profusion of specialized voluntary associations. The religious and social life of local congregations was honeycombed with voluntary associations linked to the church; these provided a range of social services and leisure activities for literally every age and gender group within the congregation, a phenomenon that in both English Canada and Quebec greatly extended the public scope and authority of the churches between 1890 and 1930. Significantly, this successful transformation of the institutional church under the impress of voluntarism in both societies ensured that the social phenomenon of a dechristianized working class was not a feature of the age of industrialization.[79]

This penetration of the religious into the social sphere through the provision of social services also lies at the core of Roberto Perin's interpretation of how religious denominations integrated immigrants into Toronto society in the immediate postwar period. Although previous historical treatments have accorded a minor, even a negative, role to the churches in the process of immigration in the mid-twentieth century, Perin's article shows that, on the contrary, religious networks played a central role not only in welcoming but also in integrating groups of new Canadians. By shifting our attention from macro-analyses that privilege political and legal aspects of immigration, to the concrete ways in which immigrants became acclimatized to Canadian society, the mediating function of the churches for those leaving the old country and arriving in the host society jumps out. This example forcefully highlights one of the constant, underlying themes suggested in the articles that comprise this volume: the tight overlap between spiritual considerations and the most practical aspects of day-to-day existence. The churches built upon the older functions served by religion in the realms of education, charity, and mutual assistance in meeting new contexts of expanded needs and demands for new strategies of social solidarity. The churches confronted contexts in which the state was inadequate and those in which they had to exercise their social action in partnership with state authorities. In both cases, the churches engaged fully with the imperatives of modernity and acquired an allegiance among ordinary people that remained extremely vital until the 1960s. The conscious attempts by the churches to involve themselves in the provision of basic physical needs (housing, food, health) and the basic social necessities of work, education, and some leisure activities underwrote what was perhaps a deeper penetration of religious values into society than had ever been hitherto seen. Although in the realm of ideas, religion in Western society was losing ground in the face of secular worldviews, in the sphere of social action the churches were able to deploy an unprecedented activism that became the foundation of their legitimacy. As Perin effectively shows, it was the ethnic churches established in Toronto that assured newly arrived central European immigrants a successful integration into their host society. Thus, it is easy to understand the popularity and importance of religion in the social and cultural life of communities of recent immigrants and especially the vitality of the parish institutions created by these groups during the postwar period. This community life, linked to a religious denomination and a clerical structure, was especially visible among immigrants but was, to some degree, more widely shared in the wider nineteenth- and twentieth-century Canadian society. However, as Perin concludes, this structure was challenged by the advances of a hypermodern temper that threatened older community and religious identities.

Gilles Routhier's article isolates another factor that limited the scope of religion in the second half of the twentieth century: its bureaucratization, which returns us to the opening contribution of Ollivier Hubert and Christine Hudon. Bureaucratization was particularly visible in Quebec, where the direct involvement of the Catholic Church in the management of society was especially strong. Thus, it is possible to draw a parallel between the way in which Vatican II was lived in Quebec and the "Quiet Revolution" of the Quebec state, while at the same time links between Quebec Catholicism and other Canadian dioceses became more strained. Both Vatican II and the Quiet Revolution seemed to be characterized by the same exaggerated expectations, but more significantly the modes of governance they evolved were highly similar, and we encounter the same actors involved in both processes of change. Both institutions, the Church as well as the state, engaged in consultation, planning, reorganization, and restructuring and generated a managerial jargon. As with the Quiet Revolution, and in a similar symbiotic movement, as if by osmosis and mutual influence, a new bureaucratic culture permeated the workings of the Quebec Church. In this way, the subsequent difficulties that afflicted the state also affected the Church: a type of top-down planning, which was certainly traditional in the Catholic Church, was aggravated by the movement towards an ultramodern style of administration that copied the public sector. While the Church was completing its bureaucratization, the essential management of social services had passed into the control of the state. This encouraged citizens to distance themselves from religion, or at least from the type of religion promoted by the most institutionalized churches. Because it was seen by ordinary people as less useful, less available, more inflexible in its structures and teachings, the Catholic Church began to visibly lose the authority that had been gradually slipping away from it for several decades.

The specific relationship between the Catholic Church and the social order that Quebec provides within the Canadian context is richly suggestive of further comparative and interdenominational studies of the ways in which the churches exercised authority in industrial societies. The treatments of Caulier, Routhier, and Fecteau and Vaillancourt either endorse or are anchored in an ongoing historiographic debate about Quebec's "exceptionalism" as a highly clericalized society in which the role of the state in the sphere of education and social welfare was limited by the presence of the Catholic Church, a level of presence unprecedented in other Western societies.[80] However, as suggested by recent work on the role of Protestant and Catholic Church institutions in shaping approaches to social welfare in English Canada, the Quebec model seems far less "exceptional." Far from following a model in which state authorities simply displaced the voluntary efforts of churches, the social service sector in English Canada followed a type of the mixed public/private model that determined the scope of the state. In terms of the power of the clergy and the institutional churches in the social sphere, the differences between English Canada and Quebec can be seen as not qualitiative but as merely matters of degree. Between 1900 and 1940, English Canadians would have been familiar with the presence of clergy and religious institutions in the promotion of social science and of social investigation methods and in the organization and management of public welfare,[81] so much so that English Canada could be characterized, in its systems of both education and social welfare, as a "Protestant" state.[82] In terms of international perspective, Quebec might appear "exceptional" if the sole point of contrast were the aggressively secularist post-1870 French republic, where assertion of a unitary republican political identity involved expunging the Catholic Church from educational institutions. If, however, the optic is the public sphere of religion in industrial society, the constitutional monarchies of Belgium, the Netherlands, and Germany provide a good deal of evidence that strong confessional control of education and key sectors of public welfare was quite compatible with building the modern welfare state.[83]

This book urges the development of interdenominational comparative perspectives in the socioreligious history of Canada. As suggested by the many paths followed by the authors in this volume, such an approach would allow us better to assess the differences in the ways in which different churches have negotiated the religious and the social. Such an approach would permit a greater attention to the profound similarities that emerge from symmetrical contexts and that, in conclusion, reveal a range of historical questions that cuts across the conventional boundaries of religious denominations. Beyond suggesting the fruitfulness of a more fully fledged attention to comparisons, these essays collectively make a larger historiographical statement. To historians who view the relationship between the churches and society solely within the framework of secularization as decline, this book suggests that, not only in Quebec and English Canada but in all Western societies, it is in the area of the social that, in the nineteenth and twentieth centuries, the churches did not simply withdraw in the face of modernity. It is on this concrete terrain constituted by the challenge of social problems, rather than in terms of abstract ideas, that the churches enhanced their social relevance and authority.

NOTES

1 Archives Nationales du Québec, Montreal, P701/3, Fonds Clerk of Penicuik, Diary, 15 March 1849. We thank Nancy Christie for these references.

2 On the ways in which the Catholic Church colonized the social terrain during the second half of the nineteenth century, see René Hardy, *Contrôle social et mutation de la culture religieuse au Québec (1830–1930)* (Montreal: Boréal, 1999).

3 For the cultural nature and significance of this shift, see Ollivier Hubert, *Sur la terre comme au ciel: la gestion des rites par l'Église Catholique du Québec (fin XVIIe-mi-XIXe siècle)* (Sainte-Foy: Les Presses de l'Université Laval, 2000): 306. For a suggestive examination of the profound differences between early-modern and ultramontane understandings and practices of religious ritual, which involved a transition between community control and a more assertive projection of authority by the clergy, see Hubert, "Ritualité ultramontaine et pouvoir pastoral clérical dans le Québec de la seconde moitié du XIXe siècle," in Jean-Marie Fecteau and Janice Harvey, eds, *La régulation sociale entre l'acteur et l'institution* (Sainte-Foy: Les Presses de l'Université du Québec, 2005): 435–47. The political aspects of this transformation, as seen in the emergence of a new mode of social regulation in Quebec, has been analyzed by Jean-Marie Fecteau, *La liberté du pauvre. Sur la régulation du crime et de la pauvreté au 19e siècle québécois* (Montreal: VLB, 2004), and by Lucia Ferretti, *Brève histoire de l'Église catholique au Québec* (Montreal: Boréal, 1999).

4 It goes without saying that future scholarship will have to pay increasingly close attention to the institutional authority and practices of non-Christian religious groups.

5 Michel Lagrée, "Avant-propos," in Michel Lagrée, ed., *Chocs et ruptures en histoire religieuse (fin XVIIIe-XIXe siècles)* (Rennes: Presses Universitaires de Rennes, 1998): 11. Lagrée's collection comprises a series of international comparisons organized around Emmet Larkin's concept of the "devotional revolution" and, because it focuses exclusively on Catholicism, itself lacks the "dimension intra-chrétienne" promoted by the editor. A more recent and more systematic comparison suggests a series of key convergences between Roman Catholic and Anglican models in this period. See Jean Baubérot and Séverine Mathieu, *Religion, modernité et culture au Royaume-Uni et en France 1800–1914* (Paris: Seuil, "Points Histoire," 2002).

6 Stephen Yeo, *Religion and Voluntary Organisations in Crisis* (London: Croom Helm, 1976): 2.

7 Robert Orsi, "Everyday Miracles: The Study of Lived Religion," in David D. Hall, *Lived Religion in America: Towards a History of Practice* (Princeton: Princeton University Press, 1997): 9.

8 Bernard Plongeron, ed., *La religion populaire, approche historique* (Beauchesne, 1976); Guy Dubosq et al., *La religion populaire. Colloque international du CNRS en 1977* (Paris: Éditions du Centre national de la recherche scientifique, 1979); Carlo Prandi, "La religion populaire: problèmes théoriques," *The Annual Review of the Social Sciences of Religion*, 4 (1980): 31–60.

9 Benoît Lacroix and Jean Simard, eds, *Religion populaire, religion de clercs?* (Quebec: Institut québécois de recherche sur la culture, 1984); Brigitte Caulier, "Le sentiment religieux," *Status quaestionis. Actes du colloque tenu à l'occasion du 25e anniversaire du Centre de recherche en histoire religieuse du Canada* (Ottawa: Université Saint-Paul, 1994): 48–59; Pietro Boglioni, "Les traditions religieuses de

l'Occident médiéval. Pensée chrétienne, religion populaire, hagiographie," in Jean-Marc Larouche and Guy Ménard, eds, *L'étude de la religion au Québec: Bilan et perspective* (Quebec: Les Presses de l'Université Laval, 2001): 193–214.

10 For an application of the regulatory model to the social history of religion in Canada, see Nancy Christie and Michael Gauvreau, "Modalities of Social Authority," in Nancy Christie and Michael Gauvreau, eds, *Intersections of Religious and Social History*, special journal issue, *Histoire Sociale/Social History*, 35:71 (spring 2003): 1–26; David Hall, "Introduction," in *Lived Religion in America*, viii.

11 See Michael Bliss, "Privatizing the Mind: The Sundering of Canadian History, the Sundering of Canada," *Journal of Canadian Studies*, 26:4 (1992): 5–17. For the first statement of the "limited identies" paradigm, see J.M.S. Careless, "Limited Identities in Canada," *Canadian Historical Review*, 50:1 (March 1969): 1–10.

12 For the "nationalist" school critique of social history, see J.L. Granatstein, *Who Killed Canadian History?* (Toronto: HarperCollins, 1998). See also the responses of A.B. McKillop, "Who Killed Canadian History?: A View from the Trenches," *Canadian Historical Review*, 80:2 (June 1999); and Bryan D. Palmer, "Of Silences and Trenches: A Dissident View of Granatstein's Meaning," *Canadian Historical Review*, 80:4 (December 1999).

13 See, for the grand synthesis based on the "normal society" paradigm, Paul-André Linteau, René Durocher, Jean-Claude Robert, *Histoire du Québec contemporain* (2 vols, *1867–1929* and *1930 au présent*) (Montreal: Boréal, 1984 and 1993). For critiques of this paradigm, see Ronald Rudin, "Revisionism and the Search for a Normal Society: A Critique of Recent Quebec Historical Writing," *Canadian Historical Review*, 73:1 (March 1992): 30–61; Jean-Marie Fecteau, "Entre la quête de la nation et les découvertes de la science. L'historiographie québécoise vue par Ronald Rudin," *Canadian Historical Review*, 80:3 (September 1999): 440–63.

14 For a critical analysis of the classic secularization theory, see Roy Wallis and Steve Bruce, "Secularization: The Orthodox Model," in Steve Bruce, ed., *Religion and Modernization: Sociologists and Historians Debate the Secularization Thesis* (Oxford: Clarendon Press, 1992): 11; Peter Berger, *The Desecularization of the World* (Grand Rapids, Mich.: Eerdmans, 1999); Danièle Hervieu-Léger, *Vers un nouveau christianisme? Introduction à la sociologie du christianisme occidental* (Paris: Cerf, 1986); Danièle Hervieu-Léger and Françoise Champion, eds, *De l'émotion en religion* (Paris: Centurion, 1990).

15 Louise Bienvenue, "Pierres grises et mauvaise conscience. Essai historique sur le rôle de l'Église catholique dans l'assistance au Québec," *Études d'histoire religieuse*, 69 (2003): 9–28.

16 Roberto Perin, "French Speaking Canada from 1840," in Terry Murphy and Roberto Perin, eds, *A Concise History of Christianity in Canada* (Toronto: Oxford University Press, 1996); Louis Rousseau and Frank Remiggi, eds, *Atlas historique*

des pratiques religieuses: le sud-ouest du Québec au 19ᵉ siècle (Ottawa: Les Presses de l'Université d'Ottawa, 1998). There is also an important current of research, generally among younger scholars, that proposes to trace a genealogy of modernity in Quebec, and thus transcending the myth of the Quiet Revolution in order to find its origins within the structures of the Catholic Church. See, for example, Lucie Piché, *Femmes et changement social au Québec: l'apport de la Jeunesse ouvrière catholique feminine, 1931–1966* (Quebec: Presses de l'Université Laval, 2003); Louise Bienvenue, *Quand la jeunesse entre en scène – L'Action catholique avant la Révolution tranquille* (Montreal: Boréal, 2003); É.-Martin Meunier and Jean-Philippe Warren, *L'horizon personnaliste de la Révolution tranquille* (Sillery: Septentrion, 2002); Numéro spécial de la revue *Société* (20/21, 1999), sur les origines de la Révolution tranquille; Stéphane Kelly, ed., *Les idées mènent le Québec: Essais sur une sensibilité historique* (Quebec: Les Presses de l'Université Laval, 2003), especially the essays by Jean Gould and É.-Martin Meunier. We should also note in this context a work that was central to this process of questioning the origins of modernity in Quebec, that of Brigitte Caulier, ed., *Religion, sécularisation, modernité. Les expériences francophones en Amérique du Nord* (Sainte-Foy: Les Presses de l'Université Laval, 1996).

17 Ian McKay, "The Liberal Order Framework: A Prospectus for a Reconnaissance of Canadian History," *Canadian Historical Review*, 81:4 (December 2000): 617–45. It should be noted in this context that McKay's emphasis on the primacy of individualism is contested by historians such as Jean-Marie Fecteau, whose *Liberté du pauvre* is more nuanced in suggesting a key collectivist and corporatist imperative within nineteenth-century liberal attempts at social regulation.

18 This view of the churches has been most effectively articulated in Canada recently in the work of Lynne Marks, *Revivals and Roller Rinks: Religion, Leisure, and Identity in Late-Nineteenth-Century Small-Town Ontario* (Toronto: University of Toronto Press, 1996). So influential is the idea of a seamless connection between the institutional churches and the middle classes among Canadian historians that one recent study of middle-class formation, Andrew Holman's *A Sense of their Duty* (Montreal and Kingston: McGill-Queen's University Press, 2001) does not include any explicit analysis of the dynamics of church life in the communities of Galt and Goderich that he studies.

19 Significantly, these two views encapsulate the dominant historical orthodoxies in both Quebec and English Canada. The "church as tradition" model, emphasizing institutional conservatism and ossification, characterizes the "normal society" model of Quebec historians. See Linteau, Durocher, Robert, *Histoire du Québec contemporain, tome 2*, 806–7; Jean Hamelin and Nicole Gagnon, *Histoire du catholicisme québécois, le xxᵉ siecle, tome 2, depuis 1940* (Montreal: Boréal, 1984). The "church as accommodator" model is most characteristic of the social history of

English Canada. The significant interpretive signposts of this literature are Richard Allen, *The Social Passion: Religion and Social Reform in Canada, 1914–1928* (Toronto: University of Toronto Press, 1973); Ramsay Cook, *The Regenerators: Social Criticism in Late-Victorian English Canada* (Toronto: University of Toronto Press, 1984); David B. Marshall, *Secularizing the Faith* (Toronto: University of Toronto Press, 1992).

20 Jeffrey Cox, "Master Narratives of Long-Term Religious Change," in Hugh McLeod and Werner Ustdorf, eds, *The Decline of Christendom in Western Europe, 1750–2000* (Cambridge: Cambridge University Press, 2003): 205–6.

21 Ibid., 208. For one preliminary parallel exercise in unmasking "master narratives" in the Canadian context, see Nancy Christie and Michael Gauvreau, "Introduction: Recasting the Postwar Decade in Canadian History," in Nancy Christie and Michael Gauvreau, eds, *Cultures of Citizenship in Postwar Canada, 1940–1955* (Montreal and Kingston: McGill-Queen's University Press, 2003): 1–37.

22 Callum G. Brown, "The Mechanism of Religious Growth in Urban Societies: British Cities since the Eighteenth Century," in Hugh McLeod, ed., *European Religion in the Age of Great Cities, 1830–1930* (London: Routledge, 1995): 243–7.

23 Brigitte Waché, *Religion et culture en Europe occidentale 1800–1914* (Paris, Belin, 2002); Jacques-Olivier Boudon, ed., *Religion et culture en Europe au 19ᵉ siècle* (Paris: Armand Colin, 2001); Hélène Frechet, ed., *Religion et culture de 1800 à 1914. Allemagne – France – Italie – Royaume-Uni* (Paris: Éditions du temps, 2001); Jean-Paul Bled, ed., *Religion et culture dans les sociétés et les États européens de 1800 à 1914* (Paris: Cned-Sedes, 2001); René Rémond, *Religion et société en Europe. La sécularisation au XIXᵉ et XXᵉ siècles, 1780–2000* (Paris, Seuil, "Points Histoire," 2001).

24 Michel Lagrée, *La bénédiction de Prométhée: Religion et technologie XIXᵉ-XXᵉ siècle* (Paris: Fayard, 1999).

25 See especially Gérard Cholvy and Yves-Marie Hilaire, *Histoire religieuse de la France contemporaine* (Toulouse: Privat, 1985–88, 3 volumes).

26 Brown, "The Mechanism of Religious Growth," 249.

27 S.J.D. Green, *Religion in the Age of Decline: Organisation and Experience in Industrial Yorkshire, 1870–1920* (Cambridge: Cambridge University Press, 1996): 200.

28 This new literature has been ably synthesized in Callum Brown, *The Death of Christian Britain: Understanding Secularisation 1800–2000* (London: Routledge, 2000), who states that "the data from 1800 to the 1960s fail to identify a period in which there was a working-class haemorrhage from congregations, tending to undermine the notion that working-class evacuation of the churches led to secularisation at any point … we are left with the conclusion that social class on its own fails to explain church decline in Britain between 1800 and 1960." (156) In the Canadian context, the statistics assembled by Lynne Marks for small-town Ontario and

by Lucia Ferretti for working-class Montreal for the late nineteenth and early twentieth centuries similarly reveal a high degree of working-class participation in churches, which included both the skilled and the unskilled. See Marks, *Revivals and Roller Rinks*, appendix C, tables 1, 2, and 3, indicating working-class majorities in each congregation, belying the overall thesis of working-class "alienation" from mainstream Protestantism. For Montreal, Ferretti's conclusions are drawn from analysis of working-class participation in devotional and voluntary associations connected with the church of Saint-Pierre-Apôtre, located in a working-class neighbourhood that progressively became more impoverished. Working-class participation and membership remained very pronounced until the 1920s. See Lucia Ferretti, *Entre voisins: La société paroissiale en milieu urbain: Saint-Pierre-Apôtre de Montreal, 1848–1930* (Montreal: Boreal, 1992).

29 Brown, *The Death of Christian Britain*, 13. For a stimulating treatment of the way in which this "discursive" Christianity was practiced in working-class communities and its relationship to church institutions, see Sarah C. Williams, *Religious Belief and Popular Culture in Southwark, c. 1880–1939* (Oxford: Oxford University Press, 1999).

30 Hugh McLeod, *Secularization in Western Europe, 1848–1914* (New York: St Martin's Press, 2000): 56–9.

31 For Spain as an extreme case of a "dechristianized" working class, see William J. Callahan, "An Organizational and Pastoral Failure: Urbanization, Industrialization and Religion in Spain, 1850–1930," in McLeod, ed., *European Religion in the Age of Great Cities*, 43–60.

32 For the dynamism of Roman Catholic religious institutions in Belgium, see Carl Strikwerda, "A Resurgent Religion: The Rise of Catholic Social Movements in Nineteenth-Century Belgian Cities," in McLeod, ed., *European Religion in the Age of Great Cities*, 61–89; for the Netherlands, in which "confessional" Catholic and Protestant religious institutions successfully organized social life and compelled a "confessional" structure of state social services, see Peter Van Rooden, "Long-Term Religious Developments in the Netherlands, c. 1750–2000," in McLeod and Ustdorf, eds, *The Decline of Christendom in Western Europe*, 117–18. A recent work that addresses the relationship between the city and religion in France is Philippe Boutry and André Encrevé, eds, *La religion dans la ville* (Bordeaux: Éditions Bière, 2003).

33 McLeod, *Secularisation in Western Europe*, 182–5.

34 Lucian Hölscher, "Secularization and Urbanization in the Nineteenth Century: An Interpretative Model," in McLeod, ed., *European Religion in the Age of Great Cities*, 263.

35 Ibid., 269.

36 Ibid., 274.

37 Ibid., 274–5. More combatively, Callum Brown has stated that definitions of religion that rely solely on social science methods like measurement of church attendance owe their intellectual lineage to late-eighteenth-century evangelical clergymen, who constructed a myth of the "unholy city" as a way of galvanizing their churches into greater organizational activity. See *The Death of Christian Britain*, 18–30.

38 Holscher, 280–1.

39 McLeod, *Secularization in Western Europe*, 286–9. See also the complex model advanced by Karel Dobbelaere, *Secularization: A Multi-Dimensional Concept* (London: Sage Publications, 1981).

40 Within the university, religious studies departments, especially that of the Département des sciences religieuses de l'Université du Québec à Montréal, have played a key role in conceptualizing this counter-interpretation.

41 Bruno Dumons, "Histoire sociale et histoire religieuse, deux soeurs ennemies. Un essai de relecture historiographique pour la France contemporaine," *Revue d'histoire de l'Église de France*, 86 (2000): 561–72.

42 Clark was a central figure in a postwar generation of Canadian academics who feared the potentially destabilizing effects of an emerging "mass culture," and, in particular, he deplored the anti-intellectualism, bad taste, and what he believed to be the lower-class character of enthusiastic brands of Protestantism that were then in the process of being eviscerated from the mainstream denominations by middle-class church leaders. For an analysis of the tenets of this postwar intellectual climate among the leaders of the United Church and influential university academics like Clark, see Nancy Christie, "'Look out for Leviathan': The Search for a Conservative Modernist Consensus," in Christie and Gauvreau, eds, *Cultures of Citizenship in Postwar Canada*, 63–94.

43 S.D. Clark, *Church and Sect in Canada* (Toronto: University of Toronto Press, 1948): xii, 169, 186, 191.

44 Ibid., 400: Clark described Methodism as becoming dependent upon "the settled residents of the community, upon the people who enjoyed a sense of status and security. Thus it ceased to be a religion which served as a revitalizing or reorganizing influence in the community among those people who lacked a sense of status or security."

45 Ibid., 431–2. This was also the conclusion offered by Clark's University of Toronto colleague, the philosopher John Irving, in *The Social Credit Movement in Alberta* (Toronto: University of Toronto Press, 1953).

46 For LeBras, see Danièle Hervieu-Léger, "'What Scripture Tells Me': Spontaneity and Regulation within the Catholic Charismatic Renewal," in Hall, ed., *Lived Religion in America*, 22–3. For the wide currency of the US "folk society" model, especially among Quebec social scientists trained at Université Laval after 1940, see the recent

discussion by Jean-Philippe Warren, *L'engagement sociologique. La tradition sociologique du Québec francophone (1886–1955)* (Montreal: Boréal, 2003): 279–95.

47 For the intellectual origins and main protagonists of this type of reasoning, see Michael Gauvreau, *The Catholic Origins of Quebec's Quiet Revolution, 1931–1970* (Montreal and Kingston: McGill-Queen's University Press, 2005).

48 For the links between these reformist priorities, the fear of a "dechristianized" working class, and the study of popular religion in Quebec, see Jean Roy, "Quelques influences françaises sur l'historiographie religieuse du Québec des dernières décennies," *Revue d'histoire de l'Amérique française*, 51:2 (automne 1997): 316.

49 Benoît Lacroix and Jean Simard, eds, *Religion Populaire, Religion de Clercs?* (Quebec: Institut québécois de recherche sur la culture, 1984): 13: "médiévale dans les structures, dans les formes, et dans les mentalités. C'est à se demander si le concile de Trente n'aurait touché que fort peu le vécu intérieur, tellement le peuple québécois a conservé ses dévotions, ses coutumes et ses rites 'médiévaux.'"

50 A number of academics believed that this largely autonomous "popular religion" survived longest among rural people and urban workers recently transplanted from the countryside. See, Fernand Harvey, "Pour une approche differenciée de la religion populaire selon les genres de vie," in Lacroix and Simard, eds, *Religion populaire*, 228; Jean-Charles Falardeau, "Religion populaire et classes sociales," in ibid., 277–95.

51 See William G. McLoughlin, *Revivals, Awakenings, and Reform: An Essay on Religion and Social Change in America, 1607–1977* (Chicago and London: University of Chicago Press, 1978): 12–23. The classic work on the subject was done by the anthropologist Anthony F.C. Wallace, *The Death and Rebirth of the Seneca* (New York: Knopf, 1970).

52 These directions have been most elegantly and powerfully expressed by Nathan O. Hatch, *The Democratization of American Christianity* (1989). However, Hatch has been critiqued for ignoring the substantial pre- and post-Revolutionary continuities in US religious life. See the synthesis by Jon Butler, *Awash in a Sea of Faith: Christianizing the American People* (Cambridge, MA: Harvard University Press, 1990).

53 G.A. Rawlyk, *The Canada Fire: Radical Evangelicalism in British North America, 1775–1812* (Montreal and Kingston: McGill-Queen's University Press, 1994): xvi, xviii.

54 William Westfall, *Two Worlds: The Protestant Culture of Nineteenth-Century Ontario, 1820–1870* (Montreal and Kingston: McGill-Queen's University Press, 1989).

55 Marks, *Revivals and Roller Rinks*, 4–5.

56 For the Marxist adoption of the notion that "popular" religion was separate from and opposed to the "elite" religion of the institutional churches, see Richard C. Trexler, "Reverence and Profanity in the Study of Early Modern Religion," in

Kaspar von Greyerz, ed., *Religion and Society in Early Modern Europe* (London: George Allen & Unwin, 1984), 249. For a sympathetic yet critical treatment of E.P. Thompson's portrayal of British Methodism, see David Hempton and John Walsh, "E.P. Thompson and Methodism," in Mark A. Noll, ed., *God and Mammon: Protestants, Money and the Market, 1790–1860* (New York: Oxford University Press, 2001), 104–8.

57 For a stimulating examination of this process at the local level, see Kenneth L. Draper, "Religion Worthy of a Free People," Ph.D. thesis, McMaster University, 2000.

58 Fecteau, *La liberté du pauvre*, 276–300.

59 Examples of scholarship that has addressed these issues in the English Canadian context include: Kenneth L. Draper, "Redemptive Homes – Redeeming Choices: Saving the Social in Late-Victorian London, Ontario," in Nancy Christie, ed., *Households of Faith: Family, Gender, and Community in Canada, 1760–1969* (Montreal and Kingston: McGill-Queen's University Press, 2002): 264–89; Patricia Dirks, "Reinventing Christian Masculinity and Fatherhood: The Canadian Protestant Experience, 1900–1920," in Christie, ed., *Households of Faith*, 290–318; Nancy Christie and Michael Gauvreau, *A Full-Orbed Christianity: The Protestant Churches and Social Welfare in Canada, 1900–1940* (Montreal and Kingston: McGill-Queen's University Press, 1996), which explores the complexities of the transition within Canadian Protestantism from a localized culture of religious voluntarism to a more centralized liberal collectivism.

60 In David Marshall's *Secularizing the Faith*, the decline or absence of revivalism is a sign of the ultimate futility and irrelevance of the institutional church.

61 Nancy Christie and Michael Gauvreau, *A Full-Orbed Christianity: The Protestant Churches and Social Welfare in Canada, 1900–1940* (Montreal and Kingston: McGill-Queen's University Press, 1996).

62 Guy Laperrière, "Religion populaire, religion de clercs? Du Québec à la France, 1972–1982," in Lacroix and Simard, eds, *Religion populaire, religion de clercs?*, 22: "au Québec, la religion populaire n'existe que par le fait des clercs, alors qu'en Europe, elle serait l'expression des survivances païennes que n'a pu déraciner le clergé."

63 Ibid., 37.

64 Emmet Larkin, "The Devotional Revolution in Ireland, 1850–75," *American Historical Review*, 77 (1972).

65 Louis Rousseau, "La conduite pascale dans la région montréalaise, 1831–1865: un indice des mouvements de la ferveur religieuse," in Rolland Litalien, ed., *L'Église de Montréal: aperçus d'hier et d'aujourd'hui, 1836–1986* (Montreal: Fides, 1986): 270–84; Rousseau, "Crises, chocs et revitalisations culturelles dans le Québec du XIXe siècle," in Lagrée, ed., *Chocs et ruptures*, 51–69, in which he stated that he

was strongly influenced by the work of Anthony Wallace and William McLoughlin. Rousseau's views were incorporated into a large-scale synthesis of nineteenth-century Quebec Catholicism authored by Philippe Sylvain and Nive Voisine, *Histoire du catholicisme québécois: tome 2: réveil et consolidation (1840–1898)* (Montreal: Boréal, 1991): 10. See also Louis Rousseau and Frank Remiggi, eds, *Atlas historique des pratiques religieuses: le sud-ouest du Québec au 19e siècle* (Ottawa: Les Presses de l'Université d'Ottawa, 1998).

66 Roy, "Quelques influences françaises," 316.

67 The major statement of Hardy's views can be found in *Contrôle social et mutation de la culture religieuse au Québec, 1830–1930* (Montreal: Boréal, 1999). See also Christine Hudon, "Le renouveau religieux québécois au XIXe siècle: éléments pour une réinterprétation," in *Studies in Religion/Studies in Religion*, 24:4 (1995): 467–89; Louis Rousseau, "À propos du 'réveil religieux' dans le Québec du XIXe siècle: où se loge le vrai débat?" in *Revue d'histoire de l'Amérique française*, 49:2 (automne 1995): 223–46.

68 In this respect, Hardy's views received powerful confirmation from the study of non-francophone Catholics in other contexts. Brian Clarke's fine study of Irish Catholicism in Toronto severely undermines Larkin's concept of "devotional revolution," as he finds a similar temporal development to Hardy's in Quebec: the clergy's views of devotion, sacramental life, and the church's authority were not largely acceptable to the laity until the late 1880s.

69 Brian Clarke, *Piety and Nationalism*; Mark G. McGowan, *The Waning of the Green: Catholics, the Irish and Identity in Toronto, 1887–1922* (Montreal and Kingston: McGill-Queen's University Press, 1999).

70 There is a tendency among Quebec historians of Catholicism to centre their attention on the priorities and projects of the clergy, which implicitly assumes a top-down model of religious change. Historians such as Jean-Marie Fecteau who examine the phenomenon of the rise of associational life have exhibited a similar tendency to assume a close link between liberal state and voluntary associations.

71 Hardy, *Contrôle social*, 228–9: "la logique capitaliste en milieu urbain."

72 On this subject, see also Brigitte Caulier, "Bâtir l'Amérique des dévots. Les confréries de dévotion montréalaises depuis le Régime français," *Revue d'histoire de l'Amérique française*, 46:1 (été 1992): 45–66.

73 On this subject there are two fundamental historiographical summaries: Lucia Ferretti, "L'Église de Montréal (1900–1950) dans les mémoires et thèses depuis 1980," in *Études d'histoire religieuse*, 59 (1993), and Louise Bienvenue, "Pierres grises et mauvaise conscience. Essai historiographique sur le rôle de l'Église catholique dans l'assistance au Québec," in *Études d'histoire religieuse*, 69 (2003): 9–28.

74 Gérard Cholvy, "Conclusion," *L'Histoire religieuse de la France contemporaine, 3, 1930–1988* (Toulouse: Privat, 1988): 484–95: "flux et reflux."

75 On this issue, and working from a comparative perspective that allows us to see
   how, even on the terrain of ideology, it is at times risky to compare the specific cases
   of France and Quebec, see Michel Lagrée, "De Veuillot à Tardivel, ou les ambiguïtés
   de la haine de la modernité," *Études d'histoire religieuse*, 67 (2001): 251–9. A subtle analysis of the history of ideas shows that, in Quebec, a certain form of liberalism was far from incompatible with a certain form of clerical discourse and social
   intervention. See also Fernande Roy, *Progrès, harmonie, liberté. Le libéralisme des
   milieux d'affaires francophones de Montréal au tournant du siècle* (Montreal:
   Boréal, 1988): 260–8.

76 For an excellent introduction to a current of research that destroyed the myth of
   clerical, conservative, and traditionalist unanimity in Quebec, see Yvan Lamonde,
   ed., *Combats libéraux au tournant du 20ᵉ siècle* (Montreal: Fides, 1995).

77 See, for example, Allan Greer, *The Patriots and the People: The Rebellion of 1837 in
   Rural Lower Canada* (University of Toronto Press, 1993); Christian Dessureault
   and Christine Hudon, "Conflits sociaux et élites locales au Bas-Canada: Le clergé,
   les notables, la paysannerie et le contrôle de la fabrique," in *Canadian Historical
   Review*, 80:3 (September 1999): 413–39.

78 Fecteau, *La liberté du pauvre*, 276–87.

79 Working-class religious experience is an immense historical terrain rich in comparative possibilities, both between Quebec and English Canada and also internation-
   ally, where the debate on working-class dechristianization has been extremely lively
   in recent years. For the historiography, see Michael Gauvreau, "Factories and Foreigners," in this volume. In English Canada, the major study remains Marks, *Revivals and Roller Rinks*, although it is limited to the period 1880–1900. Industrial
   Montreal has been better served by Lucia Ferretti's *Entre voisins*, a stimulating
   treatment of the associational life of a working-class parish between 1848 and
   1930. Given the wealth of church records available for both Catholic and Protestant congregations, the next decade should see a wealth of local studies upon which
   to build a new comparative synthesis.

80 Indeed, Fecteau's recent *La liberté du pauvre*, 342–50, while anchoring Catholic
   ideologies and practices of social intervention within the framework of a liberal society that emerged in the early nineteenth century, argues that the Church's control
   over a wide sphere of social action, colluded in by a weak provincial government, in
   fact blighted and stunted both Quebec and Canada's political possibilities by swal-
   lowing up and destroying an embryonic, supra-religious civic order, and thus preventing the emergence of a unitary system of national allegiances. The result,
   according to Fecteau, was the legitimation and cultural authority of a particularly
   harsh interpretation of liberalism, in which the "freedom" of the poor was constructed around a denial of a possible political resolution of social problems.

81 This is the argument advanced by Christie and Gauvreau in *A Full-Orbed Christianity* for the period 1900–40. More recently, a study of the management of Roman Catholic charities in Toronto, similarly disputes the claim that the welfare state was an evolutionary progression from a church-dominated voluntary sector to a modern, scientific, and secular welfare state. Welfare bureaucracies expanded by building stronger links with church charities. See Paula Maurutto, *Governing Charities: Church and State in Toronto's Catholic Archdiocese, 1850–1950* (Montreal and Kingston: McGill-Queen's University Press, 2003).

82 This characterization of child welfare initiatives in English Canada before 1930 has been offered in Nancy Christie, *Engendering the State: Family, Work, and Welfare in Canada* (Toronto: University of Toronto Press, 2000).

83 For the strong hold of confessional institutions in Belgium and the Netherlands in the nineteenth and twentieth centuries, see Strikwerda, "A Resurgent Religion," and Van Rooden, "Long-Term Religious Developments in the Netherlands." On the German case, Hugh McLeod notes that until the Nazi takeover of the 1930s, different religious confessions were given subsidies by the local authorities to provide social welfare, and, until 1919, citizens were liable to pay church taxes. In the educational sphere, church schools remained the norm until 1933. See *Secularisation in Western Europe*, 59.

I

The Emergence of a Statistical Approach to Social Issues in Administrative Practices of the Catholic Church in the Province of Quebec

CHRISTINE HUDON
AND OLLIVIER HUBERT
(translated by Yvonne M. Klein)

This essay is informed by Bruce Curtis's work[1] on the organization of Canadian censuses in the nineteenth century. Our consideration starts from the following premise: the annual reports of parish priests are to religious history and the history of the Church as it existed in the province of Quebec for thirty years what the censuses are to social-economic history and the history of the state. That is to say, they are key, if not basic, material from which it is possible to extract data susceptible to serial treatment, both diachronically and synchronously. From this point we go on to suggest that, just as the censuses were an implement of prime importance in the construction of a modern, centralized, and bureaucratic state, the annual reports could become the object of a critical analysis that would elucidate why the reports were instituted and how they were used by the Church. To be more precise, we shall try to better situate the advent of these annual reports in the history of the Quebec Church and the development of the uses of statistics and accountancy. As a beginning hypothesis, we suggest that, in a way similar to that of the state, the Catholic Church acquired tools by which to measure, categorize, and classify in order to obtain knowledge and plan its action. In the following pages, we shall attempt to unpack this information-gathering project of the ecclesiastical authorities first to find within it its gestation, then to analyze its aims and significance, and finally to reveal the "fundamentally" modern character of the administrative procedures of the Church. This essay does not intend to undertake a detailed analysis of the contents of this source, though inevitably some information of the sort will emerge. Rather, it is more a question of considering the very appearance of these annual reports in the middle of the nineteenth century in order to understand what this documentary evidence can tell us about the exercise of power by and within the Quebec Church.

THE DOCUMENTS

The annual report was a document produced by the parish priests at the instigation of the bishop. Its inception dates to the first Quebec provincial council. On 25 August 1851, the bishops adopted a decree, the council's twelfth, that required pastors to submit a report on the state of their parishes every year before 1 September.[2] Before this decree was promulgated, statistical tables regarding the state of the parishes were circulated in the Montreal diocese. They appeared in the form of questionnaires that had to be prepared for the episcopal rounds. Some of these tables date to 1841, others to 1846; the latter coincide with Bishop Bourget's round of pastoral inspections. Regardless of the obligation imposed by the first Quebec provincial council, the parish reports were not always produced annually. In this regard, certain bishops insisted on annual reports, with mixed results. In the Quebec City diocese, for example, reminders of the council's decree circulated periodically.[3] Other bishops seemed instead to have asked for the forms to be filled out about every four years, in preparation for the pastoral inspection. In some cases, the intervals between reports were even longer. The Saint-Hyacinthe archives for the nineteenth century retain a series of reports only for the years 1853 to 1855, 1862 to 1864, 1878, and 1886 to 1888. There is nothing in the clergy's correspondence or in the circular letters of the area bishops to suggest that other reports were completed by the priests and then destroyed by the diocesan authorities or the archivists.

The annual report appeared in several forms. Some were printed, others not. For example, in the Montreal and Saint-Hyacinthe dioceses, the parish priests were sent a form on which they could enter their answers in the appropriate spaces. How the questionnaires looked varied somewhat; they sometimes appeared as a text to be completed, sometimes as a statistical table in which the priest could enter numerical data. The archbishop in certain dioceses, especially Quebec City, did not have forms printed up. The parish priests got the questions and answered on tear-off sheets, either writing out the questions themselves again or simply indicating the numbers in the appropriate columns. Reports of this kind survived until at least the 1880s.

The report contained wide-ranging information about the parish and its parishioners. Some of this information was quantitative in nature. The annual report counted among other things the "parishioners," "the communicants," the "Protestants," and the schools; it indicated the value of the church and estimated the amount of the parish revenue; it gave an idea of community life in the parishes and detailed the number of persons taking their annual or Easter communion. Some reports also provided a considerable amount of qualitative information. The pastor might give some estimate of how far this or that regulation was being respected. He could say whether the fasts were being observed or how well the catechism was being followed. In certain reports, a space was provided for supplementary comments or explanations that allowed the priest to raise the problems he felt were the most pressing in his parish, to provide an account of the development of religious practices, to consider, in a general way, the religious and spiritual life of his cure or to clarify particular figures he had entered.[4] By the 1870s or 1880s, the questionnaires evolved and tended to grow more complex. Certain questions, for example those relating to the number of parishioners and communicants or to parish tithes collected, appear systematically from one report to the next. Other questions, however, appear only sporadically and seem to reflect the bishop's concern to check on the application of one or another regulation or to investigate a particular problem.

THE ANNUAL REPORT AND HISTORIOGRAPHY

It is rather surprising that no study of the annual reports in their role as instruments of power and as a means of affirming the Church has as yet been undertaken. After all, Quebec religious historiography for the last thirty years has made ample use of the priests' annual reports. The use of these reports was largely inspired by the French religious sociological work of Canon Boulard and particularly by that of Gabriel LeBras, a legal expert who proposed to historians and sociologists that they undertake a systematic investigation to become familiar with and analyze the "dechristianization" movement in France.[5] This proposal yielded a number of monographs on the French regions and dioceses.[6] The source and the method were picked up in the province of Quebec, but here different kinds of questions were asked. In an article published in the early 1970s, Serge Gagnon used the records to produce a statistical portrait of the Montreal diocese around 1860.[7] During the 1980s and 90s, Quebec scholars, especially René Hardy, Jean Roy, Christine Hudon, Louis Rousseau, and Frank Remiggi, also used them to study the religious revival movement of the nineteenth century, in order to determine its nature, chronology, and significance.[8] The analysis of these documents allowed them to construct a series measuring the rate of confession and Easter communion and follow how these practices evolved over time. Starting from the qualitative information contained in the source, Louis Rousseau and Frank Remiggi drew up maps of virtues and vices to highlight regional differences in particular periods. These two scholars have also mapped membership in devotional associations and the degree to which particular injunctions, like fasting and abstinence, were respected. Only a few historians have dealt with other elements occupying an important place in the reports, notably the data on the material condition of the Church and the financial situation of the parishes and their priests. In this regard, Jean Roy's work on priests' incomes is an exception.[9]

In all of these studies, the annual reports have been more a source, a body of historical material, rather than an object of study in themselves. Of course, the explanations and critical remarks of the authors have helped to pin down the origins of these documents, identify certain of their objectives, and give some indications about their form and the way they were filled in – in short, to take some initial steps toward an historical analysis of the reports.[10] No study, however, has to date undertaken a detailed analysis of this source not simply to situate it in the context of Quebec religion but also within the larger historical context that has been marked by the development of statistics and accounting thought, by the advent of what political scientists Jean-Pierre Beaud and Jean-Guy Provost have termed "The Age of Numbers."[11]

INSPECTION NOTEBOOKS:
PREDECESSORS OF THE ANNUAL REPORTS

Both as a procedure and as a document, the annual report had a history. It did not appear out of nowhere as a radical innovation. Diocesan systems of information and administrative control comparable to the Quebec reports were in place in many French dioceses well before they were adopted in the ecclesiastical province of Quebec. Even in Quebec, the report did not represent an altogether new approach but appeared more as a supplementary device to add to the already sophisticated mechanisms intended to oversee the clerical staff.[12]

More precisely, the report was grafted onto a very old, very effective, and well-used exercise – the pastoral inspection, also called the canonical, episcopal, or diocesan inspection. This entailed the periodic examination of the diocese by the bishop or his delegate (coadjutant bishop, archdeacon, episcopal vicar), a very standardized, delimited, defined, and well-tested procedure. The practice was ancient, but its more systematic application arose with the wave of Church reform. It would seem that the Canadian inspections appeared with the very origins of the diocesan structure. Indeed, the first volume of *Mandements, lettres pastorales et circulaires des évêques de Québec* includes the list of "confirmations by Monseigneur de Laval." The rite of confirmation, which required the presence of the bishop, usually took place in rural parishes on the occasion of a pastoral inspection. On the basis of this list, it appears evident that important tours of inspection took place in 1669, 1676, and 1681.[13] Monseigneur de Saint-Vallier (1688–1727), the second bishop of the Quebec City diocese, who laid down the real basis of the Canadian parochial system,[14] also instituted the administrative and liturgical rules for the inspection in the diocesan ritual he published in 1703 and then went on to make at least one systematic diocesan inspection himself.[15] Thus New France was in touch with metropolitan practices, especially of the northern dioceses. In the first decades of the eighteenth century, however, the absence of a bishop combined with the instability affecting the leadership of the diocese briefly interrupted the customary inspection. But by 1730 the practice was resumed and established on a basis both regular and regulated.

The inspection was a major event in the life of the parish and a principal means of wielding episcopal power. There was indeed a two-fold significance to this periodic appearance of diocesan authority in the parish. The inspection was primarily intended to check into the financial, material, moral, and spiritual life of the parish and, therefore, by implication, the quality of the work of those whose responsibility it was. But this strictly administrative dimension was cloaked, as it were, in a sophisticated ritual apparatus that was heavily laden with symbolism. Since the Council of Trent, the inspection ritual had been strictly detailed and completely standardized. This ritual regularity, which assured a certain degree of uniformity regarding the administrative procedure it supported, rested on a variety of normative sources. Among these, in eighteenth- and nineteenth-century Quebec, were the *Rituel de Québec* (1703), the *Processional romain à l'usage du diocèse de Québec* (1802) – from which an "Order of Inspection" was extracted and published separately – the *Extrait du rituel* (1836), the *Manuel de la visite épiscopal dans les communautés et paroisses du diocèse de Montréal* (1851), the *Appendice au Compendium du rituel romain, à l'usage des diocèses de la province ecclésiastique de Québec* (1851), and probably other liturgical and administrative manuals of ceremonial usages from which the bishops might draw.[16] The inspection affirmed the power of the bishop in two ways. On the administrative level, the bishop appeared as the hierarchical superior of the parish priest, who on this occasion appeared as a subordinate officer of a hierarchical organization. On the spiritual plane, the bishop was represented as the actual local incarnation of divine power. According to Saint-Vallier, the visit was in fact a Holy Day on which the people had to be convinced that they were meeting Jesus Christ in the person of their bishop so that they might be showered with blessings.[17] On both levels, we must point out, the position of the parish priest in the parish microsociology was undermined. Though the inspection was not aimed solely at the pastor but also at midwives and churchwardens and, more generally, at the parish as a whole, the weight of the inspection fell squarely on the shoulders of the priest. Beyond examining the parish properties, its finances, its souls, and its minds, the inspection was also intended to look into the conduct and work of the priest, who was, after all, responsible for the physical and spiritual condition of his parish. This aspect, which reveals genuine administrative control over personnel, is further reinforced in a diocesan context like that of Canada, where, from the very beginning, the bishop has had the power to assign parishes and arrange careers and to promote and demote priests. This inspection took on a critical importance for both the institution and its clergy.[18] Furthermore, parish assignments usually took place in the autumn, as did the pastoral inspections.

In advance of the bishop's visit, parish priests in France were required to complete a printed form that first appeared at the end of the seventeenth century in certain dioceses.[19] The practice was extended to every diocese by the middle of the eighteenth century. The forms were based on the Borromean model that the French bishops were already using for their inspections. The forms were less interested in human beings and thus in the moral and spiritual aspects of the rule but instead placed a great deal of importance on objects, real estate, and finances. As the questionnaires came into use preparatory to the inspections, the actual inspection visits themselves in France tended to become less frequent. The province of Quebec, by comparison, was different in two details. In the first instance, the printed form appeared much later than in France and was imposed more slowly, during the course of the second half of the nineteenth century. In addition, Quebec inspections, far from diminishing as they did in France, actually became more complete and more frequent. They occurred even more often in the nineteenth century than in the eighteenth.[20] Finally, the division of the original Quebec diocese into a patchwork of ever-smaller episcopal districts in all likelihood made the institution of the inspection increasingly effective.

One type of document, the inspection notebook, was kept as of 1767 and is helpful in reconstructing this history of the inspection as an increasingly frequent and sophisticated administrative procedure and in following how the bishop viewed the parish, the parishioners, and their priest. A closer description of this document will allow a better understanding of the inspection as a way of exercising control over clerical activity and as a means of gaining a knowledge about social conditions. Furthermore, these notebooks formed part of the stock of institutional memory that the bishops were absolutely bound to preserve and pass on to their successors in order to ensure administrative continuity.[21] In these notes, which were jotted down quickly over the course of the inspections and collected into very simple folio notebooks, the bishops devoted a few pages to each of the parishes they visited.[22] Their observations do not so much concern religious practices as pay greater attention to church premises, altar plate, furniture, vestments, and finances. The notes collected in the folios are brief, dry, and altogether devoid of poetry. Written down in a kind of telegraphic shorthand, they are less anecdotal than the minutes and the ordinances that accompany them, as brief as these are, especially when they concern human beings. Along with the tally of masses and the figures relating to how many were confirmed, or how much in tithes or pew rents was taken in, there are also very diverse qualitative remarks in these notebooks about furniture, real estate, pastors, vicars, housekeepers, and parishioners. We learn, for example, that one servant is too young and another undisciplined, that a certain priest owns books that are on the Index or that another is running into opposition from his parishioners. Sometimes the inspector notes down the number of parishioners who have not made their Easter duty or describes public morality – for example, slander and gossip was rife in Saint-Joseph-de-Chambly in 1768, and "an old man in Saint-François-d'Assise-de-la-Longue-Pointe was entertaining women, which caused a lot of talk" in 1773.[23]

The inspection notebook is an inconsistent source. In the same parish tour, the amount of information included can vary considerably; the earliest parish inspections are recorded in close, even minute, detail, while later ones are less well documented, as if the inspectors' initial zealous attention to the particulars of the administrative life of the parish soon gave way to a rising weariness and a desire to skip more quickly over routine and observations common to all the parishes. Greater still are the differences in the tenor and quality of the notes from one inspector to another. Some of the bishops were particularly attentive to the altar plate; others to the church furniture or the liturgical vestments.[24] For this reason, the notes allow us to reconstruct the change in the bishops' administrative policies. Different from one another as the entries may be, they bear witness to the efforts of the bishops to assert their authority and effectively manage the dioceses as areas subject to a process of institutional standardization. But they are more than this. Because they were meant to examine the dioceses and preserve the results of the supervision, because of the attention they paid to enumerating persons and things, the inspection notebooks heralded the annual report and prepared the way for what, in the second half of the nineteenth century, would contribute to the renewal of diocesan management and its improved effectiveness.

THE ANNUAL REPORT: EXTENSION OF THE INSPECTION NOTES AND NEW ADMINISTRATIVE TOOL

In terms of their historical development, the reports thus extended the inspection notebooks without replacing them. To begin with, both kinds of document comprise elements essential to the bishop's informational capital, from which he could derive an accurate and up-to-date portrait of his diocese. The diocesan administrator knew, for example, just how many people there were in each parish, how many of them could pay for the church and their pastor, and the approximate distance they had to travel to get to mass. This close familiarity with the parishes, especially in their demographic and geographic dimensions, was essential in the Quebec context where, unlike the old European dioceses, the territory was undergoing constant change. The reports, like the inspections, were intended to produce a parochial inventory – a reckoning of the parishes' material and spiritual condition.[25] The report periods were not, however, absolutely identical. Instead of preparing them once every four or five years to coincide with the bishop's tour, they were completed by the pastor every year, or at least in theory were supposed to be. Two copies of the reports were kept. One went to the bishop, while the other stayed in the parish. Thus the report also served a memorial function, somewhat like the inspection notebooks. It was a document that the bishop and the priest could consult at any time to check on the state of the parish at a particular moment.

Unlike the completely handwritten entries in the notebooks, the annual report appeared as a printed form. As we have already seen, this form had not been systematically adopted in every diocese by 1851, but sooner or later it became established. Printed forms appeared in the Quebec archdiocese in 1888,[26] and the parish priests had to pay for them themselves. In 1890, they cost ten cents apiece or six dollars the hundred. With the advent of the forms, information was arranged and presented in the most uniform way possible for every parish. This represented a major development compared to the notebooks, in which the information was never entered as a systematic list. As previously pointed out, the bishop or his secretary sometimes omitted certain details, especially toward the end of the episcopal tour. For this reason, historians have not had much recourse to this source as they are unable to draw from it data that could be statistically analyzed, such as that provided in the reports,[27] where entries had to be made for the same invariable elements. As well, especially in the statistical tables that the bishops of Montreal and Saint-Hyacinthe introduced, the number would thereafter occupy a special place. The table allowed the raw facts drawn from the narrative text to be distinctly shown. Narrative comments often appeared at the end of the questionnaire. These took the form of a simple commentary accompanying and explaining the figures. In some of the reports, the comments are really incidental. Whether and how they appeared on the form depended on the pastors. Some extremely zealous priests would produce quite substantial commentary year after year. Others are remarkable for the lack of comment in their reports or for their loose and vague remarks. There were those who appear to have made a tactical use of the report. Newly installed pastors might make fairly lengthy and sometimes quite gloomy narrative descriptions of the parish situation in their initial report. These accounts were evidently motivated by the authors' desire to throw themselves into the task at hand and to commend themselves to their diocesan superiors for the enormous work under way, thus earning the credit such devotion deserved. Later reports, on the other hand, might be much more concise. Some of them pointed out improvement, others referred to an earlier report. In answer to the question on the 1896 Rimouski form, "Do you have anything specific to add in order to provide a more exact understanding of the parish or mission and to render the bishop able to correct any abuses that may have been introduced?" one parish priest wrote in 1896, "I must repeat what I mentioned in the report of 1895."[28]

Furthermore, even the very content of what was to be investigated altered from the notebooks to the annual reports. In addition to the preference of the eighteenth- and early-nineteenth-century inspectors to confine their attention to the physical and financial condition of the parish, the report adds a decided concern with religious observance and community life that the priests now had to render in numerical form. In this way, the Church was participating in what Jean-Pierre Beaud and Jean-Guy Prévost consider "an important transformation on both the rhetorical and cognitive level. Numbers would henceforth hold a central place and a new importance. They would be used not merely to appraise the real estate holdings of the Church and the pastor's income, but could also assess religious vitality. The development expresses in a concrete fashion "the institution of the modern principle of objectivity."[29] It is witness to a growing concern – one might even say fascination – with numbers on the part of the Catholic Church that renders observation objective as well as testifying, from the clerics' point of view, to the progress and success of the parish, notions that will henceforth be expressed in terms of quantity. We see here a particularly significant aspect of mid-nineteenth-century ultramontane liturgical reform in the province of Quebec, which made a 100 percent participation in public religious observance the ultimate object of pastoral care. In order to channel an almost wholly Catholic population toward the churches and to maximize the laity's rate of participation in ritual activity, Church authorities counted not just on theological innovations like Ligurianism or new architectural details like huge churches furnished with a great many confessionals but also on a bureaucratic accountancy method of assessing effort. The questionnaire not only allowed the success of the undertaking to be measured but also, and perhaps particularly, alerted priests to new instructions and new priorities. Where the old rigorists had made access to the sacraments a privilege, the ultramontanes made it a habit. This was a very important change in the institutional culture and the new use of numbers surely made a powerful contribution to impressing the shift on the priests' minds. As well, following the example of the census and other government statistics that were instrumental in producing constructs like unemployment, poverty, or inflation, the annual report helped to develop the concept of the "practicing" Catholic, even though the concept itself was not formalized as such until the reports issuing from the 1850s. In this regard, the individual was constructed as a communicant, the Catholic as someone necessarily involved in the liturgical observances offered by the clergy. A Catholic was defined in terms of a religious exercise, the Easter or yearly communion, making it possible to decide which Catholics were "faithful" to their religious duties and which "unfaithful." The report was not merely a sign of a "modern" lay Catholicism but was an active element in the construction of a Catholic individual who, far more directly than his ancestors, was subjected to religious demands that were increasingly stifling.[30] This idea leads to a consideration of the history of internalization and to the spread of a concept of social identity founded on the criterion of intense religious observance.

Another difference between the report and the notebooks is that the figures come not from the bishop but from the pastors. The priests had to deliver a report to their superior. In the course of his visit of inspection, the bishop could verify and, if necessary, correct the information the parish priest provided. Thus the report becomes not only an inspection device but the basis for a habit of introspection. The very modalities of collecting data in the reports had the effect of developing an introspective and self-evaluative (and thus self-restraining) reflex among the parish priests. In the course of answering the questions posed by the bishop, the pastors had to engage in an examination of conscience, in a consideration of their own ministry and their administrative work. The bishop of Sherbrooke strongly stressed this aspect in 1882 when he reminded his priests of the terms of the first Quebec provincial council's twelfth decree: "Each of the questions posed provides the priest who is anxious to fulfil his pastoral ministry the materials for a serious examination of how he has carried out his duties."[31] As he filled out his report, the priest also had to take a look at his own work. The episcopal inspection retained its symbolic and administrative character – it reaffirmed the authority of the diocesan superior and provided him with the chance to check on the information furnished him by the pastor. Unlike the inspection notebook, the annual report had more than a memorial function; it also had the pedagogical function of internalizing restraint – it reminded the priest of his duties, directed his gaze toward the parish in regard to certain objectives but also in terms of certain analytical categories. In this connection, the annual reports are much like other administrative documents. As Thierry Hentsch has observed, the codes and reserved categories are meant to standardize the bases of observation but also come to "train the observers, the observed, or the respondents and end by controlling the 'phenomena' themselves."[32]

Finally, the report allowed a closer supervision of the activity of priests than had the documents arising out of the pastoral visit. The bishop could refer to it to see whether certain directives had been followed exactly. The report thus established a better verification of episcopal directives. The following example illustrates how the reports were meant to fill this objective. In the Rimouski diocese in the early 1880s, Bishop Langevin was worried about the large number of altar candles that he deemed to be of inferior quality. The bishop required that the candles be made of beeswax. He pressed the priests to buy their candles from the nuns:

> I repeat, Sirs, that you may not buy your candles from just anyone and be sure
> that it is physically impossible that they will be pure at the price they are being
> offered to you, 45, 40, down to 35 and 30 cents the pound. Buy them preferably
> from the nuns, where you will pay more but you will have the kind of guarantee
> you can hardly get anywhere else.[33]

In his 1884 questionnaire, the bishop included the following questions:

> Where do you buy your altar candles?
> What did you pay for them?
> Where do you buy the burial candles
> What happens to them after the service?

Questions of this sort reminded the priests of what the bishop required and provided the bishop with a way to follow up on his instructions. In dioceses where the reports were completed annually or more frequently than the visits of inspection, they helped to further tighten the oversight the bishop exercised on the parishes and the clergy. In this way, the head of the diocese could know who of his priests was conforming to his instructions and who was not. This information was not merely incidental but encouraged the standardization of management practices in the diocese. It also provided a first-rate resource for curial nominations as it allowed the most zealous clergy to be identified, those who most scrupulously respected liturgical formalism and were most careful in administering the parish assets while devoting themselves to establishing a perfect observance of the precept of the Easter communion, the true cornerstone of pastoral success in the period.[34]

This control over what the clergy was doing, furthered by the annual report, appeared within the context of a profound renewal of the Quebec Catholic Church. In the nineteenth century, the expression of the faith was undergoing change, with the adoption of Ligurian morality and an exuberant and festive ultramontane piety. Liturgy, clerical dress, and pious expression were Romanized. The numbers of priests and nuns grew, and they became increasingly involved in particular fields of social activity, especially relating to charity and the care of the poor, elderly, and homeless, as well as education and colonization projects.[35] Around this same period, Church structures and management styles were also undergoing change. The structures were becoming more complex as the number of dioceses increased and diocesan councils set up to assist the bishop emerged. The staffs still remained quite small, of course, and it would be an exaggeration to view them as a bureaucracy in the sense used in the sociology of organizations. Nevertheless, the presence of a staff orbiting around the bishop and of new decisional structures express the desire to govern the dioceses and parishes more efficiently and, especially, to ensure that the priests understood and applied the new directives relative to Ligurian moral precepts, the life of the community, the liturgy, the administration of parish property, and the supervision of the schools.

From the point of view of Church history, it was not by chance that this new control mechanism appeared toward the middle of the nineteenth century and no sooner. In the eighteenth and early nineteenth centuries, the issue was primarily one of "managing" a fundamentally solid and clearly distinguished religious life by means of inspections and the documents that they produced. This explains the routine nature of the documents that were first of all meant to keep the parish machine running smoothly. A series of adjustments might come out of the inspections so that the parishes might conform as closely as possibly to the Tridentine model. The inspectors thus directed most of their attention and comments to parish equipment. They tried to see that the newer parishes were gradually outfitted properly, ensured that older parishes were kept up and that the most prosperous were enhanced, and concerned themselves with their overall sound financial management. In view of these objectives, unlike Louis Rousseau, we ought not to interpret the rather repetitious nature of the inspection notes and orders or their dry and quite telegraphic style as indications of a lack of involvement on the part of the Quebec bishops in either the inspection itself or the notes and orders.[36] The appearance of the reports and the differences from the notebooks, orders, and minutes that they reveal, notably regarding the importance given to the spiritual condition of the parish and to religious observances but also to the quality of the personnel, express a change less in the intensity of the bishop's control over the parish than in the very vision of the Quebec Church as a social institution. More than ever before, this Church became centralized in its culture, hierarchical in its operations, and national in its vocation. Therefore, it had to be able to generate a massive, uniform practice, something that required bureaucratic organization and the emergence of a professional curial staff.

During the second half of the nineteenth century, the Church was producing increasing numbers of other sorts of documents, which are preserved in its archives. These include orders, minutes, proceedings, pastoral letters, mandates, circulars, and private letters. These documents were intended to define the various roles – priests, nuns, and lay persons – to be a reminder of the virtues (moral, but also administrative and technical) that should be practiced, as well as the kinds of behaviour (religious, but also professional) that should be rejected, and to check into the way in which pastors and curates were carrying out their duties. The reports thus were part of a process of amassing an informational fund to assist management. In their reports, year after year, the priests sent the bishop information that he already possessed for the most part. In their frequent reminders to fill out the forms conscientiously and answer every question, even when the answers were substantially or even exactly the same as those provided in previous years, the bishops were requiring the priests to account to them. Even more to the point, they were reminding the priests that they were subordinate to their superiors, who were keeping a careful eye on how they ran their parishes. In the same period, a number of decrees issuing from the provincial councils sought to impose norms of conduct on priests, to specify how they ought to live and behave themselves, and to mark out the limits of their powers and functions. These decrees, for example, regulate ecclesiastical meetings and examinations for young priests (1851), the management of ecclesiastical assets (1854), and clerical life (1854 and 1868). There are reminders of the obedience the priests owe to their bishop, stressing the importance of preserving the reputation of the clergy (1873), forbidding the clergy from engaging in certain occupations, most particularly medicine (1873) and trade (1878), and providing instructions on how to draw up their wills (1886).[37]

Thus, in the second half of the nineteenth century, the bishop's powers and each cleric's position in the Church and in society were specified, increasingly codified, and further asserted. In this sense, the report may be seen as one of the implements that contributed to the strengthening of episcopal power. The report, like the census of the *ancien régime*, was part of a royal administrative logic. It legitimated episcopal authority and may perhaps be seen as one of the key elements in the internal hierarchization of the clergy and in the wielding of power.

THE ANNUAL REPORTS AND THE HISTORY OF STATISTICAL THOUGHT

Let us recall that this essay was inspired by a work on the establishment of civil censuses and that one of our aims was to situate the appearance of the annual reports within the history of statistical and accountancy thought. To what degree may the annual report be compared to the census?

We see a clear parallel between governmental efforts to undertake a regular census of the population and similar efforts on the part of the Church to establish an increasingly polished informational system. Both of these undertakings were begun around the middle of the nineteenth century and both had predecessors in earlier decades. Both used intermediaries, agents in one case, parish priests in the other. Both collected diverse information in order to comprehend and intervene in those areas of interest to them, especially what affected the population and the country on the one hand, and order and public morality on the other. The state took periodic population,

agricultural, and industrial surveys, while the Church counted the number
of Catholics, Protestants, and communicants in the parishes, inventoried
the schools, evaluated Church holdings, and looked into pastors' incomes
and Church revenues. The state investigated crime and poverty,[38] whereas
the Church asked about "principal kinds of dissolution" and "most widespread vices," counted the number of taverns in the parishes, and asked
pastors about drunks, money-lenders, mistresses, or prostitutes.

Despite these evident similarities and despite the fact that the Church,
like the state, might want a better knowledge about the area and the people
in its jurisdiction, the two projects cannot be wholly integrated. The government not only collected quantifiable data on populations through its
surveys and censuses but processed them as well. It compiled the data and
established rates and averages. In short, government in the nineteenth century participated in the development of statistics through its censuses and
surveys. The Church had little recourse to statistical constructs. The information it collected from the parishes was subjected to extremely perfunctory treatment. In the reports they sent to the Vatican, the bishops provided
the total number of parishes and of Catholics in their jurisdiction. They
sent a few assessments, sometimes in figures, sometimes not, of the "state"
of the religion. But their statistical efforts went hardly further than that.
For example, the bishops did not try to establish an average number of Easter communicants in their dioceses. Nor were the reports compiled. There
were no tables bringing together the information recovered from the parishes. Moreover there were scarcely any that compared individual parishes.
On top of that, in certain cases, though these were the exception rather
than the rule, the responses from the priests were recopied into the same
register, one after the other, where an index of parish names directing the
reader to the relevant pages was the only apparatus provided to deal with
the information.[39]

Does this mean that bishops did not use the annual reports for the purposes of comparison? Not at all. Certainly this document, to the degree
that it did not prompt an exhaustive statistical treatment, tended to present
the parochial grid as a constellation and did not provide a macrosocial
description of the diocese, let alone the ecclesiastical province, as did government statistics for the nation. Of course, the figures for religious observance were not used to stimulate competition among the parishes, as were
the results of various surveys that the bishops used to make public. Nevertheless, the reports furnished a thorough knowledge of the parochial units
that allowed the head of the diocese to see where each stood and judge the
performance of the pastors. The bishop neither compiled the data nor

published it, as the figures were intended for his own use and that of his immediate staff in the assignment of parishes and in awarding promotions. Publishing the figures thus served no purpose for two reasons. In the first place, the competitive process and the habit of self-inspection that the reports encouraged worked in any event as the priests were perfectly aware that they would be judged on their responses. Secondly, in contrast to democratic governments, the bishops were not held liable for their decisions. A bishop who made arbitrary rulings and who was deemed to manage diocesan affairs unjustly would certainly be open to criticism on the part of his clergy, but his authority would remain unchallenged.

CONCLUSION

Starting from a comparison with the genesis of an instrument critical to the exercise of state power permits us to conclude by introducing the Foucaldian concept of "pastoral power" in order better to comprehend the cultural and institutional evolution revealed in this history of clerical statistics.[40] One of the key elements of pastoral power is a governmental knowledge of the social situation that is both deep and broad. This knowledge is broad, and therefore statistical, to the degree that it concerns the governed and deep because it is also individualized. In any case, if we confine ourselves to this precise aspect of modern state power, we must recognize that the evolution of ecclesiastical informational instruments seems to be in phase with those of the state. Thus, just as tools like the census and various administrative procedures were being employed in Canada to affect the state bureaucracy (the civil service) and the population in general (the citizens), the Catholic Church was at the same time and for two groups (priests and their flocks) developing and perfecting its means of investigation and constraint.

On the one hand, the exercise of a Catholic clerical governance was more successful than in the past. Indirectly it was being transmitted through the preparation of more detailed statistical reports regarding behaviour but primarily through coercing one and all by means of the ritual implements of surveillance and standardization. Of course, the confessional, that very symbol of the power wielded by the institution over the individual, had been in existence for a very long time, but it had not been used with the comprehensiveness and frequency that progressively became the norm during the nineteenth century. On the other hand, and more specifically, a more effective power was wielded over the priestly staff within the framework of a refinement of governing administrative structures: standardization of priests' training

(which became permanent), a subtle management of their careers, and a
sharpening of the oversight of their behaviour and of the mechanisms of internalizing expectation. Pastoral power was applied primarily within the institution itself. It is this intensification and this technical improvement of first
episcopal, then diocesan and administrative power, flowing from the centre
toward the periphery of the institution, that essentially allows us to make out
the history of a management control embodied initially in the inspection
visit, then in the pastoral report, but that was actually the generalization of a
clerical bureaucratic culture whose history remains largely as yet unrecorded.

NOTES

1 Bruce Curtis, *The Politics of Population: State Formation, Statistics, and the Census
  of Canada, 1840–1875*, Toronto, University of Toronto Press, 2001.
2 Jacques Grisé, *Les conciles provinciaux de Québec et l'Église canadienne, 1851–
  1886*, Montreal, Fides, 1979, 91.
3 As examples, here are two extracts, drawn from circulars dated 1875 and 1876:
  "Some reports have not as yet been sent to me. I ask the pastors to let me have them as
  quickly as possible. Some of those I have received are written in ink so faint they are
  barely legible." Again: "The Pastors would do well to remember that the annual report
  that they are to complete according to the form appearing on page 119 of the
  Ceremonial Appendix must be submitted *before the first of September*" [emphasis in
  original]. Circulars, 10 September 1875 and 15 May 1876, *Mandements, lettres
  pastorales et circulaires des évêques de Québec* (hereafter MEQ), vol. 5, Quebec,
  Chancellory of the Archbishop, 1887, 318 and 398.
4 One of them wrote: "The parish spirit is generally good. There is little enthusiasm
  for educating children. As far as the Church or charity are concerned, they are more
  miserly than generous." Archives of the Bishop of Saint Hyacinthe, IV D.4. Report
  for the parish of Saint Aimé for the year 1852.
5 Gabriel LeBras, *Études de sociologie religieuse*, Paris, Presses universitaires de
  France, 1955, 2 vols; Fernand Boulard, *Premiers itinéraires en sociologie religieuse*,
  Paris, Editions ouvrières, 1954.
6 Christine Marcilhacy, *Le diocèse d'Orléans sous l'épiscopat de Mgr Dupanloup,
  1849–1878: sociologie religieuse et mentalités collectives*, Paris, Plon, 1962; and
  Louis Pérouas, *Le diocèse de La Rochelle de 1648 to 1724: sociologie et pastorale*,
  Paris, SEVPEN, 1964.
7 S. Gagnon, "Le diocèse de Montréal durant les années 1860," in Pierre Hurtubise et
  al, *Le Laïc dans l'Église canadienne-française de 1830 à nos jours*, Montreal, Fides,
  1972, 113–27.

8 René Hardy and Jean Roy, "Encadrement social et mutation de la culture religieuse en Mauricie," *Questions de culture* 5, *Les régions culturelles* (1983): 61–78; René Hardy, *Contrôle social et mutation de la culture religieuse au Québec, 1830–1930*, Montreal, Boréal, 1999; Christine Hudon, *Prêtres et fidèles dans le diocèse de Saint-Hyacinthe, 1820–1875*, Sillery (Quebec), Septentrion, 1996; Louis Rousseau and Frank W. Remiggi, *Atlas historique des pratiques religieuses: le Sud-Ouest du Québec au XIXᵉ siècle*, Ottawa, Presses de l'Université d'Ottawa, 1998.

9 J. Roy, "Les revenus des curés du diocèses de Nicolet, 1885–1904," *Société canadienne d'histoire de l'Église catholique*, Session d'étude, 52 (1985): 51–67; J. Roy, "Le prélèvement ecclésiastique dans le diocèse de Nicolet, à la fin du XIXᵉ siècle: la fabrique," *Études d'histoire religieuse*, 67 (2001): 57–68; J. Roy,: Soutenir le prêtre" in S. Courville and N. Séguin, eds, *La paroisse. Atlas historique du Québec, vol. V*, Sainte-Foy (Quebec), Presses de l'Université Laval, 2001, 177–89.

10 Jean Roy and Daniel Robert, "Les rapports annuels des curés et l'histoire des paroisses dans la seconde moitié du XIXᵉ siècle," *Archives* 16, 1 (June 1984): 31–59. Francine Girard-Ducasse and Louis Rousseau, "Les lunettes des contrôleurs: contenus des questionnaires pastoraux montréalais avant 1880. Leur contenu et leur utilisation," *Archives* 21, 3 (Winter 1990): 47–69.

11 Jean-Pierre Beaud and Jean-Guy Prévost, *L'ère du chiffre. Systèmes statistiques et traditions nationales*, Sainte-Foy (Quebec), Presses de l'Université du Québec, 2000.

12 See "Le matériel et le personnel" in Olliver Hubert, *Sur la terre comme au ciel. La gestion des rites part l'Église catholique du Québec (fin XVIIᵉ – mi-XIXᵉ siècle)* Sainte-Foy (Quebec), Presses de l'Université Laval, 2000, 83–114).

13 *MEQ* 1, 156.

14 Alain Laberge, "L'implantation de la paroisse dans la vallée du Saint-Laurent aux XVIIᵉ et XVIIIᵉ siècles," in Courville and Séguin, eds, *La paroisse*, 17–18.

15 In his capacity as the Quebec bishop's grand vicar in 1685.

16 Regarding the preparation for the inspection and the sequence of its events, see Jean Roy and Daniel Robert, "Deux évêques trifluvians en visite: Thomas Cooke, Louis-François Laflèche et la gestion des paroisses (1852–1898)," *Études d'histoire religieuse* 57 (1990): 89–110.

17 *Rituel du Diocèse de Québec publié par l'ordre de Monseigneur Saint-Valier, évêque de Québec*, Paris, Simon Langlois, 1703, 375. The same idea appears in the mandates of the nineteenth century.

18 Clerical correspondence dealing with complaints relating to the parish priests' performance often refer to pastoral inspections, such as this example in which a pastor responded to his parishioners' complaints that he was too slow: "This is false– I am a little quicker, especially since the Monseigneur's inspection and this has been seen in the parish." His baptisms went on interminably? "This is an exaggeration; I spend less time baptizing since the last episcopal inspection." Did Sunday Mass finish

in the afternoon? "That too is very exaggerated; since Monseigneur's inspection, Mass finishes between noon and a quarter past except for once when it finished a little bit later." Archives of the Archdiocese of Quebec (hereafter AAQ), 61, *Les Écureuils* 1, 30, Gadoury to Signay, 13 October 1845.

19 For pastoral inspections and a study of that phenomenon in France see Marc Venard, *Le catholicisme à l'épreuve dans la France du XVIe siècle*, Paris, Cerf, 2000, 27–63.

20 In the nineteenth century, each parish was visited every four or five years, sometimes even every three years. J. Roy and D. Robert, "Deux évêques trifluvians," 93.

21 AAQ, 71 CD1, 164, Lartigue to Plessis, 20 March 1806.

22 The archives of the Quebec Archdiocese preserve a dozen of these little notebooks from 1767 to 1844.

23 AAQ 69, CD, 1.

24 Hubert, *Sur la terre*, 91–4.

25 Gagnon, "Le diocèse de Montréal."

26 Circulaire, 14 March 1888, vol. 7, 6.

27 The inspection notebooks do, however, provide series of great continuity, especially for financial data, which can be used within the framework of a quantitative approach.

28 Archives of the Bishop of Gaspé, D-RA-1896, Annual report of the Sainte-Anne-de Ristigouche mission.

29 Jean-Pierre Beaud and Jean-Guy Prévost, "L'expérience statistique canadienne," in Beaud and Prévost, *L'ère du chiffre*, 74.

30 See Hardy, *Contrôle sociale*.

31 Circular, 8 February 1882, *Mandements, lettres pastorales, circulaires et autres documents publiés dans l'archdiocèse de Sherbrooke*, 2, Sherbrooke, Imprimerie du Messager St-Michel, 1888, 44.

32 Thierry Hentsch, "Compter et conter: le dire de la statistique," in Beaud and Prévost, *L'ère du chiffre*, 484.

33 *Mandements, lettres pastorales, circulaires de Mgr Langevin et statuts synodaux du diocèse de Rimouski, disposés par ordre chronologique*, May 1878 to May 1887, news series no. 87, 3.

34 Hudon, *Prêtres et fidèles*, 395–422.

35 Philippe Sylvain and Nive Voisine, *Histoire du catholicisme québécoise. Les XVIIIe et XIXe siècles*. Vol. 2, *Réveil et consolidation (1840–1898)*, Montréal, Boréal, 1991, esp. 419–38.

36 Rousseau and Remiggi, *Atlas historique*, 7–8; Girard-Ducasse and Rousseau, "Les lunettes des contrôleurs," 47–69.

37 Grisé, *Les conciles provinciaux*.

38 Ian Hacking, "Biopower and the Avalanche of Printed Numbers," *Humanities in Society* 5 (1982): 279–95.
39 For example, the reports for the diocese of Saint-Hyacinthe for 1878.
40 See for example Michel Foucault, "Omnes et singulatum: Toward a Criticism of Political Reason," in Sterling McMurrin, ed., *The Tanner Lectures on Human Values* 2, Salt Lake City, University of Utah Press, 1981, 223–54.

2

Carnal Connection and Other Misdemeanours: Continuity and Change in Presbyterian Church Courts, 1830–90

NANCY CHRISTIE

First and foremost, this article concerns itself with the pace and manner in which customary social practices both resisted and advanced the transition to a capitalist, liberal social order. To do so, I have explicitly taken the institutional church – in this case the Presbyterian Church – as a barometer of cultural change with which one can trace fundamental changes in the value systems of ordinary people and elites, which in turn denote deeper social transformations occurring during the nineteenth century.[1] Whereas it is more usual for historians to examine the emergence of the capitalist order through analyses of labour relations and the growth of the state and through macrohistorical studies of the growth of the market economy, I would argue that the church, because it was an institution constructed at the confluence between the family and the state or civil society, provides a valuable entree into questions relating to the "great transformation"[2] in worldview that characterized the emergence of modern social relations. In short, this article focuses upon the church courts, institutions distinctly identified with traditional societies and evocative of a church enmeshed in pre-industrial structures of authority and community, to map the changing meaning of religiosity during the nineteenth century. Because these systems of premodern culture survived in Canada well into the 1890s and beyond, Presbyterian Kirk Sessions (or church courts) offer evidence of how cultural practices resisted the capitalist social order. However, as I shall argue, as revealed by a close analysis of their social meaning both to church leaders and to the ordinary parishioners who used them, the church courts functioned also as crucial mediators of newer mental worlds and, in this way, smoothed the transition to an urban, industrial society.[3]

This article is also an exploration in the transplantation of social practices from the old world to the new. The system of Kirk Session or church courts was part of the cultural baggage imported into the frontier settlements of early Canada. According to Rosalind Mitchison and Leah Leneman, this once efficient system of social discipline was beginning to decline in Scotland by the end of the eighteenth century, largely because of industrialization and intense urban growth. Their conclusions, however, have been disputed both by Callum Brown and by T.M. Devine, who have argued that the Kirk Sessions survived well into the 1850s, especially in rural areas, and that in various localities their ability to discipline moral irregularities may even have increased up until the 1870s.[4] Because this theocratic system of church polity had become fundamental to Protestant Scottish identity,[5] Kirk Sessions were an important aspect of immigrants' desire to replicate their social order abroad. The courts were thus imported into the Canadas and were sustained through a complex web of elite control and popular support until the last quarter of the nineteenth century, although the particular complexion of the Kirk Session changed radically from locality to locality. For example, in the district of Lachine in Lower Canada, an area settled largely by retired traders from the Hudson's Bay Company, there were virtually no disciplinary courts, as the elders of the congregation chose to regulate recalcitrant parishioners through the selective dispensation of charity to loyal church adherents. In this parish, it was difficult to find anyone wishing to undertake the duties of elder; by contrast, in the Township of Beckwith in Lanark County, Upper Canada, the elders were extremely vigilant, and this particular area remained unequalled in its obsession with fornication (to the virtual exclusion of all other offences) and in the severity of its punishments. In Hamilton, a burgeoning industrial centre, where urban sprawl characterized the parish of Knox Presbyterian, communal control of recalcitrant church members appears to have been weaker, so church elders chose to vigilantly monitor people as they became church members, knowing that families could potentially be visited and policed only once a year by elders. Moreover, in Hamilton, where concerns of work discipline were at the forefront among employers, issues of drunkenness became the centrepiece of the regulatory system.

Despite the variation among Presbyterian churches with regard to the way in which they imposed their ideal of theocratic control, it remains clear that the Presbyterian Church was a fundamental instrument of Scottish identity.[6] Its courts were punitive and signally intolerant of "scandalous" behaviour – defined as those sins that had become part of public fame through gossip and innuendo – because of the damage that might accrue to the reputation and authority of the Presbyterian Church as a whole, which

was viewed by the elders and ordinary Scots alike as a site of both spiritual
and civil citizenship. Were the Kirk Sessions reflective, therefore, of consensual social relations? Were they a venue for democratic inclinations? In
what follows, I wish to argue that while the system of social control exacted by church elders was oppressive it also provided an arena where marginal members of the community could give voice to their worldview, to
their conception of religiosity, and thereby utilize the very instruments of
dominant groups to articulate a sense of agency and even resistance. While
it is true that Canadian church elders were, as in Scotland, probably drawn
from among the "high status middle class"[7] the pathbreaking work of
Laura Gowing, Sara Mendelson, Elizabeth Foyster, and Anna Clark indicates that church courts cannot simply be seen as reflexively identified with
the interests of a male elite.[8] While the mass revolt against Rev. Wilson of
Lanark for rashly suppressing plebeian entertainments, notably dancing at
weddings, was somewhat remarkable for its resemblance to organized protest,[9] parishioners of low social status, bachelors, or illiterate and migratory servant women individually saw the Kirk Sessions as venues for both
resistance and conformity to a dominant religious worldview. From this
perspective, church regulatory practices must be seen as congeries of intersecting value systems,[10] as forums of social contestation, and church membership as the most important passport for an individual's integration into
the community. With the removal of public church courts and the increased
pattern of private visits to parishioners by the minister, the church became a
more elitist realm, where the discursive flow was controlled almost entirely
by clerics. Although the practice of public penance and the intrusion into
"private" life seems offensive to our modern sensibilities, they did provide
a forum whereby ordinary people could articulate their notions of courtship, marriage, and spirituality and thereby protect their sense of individual
or family honour.

While parishioners could selectively choose and interpret discursive texts
that dominated the religious landscape after the 1880s, these acts, because
private, were not evocative of ritualized social power. Indeed, the demise of
the church courts and the consequent privatization of social discipline by the
1880s might well be seen as representing the end of an era characterized by
more fluid social relations. Through an examination of systems of Presbyterian church discipline, we can trace the gradual shift from the church as the
protector of civil order and as an arm of the state towards a more otherworldly church in which the rhetoric of inclusiveness masks an increasing
clericalization and bureaucratization, a process that tended to increasingly
marginalize popular religiosity. Thus, by the 1880s, the diminution of lay

power associated with the church courts created a sense of greater social distance and more conflictual relations in the realms of both class and gender.

It has been noted by historians that the system of Presbyterian church courts were not officially sanctioned by the colonial authorities of British North America.[11] While true in the literal sense, in an 1835 memorandum concerning the grievances of the king's subjects in Lower Canada, Lord Gosford, Sir Charles Grey, and Sir George Gipps gave credence to the Kirk Sessions, seeing in them a means to ensure the political consent and loyalty of the potentially disaffected Scottish immigrants. In practice, as well, the relationship between the civil and church courts continued as they had in Scotland, wherein the church courts functioned as the lowest courts and where elders often functioned also as justices of the peace. Indeed, it was not unheard of for witnesses to swear before the local JP as a means to reinforce the veracity of their testimony, a practice used with particular effect in the notorious Montreal case in which one Rev. Esson was accused of consorting with prostitutes. There, another clergyman deftly utilized the status of the local JP, Peter McGill, to lend greater credence to the testimony of the two illiterate prostitutes and the male witness who claimed to have spied Rev. Esson "through a hole in the wall" – a long-standing trope in such cases where eyewitness testimony was crucial – offering money and having sexual relations twice during the night in question. In this particular case, despite the use of several affidavits authorized by McGill, the church elders quashed the charges against Esson, fearing that impugning the minister of such a wealthy congregation would be too injurious to the authority of the church as a whole.[12]

Indeed, it was the authority of the Presbyterian Church rather than the actual sanctioning of individuals that formed the dynamic of this particular relationship between church and state.[13] For example, the Presbyterian Church in Beckwith Township, Upper Canada, publicly condemned the practice of Sunday mail delivery in a petition to the legislature in 1852, and in Smith's Falls in 1842 the church censured the lockmasters for operating the Rideau Canal locks on Sunday, not only because this represented a public desecration of the Sabbath but also because opening the locks prevented parishioners access to the church.[14] However, Presbyterian elders such as those in the neighbouring community of Lanark, perhaps because of the differing political complexion of the community, drew closer limits around the boundaries of church and state and were loathe to be seen to challenge the government. For this reason, they declined to support "the formal process" of a court proceeding in the slander case of Robert Cumming against a local school trustee, even though Cumming was an elder. In order to establish clear boundaries between the domains of the civic and spiritual, the church elders publicly excommunicated Cumming for making a "public notoriety" of his accusation of intemperance against a government appointee that so directly impugned his ability to carry out the responsibilities of his office. Interestingly, in 1876, the church elders energetically disciplined this same school trustee, John Craig, for fornication, a charge of immorality unconnected to his government office.[15] Just as in the fornication case of Rev. Esson, the decision to discipline turned not upon the behaviour of the individual, which in both cases was reasonably proven, but upon the impact that a disciplinary decision would have upon the reputation of the church as an institution.

By contrast, in parishes where clergymen hoped to establish a Presbyterian theocracy, where ecclesiastical law was more powerful than civil courts, there was considerable rancour and dispute between the local magistrates and the Presbyterian clergy. In part, such disputes arose because the magistrates were largely Anglican and represented the authority of a foreign, English government and because there existed a considerable gulf between the social status of these government appointees and the Presbyterian clergymen, who for the most part were drawn from the artisanal or lower middle classes of rural Scotland.[16] For example in 1834 in Dundee, Lower Canada, the case of slander between the local representative of the crown and the Rev. Moody was rapidly settled because it "looked bad for the Minister and the Justice of the Peace to be at variance." [17] In Perth, the Rev. William Bell, a political radical and Secessionist Presbyterian clergyman, was in constant warfare with the civil courts, in part because the high status magistrates refused to bow to church law over questions of duelling, card playing, desecrating the Sabbath, and irregular sexual relations with domestic servants, all of which was viewed, from Bell's political and social perspective, as a challenge both of his middle-class sensibilities and of his ideal of establishing a theocratic form of government in the new world.[18] But, more pragmatically, Bell and other Presbyterian ministers feared that airing the dirty linen of Presbyterians in the civil courts might diminish the authority of this ethnic church and its ministers. The harshest penalty, excommunication, was brought against parishioners such as Robert Menzies who undermined the reputation of the Presbyterian Church. Robert Menzies admitted before the church elders that he had given testimony against a fellow Presbyterian in the civil court in Hamilton.[19]

The ultimate goal of the disciplinary courts was to reprove and discipline immoral behaviour, but the public process of effecting a reconciliation of the individual to the church through confession, rebuke, and admonition was a ritual of public cleansing intended to demonstrate the conformity to church rules that unified the church and its parishioners. The formalized process of church discipline was thus evocative of the church's power to enforce obedience and to adjudicate membership in the community. In the final analysis the fact that no formal recognition was granted to Presbyterian ecclesiastic courts was moot, for in practice they were generally viewed as the primary venues of justice for Presbyterian immigrants and were intrinsic to ethnic cohesion. That the church courts persisted well into the 1880s served to greatly expand the influence of the church within the civil order and thus preserved through cultural practice the elision of the secular and the profane within a polity characterized by a progressive formal jurisdictional separation between church and state. These vestiges of older confessional state structures in which religious and civil citizenship were viewed as synonymous were reinvigorated in the colonial setting principally to contain and qualify the emergence of the modern liberal state that enshrined the concept of voluntarism. Thus, when Lord Gosford, Sir Charles Grey, and Sir George Gipps, leading Whig policymakers, promoted the Presbyterian disciplinary courts as an instrument of loyalty, this implied a clear divergence from unitary Anglican notions of citizenship enunciated by Bishop John Strachan and designated an adaptive form of political organization in the Canadas that sought to harness multiple British ethnic identities to a unitary form of government, a trope that saw its fullest expression in the Macdonaldian constitution of centralized government authority balanced by semi-autonomous religioethnic cultural communities.[20] Stated another way, the Presbyterian leadership utilized the church courts as safe vessels for fostering modernity; for through the mechanism of this pre-industrial system, newer notions of evangelicalism, individualism, privacy, free-market religious voluntarism, and refurbished notions of patriarchal family formation – the fundamental tenets of liberal society[21] – could be introduced incrementally and without public controversy.

For the ordinary Presbyterian, therefore, one's notion of citizenship in the community rested fundamentally upon one's spiritual relationship to the institutional church. The spiritual and the profane were one and the same; indeed, one's spiritual reputation was key to one's wider reputation in society.[22] Hence, the admonition of Scottish fathers to their sons that the key to establishing a reputation as a man of honour and neighbourliness lay first and foremost with membership in the Presbyterian Church. While gentry notions of masculinity and the transition to adulthood was linked to one's fashionable comportment, social connections, and education, sons of artisanal, crofting, and middling families conceived of masculine honour in terms of Christian character and behaviour, what clergyman referred to as the "walk and conversation" of the elect. When immigrating to Upper Canada, the young David Gibson, a young apprentice surveyor and later grocery store clerk, found himself in a community where he had no family and where he was an unknown quantity among his neighbours. Although the act of binding himself to William Blackadder gave him some standing in the community insofar as he had to promise to be honest, faithful, and diligent and to "conform to his station," the real entree into his community was not through honest work; rather the key to achieving respectable "manhood" lay in "attending the Church regularly which will cause you to be respected above all things."[23] Thus, while it is important to stress that Scottish Presbyterians would have defined their world as primarily divided between the godly and ungodly, the priority one placed upon religion as the principal demarcator of respectability may have acquired a greater class resonance in the early nineteenth century. While class attitudes were not fully articulated, one is reminded of the subtle way in which religion shaped attitudes traditionally ascribed to labour relations. It also reminds us of the degree to which society was still defined according to a two-class model in the early nineteenth century, when concepts of middle-class behaviour were still embryonic.[24]

So interdependent were notions of spiritual and civil citizenship that Scottish immigrants went to great lengths to ensure that their minister grant them a testificat of good character, their passport to immediate membership in the Presbyterian community in the New World. The testificat iterated, among others things, where you were born and where you grew up, whether you were legitimate, had been baptized, and were in full communion with the Presbyterian Church. Because one's social status within the Scottish community was defined in terms of being "known in all things," it was incumbent upon newcomers to make a public declaration of their reputation as committed adherents, even when they had certificates of character from their former clergyman. As a result, many cases of spiritual transgression came to the fore neither through neighbourhood scrutiny nor the vigilance of the elders but by voluntary confession, which indicates that the concept of honour and the notion of moral credit through establishing public repute were not attributes esteemed solely by the gentry but were adhered to by people from the plebeian orders of Scottish society. Moreover, making presentments "by his own report,"[25] namely by a process of self-confession,[26] was sufficiently commonplace to show that this system of social discipline was important from the perspective of church leaders, who wished to utilize them to enforce conformity.[27] It was also evocative of a form of popular religious practice by which even the more marginal members of society – youth, migrants, unmarried women, and men – affirmed their legitimacy and sense of inclusion in their community.

Certainly, from the perspective of the elders, the policing apparatus of the Kirk Sessions was viewed as fundamental to their power in their community[28]; however, it also served the needs of church members themselves. Youthful migrants without family were particular desirous of using the system of public confession to establish new reputations for themselves: the newcomer William Lamb thus appeared at Session in 1844 to confess that he had fathered an illegitimate child eight years ago in Scotland, while Jane Jack, an unwed mother, made an abject confession of her past sin of fornication to the elders of St Paul's Presbyterian Church in Peterborough, even though her sin had occurred several years previously in Cobourg and she had remained in full communion since that time. Being admitted to church membership was part of one's rite of passage to adulthood, but more importantly it was a public symbol of a person's "respectable standing" in the godly community. Even those of unblemished character, such as Mrs Robert McLaren from Smith's Falls, personally approached the clergyman and willingly endured the humiliation of a full court case concerning the serious charge of adultery "to have a rumor affecting her character and standing as a member of the church cleared up."[29] Indeed, so important was church adherence to concepts of worldly success and calculations of social status that, as late as 1881, when it was accepted practice to be admitted as church members following an examination by the minister in private, men like Mr C. Hatch and Mr Cameron, from New Brunswick, elected to "testify their love to their Redeemer by publicly professing their faith in him"[30] before the entire congregation.

For these middle-class men the public manifestation of virtuous manhood was directly determined by church adherence. Likewise, women did not simply conflate honour with sexual purity; rather, their reputation as godly women took priority over the question of sexual immorality, just as church membership took precedence over other forms of civic identity. For both men and women, the principal manner by which one constructed a reputation was through membership in the church. In the early modern period, wherever church adherence was enshrined by the state, moral virtue was less an expression of popular agency, for prior to the eighteenth century one's relationship with the church was founded upon the notion of subordination.[31] By contrast, in an era of free-market religious practice defined by liberty of worship, church affiliation was no longer equated with structures of authority but was increasingly identified with concepts of equality and self-identity. Because membership in the godly community was an expression of free choice, participation in the church was assigned greater moral worth and hence the pre-eminent way by which to establish a reputation for honesty and respectability. Moreover, in an era of marked social differentiation by wealth and class position, religious faith was seen as an egalitarian force and participation in the church polity an important badge of popular religious identity rather than the machinery of an outside authority. Thus, William Mackenzie, a failing crofter in Scotland rationalized the growing rift between himself and his son, a successful clergyman in Glengarry, Upper Canada, in terms of the social distance that he saw as a function of not being "born of a higher degree"; he likewise believed that religion was the principal leveller of humanity for "all must stand to answer to a higher Judge."[32] Within these premodern court structures were appearing distinctly modern ideas about social relations and the structure of authority. While it is true that the elders and the ministers oversaw the Kirk Sessions, this form of discipline was not viewed as imposed upon them and it did not become a site of class conflict; rather, participation in the church, including what to modern eyes seems an extremely punitive system of moral regulation, was deemed by ordinary parishioners as an important facet of their notion of community and self-identity.

That ordinary Scottish migrants saw in the newly formed parish churches of Upper Canada a forum for their own class aspirations can be seen from the frequency with which church leaders were censured and called to account for a wide range of immoral acts. Since all heads of household who had made some kind of financial contribution to the church – and this could be as little as one shilling or one bushel of wheat – had a vote in the church, it was understandable that church members would interpret local church polity in terms of self-government. Further, many aspects of the social paternalism of the Old World churches was in decline in Upper Canada, where churches often equalized pew rents, thus dislodging the traditional identification between the physical template of the church seating and the social hierarchy of society as a whole.[33] Perhaps the best evidence for the increasing perception of the church as a centre of popular self-determination is the frequency with which church elites – including clergymen, elders, and precentors – were themselves policed by the common people.[34] What we see emerging is a newer kind of contractual relationship within the parish church whereby parishioners who paid believed they had an independent right to question the behaviour and duties of church leaders. Thus in 1824 Rev. McLaurin of Williamstown in eastern Upper Canada was censured in a petition signed by ninety-four parishioners not only for defrauding them of church funds but on what they considered the more serious charge of inattendance to duties. The minister's written pledge to "devote himself anew to his duties" was then publicly proclaimed from every pulpit in the presbytery.[35] In Smith's Falls in 1841 the trustees of Westminister Presbyterian were admonished for allowing Methodists to meet on church premises,[36] while in Dundee Zion Presbyterian in Lower Canada the elders were severely rebuked in 1836 for failing to regularly attend worship. They, in turn, weakly protested against this charge of "delinquency" by sarcastically retorting that "they got more good by reading their books at home."[37] Even junior officeholders were under constant scrutiny. In the Presbyterian Church at Boston, Upper Canada, in 1856 Peter McKay, the church precentor, who was handsomely paid for leading the congregation in singing the psalms, was excommunicated for having been seen drunk, to the detriment of the church; a similar case regarding the drunkness of a precentor in Carleton Place occurred in 1840.[38] Like Peter McKay, John Cam was reinstated only after agreeing "to walk worthy of his profession." In 1837 in Boston church, open social rebellion was unnecessary as plebeian Scots were well able to discipline their social betters, like the elder Mr Crighton, who was caught in a state of drunkeness.[39] Elders were particularly prey to communal vigilance as they were most commonly drawn from the wealthiest quarters of the community, unlike the precentors, who were men of more modest means.[40] Even on seemingly minor charges, such as falsely promising to sign the temperance pledge, elders were severely punished, as in the case of Mr Edmison from Peterborough in 1839. In this case, however, he seems to have been a target of disapproval because he was a young and unmarried.[41]

Was the critical gaze of ordinary parishioners a function of the social distance brought about by urbanization, and was it evidence of growing social conflict? Certainly, the social pretence of Dr McQuesten, an elder in Central Presbyterian Church in Hamilton, may have been a manifestation of growing social inequalities, especially since the charge of public drunkenness against him was brought forward by those outside the church. However, even elders like Mr Flock in smaller centres like Smith's Falls were regularly brought to account. In 1858, Flock was found guilty of "illicit intercourse" with the widow Ballantyne and for attempting to procure an abortion for her in Perth. Thus even in the absence of any real evidence of sexual relations, namely a live birth, Mr Flock was suspended because of the widespread rumours that had caused "serious detriment to the interests of religion."[42] While this case shows that the system of social regulation was not simply imposed from above, it also supports the theory advanced by Callum Brown that the social transformation of parish churches into "ecclesiastical republics" occurred first in rural rather than urban centres.[43] It also demonstrates that, once parishioners began to see their parish church as a manifestation of their control and as an expression of self-identity, they were more willing to rebuke officeholders. Their willingness to police officeholders may not have been a sign of greater class conflict; rather the desire to punish church leaders expressed their view that this was their church, and it flowed from a concern to protect its cultural authority in the wider community. What is evident is that the kind of church transplanted from Scotland was one that had already witnessed some of the modernizing changes brought about in both rural and urban areas by industrial development, had already broken with traditional notions of paternalistic cultural consensus, and now embodied newer notions of social inclusiveness grounded in contractarian concepts that governed the relationship between the parishioner and the church elite.

This vision of the church as reflecting popular and Scottish ethnic interests explains the continued efficacy of the church courts in the new world. Although these church courts encapsulated different conceptions of the relationship between moral reputation and spirituality from those of the early modern period, the Kirk Sessions, like their antecedents, preserved the notion that individual misbehaviour was injurious to the Christian community and thus a matter of public concern. The shift towards the privatization of moral regulation emerged not as function of popular or even middle-class withdrawal from the principle of congregational scrutiny; rather, it was dictated by the clericalization and professionalization of the office of the clergyman. There is considerable evidence from the professional journal of clergyman Rev. William Bell, which begins in the 1820s, of ongoing jurisdictional disputes between ministers and elders animated often by the class differential between lower- middle-class ministers and elders drawn from the local social elite. It is clear from Bell's account of his career as a Seceder clergyman that he wished to use his own system of private visiting as a means to circumvent the competing systems of communal social control – namely gossip, charivaris, and duelling, which Bell believed were condoned and engaged in by the elders.[44] The symbiotic relationship between the interests of ordinary parishioners who utilized the church courts to absolve themselves before their community and the social authority of the elders, who saw their policing role as integral to upholding their status as local elites, was frowned upon by clergymen who saw in the courts a challenge to their emerging role as professional experts.

However, by 1851, cracks were appearing in this system of lay control; ministers began to decree that, should elders hear of a case of public scandal as a result of gossip, these should be first taken to the clergymen who would resolve the issue through private rebuke and admonition. One can see as part of this assault by clergymen upon neighbourhood policing an increasing number of cases where idle gossips were themselves disciplined. In 1855 in Smith's Falls Mrs Girvin, a widow, was disciplined for having been "heard speaking publicly" about the intoxication of a Mr Dunbar, and in 1871 in Lanark a Mrs Gemell was admonished for "circulating evil and injurious report" when she accused Mr and Mrs McCurdy of milking someone else's cows. Both women were excommunicated, a punishment regularly brought against men.[45] It thus fell to the minister alone to adjudicate whether the offender had provided "satisfactory evidence of his penitence or proof of his innocence,"[46] and only if the offender was refractory (and the refractory were usually men), or the case so scandalous that it had become of common repute outside the Presbyterian community, was the case referred to Session and the elders. By the 1880s this transition from public forum to private discipline was largely complete. The decline of the efficacy of community vigilance through the Kirk Sessions was in part symptomatic of the growing authority of the professional clergy, who placed a greater emphasis on religious discourse through sermons and the production of religious literature to enforce conformity and moral self-discipline among parishioners.

Although one can uncover a slow decline in the importance of the Kirk Session as a disciplinary court down to the 1880s, it must be remarked that these courts only ever represented a small dimension of the regulatory practices within the Presbyterian Church. Historians of the early modern church courts have estimated that they had an impact upon the lives of only 5-10 percent of the population as a whole. Although we still lack a broad statistical picture for early Canada, it appears that what was critical to regulating the lives of ordinary parishioners occurred within the ambit of everyday religious practice, which included family prayers, application for church membership, securing a place at the communion table, and listening to the sermon. Applying for church membership was a very serious matter involving repeated "conversations"[47] – interrogations in private by the minister and later in public before the elders and the session.[48] Thus, Mr James Robertson, when applying to the Boston Presbyterian Church for membership in 1840, was catechized "in regard to his knowledge of the doctrines of the gospel, the sacraments of the church, experimental religion and propriety, and the session having approved of his views and walk and conversation agreed to receive him."[49]

Church members were again scrutinized in a similar manner during the run up to the communion season, which meant that every church member was examined every three months. Also, parents applying for baptism, either of themselves as adults or for their children, were subject to even more intensive probing regarding their moral character. It was at such junctures that most cases of premarital fornication were brought to light, usually by parents who confessed in order to smooth access to the sacraments for their children.[50] In addition, families were visited at least once a year by the elders, whose central aim was to expose moral dereliction, and even more frequently the minister catechized all adults within the Presbyterian community, which served, like the church courts, as a means to unite parish members by compelling conformity to church ordinances. A great number of cases of "dreadful sin" were dealt with in private.[51] In cases in which a substantial portion of the community were delinquent, "public admonition from the pulpit" was resorted to so as not to clog the machinery of the Kirk Session. Hence in Smith's Falls in 1837, where irregular church attendance had become too commonplace, parishioners were severely admonished from the pulpit by the Rev. Mr Romanes on several occasions and then privately rousted out by the elders, who called them to appear before the session if they did not repent. In large urban centres like Hamilton, where private visitation was more cumbersome, Presbyterian clergymen preferred "the united testimony" enjoined by the sermon "against prevailing error and abounding iniquity" (namely intemperance).[52] But even in rural areas, such as Williamstown in Glengarry township, the minister commonly disciplined the congregation in this manner exhorting against "irregular and rowdy" funerals and weddings, quarrelling and drinking on election day, and a wide range of "worldly" complaints: drinking; fishing, hunting, and journeying on the Sabbath; children's amusements; the practice of trading on the Sabbath; and neglect of private worship. As the minister noted, he "could enumerate many other things that have an equally bad tendency, but which are committed more privately."[53] The primary conduit of moral regulation was through precept and example in the sermon, and it was only in instances in which this failed that the session decided to "avail themselves of the laws of the country to punish the refractory."[54] The cases prosecuted in the Kirk Sessions thus represent a very tiny aspect of the church system of moral regulation and thus lend themselves best to a linguistic analysis of the mental framework it represented rather than to a statistical analysis that, in the absence of any records relating to the overall pattern of cases dealt with privately when defendents were neither refractory nor their cases sufficiently scandalous to mark them out for "public reprehension,"[55] can tell us little about the overall levels of religious conformity.[56]

MEN AND WOMEN BEFORE THE COURTS

On 21 January 1839, Anne McArthur was brought before the Kirk Session in Beckwith Presbyterian Church in the Ottawa Valley to be examined regarding the charge against her for the sin of fornication with Thomas Ferguson. After "profession of deep penitence" to the satisfaction of the elders, she was absolved and admitted to the "privileges of the church."[57] Interestingly, in this same meeting of session the elders decided to reinforce a new regime of harsher, public penitence, even though "the Laws obliging those guilty of scandalous offences to profess publicly penitence for the same, has in many Parishes become obsolete in Scotland, and has not, so far as is known to this Session, been fully acted upon in any Scotch Congregation in this province."[58]

The conclusion that immediately presents itself is that this decision to reinstate harsher forms of public humiliation was linked to a general concern to police sexual immorality among women, who since the early modern period were more regularly presented for illicit sex because it was understood that women were chiefly responsible for upholding sexual purity in society. That women were more likely to be blamed for sexual transgressions has been well documented by Laura Gowing and Mary Beth Norton, who have worked on female sexuality in early modern England and the United States respectively. Prior to the late eighteenth century, women were prosecuted more frequently for sexual impropriety than were men, and female servants, as Kathleen Brown has shown for the nineteenth century, were two to three times more likely to be punished for bastardy.[59] The central premise of this interpretation, namely that a woman's reputation was synonymous with sexual chastity, has been modified recently by a number of scholars, including Garthine Walker, Elizabeth Foyster, Faramerz Dabhoiwala, and Cynthia Herrup, who have argued that female honour was constructed in a multiplicity of ways and was not encompassed solely by the concept of sexual purity. While they agree with Gowing that there were clear distinctions drawn in the early modern period between concepts of the honest woman and the whore, chastity alone did not determine a woman's reputation; other factors, such as her socioeconomic position, piety, her role as a competent housewife, or even her reputation in the world of business came into play.[60] In particular, Garthine Walker has rightly cautioned historians on using sources like church courts, which tend to overdetermine sexual immorality as the formative ingredient in the construction of honour.

In looking to expand the ways in which historians have debated the gendered contours of honour, these historians have necessarily re-examined the ways in which masculinity and reputation were defined and shaped. Sexual reputation was just as important for men as for women in this period, especially in the church courts, where, as Martin Ingram and J.A. Sharpe have noted, unchastity was deemed to be a sin for both sexes.[61] Certainly, as I will show, the language of sexual insult continued to be used to damage women's reputation well into the nineteenth century. However, the gender dimension of sexual criminality was transformed in the nineteenth century with the rise of a revitalized patriarchal family defined around the figure of the father, who was considered responsible for the behaviour of all its members, including servants. This combined with the new evangelical code, which conflated manliness with self-control. The emerging belief in the passivity and moral innocence of women, especially in the realm of sexual relations, led to much greater levels of prosecution of men for moral transgressions.[62] Thus the decision of the elders in Beckwith Presbyterian Church to inflict harsher penalties for illicit sex was a response not to the misbehaviour of Anne McArthur but to the several acts of fornication of her partner, Thomas Ferguson, the local schoolmaster. True to the emerging Victorian code of womanhood, each of the women under question continued to be regarded as "females of unblemished character," and the focus of sexual misconduct focused upon the active male partner, the seducer. For his sins Ferguson was rebuked by the minister, suffered public humiliation before the congregation for several Sabbaths, and then was excommunicated from the church until such time that by his public behaviour he had shown that he valued "Christian principles."[63]

In attempting to analyze the gendered pattern of policing illicit sex, I will focus almost exclusively upon the Kirk Session records of Beckwith Presbyterian Church. In this particular church the cases were exclusively concerned with issues of sexual transgression at least until 1854, when intemperance was redefined as a "heinous sin," which henceforth fell within the frame of church discipline.[64] Previous discussions of the gendering of the church disciplines take a broad statistical measure of all moral offences, including intemperance. However, the latter was an overwhelmingly male offence because it had to be publicly observed in order to come within the sphere of formal court procedures. Such a methodology inevitably leads to the conclusion that women were targets of sexual policing simply because of the disproportionate number of other offences for which men stood trial. By narrowing my focus to one particular locality, where all church offences were sexual, the framework of comparison is uniform in that fornication cases are measured against one another.

Beckwith Presbyterian Church and the surrounding township of Lanark function well as a case study. The settlement was unmarked by vast socio-economic differences; variables relating to social status do not therefore interfere with a reading of gendered language. There the Scottish immigrants were drawn from the "Scotch peasantry" and displaced weavers from Perthshire and Paisley; they shared a sufficiently low standard of living that all received assistance for their passage.[65] In the new settlement, although differences in wealth existed, they were mitigated by the fact that almost everyone recorded in the marriage register was a yeoman (forty-four): there were only four gentlemen in the church, five artisans, one unskilled worker, and four middling sorts, including the clergyman. The Presbyterians of Lanark township were drawn from those smaller industrial towns where high levels of religiosity were the norm; Perth being among the top four church going towns in Scotland. For these immigrants, the church occupied a large role in their lives, and the system of Kirk Sessions and Sabbath observance did not represent merely "civil conformism but a statement of class unity and independence."[66] Moreover, because so many parishioners spoke Gaelic, the church sessions were a focus of ethnic solidarity, and conformity to church ordinances was thus a critical way in which Scottish manners and customs were preserved.

As was common in Kirk Sessions from the early modern period onwards, the most common cases of sexual transgression involved antenuptial fornication. In 68 percent (thirteen) of these cases, both spouses were interrogated; but, in those cases where only one spouse was forced to confess, only one married woman was brought to session, while one quarter of all prenuptial cases cited the male partner as the one chiefly responsible for initiating sex prior to marriage. These cases were generally treated lightly by the elders, although in Beckwith John McKenzie and Catherine Anderson were "seriously admonished." As has already been noted, Beckwith elders commonly enforced strict penalties, but in most Presbyterian churches couples were quickly integrated into the church because they were married, they had generally voluntarily confessed (hence the sin was not of common repute), and they had come forward because they wished to baptize their children. The only case of premarital sex that was severely punished was that of Alexander Stewart, when it was discovered that he had taken communion while sinning.[67] That none of these cases arose from neighbourhood gossip suggests that there communal standards of sexual morality allowed for a fair degree of latitude; and that, like the church elites, ordinary parishioners turned a blind eye to sexual relations among youth as long as they were later regularized by marriage.

The cases involving fornication that did not lead to marriage appear to better approximate the finding of Lynne Marks for Ontario and Mary Beth Norton for colonial Maryland,[68] insofar as 64 percent of the defendants named were unmarried women, while 28 percent were men (with one case in which both the man and woman stood trial together). On the surface these statistical findings seem to uphold the view that female sexual transgressions were seen to be more disorderly to the community than men's immoral sexual behaviour; however, if one considers why women were brought to trial and the pattern of punishments a very different picture emerges. It is significant that almost half the women (45 percent) voluntarily confessed their sin because they wanted to have their children baptized, and they were not pursued either by local gossips or by punctilious elders who were intolerant of plebeian sexual practices. In each of the cases in which the unwed mother came forward she was not censured. For example, when Martha McFarland "expressed deep penitence" and a desire to have her child baptized, the elder offered merely "suitable counsels and prayer" and readmitted her to the church.[69]

The remaining 55 percent of unmarried mothers who were brought to trial (and of these we do not know if they were targets of communal gossip or whether they confessed to their sins upon application either for church membership or communion) named the fathers, who were then pursued by the presiding elders. It is safe to assume that these fornicating bachelors readily confessed their guilt and paid child support, as only those cases where the men continued to deny responsibility went to trial and were recorded. We know from the 1874 case of Janet Buchanan in Dundee, Quebec, that the chief purpose of prosecuting unmarried mothers was to elicit the father's name. Upon giving birth to twins, she was persistently interrogated not because she failed to admit her sin but because she resisted naming the father.[70] Uncovering paternity was the primary focus of court proceedings; thus, while the woman was compelled to confess, the major purpose of the court proceeding was not to punish her immoral behaviour but lay in forcing the men in question and the community at large to recognize the responsibility of men as fathers and as heads of the family. In this instance, the increasing dominance of a renewed patriarchal ideal in Upper Canada, with its emphasis upon male responsibility and masculine moral probity, paralleled the moral paradigm then emerging in Quebec, recently explored by Ollivier Hubert, and the set of public mores that animated New England a century before, where, as Mary Beth Norton has explained, the pre-eminence placed by patriarchal notions of family government upon the father as the head of the family and as the guarantor of its moral worth, actually resulted in a fair degree of protection for unwed mothers.[71] As in New England,[72] in colonial Canada men were punished severely for engaging in sex outside of marriage. Indeed, behind the scenes, once found, unwed fathers would have been severely rebuked and admonished at length on the importance of marriage and family formation, especially in a community where there was no system of poor relief and where the church itself would have been financially burdened with the upkeep of bastards.

That women were deemed to be the victims of male lust is clear, because in almost every case of illicit sex, including the two cases I have found of incestuous fornication, the women were treated with leniency, and after a private rebuke before session they were readmitted to church membership. In Beckwith Presbyterian Church, only one woman was made to suffer public humiliation by being made to profess her sin before the whole congregation for several Sabbaths. She may have been punished more severely for three reasons: first, as a female servant living outside her family, she may already have been deemed more wayward and pregnancy would have meant a loss of her labour for her master; second, she may also have been brought forward by her own family, who, as cash poor farmers, would have relied upon her wages[73]; third and more importantly, she was a repeat offender.[74] The only other woman to receive the harshest punishment of excommunication was twenty-five-year-old Jane Edmison from Peterborough, who likewise was a repeat offender and, more heinous still, had slept with an Irish Roman Catholic.[75] She once again fell under the gaze of the public authorities when the census-taker in 1851 made particular note that she was an unmarried woman living in a shanty with five children!

While church leaders and the community were willing to countenance premarital sexual relations on one occasion just prior to marriage, they were not willing to turn a blind eye to repeat offenders, even if they eventually married, because of the model of moral turpitude it established among youth. Thus, Beckwith elders ascertained that Margaret McDonald's "sin of fornication" was "of an aggravated nature" because as a servant she had "fallen twice." Even though Margaret McDonald eventually married the man with whom she had slept, she was condemned to a severe public rebuke. Interestingly it was Margaret McDonald's deft ability to utilize the gendered norms of her society that eventually relieved her from humiliating herself before her fellow parishioners: as the session concluded "considering that such public appearance might possibly induce an attack of hysteria or epileptic fits to which she is represented as being usually subject the Session deem it expedient that intimation from the Pulpit be in her presence given to the congregation after service on Sabbath."[76]

For the most part, women who were found guilty of the sin of fornication were quickly absolved once they named the father. A typical case was that of the servant Margaret Stewart, who confessed to her crime when applying to have her child baptized. On 30 May 1876, when she named the father, John Bell, she was admitted into church communion, the elders "being satisfied with her religious knowledge and otherwise blameless life."[77] That she was a servant made her particularly vulnerable to either unwanted sexual advances or to idle promises of marriage, despite the fact that she worked in the home of a male relative. Unlike the civil courts, where, as Sandy Ramos has argued, women's testimony received little hearing,[78] the church courts remained an important forum for women and were instrumental in shifting the blame for moral culpability from the victimized woman to the guilty father. Where women involved in illicit sex were generally treated leniently by the church courts, moral turpitude with regard to premarital sex was harshly condemned by church elders, thus sending the message that it was men who were chiefly responsible for sexual delinquency. The only male fornicator not condemned to "stand a public rebuke" before the entire congregation was Peter McCarthur, who in 1837 voluntarily came forward to admit to having had sex with a woman from another church. Because the woman did not fall under the purview of the church courts, she could not in future demand payment from the father. The matter was allowed to pass quietly. Most unchaste men suffered the full force of church law, especially when they were seen to be moral preceptors, like Thomas Ferguson, the schoolmaster, and Duncan Ferguson, a former minister, and even these respectable members of the community suffered public rebuke and extensive "conversation" or private hectoring from the minister and the elders alike on the principles of Christian behaviour. The resolution of the 1844 case against William Sproat for having fornicated with Catherine McKay was more common: "The accused having confessed his guilt, and suspended from church until he shows greater signs of his penitence."[79] Even men like James McArthur, who was not a public officeholder, endured the humiliation of public confessing before the congregation and enduring public admonition; the message was clearly made that male sexual probity was most affirmedly seen to be the cornerstone of the social order, and responsible fatherhood a crucial component of masculinity. That these men also deemed sexual moral conduct as integral to their own sense of honour and reputation is demonstrated by the degree to which, for example, Duncan Ferguson quaked at the thought of facing a public rebuke. He was reported to have remarked that "he fears he would not be able to stand it."[80]

While married women like Margaret McDonald could feign female hysteria, the emerging modern sensibility regarding the association of maleness
with sexual desire consigned men to the role of sexual aggressors. By the
1870s this paradigm was dominant, and it was commonplace for a woman,
such as Miss Annie Mann, to be fully exculpated from church censure because she was a "victim of seduction"; Mr John Hannah, by contrast, was
charged with "grave immorality."[81] The increasing criminalization of male
sexual behaviour in the nineteenth century ensured that women were
viewed as passive victims of male lust. It was this gendered perception of
sexuality that lent verisimilitude to women's testimony and allowed them in
turn to construct narratives that built upon these cultural precepts and in
turn further embedded them in the culture. It is significant that Margaret
McGregor won her case on the sin of fornication in 1868 by her word
alone. That she could so deftly manipulate the vocabulary of truth and guilt
away from the theme of policing female morality to impugning John
McLaren for fathering her child with no supporting testimony from witnesses, and on his weak admission that he was in the habit of "frequenting
her company,"[82] shows the degree to which women were able to claim
agency and power through familiar moral discourse. In a world in which
women were being increasingly seen as a crucial component of the moral
economy of the church, it shows the degree to which men with question-
able sexual morality were seen to have little credit in the community and
that their culpability was simply assumed. More often than not, the only
avenue of male resistance was to leave the church.

NARRATIVES OF PROBITY BEFORE THE COURT

Early modern historians who have explored the complexities of how patriarchal structures functioned in the day-to-day world have, unlike historians
of the modern era, established a rich historiography that has emphasized the
way in which ordinary women could claim agency through the "small politics"[83] of the public courts, where they created exculpatory narratives. The
Kirk Sessions, which persisted into the nineteenth century, likewise functioned as a "process of negotiating the boundaries of authority"[84] for plebeian women and men. In colonial Canada, there exist few detailed accounts
of fornication cases similar to those in the early modern ecclesiastical courts,
but those that do exist were recorded because of overt male resistance to ac-
cusations by women. Because women could less easily hide the evidence of
their illicit conduct, namely a bastard child, accused mothers had to use the
repertoire of existing linguistic codes to regain their honour by portraying

themselves as victims of male lust. Here, religion served as a cultural prism both of appropriation and subversion, for women used their "otherwise blameless lives" – their nonsexual morality – to resist and reconstruct the religious codes of transgression promulgated by male religious authorities.

In order to analyse the meaning of sexual reputation as it was defined by ordinary men and women, I will examine three cases from Glengarry township in eastern Ontario, an area settled largely by Scottish settlers from the Highlands, people of little means who often were illiterate, as was the first defendant, Isabella McKenzie. Isabella, a young servant, went to live with her sister, who was ill and who had died by the time of the court hearing. Her sister had recently married Daniel McCallum. Although we do not know McCallum's occupation, he may very well have been a skilled worker, as he had his own workshop and was the master of one or two apprentices and at least two servants, his sister-in-law Isabella and one Duncan Johnston, who was accused of fathering Isabella's child. However, Johnston was not the only potential father in this case. Although McCallum was a fairly well-to-do married man, his status did not shield him from neighbourhood rumours that he had had "carnal connection" with his sister-in-law "six times, the first week after he was married to her sister, in a small stable at the back of the house," and that he had tried to purchase medicine to abort the child. Such allegations were extremely injurious to his reputation both as a husband and as an honest employer in the community. Not only did McCallum claim that he had "too much honour in him to do such a thing," but it appears that the claims of witnesses that he and Isabella had conspired to blame everything on Duncan Johnston, his employee, who had recently gone to Scotland, may very well have been true for the two brought forth witnesses who were compelled to uphold McCallum's reputation because they were also in his employ. Thus the young apprentice who, by his apprenticeship contract, would have already sworn loyalty to his master, upheld McCallum's version of events, claiming that, when a servant in the household, he had observed that Duncan Johnston and Isabella McKenzie "conversed together frequently in private at his house" and that on one occasion Mrs McCallum sent him in to roust Duncan and Isabella from a closet where they were having carnal relations. Significantly, throughout the court proceedings, the apprentice was never given a name and his identity was therefore conflated with that of his master, McCallum. Interestingly, a fellow servant in McCallum's employ, James McPherson, did not submit to the notion of paternal labour relations adhered to by the apprentice, because his testimony did not simply exonerate McCallum. Because of the persistent shortage of domestic labour in Upper Canada, servants conceived of the relationship with their employers in more free-market terms, as a contract for the exchange of labour rather than one constituted on the traditional norms of social subordination. Likewise, we can see a distinct occupational identification between young men, for McPherson adamantly defended the rights of his fellow servant Johnston. McPherson deposed that on the night in question, when the McCallum household gathered for drinks on the evening of Mary McIntire's wedding, Johnson had not slept in the house and Isabella did not sleep in the kitchen but in the bedroom with her sister and McCallum, as she usually did, thus implicating McCallum as the father of Isabella's child and confirming that this was an extremely heinous crime of incestuous fornication, one which would have likely resulted in excommunication for both partners, who would have been deemed responsible adults.

Given the potential of being condemned for having slept with her sister's husband, it was especially incumbent upon Isabella to construct a story in which she could portray herself as a woman of great moral probity who, because of her youth and innocence, was taken advantage of both by her sister and brother-in-law and by Johnston himself. First, she claimed that she had had drink forced upon her by her sister and her husband, thus demeaning their worthiness in their role in loco parentis. Second, she stated that she had sex with the defendant only on one occasion and that she had relented only because he promised marriage. To further demonstrate that she had meekly followed plebeian customs of courtship she had her brother-in-law testify that she had consulted him as to the suitability of Johnston as a husband and that she believed Johnston was going to marry her because he had offered her money. However, because the offer of money might be construed that she was a whore selling sex, Isabella added that he had also given her a brooch as a token of marriage. To further underscore that she had no hidden agenda in bringing forth this case and that she was an honest woman, Isabella refused the monthly sum awarded her by the courts for the care of her child.

When Johnston was examined, his confession that he did indeed go into a closet with Isabella was taken as confirmation of his role as the sexual aggressor, despite the fact that Johnston contended that he did so at Isabella's behest and that he believed that Isabella only wished to talk. Johnston's professions of innocence, however, carried little weight before the court. It is clear from the tone of the questions from the elders – such as whether Isabella had been led to take a drink by the older members of her family and their assumption that Johnson was guilty because of his weak admission that he may have slept that night in the house but that he could not rightly remember because of the amount of gin he had consumed – shows the gendered complexion of the social attitudes of the day, which were beginning to associate femaleness with sexual virtue. Interestingly, Isabella herself understood the way in which the consumption of alcohol would reinforce Johnston's claim of her sexual transgression. Consequently her defence hinged upon the fact that she had not voluntarily consumed spirits. In addition, even though as servants both participants were marginal to their community, the fact that Isabella was a female living under the roof of a family patriarch who was relatively wealthy lent greater credence to her stance as a victim of male lust. Gendered notions of reputation alone did not determine the outcome of the case.

However, this transition in the gendered conception of morality had not fully occurred in 1820, when the case of carnal connection between Isabella McKenzie and Duncan Johnston took place. The idea of a natural compatibility between women and their susceptibility to "religious impressions"[85] was still a contested one, a fact revealed in the split decision in this case and the fact that the elders had to enlist professional medical witnesses to uphold Isabella's story of male culpability. To prove once and for all that the servant Duncan Johnston was the father, Alexander McNaughton, a local physician, testified from the evidence of outmoded medical knowledge drawn from seventeenth-century French cases, to the plausibility of a "protracted pregnancy," whereby a woman could give birth to a legitimate child even after twelve months. He alluded also to the custom in Scotland of children born six months after marriage or ten months after the death of the husband being deemed legitimate. Like the many French widows whose cases formed the burden of McNaughton's medical testimony, Isabella McKenzie was absolved not on the basis of science but because of her "virtue and probity," which overcame the technical moral lapse of her seduction.[86]

That sexual reputation was as meaningful to men as it was to women is illustrated in the case between Alexander Grant and several female complainants in the environs of Charlottenburgh township near Cornwall. It is noteworthy that Alexander Grant was the village constable whose policing duties may well have made him an unpopular figure in the community; in this case, several fathers of the mothers of illegitimate children may have used their daughters as pawns to settle old scores, a practice that the church elders in this instance seem to have implicitly condoned. While it is clear that the accusation of the woman Sydney Glasford was fabricated because she ultimately signed an affidavit to that effect, it is probable that the testimony of several other women was dubious at best. For example, Isabella Grant (it is unknown if she was somehow related to the accused, but we know she was not his wife) had great difficulty in explaining why she took so long to come forward with her story of seduction; she responded with the non sequitur that she was reluctant because there were so many other charges against him, thus attempting to imply that he was a sexual predator in the neighbourhood. So decisive was sexual slander to notions of masculine honour that women such as Jenny Adams were willing to incur the opprobrium of adultery so as to show that Alexander Grant was so sexually promiscuous that he would make advances to married women. The final complainant, Elizabeth Edson, attested that Grant had had "carnal connexion with her sometime between the beginning and middle of November last" and that he had "repeatedly & solemnly promised to marry her *previous* to his connexion with her." Not only had Grant given her fourteen dollars, purportedly for a marriage license, along with a silver watch, but he had told her to keep the "circumstances private" until he had procured a sheriff's title for his father's property. Edson's father also swore before the court that Grant had asked for his permission to marry but that there was a further delay in the marriage because Mr Edson would be out of town on business. Even with the testimony that Elizabeth Edson was unable to marry Grant because she was already married to one John Smith, with whom she had lived for a mere five weeks, and her confession that she had thereafter slept with Grant on numerous occasions did little to tarnish her reputation as a moral and upstanding member of her congregation; but it did lead to Grant's conviction and financial responsibility for Edson's child.[87]

Although the language of sexual insult pertaining to female virtue that Laura Gowing has identified had not been eviscerated from the culture of community regulation, the aftermath of Alexander Grant's alleged sexual predations in the community forcibly illustrates the importance of situating the circulation of language within its specific context. Six years after Grant's rebuke from the Kirk elders for various sexual transgressions, Grant's wife was out with their dog herding their sheep past the house of Elizabeth Edson, one of the women who had borne Grant's illegitimate children. Betsy, as Edson was known, and her mother began hurling sticks, stones, and insults at Grant's wife, "saying that she was both a whore in this country and in the old Country, that she was a common streetwalker, that her father was destroyed by witchcraft and that her mother was a whore and that her parents had casual connection with negros, that it was best for her to take her husbands bastards and keep a regular whore house as she otherwise kept." The real target of their slander was not Grant's wife; rather, their language of female whoredom and witchcraft was a means to further castigate Grant's sexual reputation. Just as for women, men gained a wider repute in their neighbourhood once they married; indeed, having acquired a wife, the once derided village constable became a respected head of family and by virtue of his role as a father he easily gained the approbation of the elders, who readily believed Grant's story that these attacks were "without provocation." As Grant self-righteously concluded: "I demand Justice and no more from my Reverend Clergy and Elders."[88] In this period, there is an increasing convergence between the plebeian sensibility concerning the increasing importance of sexual morality in defining masculine reputation and that of church leaders, who likewise considered illicit sex engaged in by men to be more destructive of the social order than that of women.

As the nineteenth century unfolded, there was an increasing elision among both male and female church members as well as among the clergy between masculinity and sexual purity. The paradigm of female sexual passivity was well entrenched by the mid-1840s, as illustrated by the case of Isabella Urquart, a yeoman's illiterate daughter, who in 1842 accused yeoman Malcolm McGuire of fathering her female child after having had sex with her on four occasions, three times as her father's house and on occasion when returning from a ball at labourer William Hall's home at the conclusion of a bee to cut timber. Like many other women, it appears that Isabella was slow to bring forward her case – her excuse was that she had been ill – because as was common she probably had had sex with a youth who had promised marriage but, like in the case above, had been unable to either acquire land or an occupation, and so had jilted her, thus forcing her to manipulate the language of female respectability so that she might implicate a young man of dubious sexual probity. The church elders were all too willing to play along with this fiction because, in the absence of the biological father, the church would be responsible for offering charity to the injured woman. Thus, they were willing to convict McGuire on the mere shred of evidence that he had been seen walking back late at night with Isabella from the ball and the suggestion that Isabella must have had sexual congress with McGuire only because she was seen overtaking two of the female partygoers on the way home.[89]

In some respects church elders were less interested in reforming plebeian courtship practices, for, as the three cases described above demonstrate, the notion of penetrative sex prior to marriage was not the focus of clerical admonition; rather, it was a new notion of responsible fatherhood enshrined in a revitalized Victorian code of patriarchy that underscored the connection between manliness and sexual self-control. As the lenient punishments for antenuptial fornication suggest, both church leaders and parents allowed considerable latitude to youth in their courtship practices, whether carnal connection occurred in the woods, at the worship, at home, or in the closet, so long as it eventually led to marriage and most importantly to the baptism of

children. Hence, church patriarchs did not take a prurie
sexual conduct merely to suppress it. The ultimate pu
lating and monitoring male responsibility in terms of
induce men to become church members and thus reg
church coffers. In an era when the clergy were paid out of c
and when contributions were often made in kind, through paym
or barley, commodities that were often difficult to market, integra
many men as possible into the church was a matter intimately connected with
the very survival of the local churches.[90] As a response to the general poverty
of the congregation, Boston Presbyterian equalized payments to ten shillings
for all members and seven shillings for adherents.[91] In addition, fees paid by
the prospective groom went directly into the pocket of the minister, hence the
regularization of marriage went to the heart of the upward social mobility of
an impoverished, lower-class professional clergy. There was an overlapping set
of values regarding courtship practices and the importance of marriage between ordinary parishioners and the clergy, given the prevalence of couples
self-confessing "illicit" premarital sex when applying to have their children
baptized.[92] After mid-century it was common practice in cases of antenuptial
fornication that men or women came forward of their "own accord"; likewise
it was the norm for clergyman to solidify the symbolic connection between
family formation and religion by treating these "faults" with friendly exhorta-
tion "affectionately & earnestly."[93]

Of equal significance, the clergy and elders deftly played upon the importance attached to baptism, which lay at the heart of popular religion, to
compel church adherents who paid irregularly to become regular pew holders. For example, in Boston Presbyterian Church in 1837 the elders passed
the law that children would not be baptized unless their parent had not
only become church members but were also regularly admitted to communion, processes that involved intense catechizing either by the clergyman or
the elders.[94] For similar ends, elders in St Andrew's Presbyterian in New
Brunswick resumed the practice of distributing communion strictly to actual church members at benched tables, rather than generally in the pews,
"to persuade parents to bring their children to the church for baptism."[95]
So critical was the rite of baptism as a measure of "the flourishing state"[96]
of congregations that the older practice of baptizing at home was termi-
nated and the sacrament was performed only in the public precincts of the
church before the full congregation as a means of exhorting recalcitrant
parents, exceptions being made only for the aged and infirm.[97]

Given the increasing proclivity to use baptism to enforce religious conformity, the case of Alexander Murchison was not unusual. On the occasion of the birth of his first child the elders were willing to baptize it merely

he promise that Murchison would henceforth contribute financially to
e church; when, upon the birth of his second child, he had not fulfilled
is promise, the church elders severely castigated him and refused to baptize his child. His pleas of penury notwithstanding, the elders reckoned that
his circumstances were "as good as those of most of the Inhabitants."[98]

For the most part, as we have seen, both men and women generally con-
formed to church regulations regarding sexual morality, and in turn church
leaders treated youthful illicit sex with leniency. However, attempts to discipline other transgressions of church law were often forcefully resisted, especially by men. In turn, once men became particularly recalcitrant, which
they often did over issues of temperance and regular church attendance,
church leaders responded with a greater degree of severity. Hence elders
tended regularly to punish public drunkenness, even among youth, by ex-
communicating the culprit. The case of Mr Addison, who was immediately
restored to church privileges once he swore that he would refrain from
drinking in future, stands out, and one suspects that his social standing
saved him from excommunication.[99] But, when this man was again accused
of drunkenness (virtually all cases of drunkenness were the result of communal policing and vigilance, which implies a high degree of neighbourhood
abhorrence of this particular sin), the church court suspended him for six
months. This intense communal monitoring of alcohol consumption demonstrates once again that the Kirk disciplines were not merely a means of
moral regulations of the working classes by their social superiors; rather, it
shows that most of the parishioners shared the view constantly reinforced
both in sermons and through the ritual performances of public penance that
individual sins were sins against the community as a whole. However, even
more revealing of the gendered pattern of community scrutiny, most men resisted penalties for drinking and most experienced heavy sanctions of expulsion from church rites from six months to a year, at which time most
offenders had demonstrated a sincere attempt at reforming their behaviour.
The vast majority of drunkenness cases occurred at the communion table itself, for these church rites were also seen by ordinary parishioners as important community festivals to be celebrated with much dancing and drinking.
On these occasions that were the focus both of intense piety and high-
spirited frivolity, parishioners were particularly unwilling to bow to church
efforts to reform plebeian forms of leisure. Thus, when Robert Darling was
found drunk at communion in Peterborough in 1838, he stated that "altho'
he had carried the use of spirits & beer so far as to render himself talkative
& at last sick would not admit that there was anything improper in his conduct."[100] Like a large proportion of men caught drinking, Darling felt no

need to defer to church regulations and refused several demands to appear
at the church courts. The case of Robert Peacock, who had been seen "the
worse for liquor" at communion in St Andrew's New Brunswick, was typical: on 3 January 1839 he was refused a token for communion because of
this sin against the church; 30 June 1839 he was granted a token as there
was no repetition of drunkenness; but by 9 January 1842, at the St John's
day celebrations, he was once again found drunk in public and excommunicated from the church and "particularly watched."[101]

That in almost all cases of intoxication men were suspended rather than
simply admonished indicates that most men continued to flout the disciplinary process of the courts; however, these attempts at resistance were short-
lived, for excommunication meant a total expulsion from one's church
community, and in the vast majority of cases of suspension men made an attempt at conformity and often reapplied for church membership only a few
months after their conviction.[102] Most, however, were backsliders, and, as in
the case of Mrs Stevens from Hamilton, one of the few women to appear on
the charge of intemperance, who had been charged both in the police courts
(and fined ten shillings) and by the Presbyterian Kirk Session, largely on the
testimony of her husband, most intemperate parishioners experienced a continuous cycle of expulsion and readmission.[103] Just as often, even penitent
men like William Tully of Peterborough, who agreed "to walk more prudently
in time to come," expressed their disgruntlement over the severe treatment
meted out by elders for what he and other men saw as minor misdemeanours
by joining another denomination.[104]

If men resisted charges of drunkenness because they saw drinking as an
element of private leisure, beyond the bounds of church vigilance, the other
area of decisive contestation and disagreement between male parishioners
and the church leaders centred on the terrain of theological dispute. Like
the women charged for the sin of fornication, who saw in the Kirk a means
to absolve themselves of community sanction, men employed the church
courts as a means to set forth their own interpretation of the Bible with the
aim of reforming the tenets of the Church. For example, John Combe, who
like many Protestants would have been well versed in the Bible and had
been exposed throughout his life to a wide and growing literature on theological issues, powerfully demonstrated his right to speak by challenging
the minister before the assembled congregation: he "manifested an unruly
and contentious spirit in the church rejecting the first and second admonitions of the Pastor as well as private entreaty."[105] Others were more deco-
rous but no less forceful in their dissent from clerical norms. In 1848,
Mr Fotheringham from Central Presbyterian in Hamilton used his recent

election to an eldership to counter certain expressions in the Confession of Faith and the notions of predestination adhered to by the minister, while Mr Johnston Neilson, an Irish teacher and clergyman, eventually withdrew as a member of his church in Smith's Falls because when presenting his child for baptism he remained "obstinately attached to his opinion," namely that he did not believe in the Trinity.[106] Similarly, James and John Provan demanded their day in court before the elders in order to present their own views concerning the divinity of Christ and Presbyterian forms of salvation. They were eventually suspended, having already joined the Christian Brethren.[107] Even though most men who had deep disagreements with church leaders over church regulations eventually left, they frequently managed to purposely get caught in order that they could confront the despised elders face to face. Thus William Riddel, the assessor for Elmsley township, decided not to record any of the 653 Church of Scotland Presbyterians in the parish, for, as he retorted disingenuously to the church court, he believed they were all Seceders and there was no column for them on the roll![108] Because these courts so well served as forums for male dissidence they helped channel wider social contests over established authority – in this case Riddel was disputing the concept of loyalty adhered to by the Church of Scotland in the New World – onto the less politically charged terrain of theological interpretation and into an arena where ethnoreligious disputes might be resolved and kept out of the realm of newspaper discourse, which would tarnish the reputation of Presbyterianism.[109] These cases of male resistance remind historians that contests over social authority often occurred at the level of the small politics of the local parish where Riddell's ruse would have been perceived as a headlong affront to established modes of governance, and indeed this was the intent of the men who repeatedly flouted the power of the church courts.

Another focus of friction between male parishioners and the elders was the issue of irregular church attendance. Prior to the 1850s few cases for violating the Sabbath were recorded in the Session minutes; however, as ministers demanded higher wages and a more stable profession, and more substantial church buildings were becoming the norm, there was an ever greater emphasis upon regular church attendance, particularly among men who controlled the finances within their families. In almost every case of "neglect of duty" the men resisted and hence were suspended. Yet when they were readmitted they were still "seriously expostulated" by the elders, for in those months the church was without their financial contributions.[110] Previously, it had been customary both among parishioners and church leaders to focus upon church rites such as communion and baptism as the

quintessential measure of religiosity; by mid-century, however, church leaders were attempting to reconfigure religious norms towards regular Sabbath attendance, but, in turn, such interference with the prerogative of the
head of family to decide the extent of voluntary church involvement was
contested. Men who were absent from church were rigorously pursued by
church elders. For example, heads of families like John Canadine were
charged with threshing on the Sabbath and employing a hired man. Although Canadine confessed to the first charge, he adamantly resisted
church interference into the realm of market relations.[111]

Even though many men followed the lead of Canadine by leaving the
church, this was also a form of resistance that resulted in a subtle but significant shift in the boundaries of the regulatory practices of the church courts.
The message that men like Canadine were sending to church leaders – that it
was unacceptable for them to interfere with their family life – in no small
way contributed to the increasing separation between the sphere of the
church and the world.[112] This separation was, in turn, predicated upon a
wider gulf than had previously obtained between private and public forms of
behaviour; more importantly, this shift in the way in which religiosity was
defined led to a rupture in the traditional conflation between civil and spiritual citizenship that had upheld the notion of communal policing. The loss of
the church as a symbol of the civic identity of the parishioners narrowed the
boundaries of communal control. The regulatory axis of the church was
therefore limited to the domains of extramarital sex and intemperance. In the
absence of this older elision between the realms of the spiritual and profane,
which had so sustained the power of the church court to regulate morality
among its parishioners, the range of church offences became greatly limited.
It was the ongoing resistance from established, male heads of families over issues of Sabbath observance and temperance, and not the control of illicit sex,
an infraction largely of youth, which in the long term undermined the efficacy of the courts. By the 1880s, church leaders dealt with this male intransi-
gence before the church courts by shifting the burden of moral regulation
away from them and towards the creation of new institutions, such as Sunday schools, where youth could be taught early in life to internalize the tenets
of the Church, and towards a wide range of discursive practices, including
longer sermons, the production of a wider range of religious tracts, newspapers, and pamphlets specifically designed for specific age groups, principally
because these modes of regulation lay firmly in the control of church leaders.

It was the emergence of this discursive mode of regulation that marked
the achievement of modernity by the Church. On the surface, the formal institutions of the Church, namely the church courts, gave the appearance of a

society in which customary practices continued to hold sway. To a certain degree this was true, because the strength of the church courts lay with a society that continued to be defined by face-to-face relations, where community vigilance could be effectively exercised. These customary practices were also sustained by a Scottish ethnic tribalism whose traditional preoccupation with using the Kirk Sessions as a means to reinforce the unity of the group was made more intense in a colonial climate of religious pluralism. However, as this article has shown, these church courts were not mere replicas of those from the early modern period; rather, there was a coexistence of traditional religious practices and newer belief systems. Thus, the Kirk Sessions were a conduit for new paradigms of morality that focused expressly upon male sexual conduct. The creation of a national Presbyterian Church of Canada in 1876, with its modern bureaucratic apparatus located in Toronto, undermined the independence of the local parish structure and loosened the customary bonds between minister and congregation upon which the Kirk Sessions relied. Henceforth, the allegiance of an increasingly professionalized clergy lay with a centralized leadership, which relied upon discursive tools of regulation to compel spiritual conformity, thus making the Kirk Sessions obsolete. Once people believed that the authority of the Church was upheld by a powerful national edifice, it was likewise no longer deemed expedient to preserve the public process of purgation and reintegration of sinners that symbolized the corporate unity of Presbyterianism.[113]

A parallel phenomenon contributed to the decline of the church courts: the growing internalization and conformity among parishioners to church edicts, indicated by the high levels of those who acknowledged their sins *before* they could become the subject of local rumour. Increasingly, therefore, ordinary parishioners kept their sins outside the reach of public repute, thereby breaking the connection between "reputation" that was by definition a public commodity resting upon one's self-presentation to others, and the need for redress in the church courts. This privatization of moral regulation, coupled with the increasing emphasis by Church leaders upon the regulation within families by fathers and husbands, led to the silencing of women within the community. By the 1890s, as Presbyterian congregations were adopting the prevailing rhetoric of inclusivity in order to encourage "strangers" to join the church – a consequence of the spread of an evangelical ethos of church adherence – national Church leaders warned strongly against "anything bearing on the confessional or too inquisitorial,"[114] an admonition that covered not only the conduct of the formal Kirk Sessions but even the private visitation by ministers and elders. With the spread of evangelicalism throughout Canadian religious culture by the end of the nineteenth century, the focus of religiosity shifted from communal adherence to a formalized legal code of moral behaviour to an individualized determination of faith defined around a personal sense of conversion, rather than an external standard of church membership. Evangelicalism rested upon the printed word and the discourse of the clergy, not upon the oral narratives that characterized the church courts, which had given voice to the illiterate, the marginal, and the respectable alike. Although in the modern evangelical church parishioners could appropriate or personally dissent from the dominant discourse, this was a private act not evocative of social power as were the church courts, which had been a site of cultural dissidence and negotiation for even the most marginal members of the parish.[115]

NOTES

This article has been greatly improved by the suggestions generously offered by several readers. I wish to thank Michael Gauvreau, Hannah Lane, Jack Little, and Mark Noll for their enthusiasm and for their fine attention to the argument. In particular I would like to thank Sara Mendelson for sharing with me her extensive knowledge of early modern religious culture.

1 Two important articles have established the theoretical framework for this paper. See Callum Brown, "The Mechanism of Religious Growth in Urban Societies: British Cities since the Eighteenth Century," and Lucian Holscher, "Secularization and Urbanization in the Nineteenth Century: An Interpretive Model," in Hugh McLeod, ed., *European Religion in the Age of Great Cities, 1830–1930* (London and New York: Routledge, 1995). On the church as the bastion of traditional culture, see E.J. Hobsbawm, *Worlds of Labour: Further Studies in the History of Labour* (London: Weidenfeld & Nicolson, 1984): 38.

2 Karl Polyani, *The Great Transformation: The Political and Economic Origins of Our Time* (Boston: Beacon Press, 1944). For a similar interpretation of the emergence of the liberal order, see Ian McKay, "The Liberal Order Framework: A Prospectus for a Reconnaissance of Canadian History," *Canadian Historical Review*, 81:4 (December 2000). For an alternate reading of the liberal framework from the perspective of religious history and the history of the family, see Nancy Christie, "Introduction: Family, Community, and the Rise of Liberal Society," in Nancy Christie and Michael Gauvreau, eds, *Mapping the Margins: The Family and Social Discipline in Canada, 1700–1960* (Montreal and Kingston: McGill-Queen's

University Press, 2004); Nancy Christie and Michael Gauvreau, " Modalities of Social Authority: Suggesting an Interface For Religious and Social History," *Histoire
Sociale/Social History* (Spring, 2003).

3 My overall thesis, which demonstrates how cultural change occurred within the
   older structure of church discipline, accords with the theoretical trajectory of Margo
   Todd and her compelling revisionist investigation of the creation of protestant culture in Scotland in the seventeenth century. As Todd argues: "the kirk managed to
   achieve a balance between preservation and innovation in ritual and outward forms"
   (22). In this marvellous study of church sessions, Todd eschews the standard social
   control perspective to demonstrate elaborately the way in which ordinary parishioners participated in and shared the outlook of elders on the necessity of discipline for
   their conception of the godly community. In this respect, Todd shows how the church
   sessions did much more than merely monitor misbehaviour and how they also provided important social services and a sense of spiritual order. Seem Margo Todd, *The
   Culture of Protestantism in Early Modern Scotland* (New Haven and London: Yale
   University Press, 2002).

4 Leah Leneman and Rosalind Mitchison, *Sin in the City: Sexuality and Social Control in Urban Scotland, 1600–1780* (Edinburgh: Scottish Cultural Press, 1998);
   Callum G. Brown, *The Social History of Religion in Scotland since 1730* (London
   and New York: Methuen, 1987): 93–9; T.M. Devine, *The Scottish Nation, 1700–
   2000* (London: The Penguin Press, 1999): 583.

5 Todd, *The Culture of Protestantism*, 410–12.

6 On the intense ethnic cohesion of Scottish Presbyterians, see Hannah M. Lane,
   "Tribalism, Proselytism, and Pluralism: Protestants, Family, and Denominational
   Identity in Mid-Nineteenth-Century St Stephen, New Brunswick," in Nancy
   Christie, ed., *Households of Faith: Family, Gender, and Community in Canada,
   1760–1969* (Montreal and Kingston: McGill-Queen's Press, 2002): 115–16.

7 This is the term used by Callum Brown, *The Social History of Religion in Scotland*,
   151.

8 Laura Gowing, *Domestic Dangers: Women, Words, and Sex in Early Modern Lon-
   don* (Oxford: Clarendon Press, 1996); Sara Mendelson, "The Civility of Women in
   Seventeenth-Century England," in Peter Burke, Brian Harrison, Paul Slack, eds, *Civil
   Histories: Essays Presented to Sir Keith Thomas* (Oxford: Oxford University Press,
   2000): 111–25; Sara Mendelson and Patricia Crawford, *Women in Early Modern
   England* (Oxford: Clarendon Press, 1998); Elizabeth Foyster, *Manhood in Early
   Modern England: Honour, Sex and Marriage* (London and New York: Longman,
   1999); Anna Clark, "Whores and Gossips: Sexual Reputation in London, 1770–
   1825," in Arina Angerman, et al., *Current Issues in Women's History* (London and
   New York: Routledge, 1989). See also Christine Daniels, "Liberty to Complain:

Servant Petitions in Maryland, 1652–1797," and William M. Offutt, "The Limits of Authority: Courts, Ethnicity, and Gender in the Middle Colonies, 1670–1710," in Christopher L. Tomlins and Bruce H. Mann, eds, *The Many Legalities of Early America* (London and Chapel Hill: University of North Carolina Press, 2001).

9 On this point, see Nancy Christie, "'a witness against vice": Religious Dissent, Political Radicalism and the Moral Regulation of Aristocratic Culture in Upper Canada," in Jean Marie Fecteau, ed., *Agency and Institutions in Social Regulation: Towards an Historical Understanding of Their Interaction* (Les Presses de l'Université du Québec, 2005).

10 On the theme of overlapping value systems as a model of social history that dissents from top-down models of regulation, see Barbara B. Deinfendorf and Carla Hesse, eds, *Culture and Identity in Early Modern Europe (1500–1800)* (Ann Arbor: University of Michigan Press, 1993): 4; Laura Gowing, *Domestic Dangers*, 8–10; Paul Griffiths, Adam Fox, and Steve Hindle, eds, *The Experience of Authority in Early Modern England* (New York: St Martin's Press, 1996); Garthine Walker and Jenny Kermode, eds, *Women, Crime and the Courts in Early Modern England* (London: UCL Press, 1994): 3–5; Tim Hitchcock, Peter King, and Pamela Sharpe, eds, *Chronicling Poverty: The Voices and Strategies of the English Poor, 1640–1840* (London: Macmillan Press, 1997): 10.

11 See Lynne Marks, "Christian Harmony: Family, Neighbours, and Community in Upper Canadian Church Discipline Records," in Franca Iacovetta and Wendy Mitchison, eds, *On the Case: Explorations in Social History* (Toronto: University of Toronto Press, 1998): 114.

12 NAC, McGillvray Papers, MG24 I3, Discipline records, November 1829–April 24 1832.

13 On the lack of separation between individual and communal guilt within the Scottish system of church discipline, see Todd, *The Culture of Protestantism*, 174.

14 AO, Beckwith Presbyterian Church, Kirk Sessions, 12 September 1852; NAC, Westminster Church, Smith's Falls, 10 October 1842.

15 NAC, Knox Presbyterian, Lanark County, MG9 D7-11, Kirk Sessions, 4 March 1849, 30 March 1849. After the excommunication of his brother, Peter Cumming was removed from the church; 26 April 1876, the case of John Craig.

16 On the class background of Presbyterian clergyman, see Brown, "Religious Growth in Urban Societies," 251; Callum Brown, *The Death of Christian Britain* (London and New York: Routledge, 2001): 20.

17 Archives Nationales du Quebec (ANPQ), Box 334, Dundee Zion United Church, Kirk Session, 1834.

18 On these conflicts, see Christie, "'a witness against vice.'"

19 AO, Boston Church, Kirk Sessions, 6 December 1835, 13 December 1835. Not only was Menzies disciplined for testifying in a civil court, but it also appears that he had

lied, having sworn to the identity of the perpetrators of a vicious assault on the claim that they wore masks when it was a moonless night.

20 For the character of the Macdonaldian constitution, see Michael Gauvreau, "The Union of the Moderate Men," unpublished lecture, York University, January 1998, and, "Revisiting the Confessional State," paper delivered to Conference on the Social Role of the Churches/le Rôle Sociale des Egilises, Université de Montréal, November 2002. On Scottish concepts of loyalty to Britain, see Colin Kidd, "Conditional Britons: The Scots Covenanting Tradition and the Eighteenth-Century British State," *English Historical Review*, 2002, 1147–76.

21 On the role of the Protestant churches in framing modern notions of political economy and the state, see the magisterial work of Boyd Hilton, *The Age of Atonement: The Influence of Evangelicalism on Social and Economic Thought, 1785–1865* (Oxford: Oxford University Press, 1988). Seen from the vantage point of religious institutions, the emergence of the "liberal project" bears little empirical relationship to the theoretical perspective of Ian McKay, whose intellectual perspective has been overly determined by the orthodox categories of classical political economy. See McKay, "The Liberal Order Framework." Indeed, notions of individualism are not the only measure of the liberal order, but, moreover, their manifestation was not as linear as McKay has conceived them, and the very notion of the relationship between various notions of individualism was more complex and the sites for debates over notions of the "social" and "economic" were more multitudinous than the liberal project has advanced. In addition, the "others" supposedly outside McKay's liberal project may have been more imbricated in the slipstream of the emerging market economy and may have both rejected and accepted various notions of the liberal, capitalist order.

22 For continuities with earlier Scottish Protestant culture, see Todd, *The Culture of Protestantism*, which clearly takes issue with those historians who have seen an increased secularization in the culture of the Reformation, 326.

23 AO, David Gibson Papers, MS 95, James Gibson, to my dear son, 8 July 1819; "Contract for Apprenticeship of David Gibson," 12 February 1821; William Gibson to nephew David, 31 August 1821.

24 On the uses of religious cosmologies to adumbrate class perspectives, see Nancy Christie, "a witness against vice." See also Dror Wahrman, *Imagining the Middle Class: The Political Representation of Class in Britain, c. 1780–1840* (Cambridge: Cambridge University Press, 1995).

25 AO, Central Presbyterian Church, Hamilton, Session, 7 October 1858.

26 As Margo Todd has noted, self-confession resulted in less rigorous punishment and for this reason was very popular. See Todd, *The Culture of Protestantism*, 140.

27 St Paul's Presbyterian, Peterborough, Session, 8 November 1837.

28 So crucial were church disciplines to upholding the status of the elders that the elders from Smith's Falls disallowed Francis Allan's membership in a Lanark church for the reason that he would be beyond "inspection." See Wesminster Presbyterian, Smith's Falls, Session 30 September 1838.

29 NAC, Westminster Presbyterian, Smith's Falls, Session, 4 November 1860.

30 NAC, St Andrew's Church, New Brunswick, Session, 1 July 1881.

31 I have overdrawn the elitism of early modern religious practices in order to highlight the greater voluntary aspect of religious adhesion in a society characterized by high levels of religious pluralism. On the importance of ordinary parishioners in shaping early modern Protestantism, see Todd, *The Culture of Protestantism.*

32 NAC, McGillvray Papers, Vol. 7, William Mackenzie to son, John, 6 March 1822.

33 On the way in which church pews reflected the social order, see D.M. Palliser, "Introduction: The Parish in Perspective," in S.J. Wright ed., *Parish, Church and People: Local Studies in Lay Religion, 1350–1750* (London: Hutcheson, 1988): 23. Palliser says this hierarchal framework was in turn offset by the fact that church courts were supported by parishioners from all social ranks.

34 Martin Ingram has postulated that parishioners became more critical of ministers because of the growing market in religious works, which created a sense of independence among worshippers. See Martin Ingram, "From Reformation to Toleration: Popular Relligious Cultures in England, 1540–1690," in Tim Harris, ed., *Popular Culture in England, c. 1500–1850* (New York: St Martin's Press, 1995): 122.

35 NAC, McGillvry Papers, Session, 5 January 1824.

36 NAC, Westminster Presbyterian, Smith's Falls, Session, 25 January 1841.

37 ANPQ, Dundee Zion United Church, Session, 1836 n.d.

38 AO, Boston Church, Session, 9 August 1856; AO Beckwith Presbyterian Church, Session, 20 September 1840.

39 AO, Boston Church, Session, 10 June 1837.

40 For example, in the town of Williams near London, the precentor was the village blacksmith. See University of Guelph Archives, Diary of Rev. McPherson.

41 NAC, Peterborough Presbyterian, Session, 23 April 1839.

42 NAC, Westminister Presbyterian, Smith's Falls, Session, 2 April 1858. The concern by church elites for the reputation of the church led to the adultery case of Rev. Henry Esson being dismissed. NAC, McGillvray Papers, 24 April 1832.

43 Brown, "The Mechanism of Religious Growth in Urban Societies," 244.

44 On this point, see Christie, "'a witness against vice.'" The system of visitation by the minister as a means of reinforcing the religious identity of Secessionist Presbyterian congregations in the face of landlord resistance originated in early eighteenth-century Scotland. See Ned C. Landsman, *Scotland and Its First American Colony, 1683–1765* (Princeton: Princeton University Press, 1985): 59–60.

45 NAC, Westminster Presbyterian, Smith's Falls, 15 October 1855; NAC, Rev. James
   Wilson Papers, MG29 C126, 7 May 1871, Gemmill vs McCurdy.
46 NAC, Westminster Presbyterian, Smith's Falls, 4 January 1851.
47 AO, Central Presbyterian Church, Hamilton, Session, 7 April 1848.
48 NAC, Knox Presbyterian, Lanark, Session, 22 January 1849.
49 Boston Church, Session, 14 March 1840; 3 June 1842. Interestingly in the latter
   case, when women were being examined it was specified that they were judged on
   their "moral character." One should not make too much of this as men were likewise judged but the language used was one of "walk and conversation". The difference here is that the concept of the "walk" refers to one's behavior in public,
   whereas "moral character" can refer both to the private and public realms.
50 Antenuptial fornication was the most common sexual infraction brought before the
   courts throughout the whole history of the church courts. Moreover, such cases
   were often brought by self-confession and not by community suspicion. See Paul
   Hair, ed., *Before the Bawdy Court: Selections from Church Court and Other
   Records Relating to the Correction of Moral Offences in England, Scotland and
   New England, 1300–1800* (London: Elek Publishing, 1972): 232–3.
51 NAC, St Paul's Presbyterian, Peterborough, Session, 19 May 1835. In this case the
   dreadful sin referred to was that of swearing. Dancing was another sin that seldom
   came before the church courts, largely because it was so controversial and its sup-
   pression decidedly unpopular. For one of the few cases of dancing, see NAC, Knox
   Presbyterian Church, McDonald's Corners, Lanark, MG9 D7-55, Session, 28 June
   1847.
52 AO, Hamilton Central Presbyterian, Session, 18 February 1858.
53 NAC, McGillvray Papers, Session, 13 April 1834.
54 NAC, McGillvray Papers, 13 April 1834. It is absolutely crucial to see the Kirk Sessions, functioning in tandem with the sermon and other forms of suasion, as a
   means to bring about religious conformity, rather than considering them as simply a
   means to regulate sexual behaviour. For the best overall discussion on the religious
   purpose of the Kirk sessions, see Margo Todd, *The Culture of Protestantism*.
55 NAC, McGillvray Papers, Session, 1 August 1834.
56 For an excellent discussion of this problem when examining church records, see
   Margaret Spufford, "Can We Count the 'Godly' and the 'Conformable' in the Seventeenth Century?" *Journal of Ecclesiastical History*, 36:3 (July 1985): 428–38.
57 AO, Beckwith Presbyterian, Session, 21 January 1839.
58 Ibid.
59 Laura Gowing, *Domestic Dangers*, 2; Laura Gowing, "Language, Power and the
   Law: Women's Slander Litigation in Early Modern London," in Garthine Walker
   and Jenny Kermode, eds, *Women, Crime and the Courts in Early Modern England*
   (New York: 1994): 29–30; Mary Beth Norton, "Gender, Crime and Community in

Seventeenth-Century Maryland," in James E. Henretta, Michael Kammen and Stanley N. Kats, eds, *The Transformation of Early American History: Society, Authority and Ideology* (New York: Alfred A. Knopf, 1991): 141; Kathleen M. Brown, *Good Wives, Nasty Wenches and Anxious Patriarchs: Gender, Race, and Power in Colonial Virginia* (Chapel Hill and London: University of North Carolina Press, 1996): 189–92. See also John Ruston Pagan, *Anne Orthwood's Bastard: Sex and Law in Early Virginia* (Oxford: Oxford University Press, 2003): 12, 128; J. A. Sharpe, *Defamation and Sexual Slander in Early Modern England: The Church Courts at York* (Borthwick Papers, no. 58): 20. In Scotland, as Margo Todd has argued, men and women were treated equally, although the financial burden rested more firmly upon men. See *The Culture of Protestantism*, 178–9.

60 Cynthis Herrup, "'To Pluck Bright Honour from the Place-Faced Moon?: Gender & Honour in the Castlehaven Story"; Faramerz Dabhoiwala, "The Construction of Honour, Reputation, and Status in Late Seventeenth- and Early Eighteenth-Century England"; Garthine Walker, "Expanding the Boundaries of Female Honour in Early Modern England"; all in *Transactions of the Royal Historical Society*, sixth series, VI, 1996, 137–60, 201–14, 235–46; Elizabeth A. Foyster, *Manhood in Early Modern England: Honour, Sex and Marriage* (London and New York: Longman, 1999): 9. For other discussions of women's honour outside of sexual morality, see Amy Louise Erickson, *Women and Property in Early Modern England* (London and New York: Routledge, 1993): 53; Anna Clark, "'Whores and gossips': Sexual Reputation in London 1770–1825," in Arina Angerman et al. *Current Issues in Women's History* (London and New York: Routledge, 1989): 239; Leah Leneman, "Defamation in Scotland, 1750–1800," *Continuity and Change*, 15:2, 2000, 209–34; Victoria E. Bynum, *Unruly Women: The Politics of Social and Sexual Control in the Old South* (Chapel Hill & London: University of North Carolina Press, 1992): 68.

61 Elizabeth Foyster, "Male Honour, Social Control and Wife Beating in Late Stuart England," *Transactions of the Royal Historical Society*, sixth series, VI, 1996, 215–24; Ingram, *Church Courts*, 253, 285; J.A. Sharpe, *Defamation and Sexual Slander*, 10.

62 On these changes in the gendered complexion of sexual codes of honour in the nineteenth century, see John Tosh, "What Should Historians Do with Masculinity?: Reflections on Nineteenth-Century Britain," *History Workshop Journal*, 38, 1994, 183–5; Robert B. Shoemaker, *Gender in English Society, 1650–1850: The Emergence of Separate Spheres?* (London and New York: Longman, 1998): 33–5; Judith R. Walkowitz, *City of Dreadful Delight: Narratives of Sexual Danger in Late-Victorian London* (Chicago and London: University of Chicago Press, 1992): 7; Leonore Davidoff, "Class and Gender in Victorian England," in Judith L. Newton, Mary P. Ryan, Judith R. Walkowitz, eds, *Sex and Class in Women's History* (London and Boston: Routledge, 1983), on the connection between male sexuality and social disorder

and the way in which the cult of domesticity removed women from the sexual arena, 20–3. Bernard Capp believes these changes occurred much earlier, see Bernard Capp, "The Double Standard Revisited: Plebeian Women and Male Sexual Reputation in Early Modern England," *Past and Present*, no. 162, February 1999, 70–100. See also Jean C. Friedman, *The Enclosed Garden: Women and Community in the Evangelical South, 1830–1900* (Chapel Hill & London: University of North Carolina Press, 1985), who stresses that expectations for male morality were higher than those for women, which accounts for the fact that men were disciplined more frequently.

63 AO, Beckwith Presbyterian Church, Session, 14 July 1839.

64 AO, Beckwith Presbyterian, Session, 2 February 1854.

65 Andrew Haydon, *Pioneer Sketches in the District of Bathurst* (Toronto: Ryerson Press, 1925): 247.

66 For this important interpretation of the relationship between industrialization, migration, class consciousness and religion in Scotland, see Brown, "Religious Growth in Urban Societies," 252; Brown, *The Social History of Religion in Scotland*, 106.

67 For typical cases of antenuptial fornication see AO, Beckwith Presyterian Church, Session, 26 May 1837, 20 August 1837, 14 July 1839; 2 April 1843; 30 April 1843; 6 July 1853;12 August 1855. There was no change over time in the way antenuptial fornication was regarded, nor was there a distinction made along class lines, as both elders and artisans appeared before the courts.

68 Marks, "No Double Standard?"; Norton, "Gender, Crime and Community in Seventeenth-Century Maryland," 123–50.

69 AO, Beckwith Presbyterian, Session, 19 August 1855. See similar cases: 5 February 1859, 24 February 1861, 15 September 1861. The pattern for the post-1850 period was increasingly for both men and women to voluntarily come forward, thus demonstrating an increasing degree to which parishioners internalized the teachings of the Church.

70 ANPQ, Dundee Zion Presbyterian Church, Session, 29 April 1874.

71 Norton, "Gender, Crime and Community," 37.

72 Mary Beth Norton, "Gender and Defamation in Seventeenth-Century Maryland," *William and Mary Quarterly*, 3rd series, XLIV:1 (January 1987): 9; Ollivier Hubert, "The Invention of the Margin as an Invention of the Family: The Case of Rural Quebec in the Eighteenth and Nineteenth Centuries," in Nancy Christie & Michael Gauvreau, eds, *Mapping the Margins: Family and Social Discipline in Canada, 1700–1980* (Montreal and Kingston: McGill-Queen's University Press, 2004): 183–208.

73 In a cash-poor society, many farming families would have been reliant upon the wages of their female children who were put out to service for the purpose of purchasing important assets, such as a cow. On this point, see Catherine Parr Traill, *The Canadian Settler's Guide* (Toronto: McLean, 1855): 6; *A Narrative of the Rise and Progress of*

Emigration from the Counties of Lanark and Renfrew to the New Settlements in Upper Canada on Government (Ottawa: Canadian Heritage, Publications, 1978), letter Janet to sister 6 July 1821, so she can buy a cow for her family. David Tidswell has shown that in Scotland the vast majority of unwed mothers returned to their families. See "Gender, Family, work and Migration in Early Nineteenth-Century Scotland," in Pamela Sharpe, ed., *Women, Gender and Labour Migration: Historical and Global Perspectives* (London and New York: Routledge, 2001): 136.

74 AO, Beckwith Presbyterian, Session, 12 January 1840. In the case of Elizabeth McFarlane who had had sex with her Uncle Donald, she was readmitted with "special watchfulness and prayer." However when another, presumably older woman committed adultery with a relative, the Session believed she was culpable and excommunicated her for six months. See AO, Beckwith Presbyterian, Session, 27 October 1850; NAC, Knox Presbyterian, Lanark, Session, 5 June 1848.

75 NAC, St Paul's Presbyterian, Peterborough, Session, 25 August 1839.

76 AO, Beckwith Presbyterian, Session, 10 November 1839. Women may have also voluntarily confessed their sin once their children were born to avoid severe punishment, although it is more likely that they sincerely desired to have their children baptized.

77 AO, Beckwith Presbyterian Church, Session, 28 May 1876.

78 Sandy Ramos, " 'A Most Detestable Crime': Gender Identities and Sexual Violence in the District of Montreal, 1803–43," *Journal of the Canadian Historical Association*, New Series, Vol. 12, 2001, 27–48.

79 AO, Beckwith Presbyterian Church, Session, 28 April 1844.

80 Ibid.

81 NAC, Knox Presbyterian, Lanark, 25 October 1877.

82 AO, Beckwith Presbyterian Church, Session, 11 October 1868.

83 Norton, "Gender and Defamation in Seventeenth-Century Maryland," 6.

84 Mendelson, "The Civility of Women in Seventeenth-Century England," 125. See also Laura Gowing, "Ordering the Body: Illegitimacy and Female Authority in Seventeenth-Century England," in Michael J. Braddick and John Walter, eds, *Negotiating Power in Early Modern England: Order, Hierarchy and Subordination in Britain and Ireland* (Cambridge: Cambridge University Press, 2001): 60; Gowing, *Domestic Dangers*, 242; Walker, "Expanding the Boundaries of Female Honour in Early Modern England," 239, 242.

85 In 1839, Rev. William Bell had newly discovered that women were more moral than men. See NAC, Robert Bell Papers, William Bell Journal, August 1839, in which he notes: "I am acquainted with several families in the settlement, the female part of which, seems to love religion, and attend to its duties, while the male part do not. Is the female heart more susceptible of religions impressions? Or do their employments lead them to seem more sensibly their need of its support and engagements?"

86 NAC, McGillvray Papers, Session, 20 December 1820.

87 NAC, McGillvray Papers, Session, 8 April 1832. Italics are mine.

88 NAC, McGillvray Papers, Session, 10 August 1838. For another defamation suit in which attacks on the female character were a means to attack the male head of family, see AO, Boston Presbyterian, Session, 31 May 1844.

89 NAC, McGillvray Papers, Session, 1 April 1843.

90 NAC, Alexander McMartin Papers, MG24 C37, Rev. Archibald Connell to Alexander McMartin, 11 December 1827, on the difficulty of having his salary paid in wheat for which he may not get the "full store-price for wheat" and haggling with McMartin for a good price.

91 AO, Boston Presbyterian, Session, 12 January 1849; NAC, McGillvray Papers, James Harkness, St Andrew's Presbyterian, Quebec City, letter, 3 December 1822, on the precariousness of pew rents "according to the popularity and unpopularity of the minister."

92 On the importance of baptism to popular religiosity, see Keith Wrightson, "The Nadir of English Illegitimacy in the Seventeenth-Century," in Peter Laslett, Karla Oosterveen, and Richard M. Smith, eds, *Bastardy and its Comparative History* (Cambridge, MA: Harvard University Press, 1980): 183; Martin Ingram, "The Reform of Popular Culture?: Sex and Marriage in Early Modern England," in Barry Reay, ed., *Popular Culture in Seventeenth-Century England* (London: Croom Helm, 1985): 139; David. D. Hall, "From Religion and Society to Practices: The New Religious History," in Robert Blair St George, ed., *Possible Pasts: Becoming Colonial in America* (Ithaca and London: Cornell University Press, 2000): 156–9; Sarah Williams, "Urban Popular Religion and the Rites of Passage," in Hugh McLeod, ed., *European Religion in the Age of Great Cities, 1830–1930* (New York and London: Routledge, 1995): 231.

93 NAC, Knox Presbyterian, Lanark, Session, 25 July 1862; AO, Hamilton Central Presbyterian, 22 March 1861.

94 AO, Boston Presbyterian, Session, 1 May 1837.

95 NAC, St Andrew's Presbyterian, New Brunswick, Session, 27 July 1879.

96 ANQM, St Andrew's Lachine, Vol. 8, Session, 16 September 1823.

97 AO, St Andrew's Presbyterian, Carleton Place, Session, 25 July 1880.

98 NAC, McGillvray Papers, Session, 9 February 1840.

99 AO, Hamilton Central Presbyterian, Session, 8 Aug. 1870.

100 NAC, St Paul's Presbyterian, Peterborough, Session, 30 January 1838.

101 NAC, St Andrew's New Brunswick, Session, 3 January 1839; 30 June 1839; 9 January 1842. The dates would suggest that on every occasion drunkenness coincided with a holy day at the church. See also the case of William Barrie, who was "in liquor" while out and about on church business. NAC, Knox Presbyterian, Lanark, Session, 9 January 1863. The coincidence of the Presbyterian communion season

and frivolity was a well-worn theme in Scottish popular culture. For a particularly stimulating analysis of this ritual, see Leigh Eric Schmidt, *Holy Fairs: Scottish Communions and American Revivals in the Early Modern Period* (Princeton: Princeton University Press, 1989).

102 See, for example, the cases of John Halliday and Walter Gay from Hamilton, AO, Central Presbyterian, Session, 3 June 1865; and a Mr Clay in Peterborough, who, though he refused to attend the formal court session, was admonished "in secret" and thereby persuaded to reform.

103 Mrs Stevens from Hamilton was one of the few women found drunk in public. The first time she was caught by the elders, who saw her drunk on her own doorstep. She was later turned in on several occasions by her husband. See AO, Central Presbyterian, Session, 24 September 1853, 5 October 1853, 6 April 1854, January 1855, 3 April 1858, 30 April 1858. She reappears several times in the church records reapplying for church membership. Like men caught drinking, Mrs Stevens evaded the formal court; she did not overtly resist but attempted to negotiate by stating that she hoped to reform her behaviour, although she "could not promise to abandon the use of liquor."

104 NAC, St Paul's Presbyterian, Peterborough, Sesion, 25 August 1839, 10 June 1841.

105 AO, Central Presbyterian, Hamilton, Session, 12 December 1852.

106 AO, Central Presbyterian Hamilton, Session, 4 November 1848; NAC, Westminster Presbyterian, Smith's Falls, Session, 30 December 1838.

107 AO, Central Presbyterian Hamilton, 26 January 1875.

108 NAC, Westminster Presbyterian, Smith's Falls, Session, 6 October 1839.

109 Presbyterian elders wished to avoid any political implications of pitting the authority of the church courts versus that of the civil magistrates, as William Bell instigated when in a sermon he publicly castigated the local magistrates for breaking the Sabbath. The magistrates responded by using the newspapers as a venue to further politicize the act. By doing so it thus removed the issue from the purview of Presbyterian control. On this case, see Christie, "'a witness against vice.'"

110 See, for example, AO, Boston church, Session, 14 November 1841, 27 November 1842, 24 January 1859; AO, Beckwith Presbyterian, Session, 2 July 1842; AO, Central Presbyterian Hamilton, Session, 8 April 1853.

111 AO, Boston Church, Session, 18 January 1855.

112 On the identification of otherworldliness with the end of the premodern church, see Lucian Holscher, "Secularization and Urbanization in the Nineteenth-Century," 270.

113 On this point for the early modern period, Richard M. Wunderli, *London Church Courts and Society on the Eve of the Reformation* (Cambridge, MA: The Medieval Academy of America, 1981): 61.

114 AO, St Andrew's Church, Carleton Place, Session, 8 May 1992. Martin Ingram, *Church Courts*, has argued that this institution held back modernity, while this

paper has proffered the view that church courts also acted as the conduits for modern practices and values.

115 On the importance of the church courts for women, see Gowing, *Domestic Dangers*; Margaret Hunt, "Wife Beating, Domesticity and Women's Independence in Eighteenth-Century London," *Gender and History*, 4:1 (Spring, 1992): 10–33; Susan Dwyer Amussen, "'Being Stirred to Much Unquietness: Violence and Domestic Violence in Early Modern England," *Journal of Women's History*, 6:2 (Summer 1994): 70–89. For women's experience in the civil courts, see Lori Chambers and John Weaver, "Alimony and Orders of Protection: Escaping Abusing in Hamilton-Wentworth, 1837–1900," *Ontario History*, XCV:2 (Autumn 2003): 113–35.

3

Evangelicals, Church Finance, and Wealth-Holding in Mid-Nineteenth-Century St Stephen, New Brunswick, and Calais, Maine

HANNAH M. LANE

In December 1849, women from a Congregationalist church serving both St Stephen, New Brunswick, and Calais, Maine, organized an evening hotel supper to raise funds for church improvement. Their advertisement invited "the ladies and gentlemen of the community generally" at a price of fifty cents, almost two thirds the average wage of $1.25 reported for a day-labourer in the 1850 census. In response, a local newspaper endorsed a "rebuke" of this type of fundraising by a contributor who described the ideal church as a place where "The poor may go ... and not run against the arrogance of wealth. The poor widow may there put in her mite, and receive the greater blessing."[1] This was exactly the kind of event and debate that has caught the attention of historians of churches and the social order as well as nineteenth-century critics of church finance. But how typical of local churches were such events, and how directly did methods of church finance reflect social distinctions within or between congregations? In fact, fundraising efforts in the communities along the river border between St Stephen and Calais were generally less upscale; similar events in surrounding decades charged an admission price of only one tenth the 1850 daily wage figure.[2]

Nineteenth-century church finance has had a mixed press in the historical record. The promotion of "systematic benevolence," in encouraging thrift, foresight, and rational planning among churchgoers, could function as an attempt at social regulation through cultural prescription.[3] Echoing nineteenth-century critics, scholars[4] have argued that practices such as the sale or rental of pews[5] could deter the poor from church involvement. Whereas studies of public discourse explore how writers constructed a social role for churches and claimed a form of cultural authority, the latter studies investigate the social role of churches' institutional practices in inscribing distinctions based on status or wealth. In highlighting the generosity of wealthy donors, local church histories[6] may sometimes reinforce the latter argument, but denominational historians have lamented the churches' lack of authority over their congregations, deprecating low clerical salaries, churches' dependence on external support, and resistance to institutional policies.[7] As one minister noted of his first congregation in St Stephen in 1841, "their attachment to the economy of English Methodism is not that loyal. They are liberal in the support of the cause but thus wish to do it in their own way."[8]

Whether as a site of resistance to claims to authority or as a reflection or mechanism of socioeconomic differentiation, church finance has been part of several key narratives concerning the history of churches in Western Europe and North America. As established churches were rivaled or superseded by voluntarist churches financially supported by individuals or families, the model of a theoretically socially inclusive congregation produced through political coercion was succeeded by that of a potentially socially exclusive congregation produced through economic or cultural forces. By the nineteenth century, the scale and range of disparity associated with urbanization and industrialization heightened socioeconomic differentiation within or between congregations or between congregations and, in Europe, an increasingly unchurched population. These processes coincided with institutional and cultural changes within evangelicalism, and this convergence within urban churches has shaped a narrative in which older evangelical denominations such as Methodism began as "popular" movements but became increasingly "middle-class" institutions.[9]

Scholars linked these processes to secularization, variously defined and interpreted. Some revisionists have warned against sharp rural/urban distinctions; some have argued that only selective forms of secularization occurred, and at a later date, and others that periods of low or fluid church involvement had also occurred in earlier times. More specifically, some have argued that socially diverse churches persisted, or that the increased economic segregation of congregations could as easily produce socially homogenous poor or working-class churches as it could produce middle-class or elite churches.[10] Nor were the latter associated only with large industrialized cities; both socially diverse and socially homogenous churches could be found in the small towns and villages of southwestern New Brunswick along its river border with Maine.

Located at the head of the tide on the St Croix river, the parish of St Stephen, New Brunswick, and the census districts of Calais and its smaller neighbour Baring, Maine, contained several churches by the mid-nineteenth century. Before bureaucratization and the development of the modern, corporate "organizational church,"[11] local church finance was more informal and less documented, and, for these communities, sources on evangelicalism are strongest.[12] Although part of differing regional denominational structures, evangelical churches shared a similar local structure: a fluid and partly nominal ethnoreligious constituency, a congregation of casual or regular church attendees, and a smaller "Society" of church members. Although church attendance was the most common form of church involvement, it was also the least documented; however, in evangelical churches, membership was the most committed form of church involvement, and much better documented. The sources for Wesleyan Methodism on the New Brunswick side are richest, and that denomination will predominate in this study, but Presbyterian and Congregationalist churches serving both sides of the river also left membership records. For these and other evangelical denominations, additional sources also document what churches as institutions spent their money on, by what means they raised or tried to raise this money, and what controversies these efforts sometimes involved.

Meeting an acknowledged gap within the historiography of religion and society, a community study of churches' financial practices[13] can re-evaluate arguments concerning social differences between denominations or the extent of "embourgeoisement." Local church finance also illuminates the timing of broader economic processes in the northeast, such as the transition to a cash economy. This study will also point to the methodological problems raised by sources for local church finance and the difficulties of distinguishing between policy and actual practice, between promises, credit, and actual contributions, or between the internal and external sources of financial support.

Some methods of church finance, such as pew-holding or renting, could explicitly or implicitly favour more economically secure families. But churches also used various methods to counter the cultural or organizational pressures that might exclude the poor, and the relative exclusivity of pew-holding was shaped by demand and local context. The social composition of Wesleyan Methodist,[14] Congregationalist, and Presbyterian church members reflected their age profile and their larger ethnoreligious constituencies, which in turn reflected the local community itself. Wesleyan Methodists in the mill villages on the New Brunswick side and Presbyterians as a whole had the highest proportions of poor. In contrast, the Congregationalist church on the New Brunswick side of the river, formed as a result of a schism within Wesleyan Methodism, had the highest proportions of very wealthy. Wesleyan Methodist church members in the mill villages and Presbyterian church members exemplified the socially diverse church, while the Milltown Congregationalists show that the process of congregational economic segregation associated with large cities also occurred in smaller communities.

The non-aboriginal population of early St Stephen and Calais included nominally Congregationalist pre-Revolutionary settlers and denominationally diverse Loyalists.[15] The first permanent minister had gathered a Methodist congregation in St Stephen in 1785. By the end of the War of 1812, that congregation was officially part of the New Brunswick District of Wesleyan Methodists, a mission field in connection with the English Wesleyans; Methodists in Calais formed a weaker but lasting connection with the Methodist Episcopal Church. In 1825, Congregationalists formally organized a church with members from both sides of the river, in looser association with other Congregationalists in Maine. During the extensive revivalism of the 1830s, churches connected with the Maine Regular or Calvinist Baptists also organized, Episcopal Methodism recovered and grew in strength, and Wesleyan Methodism expanded into two "circuits" made up of congregations and societies of church members. Presbyterians began holding public services but did not successfully organize a church until 1854. In 1844, a Wesleyan Methodist schism in the mill villages led to the formation of another Congregationalist church, serving both sides of the river, as did Baptist and Presbyterian churches.[16]

By 1861, the Wesleyan Methodists were the single largest religious group in the parish of St Stephen, at 26 percent of the enumerated population of 5,160. Only 14 percent of this population were listed as Presbyterian, and only a minority of local Congregationalists and Baptists lived on the New Brunswick side of the river, constituting 5 percent and 7 percent of the enumerated population in St Stephen.[17] These figures for nominal religious adherence[18] have no equivalent in census returns for Calais and Baring, whose combined population was enumerated at 6,030 in 1860. Baptist and Congregationalist ministers reported that their meetinghouses could seat at least five hundred individuals, and that Episcopal Methodists reported somewhat smaller "seatings."[19]

An evangelical congregation's ability to build a "chapel" (in British North American usage) or a "meetinghouse" (in New England usage)[20] or to hire a minister was shaped by its economic context. Much less industrialized than Saint John or southwestern Maine, St Stephen and Calais were typical of the shipping, shipbuilding, and lumbering communities of the northeast. Most artisanal and commercial businesses were located in the lower villages, known also as St Stephen and Calais; lumber mills and small-scale metalwork were concentrated in the mill villages. Back settlements included subsistence and commercial farming, a few overlapping with neighbouring settlements in Charlotte County, New Brunswick, or Washington County, Maine.[21] During the first half of the century, actual specie was in short supply, and churches often received contributions in farm products, lumber, or labour.[22] As late as 1862, a minister in the parish of St Stephen noted that some contributions were "paid in produce."[23]

Ministers recognized the wider context to the economic hardships experienced by their members and supporters in this period. Between 1837 and 1857, commercial depressions and poor harvests affected both sides of the river, and Britain's move away from protected markets for colonial timber caused particular economic hardship in New Brunswick.[24] In 1842, a minister in St Stephen lamented "the unprecedented commercial distress & the consequent reduction of prices on lumber, from which the people principally obtain a livelihood." Moreover, by then, the immediate forest had been so lumbered out that firewood was scarce, and coal much "higher in price" than elsewhere.[25] These economic stresses, including poor harvests in the late 1840s, led to outmigration from New Brunswick and eastern Maine that was only partly offset by Irish immigration. In the following decades, the communities along the St Croix recovered and began to industrialize but continued outmigration, and the return of economic depression in the 1870s limited churches' accumulation of institutional wealth.

The local expenses of mid-nineteenth-century evangelical congregations varied from the minimalist rural Methodist house church to a village congregation with a building and a minister. The maintenance of a constructed, rented, or purchased house of worship was intertwined with pew-holding, discussed later in analysis of particular methods of church finance. A comparative account here of how congregations endeavoured to cover the living expenses of their ministers, in theory through salaries, reveals the varied extent of professionalization within different denominations and yet also its limited influence on local church finance. Official salaries reflected social distinctions between denominations in terms of educational expectations of ministers and regional institutional wealth or claims to status. Yet these distinctions may not have been as sharp between local congregations, when the latter failed to pay the full amount of these salaries. From the 1840s to the 1860s, local Wesleyan Methodist ministers received the basic salary of a married minister – roughly £100 or $400 a year based on the number of weeks in a particular circuit – with additional amounts based on the number and age of children. Through external subsidies, these ministers appear to have received in cash or kind what they were promised and did not have to leave with debts to local storekeepers, as sometimes occurred elsewhere. Salaries for "married with children" Episcopal Methodists were lower, and gaps between the formula and what congregations actually provided do not appear to have been filled by denominational subsidies. These gaps were not unusual; the average salary received by Maine Episcopal Methodist ministers in these years was roughly three fourths of the prescribed amount.[26] Similarly, although Baptists in Upper Mills, New Brunswick, and its neighbour Baring, Maine, offered their first minister an impressive $450 a year plus $156 for board, these smallest mill villages were never able to support their own minister.[27]

The higher salaries offered Presbyterian ministers in this period ranged from £80 to £125 ($320-$500) but depended both on the relative wealth and good will of supporters, as well as the wider denominational context. In 1844, the only Presbyterian minister for the whole of Charlotte County received £30 or $120 in actual contributions, remaining only because of grants from Scotland.[28] Another Presbyterian minister joined him just long enough to participate in the colonial ramifications of the Disruption in the Church of Scotland. After a complaint that he had not preached enough in St Stephen for the money he had received and a "rumour" that he had received money from the Church of Scotland after the Disruption, the minister publicly denied that he had only sided with the Free Church when they promised him more.[29] By 1861, a more popular minister was officially paid £125 or $500 a year but was still owed £150 from previous years; his successor was only offered £100 a year.[30]

With college and seminary degrees, Congregationalist ministers were as professionalized as these Presbyterians, and one contemporary estimate suggested their annual salaries in Maine ranged from $300 to $600.[31] In 1834, the Calais Congregationalist church promised its minister $800 but borrowed money for five years to pay arrears in his salary; particularly before 1850, a number of Maine Congregationalist churches were unable to pay the salaries they had originally offered.[32] In contrast, the wealthier Congregationalist church organized in 1846 to serve both Milltowns – New Brunswick and Maine – paid £150 or $600 a year up front, which the minister considered "the least sum that will suffice to support me comfortably & respectably."[33]

Moreover, the gap between the salaries of Methodist and Congregationalist ministers was not as wide as it appeared at first glance. Methodist ministers received additional amounts per family size, and the denomination provided modest pensions for retired ministers or the families of deceased ministers. Most significantly, both Wesleyan and Episcopal Methodists either built a "mission house" or "parsonage" or paid directly for their ministers' accommodation. In contrast, Congregationalism had no provisions for retired ministers or the families of deceased ministers, and ministers generally paid for their own accommodation in this period. Thus, although Congregationalist ministers were better educated and some claimed a higher social status than Methodist ministers, the former were not necessarily also wealthier. However, although Baptists and Presbyterians in St Stephen and Calais did not build a manse or parsonage until the 1870s, the Milltown Congregationalists bought a "parsonage" for their minister as early 1863.[34]

In theory, Wesleyan Methodist circuits also furnished their ministers' accommodations, but these furnishings were among the contentious issues in criticisms of local expenditures made by their English missionary sponsors. These expenditures show both the limits of institutional embourgeoisement at the local level and the claims of ministers to middle-class status. The St Stephen circuit steward's accounts included purely functional items for the minister's residence, but in 1843 a carpet was refused coverage, and no further furnishings were listed for ten years. When the district refused to pay for an item, the cost was picked up by the minister's family or the local church, potentially controversial, as in the case of who should pay for and therefore who would own the "stove left by Mrs Pickles at St Stephen's."[35] Of course, Mrs Pickles and her servant may not have perceived the new stove as extravagant. Keeping one servant, always a separate entry in circuit accounts, was never questioned: this was a hallmark of gentility for Wesleyan Methodist ministers, to compensate for their lesser education, lower salaries, and more modest housing than ministers of the Church of England.[36]

Congregations also collected money for local Sunday schools, but, judging by extant names or amounts, fewer individuals contributed to denominational funds, such as those for retired ministers, the families of deceased ministers, theological institutions, or missions elsewhere in the region or overseas.[37] Quite apart from private charities[38] and women's interdenominational benevolent associations, tracking formal and informal local charity from or within congregations is very difficult. During the 1840s, Methodism in Saint John, New Brunswick, followed John Wesley's original model, in which the Quarterly Meeting of lay leaders appointed a separate "Poor Steward," who together with the minister saw that the offerings from monthly communion and quarterly love feasts were distributed to the poor within the congregation and the wider community. In extant Wesleyan

Methodist records for the parish of St Stephen, no individual was identified as such until the late 1870s, but the regular stewards or the minister or an unnamed layman or laywoman may have undertaken this responsibility.[39] Similarly, the Calais Congregational church took a "collection for the poor" at its communion services held six times a year.[40] Milltown Congregational records did not specify whether they, too, followed this practice, but in 1850 an article added to their church covenant pledged members to mutual "aid in the hour of your destitution." These churches did not leave records analogous to those used in other studies: in London, England, Methodist poor funds had declined from roughly one third to roughly one tenth of annual income by the early nineteenth century, and in two late nineteenth-century Ontario towns poor funds in various Protestant churches ranged from 3 percent to less than 1 percent of annual incomes.[41]

Congregations attempted to meet the expenses of salaries, buildings, and denominational and local funds through various means: from external subsidies, from contributions outside their community or within their community but outside their constituency or congregation, and from forms of church involvement directly linked to church finance. At various times, the salaries of Wesleyan Methodist and Presbyterian ministers were subsidized by denominations in England, Scotland, Ireland, and the regional denominations of the Atlantic colonies. Individuals from other communities, including donors on both sides of the Atlantic, also contributed to Methodist and Presbyterian chapel building in St Stephen.[42] The two Wesleyan Methodist circuits in St Stephen would not be self-sustaining until the late 1860s, and one would later return to dependency. The Calais Congregationalist church was initially subsidized by the Maine Missionary Society, but the Milltown church began and remained self-supporting.[43]

Congregations raised money within the local community through collecting subscriptions from individuals or families for a particular purpose and through smaller and larger fundraising events. The collection of subscriptions was so common that one family, particularly if wealthy, might be asked to contribute to a variety of churches or voluntary societies.[44] Denominations that did not standardize salaries or provide accommodation for their ministers were most likely to use donation parties, smaller but sometimes advertised events held at a minister's home but organized by laity including "friends" from other denominations.[45]

As in other communities, women predominated among "collectors" and were the organizers of fundraising events.[46] The failure of two male lay leaders to recognize this fact inspired one letter writer not only to reproach these men but to challenge their authority. At the 1850 opening of the Presbyterian church in St Stephen after a decade of intermittent efforts, the two trustees in question thanked each other for their respective roles in bringing about this event. The irate observer protested that they had forgotten to mention that roughly half the building's costs had been raised by women: the elite women who had organized a key fundraising event and the larger number of women who had donated goods, time, or basic refreshments.[47] Moreover, the author asserted:

I believe this is the first case on record of a lawyer and broker erecting a House of Christian worship: if the record were true, I would not complain, but report says neither of these gentlemen contributed £10 ... how could these gentlemen (one of whom could have built the house from a month's profits of his saving) stand up in that assembly and assume the credit of building their sanctuary.[48]

Some women's societies on both sides of the river also engaged in varied pastoral or charitable activities,[49] but others focused only on church property. Fundraising events involved sales of food, beverages, donated items, and items produced by the organizers[50] and were not without some criticism for their "levity" and preoccupation with money.[51] Although women in poorer evangelical congregations in the Atlantic region also fundraised through these methods,[52] the expectation that a certain number of women would have time and means to make both "useful and ornamental articles"[53] assumed the presence of a certain number of economically secure families[54] not wholly occupied with the care of the very young or old. One solution for poorer congregations was to solicit donations from wealthier congregations in their region: for example, women in Halifax sent items to sales in St Stephen.[55]

These kinds of events gathered contributions from both the wider community and a church's supporters. Even allowing for exaggerated reporting, the attendance over two days at the largest Presbyterian fundraiser in the 1840s was well beyond the number of local Presbyterians and underscores the role of the wider community in financing local churches.[56] These external sources of financial support to a local congregation show that contributions received or overall institutional wealth did not necessarily directly reflect the economic resources of the congregation itself but rather those of the wider community. Thus, some methods of church finance can only be interpreted as ambiguous markers of social differences within or between congregations.

However, Congregationalist and Methodist church members might be expected to contribute more directly as part of their particular form of church involvement.[57] The former inherited the Puritan model of church support in which male church members paid the minister's salary by contributing a set proportion of the value of their property as listed in local assessments. Also advocated by some Baptists,[58] this model of originally state-mandated "minister taxes" could exempt the propertyless or calculate the proportion only on the poll tax. For example, the Milltown Congregationalist appointed a committee to calculate what to ask members to contribute based on "an ad valorem tax assessed on the property of its members." The proportion was not specified in extant sources, but a few published amounts suggest that it was a fraction of a tithe.[59]

This model did assume that most members would own property of some kind, whether they were proprietors in primarily farming and/or fishing communities or an essentially "bourgeois" church, as in Milltown, New Brunswick.[60] However, the model was only as binding as members allowed it be. According to a late-nineteenth-century retrospective, "a few paid large sums and comparatively few contributed all" that they were asked to. Eventually, even the Milltown Congregationalist church had to borrow money until a few individuals paid off the debt. Whether the Calais Congregationalist church also followed the Puritan model is not clear, but it, too, acquired debts related to minister's salaries, which took many years to pay in full.[61]

Methodists had also inherited a model for church finance from their founders. In John Wesley's model, church members were expected to contribute according to their ability at the weekly class meeting, and four times a year at the renewal of membership tickets. A penny per week per member was recommended, with wealthier members contributing on behalf of those who could not. As well ensuring a continuous recovery of local expenses, the model was intended to encourage thrift, foresight, and charity, protect congregations from dependence on the state or on "patrician endowments," and validate the "pence of the poor" equally with the "pounds of the rich."[62] This model proved controversial in both England[63] and North America, rendered "obsolete" by the expenses of institutional expansion. Especially in rural areas, Wesleyan Methodist church members and ministers in the Atlantic colonies also found it unworkable as well as unpopular.[64]

Because McColl – the long-lived founding Methodist minister in St Stephen – had been largely self-supporting, subsequent Wesleyan missionaries found it particularly difficult to persuade local Methodists to support them. Circuit accounts to 1838 were quite detailed and show that, except for McColl's successor, no other minister or lay leader collected weekly class meeting or quarterly membership ticket money in the back settlements.

However, most village class meetings collected both weekly class meeting money and quarterly contributions at the renewal of membership tickets. Circuit accounts did not break down members' contributions by class meeting but do show that contributions taken at class meetings or at the renewal of membership tickets were only a tiny fraction of circuit receipts. Moreover, the wording suggests some flexibility: "Class and Ticket Money & subscriptions in lieu thereof" or "Subscriptions at the Quarterly Renewal of the Tickets." In 1859, the minister on the Milltown circuit noted that all the class meetings paid quarterly "Ticket money" except the poorest mill village and the poorest back settlement. Only one class meeting list from the late 1870s has any indication of individual contributions on it, showing a range of small sums and that not all members contributed.[65]

Congregations of all denominations could take up public collections from regular or casual churchgoers at Sunday services, but Wesleyan Methodist circuit accounts suggest that only village congregations did so. Most of the small congregations in the back settlements gave only subscriptions and donations, although the largest and most prosperous began holding public collections during worship in 1851, but only four times a year. Moreover, in the two circuits that comprised all the Wesleyan Methodist congregations in St Stephen and a few in neighbouring parishes, public collections initially formed only a small proportion of all contributions when compared to undesignated "subscriptions and donations"; in one circuit, contributions from public collections overtook subscriptions and donations by the late 1860s, but not in the poorer congregations of the Milltown circuit.

Common to most denominations but at times controversial, the sale or rental of pews (henceforth pew-holding) was a more significant part of church finance.[66] Moreover, many dimensions of pew-holding reflected broader themes in cultural, legal, economic, and occasionally even political history. Although John Wesley had opposed pews, many urban Methodist chapels on both sides of the Atlantic had returned to family pew-holding by the early nineteenth century. In part a reaction against same-sex seating in favour of newer ideologies of family and domesticity, the timing and geography of this change varied considerably.[67] The early introduction of pew-holding as well as mixed seating into New England Methodism initiated recurring debate within US Methodism.[68] Among most evangelical denominations, the main purpose of pew-holding was to pay for and maintain a chapel or meetinghouse. At the opening of a building, wealthier individuals from other denominations also contributed to the cost of the chapel by purchasing or renting pews. For example, a deacon in the Calais Congregationalist church had in his lifetime purchased pews in a union meetinghouse in another Maine town and in the Congregationalist, Episcopal Methodist, and Baptist meetinghouses in Calais.[69] Pew-holding was an even more essential part of Presbyterian church finance: by 1861, the church in St Stephen paid the minister's salary entirely through pew rents, although churches in Charlotte County used either subscriptions or a combination of both.[70]

The question of who precisely owned a pew or, through several pews, a part of a meetinghouse or chapel, or indeed the whole building, was culturally and legally ambiguous until individual churches or denominations incorporated within a particular jurisdiction. Unlike rented pews in churches owned by trustees on behalf of either a congregation or a denomination, pews in Congregationalist, Baptist, and sometimes also Methodist church buildings were owned entirely privately. Pews might be listed with other real estate by a local property agent or among the property of a debtor passing into the hands of a creditor or to settle an estate, as in the Congregationalist deacon cited above. Individual ownership of pews could thus put the chapel itself at risk of entanglement in the debts of pew-holders and also precluded a congregation rerenting pews to recover other expenses. For this latter reason the Calais Congregationalists bought all their pews back in the 1870s and thereafter only rented them.[71]

In cases of church conflict, methods of church finance could thus determine not only on whom the minister depended for his salary but who controlled the use of a church building. In 1838, the Milltown Baptists debated hosting an Abolitionist lecturer, until the deacon who had purchased a majority of pews and thus "controlled over half the house ... decided to open the building."[72] In a more serious conflict in 1850, this same deacon led the opposition to a minister who had preached a sermon against "cram," the practice in local lumbering operations and lumber mills of paying workmen in often overpriced and damaged goods. The deacon along with other laymen were able to withhold the minister's salary, suggesting that the salary must have been originally paid by them and that the minister's supporters were not wealthy enough to provide an equivalent. When the meetinghouse was destroyed by arson, both sides accusing each other, the focus of debate shifted to who should collect from the insurance company.[73]

In nineteenth-century Methodism, chapels were supposed to be owned by the regional denominational organization – a "conference" – rather than by local pew-holders or by a single congregation. Local trustees only rented or sold the use of a pew to pew-holders. But, influenced by the New England meetinghouse model, some Methodists used the language of individual pew ownership.[74] In 1844, a number of wealthy members and lay leaders in the

Wesleyan Methodist church in Milltown, New Brunswick, quarrelled with two ministers over a variety of issues. Initially in the hands of this faction, the chapel deed was repossessed by the other trustees, after which the chapel had been destroyed by arson allegedly instigated by the anti-Wesleyan faction. The pro-Wesleyan trustees then published in local newspapers their claim to the land on which the chapel had stood and cited the Methodist interpretation of pew-holding in their defence. This conflict over property re-emerged a few years later after the death of the wealthiest lay leader loyal to the Wesleyan Methodists. Accusing their stepmother and other unnamed Methodists of undue influence, the ex-Methodists among this lay leader's sons and daughters unsuccessfully challenged his will, which had left a substantial legacy to the Milltown circuit.[75] These kinds of conflicts may well have been one of the reasons for the legal incorporation in 1853 of the Wesleyan Methodist Church within New Brunswick and the legislation's reference to the problem of "defective" language in some property deed.[76]

Whether they owned their pews outright, or bought the use of them, or rented them from trustees acting on behalf of a local congregation or a denomination, pew-holders collectively expressed ways their communities were socially organized. But how pew systems did this varied over time, by place, church, or even between a morning and an evening service. Pew-holding in eighteenth-century churches had been customary – based on gender or race, or on social or civic rank – and included designated sections for inexpensive or free pews.[77] By the early nineteenth century, this social hierarchy was redefined and sharpened in churches that shifted to market-driven methods of finance; some reduced the number of free pews and exerted more pressure on pew-holders in arrears. As churches mirrored the market economy and used more commercial methods such as auctions, churches lost control of pew prices.[78] This nearly occurred in St Stephen in 1818 but was checked by the minister: fearing "that by the people bidding so high, the poor were excluded," Duncan McColl ruled that the remainder would only be sold at the "average value sufficient to cover the expense of the building the chapel."[79]

Nineteenth-century pew-holders "proved their worldly success, confirmed their allegiance to the prevailing moral values of thrift and self-reliance," and "established their place on the social hierarchy by the price they paid for seats – a fact observable to all by the location of pews."[80] A retrospective history of St Matthew's Presbyterian Church in Halifax, Nova Scotia, quipped that a man's "credit ... was rated by his seating."[81] In St Andrew's, the nearest New Brunswick town to St Stephen, the absence of pews in the public hall initially used by Methodists had kept away higher status families who did "not like to mix with all classes."[82]

In the early 1820s, the English Wesleyan Methodist Missionary Society urged more congregations in the Maritime colonies to adopt pew rental as a means of reducing their debts, but an 1827 survey suggests that many rural chapels in New Brunswick in that period used benches instead of pews or pews with entirely free seating.[83] Debt loads varied by context, severest among poorer congregations in towns or cities with several church buildings competing for financial support. The timing of chapel building was also critical; a number were built at the end of the peak revivalism of the late 1830s, just before a decade of economic depression, poor harvests, and outmigration.[84] In order to build and finance a number of new or rebuilt chapels during the 1840s and 1850s, evangelicals in St Stephen and Calais used various methods, and their respective debts and pew systems reflected differences in the wealth of denominational groups and the effect of local context on market-driven pew systems.

The Old Ridge chapel began with thirty-eight rented pews, a free gallery, and four free pews at the front of the church, in contrast with the practice in large urban churches, where front pews were the most desirable. Records of the prices of the pews have not survived, but the amounts enabled the chapel to open without debt. Two of the four free pews were sold within a few years, a case of market demand overcoming the original intentions for the chapel.[85] However, the Old Ridge chapel was so small and the families of this settlement so interrelated that its pew-holding cannot be portrayed as replicating social structure. In other local settlements, evangelicals had small pewed chapels or an unpewed meetinghouse, or met in a schoolhouse or a private home.

Opened in 1836, the Episcopal Methodist church in Milltown, Maine, had auctioned its pews but also mortgaged the building. Ten years later, the minister at the time had reputedly walked from house to house in the general community collecting small contributions until he had enough to pay off the debt. Opened in 1846 at a cost of £950, the rebuilt Wesleyan Methodist chapel in Milltown, New Brunswick, also auctioned its pews, and by the mid 1850s had paid off its debt.[86] In contrast, the Milltown Congregationalists built their church at a cost of $8,000 (roughly £2,000) and opened it in 1849 without any debt: the pews fetched such high prices that the cost of the chapel was recovered before the auction ended. Supply exceeded demand, and twelve pews were left unsold, thus becoming de facto free pews.[87]

Pew supply also exceeded pew demand in the auction of pews for the Wesleyan Methodist chapel in Milltown, New Brunswick, but in this case the demand was also low in price.[88] Of the fifty pews in the new Milltown chapel, the class leader Abner Hill took three for his extended family, and another fourteen simply to pay for the chapel or the minister's salary. Technically, the free pews were in the back of the church, but Abner Hill essentially donated other pews in the very front and middle of the church. Stephen Hill and James Albee each rented a pew for their own use and one or two pews "for" other named families, all but one clearly related to them.[89] The remaining renters in the new Wesleyan Methodist chapel in Milltown, New Brunswick, took only one pew each, for which in some cases they had not paid anything as late as 1851. Pew records are erratic and intersperse dollars and sterling, but they suggest that some years families paid nothing towards their pledge, some might contribute firewood, others might contribute a pound a year (roughly $4). In Milltown, the highest recorded amounts came from Abner Hill and later his widow, at roughly £10 or $40 a year. If the Milltown chapel followed the practice of the St Stephen chapel in earlier decades, these amounts constituted 5 percent of their original bid or pledge.[90]

The poorest pew-holder at the 1846 opening of the Wesleyan Methodist chapel in Milltown, New Brunswick, was the "Widow Bean," and there is no indication of how she rented her pew. Her labourer sons were polled in assessments with no listed wealth of any kind until the middle 1850s; however, her millwright son-in-law had acquired some property by 1851. Another pew-holder, Jacob Libby – a young married labourer with £100 personal estate in 1846 and some real estate by 1851 – was listed on three pew lists between 1846 and 1851, yet by his name on the original 1846 list was the annotation "Nothing paid up to November 1851." Unlike churchgoers in a popular urban church with a "waiting list" for pews[91] or in very small densely packed rural chapels[92] such as that at Old Ridge, Libby and his wife were able to keep their pew because of the lack of competition from the wealthy for pews in post-schism Milltown Methodism. Moreover, in addition to gallery seating in the morning, all seating at evening services was also open. An 1856 comment on the "good attendance" at evening services and presence of "many comparative strangers ... most of whom are young men and young women"[93] suggests that the free seating and time of worship may have attracted a larger and more socially diverse congregation. If Wesleyan Methodist churches in St Stephen used the same pew agreements as those printed for the denomination's Fredericton church, unoccupied pews in the morning were opened after "the Reading of the Lessons."[94]

Elsewhere in New Brunswick, Wesleyan Methodists used a mixture of customary and market-driven pew-holding systems, which functioned in different ways according to the size and location of the church. In Saint

John, Wesleyan Methodist churches sometimes auctioned only a proportion of pews, renting others with differential rates and designating at times as many as four hundred free seats[95]; in some Presbyterian churches, individuals who could not afford to rent a whole pew could rent a single "seating" within the pew.[96] Local demand and the extent of debt shaped pew systems, as did the judgement of trustees. With low demand, bidders could ignore the most expensive seats; but even when demand exceeded supply, trustees could choose to reserve "fifty to sixty 'free seats.'"[97]

Given her poverty and the availability of free seating, why would the Widow Bean have pledged to rent a pew in the Milltown chapel? Pew-holding could sometimes be a means by which lower status families could assert their presence within the congregation and gain access to church power structures. Moreover, studies of English churches have found that pew rents were rarely paid in advance and were often in arrears or written off by the church. Churches offered differential rents on pews not just by location but also the means of the renter and set apart free seating or declared all unoccupied seats free by the opening of worship. Furthermore, the stigma of free seating was diminished by the willingness of wealthier or higher status families to sit in free seats.[98]

One pressure on congregations to raise pew prices or put more pressure on renters in arrears was the changing material culture of their buildings. Among Methodists, the transformation of urban churches began early in the century in New England,[99] but not until the 1850s in New Brunswick.[100] Shortages of seating for expanding congregations or the destruction or damage of an old building might lead to the decision to build a new one according to contemporary fashion, and mid-nineteenth-century congregations expected more physically comfortable buildings. This transformation eventually reflected the introduction of a new aesthetic: in St Stephen, the first "splendid" wooden Gothic church was built in 1849 by the newly organized Milltown Congregationalists. The Presbyterians followed with a wooden Gothic church opened in 1860–their first completed church building.[101]

However, the more dramatic changes in a few urban churches should not obscure the more gradual and modest nature of church improvement in towns and rural communities. Heated churches – by one or more rarely two stoves – were not common until mid-century, by which time perhaps one half of New England churches had some form of artificial illumination.[102] "Warming and lighting conveniences" were among the highlighted features of church improvement and new churches in St Stephen and Calais in this period. Through the chapel societies discussed earlier, women led this alteration of the interiors of both church buildings and dwellings, imitating their wider cultural role as beautifiers of domestic or private space.[103]

Mid-century church building was not without local criticism. One instalment in a wide-ranging satirical poem series published in the aftermath of the Baptist schism claimed to portray a "charming locality" on "two sides of a gently flowing river," whose "inhabitants" were "celebrated for their skill in ecclesiastical architecture":

A house of prayer stands here on every hill,
The poor, meanwhile, are ground and goaded still.
…
My father's house is called the house of prayer,
But ye have made of it a den of thieves'-
Twas so in Israel – 'tis so in St Steeves.

In other verses, the author contrasted the ideal purposes of church buildings – places where people could worship or ministers could denounce immorality without fear of reprisal–with the use of church buildings as sites of conspicuous personal or institutional consumption and display.[104]

Another short poem sequence published locally and probably by the same writer included a critique of new church-building within a portrait of a hypocritical wealthy evangelical lay leader. The latter character type had also been a subtheme in the sermon that had triggered the Baptist schism and was subsequently picked up by other local writers. Although all these writers had reacted to a local event – the Baptist schism – their themes could be found in religious discourse on economic topics published elsewhere in the northeast and in England in this period. This timing reflected both the impact of international trade depressions and the tensions between older moral economy understandings of commercial ethics and the new political economy.[105]

The concern with which this paper opened – that the poor were alienated within or socially excluded from congregations by churches' own financial practices – was also expressed by some lay leaders and ministers. When in 1845 Saint John Wesleyan Methodists debated holding their first tea meeting, most supported the concept, but cut the original ticket price from one dollar to fifty cents, suggesting that accessibility was also an issue. With regard to the Methodist model for church finance based on collecting contributions at weekly class meetings or membership renewal, an 1872 writer claimed that most ministers had not enforced the model; "poor people and persons in quite moderate circumstances with large families" resisted becoming members or ceased to attend class meetings rather than "confess their poverty."[106] Critics of pew-holding contrasted its social distinctions with the open seating of camp meetings, or noted that the poor paid a much higher proportion of their income in pew rent than did the wealthy.[107] Nevertheless, historians of English churches have noted that even some working-class churches resisted the abandonment of pew-holding, fearing the loss of key income or perceiving free pews as an attempt to take power away from laity who exercised a property-based vote in chapel business.[108] The latter was a theme of debates over bills concerning Church of England properties[109] and the incorporation of Presbyterian churches, including the one in St Stephen.

This latter debate shows how the relationship between church involvement and finance shaped church polity. The Presbyterian church in St Stephen first tried to incorporate in 1855, but the bill was defeated because of objections to three different wordings. The first version stated that only male church members or "communicants" could become or elect trustees, while the second merely reduced the number of eligible trustees or voters to those who were both communicants and pew-holders. The third version included non-member pew-holders among those eligible to become or vote for the trustees, but still allowed non-pew-holding church members to become or vote for trustees and this latter point also proved contentious. The St Stephen Presbyterians then focused, along with others, on achieving New Brunswick-wide incorporation of Free Church Presbyterians, but, in 1857 and 1858, legislation qualifying male contributors to the minister's salary to be or vote for trustees was also defeated.[110]

Fuelled in part by ongoing Free Church/Church of Scotland tensions, the public opposition does not appear to have come from St Stephen itself but from Presbyterians elsewhere in the county and from members of the House of Assembly. The bill's opponents interpreted the earlier wordings as taking power away from the pew-holders and giving too much power to the clergy, and their rhetoric echoed historic and recurring debates within the Presbyterian tradition. Why did these critics of the initial Presbyterian incorporation bills in New Brunswick ignore or dismiss the male church members from the question so easily? The low proportion of men among Presbyterian church members meant that only a small number of members would have been eligible to be trustees or their electors, and in conflicts over the Disruption trustees and elders had often formed opposite sides. Only church members could sign the call for a minister, and thus might be more sympathetic towards him.[111]

The rhetoric of one Presbyterian opponent to the 1855 bill concerning the St Stephen church suggests another reason why these men dismissed the potential power of male communicants as checks to the minister: perceived differences between the social range of men who might be church members and that of men who were regular contributors: "A transient person, one working for a few days in a shipyard, for instance, being a communicant, would have a voice in the affairs of the church, when a permanent resident and a Pewholder would be entirely excluded."[112] In 1857, another objector claimed that "the Minister would have it in his power to call on every penny a week contributor whenever he wished his stipend to be increased, and thereby swamp the Electors being pew or seat holders."[113] The bill finally passed in 1859, after qualification as an elector or trustee was limited to men who had actually contributed (as opposed to promised) ten shillings or more annually to the minister's salary in any form, including pew rent.[114] Whereas a propertyless male church member could have qualified as an elector or trustee in St Stephen under the 1855 bill, such a man was excluded under the wider 1859 legislation, as of course were most church members, because they were women.

Since none of the relatively few local and lay voices in these debates over church buildings, finance, and polity were ever named, determining whether churches' expenses and methods of fundraising deterred the poor from church involvement must be done indirectly. Records do not exist for the most common form of church involvement – casual or regular church attendance – but do exist for the most committed forms of involvement in Wesleyan Methodist, Presbyterian, and Congregationalist congregations: lay leadership or church membership. Was the partial use of the Wesleyan or Puritan models for church finance in St Stephen and Calais reflected in the underrepresentation of the poor among Wesleyan Methodist or Congregationalist church members? Did Presbyterian church members come from the same socioeconomic groups as their lay leaders or electors, as the latter were defined under the new legislation?

The following analysis is based on linking Wesleyan Methodist, Presbyterian, and Congregationalist records of lay leaders and church members, census returns for Charlotte County, New Brunswick, and Calais and Baring, Maine – the latter reporting real and personal estate by 1860 – and assessments for the parish of St Stephen. Thus the following discussion considers only members in the Wesleyan Methodist churches on the New Brunswick side of the river but not the members of the Episcopal Methodist churches on the Maine side of the river. Only one Presbyterian church served both sides of its river, and nearly all of its members or lay leaders could be linked to St Stephen Parish assessments; only a few Presbyterian members were in Calais in 1850, and some enumerated there in 1860 had previously resided in St Stephen. Birthplaces and church records show that a number of immigrant Presbyterians in Calais became Congregationalists, a pattern that also occurred elsewhere in Maine. The two Congregationalist churches – one located in Calais and the other in Milltown, New Brunswick – also served both sides of the river; thus, although the discussion of rates of membership among Congregationalist adherents can focus only on New Brunswick residents enumerated in the New Brunswick census of 1861, the discussion of the social composition of Congregationalist church members will include both sides of the river.

Assessments and US census returns provide a symbolic but systematically obtained representation of relative wealth–a representation of differences rather than an accounting of assets or income. For the purposes of taxation and voter eligibility, St Stephen assessments listed most males over twenty, local real estate – which assessors were in a position to evaluate – and local personal property, often underreported or undervalued. The enumerators of the 1860 census asked household heads to estimate the real and personal property owned by each individual within the household regardless of where that property was owned[115]; here, respondents had less incentive to underreport their wealth and may have sometimes overreported it.[116] As assessments and US census returns did not refer to the same kind of wealth and portrayed this wealth in different ways, the analysis of St Stephen assessments and Calais and Baring census returns is kept separate in the following tables.

Because most evangelical church members and a few Wesleyan Methodist pastoral leaders were women, analyzing their socioeconomic composition as represented by wealth-holding required linking members and leaders to one or more relatives, and then linking these families to information on wealth from assessments or US census returns. Enumerated or assessed wealth was then summed per family and treated as a socioeconomic characteristic of individuals within the family. As most of the analysis is of assessments for the parish of St Stephen, the wealth groups used below are derived chiefly from the property requirements for voting or election to political office in New Brunswick. Wealth-holding in the villages was more stratified, symbolizing a wide range of assets; wealth-holding in the back settlements was much less likely to include personal estate or income and generally represented a farm. For these reasons, and the evidence cited earlier that the pressure on Methodist members to contribute regularly to the church was less in the settlements, the villages and back settlements were analyzed separately. This distinction enabled a further simplification: the use of summed totals of assessed real estate, personal estate, and annual income for individuals or families.[117]

Using these combined sources in this way enabled the inclusion of women – the majority of church members – who were generally more demographically diverse than male church members, most of whom were older, married men. Given that wealth-holding tended to increase somewhat with age (although sometimes declining in old age), analysis only of male church members presents a distorted image of the social composition of evangelical churches. Finally, a larger number of men and women could be linked to at least one assessment over time than could be linked to a census return or assessment in a single year.

As all the following analysis will show, instead of reflecting the exclusion of the poor from church membership, the social composition of both lay leaders and church members most obviously reflected that of the ethnoreligious groups from which these members came.[118] Individuals whose family roots lay in the first or second generation of European settlement of a particular community came from families whose grandparents or great grandparents had first access to the best land and time to develop it and, if economically successful, also accumulate and invest property. In St Stephen, no new back settlements were formed after the 1820s, although elsewhere in Charlotte County, transiency and waves of British immigration created a somewhat more fluid rural social structure. Although Catholics included the largest number of recent immigrants, Presbyterians in St Stephen and Calais included not only descendants of Irish or Scottish Presbyterian Loyalists but also more recent immigrants, predominantly Irish. Wesleyan Methodists had a fairly small proportion of immigrants from the British Isles, although because of their age they were overrepresented among church members and lay leaders.

Congregationalists included very few immigrants, except for a few former or future Presbyterians but, along with Wesleyan Methodists, included a number of families of pre-Loyalist origin. Wesleyan Methodists and even more so Congregationalists had a demographic core of early settled and more prosperous families: for families still resident in 1861, those who had survived and persisted through the economic stresses of the previous decades. Moreover, a number of old Congregationalist families – some intermarried with old Episcopalian families – reflected these denominations' historic associations in coastal communities with mercantile and official elites.[119] In short, the Congregationalists were the wealthiest ethnoreligious group, and in St Stephen, unlike other communities with larger Scottish populations, the Presbyterians were the poorest.

Analyzing lay leaders necessarily involves relatively small numbers, and for this reason the very few documented lay leaders in the two Congregational churches for this period are excluded from table 1. Wesleyan Methodist and Presbyterian churches both distinguished pastoral lay leaders–Methodist class meeting leaders or local preachers and Presbyterian elders – and financial officers–stewards or trustees. Laymen occupying both kinds of positions are counted as pastoral leaders in the following table. In both denominations, pastoral leaders were always church members, but financial officers might include men in the congregation who had not formally joined the church. As table 1 shows, among Wesleyan Methodist lay leaders in villages active between 1854 and 1881 and linked by self or family to one or more parish assessments between 1854 and 1863, most were in the middling or higher wealth groups; in fact, some poorer lay leaders had left the parish by these years, chosen for the purposes of comparison with the Presbyterians.

As already noted, the legislation incorporating the Free Presbyterian Church in New Brunswick specified that only men who gave ten shillings a year or more to the minister's salary could be or vote for trustees. In fact, this requirement does not appear to have substantially excluded poorer men from qualifying as electors in St Stephen, though whether they provided the ten shillings in actual cash or in lumber, farm products, or labour is not specified in the records. Forty-eight Presbyterian men from the villages on the St Stephen side of the river were elders, trustees, or their electors between 1854 and 1864 or between 1872 and 1882 and could be linked by self or family to parish assessments in these years. The very few men who were elders–an ordination for life usually of an older man–or trustees–men who managed the chapel and were elected annually–were from the higher wealth groups. Nonetheless, 40 percent of the electors were in the lowest wealth groups.[120]

As in other communities, lay leaders were expected to be older and wealthier or higher-status men[121]; nevertheless, commentators sometimes acknowledged the economic as well as spiritual influence of female lay leaders.[122] Although excluded from or underrepresented in various forms of lay leadership, women were the majority of members in these churches. Wesleyan Methodist, Congregational, and Presbyterian churches shared similar but not identical criteria for church membership. All three required private or public expression of religious experience in the language of evangelical conversion to clergy and lay leaders. But their official theological understandings of this language and psychological process varied; and religious obituaries for Wesleyan Methodists also suggest that this understanding

Table 3.1
Wesleyan Methodist or Presbyterian lay leaders and Presbyterian electors active 1854–1881
in St Stephen and linked to at least one parish assessment 1854–1863

	Wesleyan Methodists	
Total assessed wealth	Pastoral	Financial Officers
0	12.5%	14%
£10-99/$40-399		11%
£100-299/$400-1199	25%	22%
£300-1499/$1200-5999	50%	44%
£1500-22,500/$6,000-90,000	12.5%	8%
N	16	36

	Presbyterians		
Total assessed wealth	Elders	Trustees at least once 1855–1881	Electors but never trustees 1855–1881
0			24%
£10-99/$40-399	20%	9%	16%
£100-299/$400-1199	40%	36%	32%
£300-1499/$1200-5999	40%	46%	24%
£1500-22,500/$6,000-90,000		9%	3%
N	5	11	37

varied among individuals and among those who wrote about them for religious publications. Wesleyan Methodist members also included those who were still seeking conversion, whereas Congregationalist and Presbyterian members needed to show that they were genuinely and firmly converted. Wesleyan Methodists joined a class meeting–a private devotional group–and remained members by attending this class meeting, though some ministers waited up to two years after an individual had ceased to attend class before dropping them from the membership. Presbyterians retained their church membership by being admitted to communion at least once a year. In the Congregationalist tradition, church membership was a covenant between members that could only be mutually and formally dissolved, so members included non-residents who had not yet joined another church. Yet despite these differences, these denominations cooperated in joint prayer meetings and revivals, and, most significantly, accepted transfers of members from each other's societies.[123]

The single year approach was essential for analyzing rates of membership among different socioeconomic groups within a probable constituency for a particular church: those enumerated in St Stephen in 1861 as nominal adherents of that church's denomination. As few evangelical church members joined before age fifteen,[124] those enumerated in 1861 as aged fifteen or over were defined as this age group for this constituency of potential church members. Wesleyan Methodists had organized class meetings in the settlements, and, although some of these members had moved to the villages by 1861, others had not. Thus, of 990 Wesleyan Methodist church members listed in rural or village class meetings within the parish of St Stephen between 1840 and 1881, only 141 were enumerated within the villages in 1861 as Methodist adherents aged fifteen or over and could also be linked by self or family to parish assessments 1860–62.[125] More Presbyterians lived in the villages, and, of 279 Presbyterian known church members within the parish of St Stephen between 1854 and 1882, sixty-three were enumerated within the villages in 1861 as Presbyterian adherents aged fifteen or over who could also be linked to parish assessments 1860–62. Most Congregationalist church members between 1825 and 1881 lived on the US side of the river, and only seventy were enumerated in villages on the New Brunswick side in 1861 as Congregationalist adherents aged fifteen who could also be linked to parish assessments 1860–62. As these small numbers of village church members enumerated in St Stephen in a single year show, church members were as transient as their communities.[126]

As table 2 shows, 27 percent of all of the Methodist group of adherents in villages and linked to assessments were Wesleyan Methodist church members in one or more years between 1860–62. Of these Methodist adherents, 19 percent were former or future church members, and 54 percent were never members in the St Stephen circuit between 1840 and 1881 or in the Milltown circuit between 1849 and 1881. In contrast, with complete church records from an earlier date and easier terms of continued church membership, Congregationalist church members were most readily linked to census returns and assessments, producing the highest rates of church membership of the three groups of adherents analyzed in table 2.

The much lower rates of church membership among Presbyterians linked to assessments reflect several factors. The church was not organized until 1854, with only two communion services a year and no regular ministry, which reduced the number of times a record of communicants was kept; as well, records in the mid 1860s are incomplete. Finally, in the Presbyterian tradition, membership was so serious a decision and taking communion after any spiritual declension so serious a sin that Presbyterians tended to join churches at an older age than Methodists or Congregationalists.[127]

Table 3.2
Church Members and Adherents age 14 or over enumerated in villages
St Stephen, 1861 and linked to parish assessments 1860–62 by self or family

Except for those in brackets, % are the percentages of member/adherent groups
in wealth groups.

	Adherents enumerated as Methodists in 1861				
Total assessed wealth	Members 1860–62	Members 1840/49–59	Members 1863–81	Never Members 1840/49–81	All Adherents
0	13%		12%	13%	12%
£10-99/$40-399	12%	20%	7%	22%	17%
£100-299/$400-1199	29%	47%	46%	26%	31%
£300-1499/ $1200-5999	43%	27%	21%	28%	31%
£1500-22,500/ $6,000-90,000	2%	6%	14%	11%	9%
All Methodist adherents	83 (27%)	15(5%)	43 (14%)	170 (54%)	311

	Adherents enumerated as Presbyterians in 1861			
	Members 1854–62	Members 1863–82	Never Members 1854–64, 1867–82/ Not linked 1865–66	All Adherents
0	22%	37%	33%	31%
£10-99/$40-399	12%	16%	16%	16%
£100-299/$400-1199	38%	10%	30%	30%
£300-1499/ $1200-5999	22%	37%	18%	20%
£1500-22,500/ $6,000-90,000	5%		3%	3%
All adherents	40 (16%)	19 (8%)	184 (76%)	243

	Adherents enumerated as Congregationalist in 1861				
	Members 1860–62	Members 1825–59	Members 1863–81	Never Members 1825–81	All Adherents
0-£99/4399	8%	No lapsed members were enumerated in 1861		17%	11%
£100-299/$400-1199	20%		21%	27%	23%
£300-1499/ $1200-5999	39%		64%	35%	40%
£1500-22,500/ $6,000-90,000	33%		14%	21%	26%
All adherents	66 (45%)		14 (10%)	66 (45%)	146

Among Methodist adherents whose names never appeared on extant membership records, the proportion of those without any assessed wealth or in families without any assessed wealth reflected the proportion of this wealth group among all adherents. The next-to-lowest wealth group was overrepresented among never-member adherents, reflecting the fact that in villages these amounts in assessments referred to wages or small amounts of personal property most commonly linked to younger men living on their own, and young men in general had the lowest rates of church membership. The proportions of each wealth group among Presbyterian adherents never linked to extant membership records between 1854 and 1882 almost mirrored the proportions among all Presbyterian adherents in 1861. Among both Methodist and Presbyterian adherents, at least one of the middle wealth groups was overrepresented among current church members. As the poor were underrepresented among Congregationalist adherents, they were barely present among those who were also Congregationalist church members.

Since very few of these members left texts portraying their reasons for joining evangelical churches in these decades, one can only speculate about what these patterns might represent. In religious obituaries, spiritual reasons and family influences explained an individual's initial desire to seek conversion, the conversion itself, or the sometimes separate decision to join a church. The greater ability to contribute regularly to the church was clearly not enough to persuade more than a few very wealthy Methodist adherents to attend village class meetings, although a larger proportion of wealthy Congregationalist adherents did also become Congregationalist church members. Middling wealth groups may have been overrepresented because church membership may have been a stronger element in middling or middle-class social identity. Yet if this cultural association was in the minds of St Stephen and Calais evangelicals, it was not strong enough to persuade more than one half of Methodist adherents, one-third of Presbyterians, and three-fifths of Congregationalists in middling wealth groups to become church members. In this period, even ministers and lay leaders among the relatively wealthy Congregationalists still held views on leisure activities that were at odds with the popular culture of all social groups.[128]

However, demographic differences between wealth groups and between church members and never-member adherents clarify these patterns further. Poorer adherents included a higher proportion of the young, who were less likely to join churches, evident in the age distributions of the current member and never-member groups. As table 3 shows, the median ages of higher wealth groups were higher than those of lower wealth groups, and the median ages of current church members were higher than those of never-member adherents.

Table 3.3
Median Ages in 1861 of Evangelical adherents age 14 or over enumerated
in villages, St Stephen and linked to parish assessments 1860–62 by self or family

Total assessed wealth	Wesleyan Methodist Members 1860–62	Methodist Adherents, Never Members 1840/49–81
0-£99/$399	age 34 (52nd percentile)	age 26
£100-299/$400-1199	age 35	ages 26–27
£300-1499/$1200-5999	age 42	ages 29–30
£1500-22,500/$6,000-90,000	(N=2)	age 20 (N=18)

	Presbyterian Members 1854–62	Presbyterian Adherents, Never Members 1854–64, 1867–82
0-£99/$399	age 36	age 27
£100-299/$400-1199	age 37 (53rd percentile)	age 30
£300-1499/$1200-5999	age 45 (55th percentile)	age 26 (49th percentile)
£1500-22,500/$6,000-90,000	(N=2)	age 49

Linking church membership records to assessments in other years enabled the inclusion of individuals not enumerated in St Stephen in 1861, and comparison of Wesleyan Methodist, Presbyterian, and Congregationalist members. As table 4 shows, Wesleyan Methodism predominated in the more socially homogenous back settlements of the parish of St Stephen. There, the wealth-holding of Wesleyan Methodist church members reflected that of adherents generally, most of whom were Methodists. Many of these farms were very modest: in the 1861 agricultural schedule, farms valued at £100 or $400 contained fifteen or fewer improved acres, roughly 60-70 acres unimproved, and a few livestock. Because this analysis includes the more transient, the poor are more visible in table 4, with 30 percent of Wesleyan Methodist members in villages between 1854 and 1866 linked to assessments of less than £100.

Half of Presbyterian members in villages in St Stephen between 1854 and 1866 linked to parish assessments were in the lowest wealth groups, compared with only 9 percent of the Congregationalists linked to parish assessments, as shown in table 5. Congregationalists linked to parish assessments – almost all associated with the church of Milltown, New Brunswick – were also more elite than Congregationalists enumerated in Calais in 1860 or 1850. At the other end of the scale, whereas parish assessments did not record any wealth below £10 or $40, the Calais census listed smaller amounts that appear in this table within the second wealth group for a number of Congregationalists.

Table 3.4
Church members linked to contemporary assessments for the parish of St Stephen assessments

Wesleyan Methodist Members 1840/49–53		
Total assessed wealth	Back Settlements	Villages
0	10%	15%
£10-99/$40-399	6%	4%
£100-299/$400-1199	64%	30%
£300-1499/$1200-5999	20%	42%
£1500-22,500/$6,000-90,000		8%
	N=91	N=157
Wesleyan Methodist Members 1854–1866		
0	6%	17%
£10-99/$40-399	9%	13%
£100-299/$400-1199	52%	35%
£300-1499/$1200-5999	33%	30%
£1500-22,500/$6,000-90,000		5%
TOTAL	N=116	N=212

Presbyterian church members 1854–66		
Total assessed wealth	Back Settlements and the Ledge (a farming/shipbuilding community)	Villages
0		29%
£10-99/$40-399		11%
£100-299/$400-1199	69%	33%
£300-1499/$1200-5999	31%	23%
£1500-22,500/$6,000-90,000		3%
	N=13	N=90

The contrast between the Congregationalists in the New Brunswick mill villages with the Wesleyan Methodists in these villages is even starker for the years after the conflict and before the economic upswing in the 1850s. The Milltown Congregationalist church had been founded by thirty church members, half of whom were former Wesleyan Methodists from the 1844 schism. Differences in the salaries and chapel finance of the Wesleyan Methodists and Congregationalists in Milltown, New Brunswick, were paralleled in the social composition of their memberships: Wesleyan Methodist members in the mill villages within the Milltown Circuit were not only generally poorer than Congregationalists but also generally poorer than the Wesleyan Methodist members elsewhere in the parish.

Table 3.5
Congregationalist church members 1854–66 in St Stephen and Calais

	St Stephen Parish Assessments		Calais Census returns	
	Back Settlements	Villages	Personal and Real Estate in 1860	Real Estate in 1850
0	33%	1%	4%	30%
£10-99/$40-399		8%	15%	5%
£100-299/$400-1199	50%	27%	20%	26%
£300-1499/$1200-5999	17%	38%	44%	30%
£1500-22,500/ $6,000-90,000		26%	17%	9%
N	6	117	195	43

Table 3.6
Methodist and Congregationalist church members in the mill villages

	Members of Methodist class meetings in Union Mills, Milltown, and Upper Mills, New Brunswick, 1849–1853		Milltown Congregationalist church members 1846–53 (transferring Congregationalists, former Methodists, and new members)	
	Assessed Wealth in the parish of St Stephen	Real Estate enumerated in Calais, 1850	Assessed Wealth in the parish of St Stephen	Real Estate enumerated in Calais, 1850
	N=77		N=63	N=22
0	22%	(N=1)	10%	41%
£10-99/$40-399			8%	9%
£100-299/$400-1199	34%		17%	32%
£300-1499/ $1200-5999	36%		27%	18%
£1500-22,500/ $6,000-90,000	8%		38%	

Wesleyan Methodist ministers attributed the financial difficulties of the Milltown circuit not only to the loss of wealthy members in the schism and the cost of rebuilding the chapel after its arson but also to the social composition of the congregation itself: "The support of our church in this place is derived from a very small number whose means are extremely limited."[129] As table 6 shows, Wesleyan Methodists were not without church members from wealthy families, nor did the Milltown Congregationalists exclude the propertyless. But, overall, in the mill villages most Wesleyan Methodist church members came from the lower wealth groups, and most Congregationalist members came from the two highest.

Thus, the Milltown Methodist schism in 1844 initiated the process of congregational economic segregation in local evangelicalism. In large cities in the northeast, residential segregation by wealth had led to increasing social differentiation between churches within the same denominational tradition.[130] On a smaller scale, congregational economic segregation could also occur when communities grew large enough to sustain multiple churches. In Milltown, New Brunswick, a wealthy Congregationalist church emerged out of a socially diverse Methodist church. The financial practices of the two churches, along with the original schism and of course the economic context itself, were the mechanisms of socioeconomic differentiation between them. And for at least one Methodist minister, churchgoers themselves had inscribed the community's social distinctions: writing in 1874, he claimed that newcomers attended the Congregationalist church for nonreligious reasons – the Milltown Congregationalists had "social position, wealth and show" – and he stated that "If you attend the Methodist Church you must not expect to move in our circle."[131]

Evangelical church finance in these communities illustrates a number of economic changes associated with modernization. Church accounts show the gradual transition from a credit to a cash economy, though the persistence of donation parties suggests that church finance could also be understood as reflecting some dimensions of a gift economy. The new incorporation legislation for Presbyterian and other churches in these years, specifying that trustees' powers were now more limited but that their responsibilities were now also less risky, reflected the development of limited liability as both a legal and as a more widely understood cultural concept. The history of church finance also relates to ongoing debates over the definition, timing, and extent of a "market economy" in the northeast and over the possible influences of economic changes on patterns of individual behaviour or private or public discourse.[132] The history of pew-holding suggests tangible, but varied, patterns and speculative interpretations. The shift from customary pew-holding systems to market-driven systems was sometimes resisted by clergy or lay leaders, but at other times accepted. To complicate this picture further, in some circumstances, local market forces through the supply and demand of pews ironically undercut the cultural influence of the market economy on pew-holding systems.

For both past commentators and historians, the new forms of consumption most associated with urban churches – larger, more expensive buildings and more comfortable or decorated interiors – were the most prominent and novel markers of change in nineteenth-century evangelicalism. Yet the persistence in smaller communities such as St Stephen and Calais of relatively low salaries for some evangelical clergy when compared with those of their ministerial colleagues, of debts owed to ministers or on chapels, and of reliance on external subsidies caution us against overstating the wealth of evangelical churches as institutions in this period when compared with earlier decades. Although, with regard to Methodism, some have suggested that the financial problems in the Maritime colonies were exceptional and the result of "poor management,"[133] similar problems occurred elsewhere and not only among Methodists.[134] Historians must also remember that new church-building may at times be more a reflection of access to credit than of actual institutional wealth in hand.[135] Church buildings were paid for not just by their congregations but by their larger communities through extracongregational fundraising of various kinds. The financing of church buildings may ultimately have been less problematic than the financing of salaries and denominational structures; for local laity, "Buildings were tangible assets; preachers and missionaries were speculative investments."[136]

Although among Methodists the financial troubles of the circuits in St Stephen increased the cultural pressure on local Methodists to contribute to their churches, the flexible interpretation of both pew-holding agreements and John Wesley's model for church finance may have countered this pressure. Similarly, although perhaps more male Presbyterians might have participated in electing their trustees had the legislation for incorporation passed in the version that had not specified a set contribution, a surprising number of Presbyterian men without any locally assessed property did manage to qualify. Nevertheless, the debate over eligibility defined by church membership or by financial contributions reflected tensions that also occurred elsewhere in this period between the ideal of the church as solely a spiritual community and the modern organizational church.[137]

This paper's findings point to the importance of recognizing a continuum between social diversity and various kinds of social homogeneity. As represented by assessed or enumerated wealth, Wesleyan Methodist church members in the villages were the most socially diverse. Wesleyan Methodists in the back settlements and Presbyterians in the villages were more concentrated among lower wealth groups. Both denominations, and even more so the Congregationalists, did include very wealthy individuals or families among their members or pew-holders. The significant financial support given by wealthy layman and laywomen may have eased the pressure on poorer members, even as it rendered churches more dependent on and perhaps also controlled by elites.[138] The inclusion of the poorest in an institution that wished to support a minister and his family and heat a chapel through winter required also the inclusion of the wealthiest. These churches relied on both the "pence of the poor" and the "pounds of the rich."

NOTE ON SOURCES

The quantitative analysis in this paper is based on machine readable versions of the complete manuscript census returns for St Stephen, New Brunswick, 1851–71, selected St Stephen parish assessments 1841–62, and the following church records, all on microfilm at the Provincial Archives of New Brunswick: pew, baptismal, marriage, membership, and Quarterly Official Board records for the St Stephen and Milltown Wesleyan Methodist circuits; records of the Congregational Church, Milltown, New Brunswick, and of the Presbyterian Church, St Stephen. Some Methodist deeds and early pew records are located in the Ganong Collection at the New Brunswick Museum. A copy of the membership records of the Congregational Church, Calais, Maine, is at the Maine State Historical Society, Portland; see also *Historical Sketch of the First Congregational Church, Calais, Maine, with Confession of Faith, Covenant, Rules and Catalogue of Members to May, 1877* (Boston: Thomas Todd, 1877).

Further demographic or wealth information was obtained by consulting assessments in other years, the 1881 St Stephen census, St Stephen Rural Cemetery Records, the marriage register kept by George Stillman Hill, Charlotte County marriage records 1835–44, Charlotte County probate records 1835–61, and newspapers. I am also indebted to Gail Campbell for access to her data for other Charlotte County parishes 1851–71 and Charlotte County Marriage records 1845–71. Marriage records kept by the town of Calais and the Calais and Baring census returns 1850–60 are on microfilm at the Maine State Archives. Directories and family histories were also used and are listed in "Methodist Church Members, Lay Leaders and Socio-Economic Position."

NOTES

1 *Calais Advertiser* (henceforth CA), 19 December 1849, 2 January 1850.
2 CA, 7 June 1848; 23 September 1852, 17 December and 2 July 1857.
3 Neil Semple, *The Lord's Dominion: The History of Canadian Methodism* (Montreal and Kingston: McGill-Queen's University Press, 1996): 209–10; Jane Garnett, "'Gold and the Gospel': Systematic Beneficence in Mid-Nneteenth-Century England," in *The Church and Wealth*, eds W.J. Sheils and Diana Wood, *Studies in Church History*, 24 (Oxford and New York, B. Blackwell, 1987): 347–58.
4 Callum G. Brown, "The Costs of Pew-Renting: Church management, Church-Going and Social Class in Nineteenth-Century Glasgow," *Journal of Ecclesiastical*

History, 38 (1987): 347–61; Lynne Marks, *Revivals and Roller Rinks: Religion, Leisure, and Identity in Late-Nineteenth-Century Small-Town Ontario* (Toronto: University of Toronto Press, 1996): 59–64; Marguerite Van Die, "'The Marks of a Genuine Revival': Religion, Social Change, Gender, and Community in Mid-Victorian Brantford, Ontario," *Canadian Historical Review* 79 (1998): 543; Mark S. Schantz, *Piety in Providence: Class Dimensions of Religious Experience in Antebellum Rhode Island* (Ithaca: Cornell University Press, 2002): chapters 1 and 4.

5 These two terms were often used inconsistently or interchangeably, rent sometimes referring to an amount towards the original sale price.

6 Rev. L.B. Gibson, *History of St Stephen Presbyterian Church* (St Stephen, 1909); Clara Rideout, *Notes on the History of the First Congregational Church Calais, Maine* (Calais Advertiser Press, 1925); Winfield Milligan, *A History of the First Methodist Episcopal Church of Calais, Maine* (Calais, 1935); Ellen Gregg, *Kirk-McColl 1785 to 1980* (St Stephen: Print'N Press, 1981).

7 Goldwin French, *Parsons and Politics: The role of the Wesleyan Methodists in Upper Canada and the Maritimes from 1780 to 1855* (Toronto: The Ryerson Press, 1962): 87–8; Semple, 103–4; Mervin M. Deems, *Maine-First of Conferences: A History of the Maine Conference-United Church of Christ* (Bangor: Furbush-Roberts Printing, 1974): 37–9.

8 Journal of Henry Daniel, 1841–47 (New Brunswick Museum).

9 In addition to French and Semple, see G.A. Rawlyk, Introduction, *Aspects of the Canadian Evangelical Experience*, ed. G.A. Rawlyk (Montreal and Kingston: McGill-Queen's University Press, 1997); and John H. Wigger, *Taking Heaven by Storm: Methodism and the Rise of Popular Christianity in America* (New York: Oxford University Press, 1998).

10 See Hugh McLeod, ed., *European Religion in the Age of Great Cities* (New York: Holmes & Meier, 1996); David Lyon, "Introduction," in Lyon and Marguerite Van Die, eds *Rethinking Church, State, and Modernity: Canada between Europe and America* (Toronto: University of Toronto Press, 2000): 3–19; Nancy Christie and Michael Gauvreau, "Modalities of Social Authority: Suggesting an Interface for Religious and Social History," *Histoire Sociale/Social History,* XXXVI, 71 (May 2003): 1–30; Gustavo Benavides, "Modernity," in *Critical Terms for Religious Studies,* ed. Mark C. Taylor (Chicago and London: The University of Chicago Press, 1998): 189–97; Robert Wuthnow and Tracy L. Scott, "Protestants and Economic Behavior," in *New Directions in American Religious History,* eds, Harry S. Stout and D.G. Hart (New York and Oxford: Oxford University Press, 1997).

11 John D. Thomas, "'The Christian Law of Living': The Institutionalization of Christian Stewardship in The Methodist Church (Canada, Newfoundland, Bermuda) 1883–1925," in *Papers: Canadian Methodist Historical Society,* 1991–92, 109–28.

12 This paper is based partly on chapters 7 and 8 of "Methodist Church Members, Lay Leaders and Socio-economic Position in Mid-Nineteenth Century St Stephen, New Brunswick" (PhD thesis, University of New Brunswick, 2004) and "'The Pence of the Poor and the Pounds of the Rich': Methodist Church Finance and Wealth-Holding in Mid-Nineteenth-Century St Stephen, New Brunswick," *Papers: 1997 and 1998* (Toronto: Canadian Methodist Historical Society, 1999): 90–116.

13 Mark A. Noll, Introd. to *God and Mammon: Protestants, Money, and the Market, 1790–1860*, ed. Noll (New York: Oxford University Press, 2001): 10.

14 Confusingly, St Stephen census returns did not always specify that an enumerated Methodist was a nominal adherent of Wesleyan Methodism on the New Brunswick side or of Episcopal Methodism on the Maine side. Moreover, some Methodist adherents on the New Brunswick side may have been members in Episcopal Methodist churches located on the Maine side of the river, but the latter's records have not survived. Judging by the relatively few Maine residents found in Wesleyan Methodist records, the number who crossed the river, at some points paying a toll, when there was a church in the same tradition within their own community were relatively few.

15 I.C. Knowlton, *Annals of Calais, Maine, and St Stephen, New Brunswick* (1875; rpt St Stephen): 10–14; T.W. Acheson, "A Study in the Historical Demography of a Loyalist County," *Histoire Sociale/Social History*, (April 1968): 53–6; and "New Boston to New Brunswick: Anonymous Loyalists in New Hampshire," *Acadiensis*, XXVII, 1 (Autumn 1997): 3–26.

16 In addition to Knowlton, Rideout, and Gibson, see T.W. Acheson, "Duncan M'Coll," *Dictionary of Canadian Biography*, VI (Toronto: University of Toronto Press, 1987): 429–32.

17 *Census of the Province of New Brunswick* (Saint John: George W. Day, 1861).

18 "Adherent" or "adherence" follow nineteenth-century usage and refer to what was recorded on census returns; see Hannah M. Lane, "Tribalism, Proselytism, and Pluralism: Protestants, Family, and Denominational Identity in Mid-Nineteenth-Century St Stephen, New Brunswick," in Nancy Christie ed. *Households of Faith: Family, Gender, and Community in Canada 1760–1969* (Montreal and Kingston: McGill-Queen's University Press, 2002): 103–37.

19 See "Social Statistics," Censuses of Calais and Baring, 1850 and 1860; and Paul Goodman, "A Guide to American Church Membership Data Before the Civil War," *Historical Methods Newsletter*, 10 (1977): 183.

20 Both words were gradually superseded by "church" in later decades; see Jane C. Nylander, "Toward Comfort and Uniformity in New England Meeting Houses, 1750–1850," in Peter Benes ed., *New England Meeting House and Church: 1630–1850* (Annual proceedings: Dublin Seminar for New England; Boston: Boston University, 1979): 86.

21 In addition to "Methodist Church Members," chapter 2, see Harold A. Davis, *An International Community on the St Croix (1604–1930)* (1950; rpt Orono: University of Maine, 1974), and T.W. Acheson, "Denominationalism in a Loyalist County: A Social History of Charlotte County, NB" (MA thesis, University of New Brunswick, 1964).

22 Calvin Clark, *History of the Congregational Churches in Maine: Volume One* (Portland: The Southworth Press, 1926): 201–2, 249; Rideout, 9; French, 201; William Howard Brooks, "The Changing Character of Maritime Wesleyan Methodism 1855–1883" (MA thesis: Mount Allison University, 1965): 51; *The Provincial Wesleyan* (henceforth TPW): 31 May 1851; Minutes, New Brunswick District of Wesleyan Methodist Missionaries (henceforth NBDM), 1826–28.

23 Except for a brief gap in the 1830s and another in the 1860s, accounts for the Wesleyan Methodist St Stephen Circuit are complete from 1831 on; separated from the former circuit in 1838, Milltown Circuit Accounts are missing before 1855. The list of contributions is found with Milltown Membership Records, 1862.

24 See NBDM, 1842, 1844, 1846; Enoch Wood to Wesleyan Missionary Society Committee (henceforth WMSC), 16 February 1844; Richard Knight to WMSC, 30 January 1847, and 9 May 1848; TPW, 6 July 1850; see also J.I. Little, *Borderland Religion: The Emergence of an English-Canadian Identity, 1792–1852* (Toronto: University of Toronto Press, 2004): 172.

25 Spiritual report, St Stephen Circuit, 1842; NBDM, 1841.

26 By the official formula, the two ministers in Milltown, Maine, and the village of Calais the late 1840s should have received respectively $240 and $390, but the latter minister received only $288.59; see Knowlton, 40; Rev. Stephen Allen and Rev. W.H. Pilsbury, *History of Methodism in Maine, 1793–1886* (Augusta: Charles E Nash, 1887): 62, 122, 133, 137, 267–8; and David Hempton, "A Tale of Preachers and Beggars: Methodism and Money in the Great Age of Transatlantic Expansion, 1780–1830," 134.

27 Clifford G. Chase, *A History of Baring*, (1925, reprinted 1950): 14–15; see also Milltown membership records, and TPW, 15 May 1856.

28 F.E. Archibald, "Contribution of the Scottish Church to New Brunswick Presbyterianism from its Earliest Beginnings until the Time of the Disruption, and Afterwards, 1784–1852" (PhD thesis, University of Edinburgh, 1932): 80, 119–20.

29 *Standard* (St Andrew's, New Brunswick), 3 September 1845, 1 October 1845, 17 December 1845.

30 *Minutes of the Synod of the Presbyterian Church of New Brunswick* (Saint John, 1861–62); Gibson, 19.

31 Clark, 185, 244; *Christian Mirror* (Congregationalist, henceforth CM), 4 February 1841.

32 CM, 5 September 1839; Clark, 186–7; Rideout, 10; see also Donald M. Scott, *From Office to Profession: The New England Ministry 1750–1850* (Philadelphia:

University of Pennsylvania Press, 1978): 113,120; Michael D. Carter, *Converting the Wasteplaces of Zion: The Maine Missionary Society 1807–1862* (Wolfeboro: Longwood Academic, 1990): 71–2; Little, 70–1, 79.

33 Records of the First Orthodox Church of Milltown, New Brunswick (henceforth Milltown Congregationalist records), 1847.

34 CM, 4 February 1841; Clark, 146–7; Gibson, 44; Knowlton, 81; E.H. Balkam, "The Congregational Church: The History of the Milltown Society," *St Croix Courier* (St Stephen), 7 January 1897.

35 St Stephen Circuit Accounts; Journal of the New Brunswick District Meeting, 1843–44; for similar conflicts elsewhere, see Little, 168.

36 R.D. Gidney and W.P.J. Millar, *Professional Gentlemen: The Professions in Nineteenth-Century Ontario* (Toronto: University of Toronto Press, 1994): 116–19.

37 For Wesleyan Methodists in St Stephen, see circuit totals reported in NBDM and after 1855 the Saint John District Meeting Minutes; for Congregationalists, see Rideout, and S.H. Keeler, *A Semi-centennial Discourse, delivered at Calais, Me., June 3, 1879* (Calais: J.A. Sears, 1879), and contributions from the Calais or Milltown, New Brunswick churches published intermittently in CM. For Presbyterians, see the Minutes of the Synod of New Brunswick, cited above.

38 As studies have noted, obituaries did not routinely cite their subject's charitable activities, suggesting that some were more charitable than others, and in St Stephen such obituaries sometimes concerned individuals of very modest means; see Lynne Marks, "Indigent Committees and Ladies Benevolent Societies: Intersections of Public and Private Poor Relief in Late-Nineteenth-Century Small-Town Ontario," *Studies in Political Economy*, 47 (Summer 1995): 65; TPW, 19 July 1855; one writer on church finance argued that ministers were also expected to assist "his poor members"; see TPW, 2 March 1870.

39 Rev. Robert Cooney, *Autobiography of a Wesleyan Methodist Missionary* (Montreal: E. Pickup, 1856): 199; Milltown Circuit, Quarterly Board Minutes,1878; see also TPW, 7 November 1879.

40 *Historical Sketch of the First Congregational Church, Calais, Maine, with Confession of Faith, Covenant, Rules and Catalogue of Members to May, 1877* (Boston: Thomas Todd, 1877): 14.

41 Gareth Lloyd, "Eighteenth-Century Methodism and the London Poor," in *The Poor and the People Called Methodists 1729–1999* (Nashville: Kingswood Books/Abingdon Press, 2002): 130; Marks, "Indigent Committees," 75–6.

42 *British North American Wesleyan Methodist Magazine* (henceforth BNAWMM). May 1846; T. Watson Smith, II, *History of Methodism in Eastern British North America* (Halifax: Methodist Book Room, 1877): 342; *Christian Visitor* (Saint John), 7 July 1864.

43 In addition to St Stephen and Milltown Circuit Accounts, see Rideout, 9, and Keeler, 14–16.

44 See "Methodist Church Members," chapter 7.

45 CA, 29 October 1846; see also CM, 25 February 1841, CA, 28 April and 17 November 1859; *Standard*, 22 October 1841, 18 March 1857; *Frontier Journal* (Calais, henceforth FJ), 8 December 1846; TPW, 7 Oct 1868; among local Wesleyan Methodists, a donation party does not appear as a separate listing in St Stephen Circuit Accounts until the 1860s.

46 Clark, 246–54; Carter, 36; Marguerite Van Die, "Revisiting 'Separate Spheres': Women, Religion, and the Family in Mid-Victorian Brantford, Ontario," in Christie ed., *Households of Faith*, 249–50; Marks, 65–8.

47 *Standard*, 27 August 1845; CA, 13 and 27 August 1845.

48 *Standard* (St Andrews, New Brunswick), 11 and 28 January 1852. The writer may have known the men personally: despite the disparaging allusions to their occupations, the sting of the rebuke was softened in the conclusion addressing them by name: "O Jemmy! O Sammy! Where was your gallantry – where your manhood on that occasion."

49 Keeler,19; Rideout, 20; Milligan,15; CM, 16 December 1840, 14 January 1841, 9 February 1851; TPW, 15 May 1856.

50 In addition to circuit accounts, see BNAWMM, February 1846 and TPW, 21 February 1852, 30 November 1854.

51 TPW, 23 October 1856; for similar debates later in the century, see Marks, 77–9.

52 David Sutherland, "Race Relations in Halifax, Nova Scotia, During the Mid-Victorian Quest for Reform," *Journal of the Canadian Historical Association/Revue de la societé historique du Canada* (1996): 43.

53 CA, 2 July 1857.

54 Marguerite Van Die, "'A March of Victory and Triumph in Praise of "The Beauty of Holiness"': Laity and the Evangelical Impulse in Canadian Methodism, 1800–1884" in G.A. Rawlyk ed., *Aspects of the Canadian Evangelical Experience*, 87; Marks, 72.

55 TPW, 3 February 1853; Methodists elsewhere also solicited donations from throughout the region for their sales; see TPW, 30 October 1856.

56 *Standard*, 27 August 1845; CA, 13 and 27 August 1845.

57 And sometimes also Presbyterian church members, see Nancy Christie, "Carnal Connection and Other Misdemeanors."

58 Henry S. Burrage, *History of the Baptists in Maine* (Portland: Marks Printing House, 1904): 193; Little, 967, 101.

59 CM, 29 April 1841; CM, 9 February 1851; Knowlton, 64.

60 Acheson, "Denominationalism,"139.

61 In addition to Balkam, see Rideout, 10–11.

62 TPW, 31 May 1851; 16 April 1857, 28 May 1857.

63 See "Methodist Church Members," chapter 7; Michael R. Watts, *The Dissenters: Vol. II The Expansion of Evangelical Nonconformity* (Oxford: Clarendon Press, 1995): 236–7; and David Hempton, "A Tale of Preachers and Beggars: Methodism and Money in the Great Age of Transatlantic Expansion, 1780–1830," in Noll. 126–8.

64 French, 65–6; NBDM, 1840, 1841, 1845, 1846, 1848; Allen and Pilsbury, 24; TPW, 13 July 1850, 31 May 1851, 13 October 1853, 11 and 29 December 1853.

65 In addition to circuit accounts, see McColl's journal published in BNAWMM, 1840–42; Spiritual Report, St Stephen Circuit, 1831; Milltown Membership Records, 1859 and 1878.

66 Noll, 9–10; Michael S. Franch, "The Congregational Community in the Changing City, 1840–70," *Maryland Historical Magazine* 71 (1976): 370.

67 Watts, 169–71, 299; James Mudge, *History of the New England Conference of the Methodist Episcopal Church 1796–1910* (published by the Conference, Boston 1910); 413; Dale Gilbert Jarvis, "Gender Segregation and Sacred Architecture: A Study of George Street Methodist Church, Peterborough, Ontario," *Canadian Folklore Canadien* 17 (2) 1995, 111–24.

68 Allen and Pilsbury, 89, 92, 241–2; Mudge, 82–3, 92.

69 Knowlton, 60; CA 5 March 1851. Similarly, two lists of pew-holders for the Episcopal Methodist chapel in Milltown, Maine included lay leaders from the Wesleyan Methodists; see CA, 6 May 1847; FJ, 9 October 1850.

70 Minutes, Synod of New Brunswick, 1861–64 cited above. For similarly varying methods of church finance and ministerial salaries in Free Presbyterian churches in Canada East and West in this period, see Richard W. Vaudry, *The Free Church in Victorian Canada 1844–1861* (Waterloo: Wilfred Laurier Press, 1989): 100–1.

71 Nylander, 97; CA, 30 April 1845, 26 January 1842; T. Watson Smith, II, 337; Rideout, 11.

72 Knowlton, 80.

73 Knowlton, 80; CA, 11 September 1850; FJ, 4 September 1850; 10 October 1850.

74 See for example the wills and probate records for three Wesleyan Methodist lay leaders, John Brown, Abner Hill, and Stephen Hill in Charlotte County Probate Records.

75 For the details and documentation of both the Baptist and Wesleyan Methodist schisms, see "Methodist Church Members," chapter 6.

76 TPW, 19 May 1853; see also J.I. Little, "The Methodistical Way: Revivalism and Popular Resistance to the Wesleyan Church Discipline in the Stanstead Circuit, Lower Canada, 1821–1852," in *Studies in Religion/Sciences Religieuses*, 31, 2 (2002): 177–9; and *Borderland Religion*, 174–5.

77 See for example, the early pew plans for Christ Church, Fredericton (MC223, PANB) and the initially wholly customary pew systems discussed in Ollivier Hubert, "Ritual Performance and Parish Sociability: French-Canadian Catholic Families at Mass from the Seventeenth to the Nineteenth Century," in Christie ed. *Households of Faith*, 39–43.

78 Brown, 347–55; Ann C. Rose, "Social Sources of Denominationalism Reconsidered: Post-Revolutionary Boston as a Case Study," *American Quarterly* 38 (Summer 1986): 253–4.

79 BNAWMM, January 1842, 11.

80 Brown, 61; see also Watts, 232.

81 Barbara C. Murison, "The Kirk versus the Free Church: The Struggle for the Soul of the Maritimes at the Time of the Disruption," in Charles H.H. Scobie and G.A. Rawlyk eds, *The Contribution of Presbyterianism to the Maritime Provinces of Canada* (Montreal and Kingston: McGill-Queen's University Press, 1997): 22.

82 Cited in Craig Walsh, *A Look at St Andrews Methodism to 1925* (Wesley United Church, St Andrew's, NB, 1996): 12.

83 NBDM, 1827; see also TPW, 2 September 1857.

84 Semple, 104; by the end of the 1840s, the oldest Saint John church had repaid off all its debt; in addition to Cooney, see Geo. A. Henderson, *Early Saint John Methodism and History of Centenary Methodist Church*, (Saint John, NB: G.E. Day, 1890): 45–51.

85 Pew Records for the Old Ridge chapel are part of the records of the St Stephen Circuit at PANB; see also *Standard*, 20 August 1851.

86 Milligan, 9; CA, 25 February 1847; Cooney, 163.

87 In addition to Balkam, see CA, 18 January 1849.

88 BNAWMM, February 1846, 357; Pew Records for the Milltown chapel are part of the records of the Milltown circuit at PANB.

89 It is not clear whether Albee and Hill expected to collect from these individuals or whether they were donating pews on behalf of their extended families.

90 Undated pew lists for the St Stephen circuit from roughly the 1820s or early 1830s are in the Ganong collection at the New Brunswick Museum.

91 Cited in Margaret I. Campbell, *No Other Foundation: The History of Brunswick Street United Church* (Hantsport, NS: Lancelot Press, 1984): 218.

92 Aubrey M. Tizzard, *Methodism, A Flame: Dorchester, New Brunswick* (Newtonville, ON: R. & A. Tizzard, 1978): 17–19.

93 CA, 22 July 1852; TPW, 15 May 1856.

94 Reproduced in Anita Jones, *The Story of Wilmot United Church 1791–2002* (Fredericton, New Brunswick: Wilmot United Church, 2002): 40.

95 TPW, 12 February 1857; Henderson, 45–51; a copy of the Regulations for the sale and occupancy of pews, in the Guildford-Street Wesleyan Chapel, Carleton, is located in CIHM (one page undated, but preceding decimal coinage).

96 D.F. Hoddinott, *From Whence We Came* (Newcastle, NB: Walco Print & Litho, 1979): 43.

97 Tizzard, 12–15; Shirley A. Dobson, *The Word and the Music: The Story of Moncton's Central United Church and Its Methodist Roots* (Moncton and Sackville: Central United Church and the Tribune Press, 1994): 76.

98 S.J.D. Green, *Religion in the Age of Decline: Organisation and Experience in Industrial Yorkshire, 1870–1920* (Cambridge: Cambridge University Press, 1996): 148–51; Mark Smith, *Religion in Industrial Society: Oldham and Saddleworth, 1740–1865* (Oxford: Oxford University Press, 1994): 70–3, 159; see also Watts, 230–2.

99 In addition to Allen and Pilsbury, see Carwardine in Noll 78–9, and Richard L. Bushman, *The Refinement of America: Persons, Houses, Cities* (New York: Vintage Books, 1992): 337–52.

100 T.W. Acheson, "Methodism and the Problem of Methodist Identity in Nineteenth-Century New Brunswick," in Charles H.H. Scobie and John Webster Grant eds, *The Contribution of Methodism to Atlantic Canada* (Montreal and Kingston: McGill-Queen's University Press, 1992): 118; Gregg Finley and Lynn Wigginton, *On Earth as it is in Heaven: Gothic Revival Churches of Victorian New Brunswick* (Fredericton: Goose Lane Editions, 1985): 87.

101 CA, 18 January 1849, 3 December 1851; CM, 9 February 1851; *Standard*, 5 September 1860.

102 Nylander, 88 and 93; Clark, 349–50.

103 BNAWMM, February 1846, 356; TPW, 21 February 1852, 3 February 1853, 26 January 1854, 16 August 1855; Marks, 68–9.

104 FJ, 20 November 1850.

105 FJ, 5 June 1851; 19 June 1851. The local and wider cultural context to these texts is discussed in "Methodist Church Members."

106 Henderson, 72; TPW, 6 October 1872; see similar claims among English Wesleyans cited in Watts, 70.

107 TPW, 16 July 1852; 16 October 1875; CM, 16 August 1870.

108 Mark Smith, 72–3.

109 G.E. Fenety, *Political Notes and Observations* (Fredericton, NB: S.R. Miller, 1867): 154–62; for this reason, pew renters also resisted shifts from pew owning to pew renting; see Little, *Borderland Religion*, 185.

110 New Brunswick, *Synoptic Reports of the Legislative Assembly*, 1855, 1857; *Journal of the Legislative Assembly*, 1858, 1859.

111 Vaudry, 23–4; Murison, 26–31.

112 New Brunswick, *Synoptic Reports of the Legislative Assembly*, 1855.

113 New Brunswick, *Synoptic Reports of the Legislative Assembly*, 1857.

114 The quotes are from the Synoptic Reports cited above; the final legislation is in Acts of the Province of New Brunswick, 1859, 22 Cap. VI.

115 See "1850 Census: Instructions to Marshals and Assistant Marshals," "1860 Census: Instructions to the Marshals," Integrated Public Use Microdata Series (IPUMS), Minnesota Population Center, University of Minnesota (www.ipums.umn.edu/usa/index.html).

116 In addition to "Methodist Church Members," chapter 3, see Jack S. Blocker, "Bias in Wealth and Income Records: an Ohio Case Study," *Historical Methods* 1996 29 (1): 25–36.

117 Co-resident families were identified from census returns; other families were reconstituted from baptismal and marriage records; this and the following paragraphs are discussed and documented more fully in "Methodist Church Members," chapters 3 and 8.

118 The most recent review of studies on ethnicity, religion, and wealth in nineteenth-century Canada is Peter Baskerville, "Did Religion Matter? Religion and Wealth in Urban Canada at the Turn of the Twentieth Century: an Exploratory Study," *Historie sociale/Social History* XXXIV (May 2001): 61–96; see also Little, 21–4.

119 In addition to Acheson and other works cited in "Methodist Church Members," see Stephen A. Marini, "Religious Revolution in the District of Maine 1780–1820," in Charles E Clark, James S. Leamon, and Karen Bowden eds, *Maine in the Early Republic: From Revolution to Statehood* (Hanover and London: University Press of New England, 1988): 143.

120 For similar patterns, see Peter Hillis, "Church and Society in Aberdeen and Glasgow, c. 1800–c. 2000," *Journal of Ecclesiastical History* 53 (2002): 722–3.

121 See Stuart M. Blumin, "Church and Community: A Case Study of Lay Leadership in Nineteenth-Century America," *New York History* 56 (1975): 393–408; R.W. Ambler, "The social composition of church leadership: nonconformist trustees in Lincolnshire, 1800–1870," *Bulletin of the John Rylands University Library of Manchester* 75, 1 (1993): 133–56.

122 Keeler, 17–18.

123 In addition to "Methodist Church Members" and "Tribalism, Proselytism, and Pluralism," see also General Conference of the Congregational churches of Maine, *A Manual of Congregationalism* (Portland: Hyde and Lord, 1848, reprinted in 1859) and annual reports from the Washington County Conference published in the *Christian Mirror*.

124 See "Methodist Church Members," 165.

125 Records for class meetings on the St Stephen Circuit date from 1840 and for the Milltown circuit from 1849; one class meeting within the parish of St Stephen became part of the neighbouring parish's circuit for which no records survive from this period.

126 Moreover, some members were not adherents of the same denomination as their church, some members in the 1870s were under the age of fifteen in 1861, and others could not be linked to parish assessments between 1860 and 1862;

see "Tribalism, Proselytism, and Pluralism" and "Methodist Church Members," chapters 4 and 5.

127 See "Tribalism, Proselytism, and Pluralism."

128 In addition to "Methodist Church Members," see Carter, 17.

129 Spiritual Reports, Milltown Circuit, 1850.

130 Michael S. Franch, "The Congregational Community in the Changing City, 1840–70," *Maryland Historical Magazine* 71 (1976): 370–9; Jane Greenlaw, "Choix Pratiques et choix des pratiques: le non-conformisme protestant à Montréal (1825–1842)," *Revue d'histoire de l'Amérique française* 46, 1 (1992): 98–9, 106.

131 TPW, 20 April 1874.

132 See *The Market Revolution in America: Social, Political, and Religious Expression, 1800–1880*, eds Melvyn Stokes and Stephen Conway (Charlottesville and London: University Press of Virginia, 1996).

133 Semple, 103–4.

134 TPW, 21 August 1856; Mudge, 70–3.

135 See Watts, 227–8.

136 Hempton, "Methodism and Money," 138.

137 See John Webster Grant, *A Profusion of Spires: Religion in Nineteenth-Century Ontario* (Toronto: University of Toronto Press, 1988): 176–85; Curtis D. Johnson, *Islands of Holiness: Rural Religion in Upstate New York, 1790–1860* (Ithaca: Cornell University Press, 1989) chapters 12–13. In the 1850s, a majority of Free Church Presbyteries in Canada East and West rejected a proposal that only church members could be voters or managers in financial matters; however, another perspective within these debates was in favour of elders remaining apart from the financial affairs of the church for spiritual reasons; see Vaudry, 89–90.

138 For a similar argument, see Hempton, "Methodism and Money," 131–2.

4

Finishing Badly: Religion, Authority, and Clergy in Late-Victorian London, Ontario

KENNETH L. DRAPER

INTRODUCTION

This paper explores the contours of the religious authority of the Protestant clergy in the late nineteenth century. This exploration will proceed by way of three stories of failure. Historians have been criticized for privileging the winners in history, but it is not primarily to redress any perceived imbalance that these stories of failure are offered. What is of interest are the conflicts and fractures of power as three clergymen and the various parties arrayed against them marshal the past and the future, and lay expectations and clergy prerogatives, to negotiate the advances and retractions of their authority. In the process, something of the geography upon which religious authority was contested begins to take shape.

The relation of religious authority to the study of English-speaking Canada in the late nineteenth century has recently become a matter of some interest.[1] A venerable tradition of historiography has suggested that the social authority of religion in this period was inevitably in decline in the face of modernization and scientific advance.[2] Thus, discussions of religious authority were plotted as a series of defeats as secularization claimed cultural and social ascendancy. Over the last decade and a half this narrative of decline has been successfully revised in important studies by John Webster Grant, William Westfall, Michael Gauvreau, Marguerite Van Die, and Nancy Christie.[3] Out of this work clear evidence of the persistence of religious activity has emerged. Nineteenth-century English-speaking Protestantism, at least in Ontario, presents itself in this scholarship as culturally confident, numerically strong, architecturally ubiquitous, intellectually sophisticated, and socially engaged.

Table 4.1
The Religious Population of London, Ontario, 1871–1891

	1871		1881		1891	
	N	%	N	%	N	%
Baptist	713	4.5	885	4.5	1036	4.6
Church of England	5282	33.4	6502	32.9	6720	30.2
Congregational	377	2.4	489	2.5	354	1.6
Methodist	3941	24.9	4952	25.1	6367	28.6
Presbyterian	2678	16.9	3257	16.5	3605	16.2
Roman Catholic	2700	17.0	3284	16.6	3450	15.5
Other Christian	70	.5	259	1.3	410	1.8
Non Christian	63	.4	51	.25	145	.65
Not Given	2	–	67	.35	195	.85
TOTAL POPULATION	15826	100	1974	100	22282	100

Source: Canada Census, 1871, 1881, and 1891.

This characterization would fit London, Ontario, in the 1880s and 1890s. The general religious character of the London population in this period is illustrated in table 1. Although many Londoners did not attend church regularly, few did not regard themselves as adherents of one of the major denominations. The statistics for London closely resemble those compiled by John Webster Grant for Ontario as a whole, although London had a significantly higher proportion of Anglicans (33.4 percent in 1871, compared to 20.4 percent in Ontario in that same year). As a consequence of this local Anglican strength, the other denominations were relatively less strong in London than in the province as a whole. Beyond identification with Christian groups, Londoners contributed to fifty church construction or renovation projects during this period, significantly shaping the city's streetscape. Religiously motivated Londoners operated a soup kitchen, founded an Orphan's Home and a Home for the Aged, established local chapters of the Young Men's Christian Association (YMCA), the Women's Christian Association (WCA), the Women's Christian Temperance Union (WCTU), and the Young Women's Christian Association (YWCA). Individual congregations sponsored literary societies, missions circles, benevolent societies, Bands of Hope, Ladies Aids, and young peoples' groups. The quantity, range, and influence of religiously motivated activity was on the rise as London approached the twentieth century.[4]

This evidence of persistence, or even advance, opens the question of the religious authority upon which all of this activity was premised. The present study proposes to make a contribution toward this question. Stories of failure would seem to support some version of religious decline rather than to promote an understanding of this confident religious culture. However, the argument here will be that these failures illustrate a diffusion of authority away from clergy and ecclesiastical institutions toward an increasingly demanding religious population. This diffusion should not be understood as a decline in religious belief, as assumed by proponents of the secularization thesis, but rather as the emergence of an activist, religiously motivated laity for whom religion was an increasingly important vector of identity.[5]

LOCATING CLERGY AUTHORITY

The place of the church in society was under active negotiation in late Victorian Canada. Calls for disestablishment in Britain and the post-confederation emergence of Canada as a liberal society were subverting the established place of Christianity. The churches and their clergy were, for the most part, promoters of a national vision of Canada as a free and democratic society and worked to articulate new claims for religious authority as voluntary institutions contributing to the public good through the construction of Christian character.

After the 1850s, church and state were officially separated; however, habits of thought and action continued to provide underlying connections. The churches were widely viewed as being essential to the peace of the state and prosperity of the populace. Religion was accorded a place in the social order, though a voluntarist discourse seriously undermined its claims to public authority. In 1839 Lord Durham observed that self-government would not be successful unless the religious welfare of the citizenry was attended to.[6] The nature of that attention was still being worked out in the 1870s and 1880s. Local congregations subscribed to distinct theological traditions regarding the nature of the church, yet all these traditions were being pushed to adopt remarkably similar activities. As the churches responded to social and cultural transition, new programs, new governing structures, and new attitudes to church finance were devised.[7] The traditional concern of the church for the poor and outcast was instrumental in the creation of an outspoken and socially prominent Protestant lay leadership. Grounded in a construction of evangelical harmony and good works, a host of religious institutions including the YM and YWCAs, the WCTU, orphans' homes, and a variety of religious societies worked to establish and protect Protestant values as the definition of the common good. Despite the support of the churches for these efforts, it was becoming clear that interdenominational activities were competing for the wealth and volunteer effort of parishioners' and undermining churches as the institutional expression of the Protestant community.

The position of the clergy was as contested as that of the church in the transition to liberal democracy. In traditional church models, reflected in Anglican and Presbyterian practice, the clergy were "learned" gentlemen deriving status from their connection with local ruling elites as well as from the ministrations of the church.[8] Ministers of the "dissenting" churches were among the most persistent critics of clergy privilege. They presented themselves as "of the people" – simple ministers of the Gospel against the state supported establishment.[9] The rhetoric of liberalism and religious voluntarism undermined the traditional authority of the "established" clergy in their congregations and in public. By the late Victorian period, however, the battles of the 1840s and 1850s were over and the perception of the "dissenting" clergy was in transition as well. By the 1870s and 1880s, Methodism, a former leader in the fight against establishment in Upper Canada, considered itself a national church in waiting.[10] The heroic days of circuit-riding were happily in the past and Methodist ministers were aspiring to a status that befitted their position as spiritual leaders of the community. Much the same could be said for Congregationalists and Baptists, who could now join with their ministerial brethren in regarding the ministers of the Salvation Army and Latter Day Saints with suspicion and contempt.[11] The traditional accounts of clerical authority had largely been eroded, attention in this study is paid to the new contours of authority that empowered the activist clergy of this period.

The rhetoric of voluntarism and religious liberty that undermined historic patterns of religious authority provided the basis of an Evangelical Protestant discourse that found a new legitimation for religious authority. This discourse expressed itself in what Goldwin French identified as the evangelical "creed."[12] The most significant advantage of this "creed" was that it was not credal. It provided a powerful language of consensus that pointed toward broad areas of shared activity and concern without requiring unanimity. Thus, as good citizens of a liberal society, the clergy and their parishioners could work together toward common ends without having to agree on doctrine or ecclesial practice. The particularity of denominational traditions seemed to be transcended in the vocabulary of the evangelical creed and, thus, a common voice was found in public despite very real underlying differences.

The religious history and culture of the London area were founded on a thoroughly evangelical basis in the early 1830s by the efforts of two pioneer missionaries, Presbyterian William Proudfoot and Anglican Benjamin Cronyn. Cronyn, an Irish Low Churchman, and Proudfoot, a minister of the United

Secessionist Church, had both been influenced by British evangelicalism.[13] Cronyn's victory over A.N. Bethune, the High Church candidate, in the first Episcopal election in Canada underscored the firmly evangelical character of the new Diocese of Huron.[14] The founding of Huron College in 1863 ensured the Diocese a source of reliable evangelical clergy, untainted by what Cronyn considered the dangerous influences at work at Trinity College.[15] William Proudfoot introduced a voluntarist and evangelical Calvinist Presbyterianism to London.[16] In 1844, to provide a Canadian-born clergy, Proudfoot established a Divinity Hall in London. Although the Hall was later moved to Toronto and eventually merged with Knox College, Proudfoot's influence was strongly felt. From 1832 to 1890, first he, and then his son, pastored the church he founded. Although Cronyn and Proudfoot shared evangelical convictions, they were pioneering missionaries for different representations of the Kingdom and personal, political, and religious differences led to deep animosity between them.[17] However, London's religious development was thoroughly evangelical, a characteristic the advent of evangelical Methodist and Baptist works only served to intensify.

The evangelical discourse, which provided a common language of clergy authority, insisted that true religion was a matter internal to the individual heart and mind. Underlying the mundane was a deeper reality in communion with the divine and providing meaning and authenticity to thought and actions.[18] Access to this spiritual dimension came through conversion and inner change. In this sense, religion was private, denoting some inner reality that could not be constrained or regulated from outside. Religious regulation, characteristic of established churches, was understood by the evangelical creed to be detrimental to this essentially inner religion. True religion was fostered in private, and home and family were believed to be the appropriate context in which spiritual life could mature.[19] This form of spirituality provided authority for the clergy as promoters and proponents of much sought after spiritual authenticity. Nonetheless, they themselves were outsiders whose entrance into the spiritual lives of their parishioners was in support of the integrity of home and family and in defence of religion in this personal private space.

The development of Christian character was a private responsibility; however, liberal society was constructed of private individuals, and thus personal integrity was considered to be the source of social well-being. The social benefit of Christianity to liberal society was to lay in its promotion of nation-building and good citizenship, and London's clergy were quick to make these connections. The blessings of God, for which Londoners were to be thankful, were enumerated by Rev. James Ballantyne of Knox Presbyterian in a Thanksgiving Day sermon as "peace, laws made by ourselves, the choice of those who fill positions of authority, civil and religious liberty." These benefits were not bestowed promiscuously but depended upon the state instilling Christian morality in "preparation for the duties of citizenship." Failure to pay adequate attention to this prerequisite for democracy was to "invite a reign of irresponsibility and immorality,"[20] or, as Rev. W.R. Parker expressed the same message more positively, "A prosperous country must sustain a pure, vigorous and evangelical church."[21] Throughout this period, the clergy in London agitated for or against legislation, quite clearly using their position as ministers of the Gospel to rally support.

The clergy's claim to authority in public was premised on their claim to serve the public good. Both claims promised measurable and tangible results. In private the church and the home would produce Christian character, and, in public, Christian influence would ensure peace, prosperity, and good government. Thus what Canada needed was not less but more religion in its public life. No claim to authority could be made by the clergy based on their status. Instead, they appealed to their ability to inculcate Christian righteousness in individual citizens, thereby producing by indirect means a prosperous, secure, and Christian Canadian public life.[22]

These transitions in the place of religious authority in society had far-reaching implications for congregational life. Authority in congregations was tied up in historic traditions, theological commitments, patterns of church government, and the interpersonal connections between pastor and people. Clergy claims to instil Christian character in the most private and interior religious space that evangelical thought and practice so valued offered a powerful source of spiritual authority. However, access to this private space was not the privileged prerogative of the clergy. The home, the family, and the proliferation of religiously motivated lay activities all claimed to act in this sacred space. New structures of authority were emerging offering new opportunities for pastors who could marshal them effectively. At the same time, the transitions and intersections of religious and clerical authority were unstable, and this made failure particularly easy. The three stories that follow illustrate the difficult terrain on which pastors laboured to fulfill their callings and congregations aspired to attain spiritual well-being.

REV. TIMOTHY O'CONNELL AND THE TRIUMPH OF THE EVANGELICAL CHURCHMAN

A rather remarkable incident occurred in London's Chapter House, the Anglican pro-Cathedral, in December 1884. The Rev. Timothy O'Connell, rector of the Cathedral parish of the Holy Trinity, prepared to begin the service Sunday morning, 7 December. At that moment, Mr George McNab, the Dean's churchwarden, accompanied by Detective Phair, acting under the authority of the mayor, proceeded down the aisle intent on preventing O'Connell from conducting the service. O'Connell was thereupon arrested for disorderly conduct and disturbing public worship.[23] The arrest of O'Connell was precipitated by a series of events signalling his inability to conform to the evangelical standards of his congregation. The charge of disturbing public worship was laid after Bishop Maurice Baldwin "inhibited" O'Connell, suspending his authority to perform his sacred duties, pending an investigation of incidents of drunkenness and erratic behaviour.

As the day progressed, it seems the charge of disturbing public worship began to look a little farfetched to those involved. The judge at the subsequent civil suit against Mayor Hyman pointed out that, if O'Connell was conducting worship, he could not be disturbing it, and, if he was not, there was no worship to be disturbed.[24] Whatever the reason at the time, O'Connell was released later in the afternoon, whereupon he returned to his boarding house, locked himself in, called for the city's leading Orangemen to request protection and began either to drink heavily (the report of his guests) or to liberally self-administer some medicine his doctor had prescribed (his own report). Under the influence of one (or both) of these substances, he kept the household up most of night with shouts and banging on stovepipes with a heavy walking stick. On this and other occasions O'Connell was seen brandishing a revolver, which, several witnesses reported, was loaded. This impelled his landlord, one William Shoebottom, to enter a charge of insanity, and, by noon on Monday, O'Connell was once again in jail.[25]

Details of the story emerged over the next year through newspaper reports, public meetings, and hearings before the Police Magistrate, an ecclesiastical Court of Triers, and a series of civil suits.[26] Timothy O'Connell, an enthusiastic Irish Anglican clergyman most recently of Nebraska, arrived in London in April 1883. Shortly before his retirement, Bishop Isaac Hellmuth appointed O'Connell rector of the Cathedral congregation of the Holy Trinity, and all indications were that the appointment would be satisfactory to all. O'Connell was described, even by his later opponents, as a compelling preacher and organizer, inaugurating a Literary Society and a Girls' Friendly Society under the auspices of the parish. Shortly after O'Connell's installation, Dean Michael Boomer was taken seriously ill increasing the responsibilities of the new rector. In recognition of his vigorous pursuit of his pastoral duties and his increased workload due to the Dean's sickness, O'Connell's annual salary was raised in a relatively short period from $800 to $1,200 to $1,400. All of this presaged a long and successful tenure for O'Connell as rector of the Cathedral parish.

The first indications of trouble came in March of 1884 with reports of public drunkenness, even at parish events. Such reports escalated through the summer and into the fall, leading to an agreement that the vice-president would chair subsequent meetings of the Literary Society in O'Connell's place. Despite this agreement, O'Connell demanded the chair at the October 1884 meeting of the Society, causing an incident involving police intervention. In the end, O'Connell was granted his request and used the privilege to deliver an impassioned denunciation of the Scott Act, a version of local option prohibition then in force in Ontario but not in the city of London. O'Connell's agitation and distraction increased throughout the fall, leading him to take into his confidence churchwarden and local attorney George McNab and Police Chief Williams. To both these men, who would have roles in the coming drama, O'Connell confessed to troubles in Nebraska that resulted in his being kidnapped by his wife's family and confined to an insane asylum from which he was able to escape with the assistance of a fellow Orangeman. McNab and Williams were then sworn to protect O'Connell as he was convinced that agents had been sent to London to again kidnap him and return him to the asylum. Already McNab had received numerous complaints from members of the parish and a formal petition demanding action on O'Connell's drunkenness. At this point, McNab felt duty bound to lay all of this before Bishop Maurice Baldwin and demand O'Connell's removal. Baldwin met with O'Connell and suggested he take an extended holiday. When O'Connell refused, it was more forcefully suggested that he quietly resign to avoid the scandal of disciplinary action. Again O'Connell refused, and the bishop issued the inhibition, which was delivered to O'Connell on Saturday, 6 December, but returned to the bishop unopened. Thus, the events of Sunday morning, 7 December, were set in motion.

The aftermath of the arrest was as complex as the lead-up. O'Connell was arrested three times: once for disturbing public worship on 7 December but not charged; again on 8 December for insanity and being dangerously at large, the charges eventually being dropped; and finally on 21 December, while on bail pending a hearing on the insanity charge, for drunk and disorderly behaviour for which he was found guilty. In January 1885, he was to face a Court of Triers convened by Bishop Baldwin to consider the charges brought against him by his congregation. After objecting to the conduct of the proceedings and the composition of the Court, O'Connell withdrew leaving the Triers to find him guilty *in absentia* for a series of fourteen charges.[27] Bishop Baldwin then withdrew his clerical licence, an action that led to civil suits being brought against Baldwin, McNab, and several others for wrongful arrest and wrongful dismissal. In the civil action against Mayor Hyman, O'Connell won $600 and expenses because it was determined that Hyman had authorized the original arrest.[28] The action against Baldwin was resolved with a compromise in which Baldwin was to provide letters of reference to other dioceses if O'Connell would "conduct himself as a clergyman for three months."[29]

The pastoral difficulties of Rev. Timothy O'Connell were public as well as religious. The drama itself played out in boarding houses, on the streets of London, in the stores and at the weddings of prominent citizens, and, of course, in the sanctuary of the Chapter House. The most extraordinary aspect of this conflict between congregation and pastor was the role of the police and the courts. On no less than four occasions the police were called to intervene, and it was left to the courts of the state to provide the rather ineffective resolution to the conflict. It would have been quite unimaginable for the Presbyterians or the Congregationalists, the other participants in these stories of failure, to look to the state or appeal to the public to work out their pastoral disputes. The Cathedral Congregation of the Holy Trinity expected that the secular authorities had an obligation to protect their religious institutions, even against their own pastor. When George McNab and other key leaders were convinced that O'Connell intended to ignore the bishop's inhibition, they turned to Mayor Hyman and Police Chief Williams to enforce the order. As the courts would later make clear, the police had no authority to do what they did as was evident in the confusion about what the charge against O'Connell should be. For these evangelically oriented Anglicans, it would seem that drunken, boisterous behaviour by a clergyman could best be explained by insanity; this conclusion was confirmed by McNab's knowledge of O'Connell's previous committal.[30] For his part, O'Connell evidently had more faith in the civil courts than he did in the ecclesiastical one. He repeatedly called on the courts of the state to vindicate his rights as a clergyman of the Church of England against the church itself.

Were this drama to have unfolded a couple of centuries earlier and in London, England, rather than London, Ontario, it would better fit the received narrative of religious authority. It is clear that among prominent Anglican laymen, however committed they were in some respects to voluntarism and a separation of the church and state, an expectation remained that the state would protect their religious interests. Patterns of authority reaching centuries into the past wove together the power of state and church to ensure a strong state and a pious people. O'Connell's public flaunting of behavioural expectations for the clergy could undermine the piety of the people and thus, in their minds, sanction the kind of action by the state McNab demanded.

O'Connell also made an appeal to past expectations in his defence. In his view the evangelical obsession with total abstinence was an unhappy innovation out of step with both the traditional expectations for clerical sociability and his own convictions. While consistently denying that he was drunk, O'Connell made no secret of his drinking or his impatience with any form of prohibition. In the course of the civil suit against Bishop Baldwin, O'Connell's lawyer quipped that learning to drink was part of the training of an Anglican clergyman. Apparently, this pastoral skill had not made it into the curriculum of the solidly evangelical Huron College, nor was it fully appreciated by O'Connell's congregation.

In the O'Connell case, religious authority was intersected by past and present and by secular and ecclesiastical claims in complex ways. O'Connell's enthusiastic and active ministry gained him early favour with his congregation and support for his enterprises; however, his religious authority slipped markedly with stories of drinking, insanity, and some fairly aggressive behaviour involving a revolver. After these incidents, the congregation of the Chapter House was convinced that O'Connell lacked the marks of character that would qualify him to serve as their pastor. After his arrest, O'Connell had no support from his former congregation and what solace and support he received came from other denominations.[31] Once it was decided that O'Connell had to go, churchwarden George McNab worked with speed and deliberation. The bishop was willing to inhibit O'Connell, but McNab did not trust the ecclesiastical process. His action to call in the police to arrest O'Connell in his pulpit was not a simple throwback to some earlier intermeshing of church and state. It should be read as an assertion of lay power to act more quickly and effectively to protect the sacred event on that December Sunday than the slow and arcane ecclesiastical procedures. As an attorney McNab assumed that his professional expertise could resolve the issue with the kind of dispatch the bishop was unable to provide. This is not a story of the church using the state to deal with a difficult clergyman, but a case of lay action circumventing the procedures of the church, assuming lay authority to be more effective in protecting the religious sensibilities of the congregation from the ministrations of an unworthy pastor. The outcome, after the civil suits of 1886, was really rather embarrassing for both church and state.

THE REV. DR PROUDFOOT AND THE DISCOURSE OF CHURCH AND YOUTH

By the spring of 1889, the Rev. Dr John J.A. Proudfoot had enjoyed a successful ministerial career by any standard. The rev. doctor's father, pioneer missionary Rev. William Proudfoot, had established the first Presbyterian Church in London in 1833. J.J.A. Proudfoot was ordained in 1848, and in 1851, upon his father's death, he was called to the pulpit of First Presbyterian Church, where he served the congregation for thirty-eight years. In conjunction with his pastoral duties, Proudfoot served from 1851 to 1861 as Presbytery Clerk and concurrently from 1851 to 1876 as secretary of the Home Mission work. From 1867 until his final retirement in 1901 at age eighty, he was lecturer in Homiletics, Pastoral Theology, and Church Government at Knox College in Toronto.

In all of these ways Proudfoot had the marks of an exemplary pastor who served his congregation and the wider church to everyone's evident satisfaction. However, in early 1889 a decided change in the congregation's evaluation of their pastor's efforts on their behalf became public. A report appeared in the London *Free Press*, rehearsing Proudfoot's virtues and attainments but also detailing complaints attributed to a growing section of the congregation.

Some of the members of the congregation are not slow in expressing the opinion that under Dr Proudfoot the church presents no attraction to the young people; that the minister neglects the social duties of his office, and the distance he lives from the city renders his oversight of the flock almost impossible. They also say that the Church is losing ground through the alienation of the younger members and children, and charge this to the pastor's neglect, occasioned in part by the preoccupation of other duties, and in part to constitutional qualities and advancing age.[32]

Since his appointment at Knox College in 1867, Dr Proudfoot had divided his time between Toronto and London. Typically weekdays were spent in Toronto, with Proudfoot returning to London on Friday night for prayer meeting and preaching twice on Sunday.[33] Both Proudfoot and his congregation had, for many years, understood these activities, together with the occasional public lecture, to comprise his pastoral duties. The combination of Proudfoot's advancing age (he was sixty-eight), absence, and his lack of interest in anything beyond the task of preaching, convinced many in the congregation that they needed a younger, more energetic man to maintain the interest of their children.

A proposal was brought forward to hire a younger man as an assistant to Proudfoot to carry "the heavier work of the church," giving the older man leave to pursue his wider interests. As the details of the proposal began to emerge, it was not at all clear that the younger man would be an assistant. It was suggested that Proudfoot's salary be reduced to $600 a year and the assistant be given $1,200, the amount then being paid to Proudfoot. The division of duties in the proposal had Proudfoot preaching once on Sunday and the "assistant" having charge of all other aspects of church work. One member of the congregation later suggested that the intention was to provide their venerable pastor with an honourary role. Proudfoot immediately read this as a thinly veiled scheme to push him out, considered the offer an insult, and flatly turned it down, charging those presenting the request with spitefulness.[34]

Having come this far, the disaffected members of the congregation were not willing to leave the matter. A congregational meeting was held Thursday, 4 July 1889, with Dr Proudfoot presiding, to officially act on the proposal. On this occasion, Proudfoot reiterated his opposition to the offer of an "assistant" and expressed his confidence that his congregation would not allow such a scheme to move forward. In response, Robert Reid, long-time member of the Board of Managers and chair of the committee that had drafted the proposal, spoke of the crisis First Presbyterian was facing. Reid made the points that the church was situated in a city where there were lots of churches and that "it was necessary to provide all attraction possible with a consistent observance of Christian laws." Even Proudfoot's preaching, the skill he imparted to aspiring ministers studying at Knox, was regarded as endangering the future of the church. Reid relentlessly continued, "that the very large proportion of the young people were dissatisfied with the doctor's preaching was no secret, and many of them had gone to other churches, and still others had signified their intention of following the same course if Dr Proudfoot remained." In response to the charges of spite, Reid argued that those involved were motivated only by "a desire to do what was best in the interests of Presbyterianism and of the Church."[35] It was clear by this exchange that the current arrangement was untenable; however, the graceful compromise in the guise of an assistant had now been publicly rejected, and the congregation was not willing simply to push Proudfoot out. A committee consisting of the Session and the Board of Managers was appointed to devise a solution to the impasse and report back to the congregation.[36]

Upon meeting together and waiting upon the doctor, it was determined that, while Proudfoot found the previous proposal humiliating, if asked, he would be willing to resign to preserve the peace. The committee met again and determined by various means to raise $3,000 to present to Proudfoot on his retirement. However, rather than meet with the committee to discuss such an arrangement, Proudfoot informed them that he would lay his resignation before the Presbytery at their September meeting. It appears that, when he did so, he made it clear that his resignation was offered under considerable duress. Rather than accept the resignation and declare the charge vacant, as the members of the committee had anticipated, the Presbytery struck its own committee to investigate and determine if another solution might be found. This led to an angrily worded circular dated 25 September, appearing in the press 3 October.

A meeting of the congregation with the Presbyterial Committee was held on the afternoon of 4 November 1889.[37] At this meeting any rehearsal of grievances against the pastor was ruled out of order. This seemed heavy handed to some members of the congregation who expressed frustration with the intrusion on congregational affairs. The chair reminded those present that this was how Presbyterian government worked and that the meeting was to focus on finding a settlement. In the minds of the Committee of the Presbytery this would preferably involve a continued role for Proudfoot. To that end the proposal offering an assistant was reintroduced as a motion. Sentiments among the congregation seem to have moved in the direction of a fresh start, and, when the vote was called, the motion was lost. But this left the situation exactly as it was after the July meeting. The Presbytery continued to be involved, and on Sunday, 8 December, a congregational meeting was convened chaired by Presbyterial representative Rev. Alex Henderson. A statement very complimentary to the work and character of Dr Proudfoot was read along with an undertaking on the part of the church to provide a $2,000 gift in recognition of his years of service. This motion was carried unanimously, and, at the 10 December meeting of the Presbytery, Proudfoot's resignation was officially accepted, and the pulpit declared vacant as of 15 December 1889. The matter was now finally put to rest.

The Rev. Dr John Proudfoot seemed genuinely surprised and confused by the revelations of May 1889. The expectations connected with pastoral ministry had changed during his extended pastorate, and Proudfoot had not moved with the times. This was particularly evident when his ministry was compared to that of other clergy in the city.[38] The image of the pastor as scholarly divine delivering the Word twice on Sunday and baptizing, marrying, and burying as called upon was already out of date. The voluntarist church demanded an activist clergy involved in ministering to the poor, supporting missionaries, providing uplifting lectures and entertainment, and, perhaps most importantly, retaining the interest of the young. It was the concern that the church provide the "attractions" that would ensure the incorporation of the next generation that preoccupied church adherents more than any of the others.[39]

The powerful force sweeping away Proudfoot's forty years of faithful service came from the future; perhaps more accurately from the conviction that a particular kind of church program was necessary if the young were to be integrated into the life of the church. Even Proudfoot's most pugnacious critic, Robert Reid, claimed personal affection for him and, throughout the proceedings, displayed a certain amount of deference. Once it was clear Proudfoot would leave, Reid became as vocal and eloquent with his praise as he had formally been with his criticism. This gives credence to his contention that it was the long-term health of the church and not personal animosity that motivated the difficulties.[40] What made this situation difficult and quite different from the response to O'Connell was the real loyalty and genuine affection many felt for Proudfoot. By the November meeting it was becoming clear that even Proudfoot's supporters had concluded it was time for him to retire.

In the O'Connell story, ecclesiastical procedures were subverted by actions taken by secular authorities. In the Proudfoot case, the lay leaders of the movement against Dr Proudfoot were suspicious of the proceedings of the Presbytery, and the circular dated 25 September expressed concerns that the process was moving backward. However, the moderating role of the representatives of the Presbytery allowed the various factions of the congregation to reach what was presented as a unanimous position, also acceptable to Proudfoot. The congregation's complaints against Proudfoot were maintained with frankness and tenacity from May, when they were first raised publicly, through to December, when the situation was finally resolved. It seemed to many adherents of First Presbyterian that the only way to save the church was to force Proudfoot out. They stuck to this position in the interest of the future despite a more than sixty-year Proudfoot legacy. To the congregation, providing for the religious needs of the young outweighed the religious authority of the past, and, with the mediation of the Presbytery, Proudfoot's resignation was confirmed. The congregation's hard line was vindicated in the rapid success of Rev. W.J. Clark, a recent graduate of Knox College. Mr Clark preached his first sermon in July 1890 on the need for enthusiasm in the ministry and soon implemented a full slate of church activities.[41]

REV. ROBERT WALLACE AND THE DISCOURSE OF INTENSIFICATION

Congregationalist pastor Rev. R.W. Wallace was a man of great energy and ability. In the 1870s, long before Rev. Dr Proudfoot's difficulties, Wallace

was providing a model for the new activist pastor. He achieved prominence
with the local press and was often the source newspapers cited for a religious response to current issues. His references to the priority of private
judgement and his non-dogmatic moral wisdom made him an ideal public
religious figure. Wallace's Sunday evening lectures held at the Congregational Church were well attended by members of the wider community. Innovative plans were devised to reach out to the poor and neglected through
a visitation system. Despite all the marks of a successful ministry, Wallace
surprised his congregation by tendering his resignation after the Sunday
morning service on 10 August 1879.

Thursday evening, 14 August, the congregation met to hear the reasons for
their pastor's resignation. Wallace suggested that his actions should not have
come as a surprise, as a number of events had been leading in this direction
for some time. Indeed, as early as June 1878, he had expressed his concerns
and was dissuaded from resigning at that time only by the intervention of
several friends. Wallace wanted to make it clear that his resignation was not
due to any of the usual causes. His resignation did not mean he wanted to
leave, was unhappy with the salary, was headed somewhere else, or had a
quarrel with the church. He simply felt he needed more cooperation from
members of the congregation if the church was going to prosper.[42]

Wallace went on to carefully itemize his frustration with the lack of dili-
gence to Christian duty characterizing the majority of the congregation.
Here the report of the meeting found in the London *Free Press* is quoted at
some length:

Many [in the congregation] were doing nothing. Scarcely a person, young or old,
came forward with a request that something might be found for them to do ... This
he could not understand. Many young men in the church never came to him to ask
counsel about their own souls or those of their friends, and out of the 220 or
230 members, the average attendance at prayer meeting had been very low ... The ladies, although there were a faithful few, were not as enthusiastic in their work as necessity demanded, and the attendance at the Lord's Supper every month did not show
an average of over 100. There was a vast amount of thoughtlessness or indifference in
the church, which he had found himself unable to remove, not withstanding the most
strenuous efforts and earnest prayers. He was ambitious and wished the church to be
talked about, that there might be a large harvest of souls for Christ. Under these circumstances any other man would have acted as he had done, and he felt there should
have been no surprise on the part of his congregation. He was alone in his work.[43]

For Wallace, this lack of participation was particularly serious given the underlying principles of Congregationalism. As a consistent and outspoken

advocate of religious independence, Wallace expected his parishioners to match his vigour in pursuit of these principles. In dedicating the new Congregational church in August 1876, Wallace had set the standard very high.

... We dedicate our new building to the service of God. We yield it up – primarily – to the work of evangelization, which our Master has ordained and organized ... We consecrate it to humanity in the best and heartiest acceptation of the term ... Here every moral reform shall find a home ... We set it apart – secondarily – to the dissemination of the principles of Congregational independency ... Whatever good can come to us from any quarter we shall welcome, and, we shall ask no permission from Synod, or Presbytery, or Conference, or Union to make it our own. Here no creed shall interfere with the rights of personal investigation or put a fetter on conscientious action.[44]

The church was to be an active agent in London for evangelism, reform, independent thought, and conscientious action. Anything less would be a betrayal of the high calling Wallace believed the congregation had been blessed with.

Wallace's difficulties appear to be the mirror image of Proudfoot's. Here an activist pastor feels forced to resign due to the inactivity of the congregation, while, in Proudfoot's case, an inactive pastor was forced to resign by an activist congregation. Wallace's rhetorical denunciation of an inattentive, even irreligious congregation would seem to support the narrative of religious decline.[45] However, a review of his pastorate makes the notion of decline implausible as an explanation. Wallace arrived in London in June 1871 to pastor a church with a membership of 130 housed in a small frame building. In 1876 and at a cost of over $25,000, a two-hundred-member congregation moved to a large brick church on a prominent corner of Dundas Street.[46] Records of the Congregational Association for 1880, the year Wallace actually left London, puts average Sunday attendance at seven hundred, and the 1881 census records 489 Congregationalists, the high point for the nineteenth century. What prompted Wallace to resign was not decline but growth lagging behind elevated expectations. Moreover, it seems fairly certain that Wallace was not intending to leave when he tendered his resignation in August 1879. He made it clear he was still committed to the church and wanted to stay but could only stay if accorded the cooperation he regarded his due.

Two congregational meetings were held to deal with the matter of the pastor's resignation.[47] Both resolved to request the pastor to withdraw his resignation, and both expressed hopes that "all would unite in helping the Pastor in the future" in some vague way, but neither addressed the specific frustrations raised by Wallace at the 14 August meeting.[48] At the special meeting held 21 August to formally act on the resignation, the issue of pastoral visitation emerged. Few details were given, but a separate motion was required promising to consider the subject of visitation at a future date, seemingly to ensure the passage of the motion declining to accept the pastor's resignation.[49] At least some members of the congregation were inclined to accept the resignation, or perhaps to turn Wallace's tactic back on him and use this opportunity to win some concessions from the pastor. Wallace's letter withdrawing his resignation, dated 23 August 1879, reinforces this reading. In it he expresses his pleasure at the unanimity of the request to withdraw the resignation but goes on to thank those involved for raising the "vexed question of pastoral visitation." Wallace indicates that he recognizes this issue as a criticism of his ministry by assuring them that "no one of you will ever forfeit my friendship by telling me of my lacks, or advising me of what will help me in my preaching, in my social work, or in my life." He promised to spend an evening discussing the issue of visitation in the near future and ends the letter with a fresh dedication of himself to the spiritual welfare of the people.[50] However, no new level of cooperation or an acceptable resolution regarding pastoral visitation was evident in the subsequent months and in August 1880 Wallace resigned again, this time having already secured a charge to two mission churches in Detroit.[51]

Unlike O'Connell and Proudfoot, Wallace was not forced out by his congregation. If anything, it was his ambition and inability to bring his congregation into his vision for the ministry of the Church that led to his resignation. The resignation may be an indication that Wallace believed he had failed to stimulate in his congregation the spiritual character on which clergy authority moved. He wanted his church to be well known for its work in behalf of the Kingdom of God. Hence, Wallace gave his energies to preparing lectures, writing columns for the newspapers, building a large church, and a variety of outreach schemes that required a steady stream of motivated volunteers to succeed. The congregation followed Wallace in much of this, but with everything achieved there was more to do. When sufficient numbers of volunteers did not materialize to sustain the rapid growth and new initiatives, Wallace blamed it on religious indifference and preached all the harder for active attention to Christian duty. This Wallace believed to be the work of the church, but the people wanted their pastor to visit them. What seemed to be lacking was a measure of personal spiritual influence. A plausible reading of this situation might be that the issue of pastoral visitation was raised because the congregation wished their pastor to focus more on them and not merely to badger and threaten them into ever greater levels of church work.

Although in the vanguard of an emerging model of the successful pastor, Wallace was as out of touch with the expectations of his people as Proudfoot.

Congregationalist principles of democracy worked effectively to mask the power relationships in play between Wallace and his congregation. Without an appeal to an external governing body, the pastor and people were on their own to work through their differences. Interestingly, both re-sorted to the same tactic to bring about the desired result – the withdrawal of their labour. Wallace was wholly dependent upon the volunteer labour of the congregation if his vision for the church was to be achieved. Whatever their level of piety and spiritual vitality, the most effective means of redi-recting the considerable energies of their pastor was to stay at home and al-low the pastor to manage his great schemes on his own. On the other side, the resignation of a Congregationalist pastor placed the people in an un-comfortable position. With no bishop to appoint or presbytery to moderate a call, it could take considerable time and energy to find a suitable pastor. Thus, the threat of resignation carried considerable weight. What seems clear is that the threat was powerful enough to elicit promises of full coop-eration but not necessarily the full-hearted commitment Wallace desired. So, an uncomfortable situation persisted for another year until a sincere resignation was submitted and accepted.

Among the Congregationalists, the pastoral connection was premised upon a mutual sense of the will and direction of God between pastor and people. This construction of the pastoral relation rejected a priestly model that created clear distinctions between the clergy and laity. Among Lon-don's evangelical Anglicans and Presbyterians, an acceptance of the Protes-tant concept of the "priesthood of all believers" had begun to subvert this distinction; however, a tradition of deference ensured some vestige of au-thority for their clergy. Neither theology nor tradition elevated Congrega-tionalist pastors above their flocks. Successful pastors were effective in acting in the role of religious friend and guide. A perceptive London *Free Press* reporter commented that the fortunes of the Congregational Church rose and fell with the quality of its pastor.[52] Of all denominations in Lon-don, the Congregationalists gave their pastors the least religious authority but were the most dependent upon their pastors for prosperity. This made the relationship between them inherently fragile and unstable.

CONCLUSION

In some ways there is nothing new here. As Olliver Hubert has observed, congregational scrutiny of clergy was as active in the eighteenth century as the nineteenth, and one does not have to look very far in any century to find examples of conflicting expectation between pastors and congregations.[53] However, religious authority of clergy and their people increasingly traversed the shared goal of the spiritual transformation of individuals and, through this means, of communities. These stories of failure indicate the degree to which the valoration of personal religion shifted authority toward members of the congregation.

It is clear that appropriate attention to congregational expectations was essential to the success of the clergy. Gidney and Millar describe a transition within all of the older professions that increasingly defined professionals as purveyors of expert services, without the cultural authority once accorded learned "gentlemen."[54] The troubles of O'Connell, Proudfoot, and Wallace indicate that this transition was well underway in London. The clergy had used the evangelical discourse of personal and deeply interior religion to authorize their ministry. Evangelical rhetoric had been fused to this new professionalism to define the clergy as providers of expert spiritual services to their congregations and communities. Clerical authority would now correspond closely with the spiritual development of the flock and, in particular, the young. In none of the narratives of failure was there an appeal to the sacred nature of the clerical office itself. Each congregation, spanning the ecclesiastical world from episcopal to congregational forms of government, treated its clergy as a professional to be evaluated on the basis of how well he provided the required service.

While these three cases are in no way exhaustive, the rhetorical shape of expectations for the professional services provided by clergy begins to emerge. In evangelical London, clergy were to maintain a certain dignity, quite incompatible with O'Connell's pistol toting drunken paranoia. Such behaviour reflected badly on the consumers of his services and modeled a character that did not inspire the young to virtue. This required immediate, even pre-emptive action. Perhaps the most powerful rhetoric at the disposal of both clergy and congregations turned on the necessity of passing the faith to the next generation. If the services of a minister could deliver this, as it seemed O'Connell was doing early in his tenure, clerical authority was assured. However, in the case of Proudfoot, and O'Connell after his arrest, authority evaporated when the piety of youth was at risk. On the other side, activist pastors powerfully marshalled the rhetoric of intensification, calling for ever more strenuous demonstrations of commitment. Congregations rallied to calls for Christian action and spiritual vigour. Without the intangible quality of a strong relational connection, this rhetoric of intensification became the overzealous badgering of a pastor who could no longer inspire people to mission.

Congregational initiative is another component of these stories. The shift in authority toward the laity is quite evident in each case. In the O'Connell case, the congregation subverted the authority of the bishop to discipline his clergy. Robert Reid rallied the congregation in demanding an activist pastor and resisted attempts of the Presbytery to find a continuing role for Proudfoot. Wallace's problems began with his resignation; however, the tables were turned as the congregation took the opportunity to critique his failure to visit them. The congregations also exhibited a suspicion of, or impatience with, the institutional practices of their communion, believing, as their actions would indicate, that lay initiative was more efficacious that ecclesiastical.

It is also striking that action taken against the clergy was in no way a rejection of religion or evidence of a loss of faith. Indeed, in each case, the action was in defence of some spiritual value central to lay identification with their faith. Churchwarden George McNab was determined O'Connell should not conduct the service after McNab became convinced that O'Connell was unworthy of his pastoral calling. The extraordinary measures taken by McNab, Mayor Hyman, and Detective Phair were to preserve the sacred nature of the Anglican service. Proudfoot ran afoul of his congregation, many of whom he had baptized and married, because he was not sufficiently attentive to the religious infrastructure required to attract and build the character of the young. Reid and Proudfoot's antagonists were convinced that the spiritual well-being of the next generation of faithful was the chief responsibility of the clergy. Wallace, on the other hand, was attentive to the infrastructure of ministry to the exclusion of the personal relationships his congregation required of their spiritual guide. In each case, the congregations are revealed as demanding consumers of the spiritual services necessary to instil Christian character and ensure the future of church and nation. The significance of these stories of failure may be that lay people had come to consider themselves the guardians of spiritual values and were able to wield considerable religious authority, when necessary, against their clergy and churches.

NOTES

1 Nancy Christie and Michael Gauvreau, "Modalites of Social Authority: Suggesting an Interface for Religious and Social History," *Histoire sociale/Social History* 36, no. 71 (May 2003): 1–30.

2 A.B. McKillop, *A Disciplined Intelligence: Critical Inquiry and Canadian Thought in the Victorian Period* (Montreal and Kingston: McGill-Queen's University Press,

1979); Ramsay Cook, *The Regenerators: Social Criticism in Late Victorian English Canada* (Toronto: University of Toronto Press, 1985); and David B. Marshall, *Secularizing the Faith: Canadian Protestant Clergy and the Crisis of Belief, 1850–1940* (Toronto: University of Toronto Press, 1992). Marshall has provided a review of this debate, in which he argues for the cogency of secularization for understanding the nineteenth century, in "Canadian Historians, Secularization and the Problem of the Nineteenth Century," Canadian Catholic Historical Association, *Historical Studies* 60 (1993–94).

3 John Webster Grant, *A Profusion of Spires: Religion in Nineteenth-Century Ontario* (Toronto: University of Toronto Press, 1988); Michael Gauvreau, *The Evangelical Century: College and Creed in English Canada from the Great Revival to the Great Depression* (Montreal and Kingston: McGill-Queen's University Press, 1991); William Westfall, *Two Worlds: The Protestant Culture of Nineteenth-Century Ontario* (Montreal and Kingston: McGill-Queen's University Press, 1989); Marguerite Van Die, *An Evangelical Mind: Nathaniel Burwash and the Methodist Tradition in Canada, 1839–1918* (Montreal and Kingston: McGill-Queen's University Press, 1990); and Nancy Christie and Michael Gauvreau, *A Full-Orbed Christianity: The Protestant Churches and Social Welfare in Canada, 1900–1940* (Montreal and Kingston: McGill-Queen's University Press, 1996).

4 For the growth of lay religious activity see Kenneth L. Draper, "Religion Worth of a Free People: Religious Practices and Discourses in London, Ontario, 1870–1890," (PhD diss., McMaster University, 2000), chapters 4 and 5, and Marguerite Van Die, "A March of Victory and Triumph in Praise of 'The Beauty of Holiness:' Laity and the Evangelical Impulse in Canadian Methodism, 1800–1884," in *Aspects of the Canadian Evangelical Experience*, ed. G.A. Rawlyk (Montreal and Kingston: McGill-Queen's University Press, 1997): 84–6.

5 For a recent challenge to the chronology of secularization, see Callum G. Brown, *The Death of Christian Britain: Understanding Secularization, 1800–2000* (London: Routledge, 2001). For a discussion of religion and identity, see Draper, "Religion Worthy of a Free People," 25–31.

6 Gerald M. Craig, ed., *Lord Durham's Report: An Abridgement of Report on the Affairs of British North America by Lord Durham* (Toronto: McClelland & Stewart, 1963): 73. For a discussion of the Durham on religion see Janet Ajzenstat, *The Political Thought of Lord Durham* (Kingston and Montreal: McGill-Queen's University Press, 1988): 38–40.

7 Draper, "Religion Worthy of a Free People," chapters 2 and 3.

8 R.D. Gidney and W.P.J. Millar, *Professional Gentlemen: The Professions in Nineteenth-Century Ontario* (Toronto: University of Toronto Press, 1994): 16–7.

9 Egerton Ryerson, *The Clergy Reserves Question* (Toronto: J.H. Lawrence, 1839; reprint, Ann Arbor, MI: UMI, 1981).

10 William Magney, "The Methodist Church and the National Gospel, 1884–1914," *The Bulletin* (United Church of Canada/Victoria University Archives [UCA], 1969), and Neil Semple, *The Lord's Dominion: The History of Canadian Methodism* (Montreal and Kingston: McGill-Queen's University Press, 1996): chapter 8.

11 For a variety of attitudes regarding the coming of the Salvation Army to London, see "The Question of the Day: The Clergymen of London and Surroundings," *London Advertiser*, 17 July 1884. Clergy opinion on the Latter-Day Saints was not as systematically solicited, however; see the letter to the editor by Rev. James Cooper, "The Latter Day Saints," *London Advertiser*, 29 March 1876. Also see James Penton, "The Response to Two New Religions in Canada in the 1880s: The Latter-Day Saints and the Salvation Army," *Proceedings of the Canadian Society of Church History* (1987).

12 Goldwin French, "The Evangelical Creed in Canada," *The Shield of Achilles: Aspects of Canada in the Victorian Age*, ed. W.L. Morton (Toronto: McClelland & Stewart, 1968): 15–35. Attention has been given to the influence of evangelicalism on Canadian history in recent years, see in particular George Rawlyk, ed., *Aspects of the Canadian Evangelical Experience* (Kingston and Montreal: McGill-Queen's University Press, 1997).

13 Alfred H. Crowfoot, *Benjamin Cronyn: First Bishop of Huron* (London: Synod of the Diocese of Huron, 1957). On Proudfoot see John S. Moir, *Enduring Witness: A History of the Presbyterian Church in Canada* (Eagle Press, 1987), 84–5, and "The Proudfoot Papers," *Transactions of the London and Middlesex Historical Society*, part 6, 1915. For an excellent introduction to British Evangelicalism, see David Bebbington, *Evangelicalism in Modern Britain: A History From the 1730s to the 1980s* (Grand Rapids: Baker, 1992).

14 See Curtis Fahey, *In His Name: The Anglican Experience in Upper Canada, 1791–1854* (Ottawa: Carleton University Press, 1991): 255.

15 Crowfoot, *Benjamin Cronyn*. Also see Benjamin Cronyn, *Bishop of Huron's Objections to the Theological Teaching of Trinity College* (London, C.W., 1862), and *The Protest of the Minority of the Corporation of Trinity College, Against the Resolution Approving of the Theological Teaching of that Institution* (London, C.W., 1864).

16 Moir, *Enduring Witness*, 84–5.

17 William Proudfoot, "The Proudfoot Papers, Part XI," *Transactions of the London and Middlesex Historical Society* (1922), 90–1, and Crowfoot, *Benjamin Cronyn*.

18 Richard Rabinowitz, *The Spiritual Self in Everyday Life: The Transformation of Personal Religious Experience in Nineteenth-Century New England* (Boston: 1989): 237.

19 The relation of religion and family is explored in the contributions in Nancy Christie, ed., *Households of Faith: Family, Gender, and Community in Canada, 1760–1969* (Kingston and Montreal: McGill-Queen's University Press, 2002). Also see Marguerite Van Die, "'A Woman's Awakening': Evangelical Belief and Female Spirituality in Mid-Nineteenth-Century Canada," in *Canadian Women: A Reader* (Toronto: Harcourt Brace, 1996).

20 See the sermon by James Ballantyne in "Thanksgiving Sermons," *London Daily Free Press*, 8 November 1889.

21 "Twelfth of July Sermons," *London Advertiser*, 12 July 1875.

22 For examples of London clergy in the period working for civic righteousness, see Draper, "Religion Worthy of a Free People," 266–78.

23 "Arrested in His Pulpit, Rev. Mr O'Connell Charged with Disturbing Public Worship," *London Advertiser*, 8 December 1884.

24 "O'Connell vs. Hyman," *London Daily Free Press*, 21 January 1886.

25 "Re-Arrested," *London Advertiser*, 9 December 1884.

26 See reports in the *London Daily Free Press*, 22, 23 January 1885, 10, 11, 16 February 1885, and "Evidence Before the Police Magistrate," *London Advertiser*, 27 December 1884. For O'Connell's defence against the charges against him see "Who's Safe?" *London Daily Free Press*, 3 January 1885, "Letter from Jail," *London Advertiser*, 11, 15 December 1884, and "O'Connell's Defence," *London Advertiser*, 17 February 1885.

27 "The O'Connell Case," *London Daily Free Press*, 10 February 1885; "The O'Connell Case," *London Daily Free Press*, 11 February 1885; and "O'Connell's Sentence," *London Daily Free Press*, 16 February 1885.

28 "O'Connell vs. Hyman," *London Daily Free Press*, 21 January 1886.

29 "O'Connell vs. Hyman," *London Daily Free Press*, 21 January 1886; "O'Connell v. Baldwin," *London Daily Free Press*, 22 January 1886. A report appeared in the *Free Press* in May 1886 that Rev. O'Connell was inhibited in Baltimore on the basis of the incidents in London. "O'Connell's Ill Fortune, He is Again Inhibited from Preaching in Baltimore," *London Daily Free Press*, 11 May 1886.

30 The full story would provide an interesting case study for a Foucauldian analysis of the uses of insanity in establishing and maintaining community standards of behaviour. Michel Foucault, *Madness and Civilization: A History of Insanity in the Age of Reason* (New York: Vintage, 1988).

31 "Rev. Mr O'Connell's Second Letter," *London Advertiser*, 15 December 1884 and "Christianity: Ye Gods!" *London Advertiser*, 16 December 1884.

32 "First Presbyterian Church," *London Daily Free Press*, 21 May 1889.

33 Fred Landon, *A History of the First Hundred Years of the First United Church, London, Ontario (formerly the First Presbyterian Church) 1832–1932* (London, Ontario: n.p., 1932): 20. Landon explains how the work of the church was accomplished in the absence of Proudfoot. "The work of the church would probably have been seriously handicapped by the pastor's absence but for the fact that the women of the church organised and did much of the visiting, a faithful group serving in this way for many years."

34 "Pastor and People," *London Daily Free Press*, 5 July 1889.

35 "Pastor and People," *London Daily Free Press*, 5 July 1889.

36 "Pastor and People," *London Daily Free Press*, 5 July 1889.

37 Events recounted in this paragraph come from the circular "Dr Proudfoot's Resignation," *London Daily Free Press*, 3 October, 1889, or the report of the congregational meeting "Pastor and People" *London Daily Free Press*, 5 November 1889.
38 Draper, "Religion Worthy of the Free People," 126ff.
39 Marguerite Van Die argues that the vibrant evangelical culture she describes in the
   1850s, 60s, and 70s, underwent a decline in the 1880s due to an inability of the
   older generation to get their children to follow in their footsteps, "'The Marks of a
   Genuine Revival': Religion, Social Change, Gender and Community in Mid-Victorian Brantford, Ontario," *Canadian Historical Review*, 79, 3 (1998): 561–2. The
   evidence from London indicates that this possibility was constantly on the minds of
   the faithful and that the many programs that came into being in the 1880s and 90s
   were intended to attract the young.
40 "All's Well that Ends Well," *London Daily Free Press*, 9 December 1889.
41 "Ordained and Inducted," *London Daily Free Press*, 3 July 1890, and Fred
   Landon, "A History of the First Hundred Years of the First United Church," 25–9.
42 "Congregational Church, Rev. R.W. Wallace's Reason for Resigning," *London
   Daily Free Press*, 15 August 1879.
43 "Congregational Church, Rev. R.W. Wallace's Reason for Resigning," *London
   Daily Free Press*, 15 August 1879.
44 "Church Opening," *London Advertiser*, 28 August 1876.
45 Callum Brown suggests that much of the validity of the secularization thesis
   comes from a tradition of preaching against the supposed irreligion of the age. This
   clergy strategy worked to create a compelling sense of spiritual danger, thereby increasing the immediacy of the need for salvation (*The Death of Christian Britain*,
   18–30).
46 "'Tis Forty Years Since," *London Daily Free Press*, 17 May 1877.
47 Congregational Church, London, Ontario, Minutes of Congregational Meetings,
   14, 21 August 1879 (UCA).
48 Congregational Church, London, Ontario, Minutes of Congregational Meetings,
   14 August 1879 (UCA).
49 Congregational Church, London, Ontario, Minutes of Congregational Meetings,
   21 August 1879 (UCA).
50 "Congregational Church," *London Advertiser*, 25 August 1879.
51 Congregational Church, London, Ontario, Minutes of Congregational Meetings,
   21 August 1880 (UCA).
52 "Congregationalism," *London Daily Free Press*, 14 June 1875.
53 Olliver Hubert, "Ritual Performance and Parish Sociability: French-Canadian
   Catholic Families at Mass from the Seventeenth to the Nineteenth Century, in
   Christie, ed., *Households of Faith*, 37–76.
54 Gidney, *Professional Gentlemen*, 379–84.

5

Developing Christians, Catholics, and Citizens: Quebec Churches and School Religion from the Turn of the Twentieth Century to 1960

BRIGITTE CAULIER

Three institutions had long been the basis of education: family, church, and school. In the nineteenth century, the school became increasingly state-coordinated and centralized. Faced with the need to develop a mode of instruction that would allow individuals to enlarge their ability to participate in social progress, Western societies placed a greater confidence in the school than in the family to instruct and even to raise children. It was felt that families lacked the necessary training or were too busy to do the job properly. As a result of this redirection of responsibility over what was taught, the Churches feared losing control over the formation of conscience. As the world became less subject to religious interpretation and as secularization advanced, the Catholic Church became increasingly concerned. The collective vision held fast and became established by the schools. In France, an address by Rabaut Saint-Étienne to the Convention in December 1792 gives us a snapshot of the situation the Ancien Régime faced regarding the realignments that were yet to come:

Is there a way, soon, in the near future, to communicate simultaneously uniform and common impressions to all the people of France that will have the effect of making them all worthy of the Revolution? … That secret has been well known to the priests who, through their catechisms, their processions, their missions, their pilgrimages, their statues, their paintings, and everything else that nature and art put at their disposal, led mankind inevitably in the direction the priests intended.

It follows from this observation that it is necessary to distinguish public instruction from national education. Public instruction enlightens and exercises the mind; national education forms the heart; the first provides light and the second virtue. National education is food for all; public instruction is the share of the few. They are sisters, but national education is the elder.[1]

The French school contained and transmitted the vision of a republican and secular society conveyed especially in the moral lessons and civic instruction that excluded religion and the intervention of the Catholic Church. From which academic tasks was the Church not excluded? What role did it take for itself in the social vision valued by the school? The Canadian experience provides evidence of active Churches' intervention in the directions taken by a system of public education.

WHAT DO NORMS TELL A HISTORIAN AND HOW SHOULD WE INTERPRET THEM?

In the Province of Quebec, the public system took shape within the difficult context of linguistic duality. The issues of identity that bulked so large were expressed in demands for a confessional system. Anglophone Protestants, especially members of the smaller denominations, feeling that they would remain a minority in Quebec, played the denominational card in order to preserve their identity.[2] As Jean-Pierre Charland has shown,[3] it was following various fruitless attempts on the part of the liberal bourgeoisie that the school system was constructed within the framework of an increasingly stressed confessionalism. The Catholic Church did not have the initiative nor did it immediately dominate the school system that was under formation in the nineteenth century. Hard and fast, uncompromising confessionalism was established for good in 1875 when the Ministry of Public Instruction was abolished and Catholic bishops took seats *ex officio* on the Council of Public Instruction. This same law extended an increased autonomy to Protestants. Though Catholics and Protestants (for which read francophones and anglophones) might have been eager to keep their children separate in the classroom, they were united in a shared notion of an altogether Christian school system. Thus the repeated refusal to set up Jewish school commissions. The school belonged to Christianity, as did the society from which it came. This idea also prevailed in the school systems of the Canadian provinces that did not go the route of the denominational school, like Ontario. The school was charged with inculcating moral, religious, and social values that reflected the insistence on charity, propriety, and all the attitudes and behaviours that these values embodied.

In the period under consideration, Quebec churches viewed the question of school instruction from much the same point of view. The Code of Public Instruction, the general directions that accompanied the new curricula, and the directives to schoolteachers are all documents that inform us of what the Churches had in mind. The specificity of this school system did not seek to impose uniformity on every pupil. It was not a question of creating unanimity, of a collective vision that would override political or religious divisions in favour of a political system, as in France. There was no common theory. Further, the system was there to protect the anglophone Protestant minorities in Quebec in relation to the francophone Catholic majority in the province as well as the francophone Catholics in an anglo-Protestant Canada. In a context such as this, comparing the separate curricula is indispensable in order to understand the division between the groups and how it was maintained in a situation in which identities were fragile.

Historians have often remained cautious regarding the analysis of normative data, emphasizing that these may never have been actually in use. In the area that concerns us here, the gap between the norm and the reality seems quite narrow for a number of reasons. The Quebec public school provided a religious education that was organized as a subject and that was integrated into the students' academic course with its schedule, exercises, evaluation, and notional content. The two Confessional Committees, Catholic and Protestant, in charge of the curricula entrusted subcommittees whose members they selected, essentially ecclesiastics and religious on the Catholic committee, to develop them in considerable detail. The programs were revised, clarified, or even totally rewritten according to the requirements of course development and pedagogical need.[4]

The files detailing the programs that resulted from broad consultations in which the religious authorities who were involved in Catholic education made their voices heard reveal the societal diagnoses of these elites and the orientations they preferred, extending to the social relations between the sexes. These files contain what was thought about the creation of upper primary grades and about the sexual division of programs. The file dealing with religion is a condensation of the justification for sexual segregation in the religious training and observances for boys and girls. Whether or not these norms were applied, their changes over time does indicate broad societal shifts as well as indicating the degree of uneasiness or certainty experienced by the elites and educational decision-makers.

The textbooks provide a view of the way general mottos were transmitted, the better to embed them in the classroom. The importance of religious examples in the teaching of other subjects is obvious. It is not altogether accurate to say that these manuals were not actually used by the children. In the files specifying curricula at the end of the nineteenth century, Catholic school authorities were complaining that, on the contrary, teachers were happy to make the children learn the manuals by heart. In 1891, the subcommittee in charge of program examination deplored the teachers' failure to explain the material: "In almost every school, teaching a subject is the equivalent of teaching the manual by rote to the pupils."[5]

One might also argue against placing too much weight on this particular collection of documents on the grounds that the programs are often too thick to be viewed in their entirety. That is certainly true to a large extent. But the historical fact is that teaching in those times was eminently a matter of performance. Classroom doors had to be left ajar. The lessons, teachers' choices, and their inflections or individual stances could not be left open. We have used several accounts by students, parents, and inspectors – with all the limitations they involve. We also know that the programs were handed to the teachers and that the pedagogical journals carried specific adaptations of them. Along with the manuals, they represent evidence that most closely approximates the actual education of the period, most particularly in the francophone Catholic schools. Over time, they became more and more specific and complete.

Additionally, we are dealing with a period when there was a collective belief in a received truth. There was one truth; it was pronounced in the schools, in the family, and in church. The ecclesiastical authorities had ways of seeing that it was respected. Within the discourse that these three institutions took turns to convey, there were no or few breaches, no or little disagreement. Even though certain anxieties emerged in the 1930s, control over Quebec Catholics seemed to have reached its peak.[6] Compulsory education fostered a complete transfer of religious education and preparation for receiving the sacraments into the public school.[7] Furthermore, the educational authorities supervised and inspected teachers. All in all, the teaching staff was left with little initiative, and additionally, in the Catholic schools, it was often drawn from religious communities.

Confessionalism thus coloured the Quebec educational project from the outset. It was meant to mold men and women who had to fit into a particular society. The school both produced and partly reproduced a society based on an anthropology specific to itself and that contributed to its identity.[8] As well as the religious textbooks, like catechisms, that provided what one needed to know to achieve salvation but that also instilled a vision of the world and of social relations, the general directives addressed to teachers gave a notion of the grand principles and attitudes to be adopted with the pupils. In remaining especially attentive to the elementary school, a standard was reached that involved the largest number of children at an age when they were most open to indoctrination.

TEACHING AND SHAPING CATHOLIC CITIZENS

The school has been a powerful vector to convey values, as lessons and teachers' attitudes reflect values that the textbooks implanted in stories, readings, and pictures. The items that appeared in the classroom often symbolically supported those values. They reinforced this fundamental affirmation of a Catholic social identity. Just as every school in France bears the words "Liberty, Equality, Fraternity" over its door, the classrooms of the Quebec Catholic schools reflected religious affiliation. As iconographic reinforcement occupies an important place in Catholicism, we expect to find classrooms decorated with religious images. Since the 1888 syllabus, compulsory schoolroom furniture included at the very least a crucifix or cross and a framed picture or statue of the Virgin. These continued to figure in the regulations of the Catholic Committee and the annual class photographs indicate that these simple requirements were frequently surpassed. In addition, prayers opened and closed every school day and the school calendar was adapted to the needs of training. In order to permit pupils to devote themselves fully to the preparation for their first Communion in the parish, teachers were required to leave time for these in their homework and timetables. When the age for first Communion was established at the age of reason (generally seven) by Pope Pius X in *Quam singulari*, weeks of intense preparation for the solemn event were held that meant that school was over for the most part.[9]

In the twentieth century, these general denominational signposts no longer seemed to be sufficient for those who were drafting a new curriculum, approved in 1922 and applied the following year. Its statement of general principles gives an idea of the new concerns of the Catholic Committee:

Religion is not merely a subject to be taught in the hours allotted to it; it is also an element in moral and religious development and must be *lived* every hour of the day. The atmosphere in the school must be a religious one. Religious and moral ideas must be present in the curriculum, in relations between the pupils, in the teacher's thinking, in how discipline is enforced and even in how the classroom is furnished. Through all these means, religion must penetrate the soul to become a source of thoughts, a regulator of feelings and a principle of action.[10]

It was no longer a matter of teaching religion but of shaping children by means of religion. Moreover, the drafting of this curriculum, which began in 1917, was affected by the difficult context of the period. Good citizenship had to be added to the internalization of Catholicism. Along with the prayers that bracketed the school day, morning, and night, students also had to sing "O Canada," the national anthem, at least once a week.[11] This association is found in the statement of principles that introduces the teacher's guide to applying the curriculum. Instructors were to see to the "creation of moral initiatives producing the principles of life for the Christian and the citizen." They also had to "give the child fundamental religious knowledge and cause him to develop from it the habits of a lifetime … here we find the basis on which to educate the Christian, the man, the citizen. This is the basis that must be laid down in the soul in primary school."[12] All the subjects had to be unified – class dictation should thus both provide agricultural information and a moral lesson. From both sacred and Canadian history, children were to discover heroes who could act as models for their moral progress. It was no longer just a matter of awakening children to their faith but of making them internalize their moral duties, as the school had to shape children for life. This curriculum that would prove extremely innovative in its integration of its pedagogical principles from the school all the way to the important stage of teacher training and development emphasized the reinforcement of a moralistic training through religion. This emphasis may have occurred because lay teachers, although they lacked the authority of being ordained, were responsible for explaining the catechism.[13] Or perhaps it was just a matter of making sure of a more articulated moral training in a society that was moving in the direction of urbanization. The other aspect of this curriculum consisted of a refusal to give greater weight to scientific and technical instruction,[14] in favour of a minimal program adequate for the largest number of children.

The revisions made to the curricula during the 1930s did not give rise to such statements of principles, being more concerned with specific instructional directions for each subject. It was not until after the Second World War that guiding principles appear once more in the curricula. A revision dealing with the elementary schools and prescribed by the Catholic Committee in December 1942 was progressively introduced beginning in 1946. In the meantime, a law requiring compulsory school attendance was finally passed in 1943, following a debate that had begun in 1875. Now children were required to attend school until the age of fourteen. The primary school curriculum was now directed at "the formation of the man, the citizen, and the Christian." From this generalized Christianity, it moves quickly to a denominational affirmation: "A school will be indeed Catholic to the degree that it strives in every way to cause the child to imitate Jesus Christ in his thoughts, judgements, and deeds."[15] A set of equivalences was established that was vigorously repeated in the curriculum for the secondary years, which had been finally divided from primary school instruction in the 1950s. In so hazardous a period, when teenagers were increasingly rebellious, teachers had to be motivated if they were to produce sturdy Catholics. The aim of Catholic educators thus consisted of "cooperating with divine grace to develop perfect Christians, Catholics, that is, complete men of genuine character."[16]

The Catholic curricula entailed a hierarchical arrangement of subjects that placed religion at the head of the disciplines. This was not, in our view, a matter of making a simple declaration of principles but rather a constant reaffirmation of what legitimated the teaching of other subjects. In the final quarter of the nineteenth century, as syllabuses became more and more detailed, each publication from the Catholic Committee allowed this subject-matter hierarchy to be reasserted. Religion, then moral and religious instruction, but also religious instruction and moral education, depending on the changing terminology within the same program, always appeared in the first place. The tone was set in 1888: "Teaching religion must always come first among the subjects in the course of studies and must be given in every school."[17] In the first half of the twentieth century, as courses in education grew and became more specialized, religion continued to appear in the list of obligatory subjects, invariable and everywhere.

Course material was in fact subdivided into several subtopics; it contracted or grew depending on the significant dogmatic and ideological modalities. To simplify the discussion, let us think primarily of the first six years (seven after 1937), which roughly corresponded to the elementary level, toward the end of the period.

The first years of school were devoted to learn catechism. In 1879, the first two years featured an abridged catechism; in grades 2 and 3, the little catechism was to be absorbed. In grade 4, which at the time marked the end of the elementary level, they started on the large catechism. The three years of model school, as the upper primary grades were then termed, continued this study. A little less than a decade later, teaching catechism was revised so that it consisted of oral instruction in the first year, the abridged little catechism in the next year, and the little catechism itself in the third and fourth years. After a year spent reviewing in grade 5, the students started in on the large catechism in grade 6. With the new catechism of 1888, which remained in use for a very long time (about fifty years), these large distinctions disappeared and it was taught throughout the whole six years (seven at the end of the 1930s, when the preparatory course was incorporated into the elementary level). The 1951 Catholic catechism, the last in question and answer form, changed nothing as far as school instruction at this level went. The alterations to the program beginning at the end of the nineteenth century were concerned with how to make sure the contents of the catechism were absorbed. The book was incontrovertible. It announced the duties owed to God, to the Church, and to one's neighbours. If it provided the knowledge essential for salvation, it also instilled principles of moral behaviour, models of how to live in society and in the parish community. This body of information to be memorized, which led to a diploma in religious instruction, was clarified by the material appearing in the secondary topics.

These became part of the religious instruction program and underwent revisions. They considerably enriched and enforced the absorption of the catechism. A solid trio appeared throughout the nineteenth century and a good part of the twentieth: prayers, catechism, and sacred history, though the relationships among these were not immediately formalized. In 1879, prayers were lodged in the beginning year, while sacred history, enlivened by little stories, began in grade 1 and went all the way to Old Testament in grade 6 and to the life of Jesus in 7. The reading program included *Devoirs du chrétien* (Duties of the Christian), beginning in grade 2, to which Latin readings were added in grade 3, all of which continuing until grade 6. These Latin readings consisted of elementary instruction in the prayers and the Latin Mass. In the 1920s, the prayers took over the contents to go beyond the strictly formal aspect of a correct pronunciation in church. In this way, the structure of public schooling contributed to the socialization of the children on the religious level. It was intended to make them into active and, if possible, diligent parishioners. In view of the secondary material associated with the religious program, the entire socialization of children appears to fall under the jurisdiction of religion. Thus, after 1888, the teaching of deportment was folded into religious instruction. In the earlier program, manners were taught as object lessons as the occasion arose. Now the pupil would learn how to behave properly at home, in public, and in church. Hygiene was added to all this in 1922 for the first four grades. In grades 5 and 6, hygiene and deportment were removed from the supplementary material, leaving room for the Gospels and the establishment of the Church. The mastery of the body was an essential element for the Catholic Church, as it was the key to moral control, the body being the site of impulses that had to be tamed.

In the late 1930s, sacred history returned in what now became grades 6 and 7, and the complete text of the Gospels, in a JOC (Jeunesse Ouvrière Catholique) edition, was added.[18] The great innovation in the troubled and uncertain years of 1937–38 were "lessons in good citizenship that would provide a pretext for the teaching of religion and morality"[19] in grades 1–5. In grade 6, the older students would work on individual morals; they studied their obligations toward their bodies and their souls. Civic-mindedness followed from morals and could not be separated: "Good citizenship is thus an ethic that can be divided into individual morality, family morality, and the morality of the school, and national and international politics. The program is drawn up in conformity with this division."[20] It was a question of living a Christian life, and, to do that, one must:

a) avoid mortal sin and remain in a state of grace;
b) attend mass every Sunday and on Holy Days of Obligation;
c) go to confession and communion often;
d) never neglect prayers;
e) always be obedient, polite, studious, pious, and charitable.[21]

In grade 7, the civics program took on some of the aspects of other subjects and dealt with individual behaviour.

Lessons in deportment accompanied religious instruction from grades 2 to 5, consisting of a direct extension of Christian principles as applied to behaviour. But, for students in grades 6 and 7, specific time was left for it in the timetable in order to complete their education. The increased demands that ran through the 1937–38 revised curriculum are particularly expressed in regard to the new program of complementary courses. The Catholic Church believed itself to be under threat and fought back. The tone it used reveals a sense of controversy. Students were being prepared to live in a society that was hostile to religion. We need only consider the twin objectives for the sacred history program in the complementary course outlines for the primary schools: "a) To demonstrate that the Catholic Church was instituted by God; b) To serve as an argumentative defence against the principal objections to religion. Indeed … this instruction develops religious pride; it prepares the students to defend their religion intelligently on the frequent occasions that it may be attacked."[22] In grade 8, the period from prehistoric times to the Middle Ages was studied. The following year dealt with the period from the Middle Ages to the modern times, until the Lateran accords. In citizenship education, in the first of these grades the students worked on morality in the family and the school; the following year turned to morality in society, putting forward the Catholic point of view on equality, individual liberty of conscience, and freedoms of religion, work, association, and the press. There was an equal insistence on the necessity for education and proper child-rearing. To prepare future mothers and fathers, certain ideas of how to bring up young children had to be transmitted. The grade 12 philosophy program, devoted exclusively to moral philosophy, went more thoroughly into apologetics. Catholic theories were presented about the origin of human beings, for example, the refutation of evolutionary theory. Specific topics included, among others, suicide, alcoholism, unbridled fleshly desires, homicide, property rights, social issues, the family, and feminism – true and false, of course – denominational and neutral schools, universal suffrage, the death sentence, and so on. Of course, it was the social views of the Catholic Church that were unequivocally defended in the public schools it controlled.

The last curriculum for religion at the primary level (introduced in 1946, it lasted, with modifications, until the 1960s) brought together prayers, catechism, and sacred history. Deportment was separated, allowing very specific instruction in the rules of good manners in the home, at school, in church, on walks, for social engagements, and in correspondence. Socialization was thus always formalized in school instruction. Moral training remained an independent subject but taught in a strengthened curriculum that had as its objective to teach the children their obligations toward God, their neighbours, and themselves. This new program encompassed patriotism and citizenship.

It was with this reform in the 1940s that anglophone Catholics achieved autonomy in the matter of the syllabus. Until the end of the 1930s, the Catholic Committee had produced only French course outlines. Then they proceeded to official translations instead of relying on literal translations that were carried out one way or the other in the school commissions. This absence of specific programs for the anglophone Catholic populations might be seen as a sign of a desire for complete assimilation into a common culture. It was nothing of the sort. The textbooks that were authorized for public education made the difference, including the catechism, which was not always the same as the one approved by the bishops. Morever, the smallness of the clientele of the English Catholic schools, especially in the twentieth century, encouraged them to come under the influence of the United States. This tendency, found elsewhere among Canadian Catholics, was reinforced during the construction of the first strictly anglophone Catholic program in 1948. The choice of required texts reflected the integration of the English Catholic sector into the sphere of influence of the US textbook and its dependence on it.

A single course comprised religious instruction for children in the English Catholic school. It was subdivided into prayers, Bible history, mass, the liturgical year, and catechism. Teachers found themselves obliged to see that the contents of the religious instruction were assimilated and internalized: "All religious instruction is based upon four main aims which *must* be attained if the lesson is to be effective. The teacher is not free to strive for any less than all four of these aims in his or her work. These four aims are to bring the pupil 1) to understand, 2) to appreciate, 3) to remember, 4) to practice his religion."[23]

In sum, for the period under consideration and for all Quebec Catholic children, francophone and anglophone alike, attending public school, religious instruction was compulsory and was taught for a number of hours in the week. All in all, the confessional Catholic system rested on religious instruction that was heavily present in its particular curricula, an instruction that happily spilled over into other courses in order to reinforce the message. One need only look at the textbooks that were used.[24] Though the societal view claimed to be Christian, we observe the degree to which it was in fact part of a clearly identified and closely limited Catholicism. The Catholic Committee relied on the school to transmit to future citizens an essentially Catholic perspective on the world. Respect for authority and for the social order was learned very young, while behavioural conformity was acquired from the teacher's example and through lessons and practice.

THE PROTESTANT SCHOOL, SHAPER OF DEMOCRATIC CITIZENS?

In the Protestant sector, confessionalism was expressed quite differently from what we have seen on the Catholic side. In order to respect denominational freedom of choice, the religious content was conceived more loosely. Three fundamental articles appear in the entire period and are part of the reform in the 1960s. Conscientious objection was affirmed from the outset: "Religious instruction shall be given in every public school; but no one may require a student to read or study a religious text or take part in any devotional or religious exercise of any sort to which his parents or guardians have registered an objection in writing."[25] The school commissioners and the school officials were obliged to supervise the application of this clause.

The Protestant Committee, so as not to come into conflict with different denominational sensitivities, naturally opted for the Bible as a textbook. Thus it was agreed, regarding sacred history, that "the teaching of sacred history is part of the curriculum at every level of the Protestant school system and, in order to teach this material, the Bible shall be used as the text, but no denominational teaching shall be given in the Protestant schools."

In practice, Protestant school denominationalism was demonstrated every day: "Every Protestant school shall open each day with a reading of a passage from the Bible and by the recitation of the Lord's Prayer."[26] This article is also found in the regulations dealing with the obligations of teachers. In 1899, several details were added to the second article, specifying that the first half-hour of class should be devoted to opening exercises, moral instruction, and sacred history. The use of Holy Scripture is mentioned, but so are authorized textbooks.[27] Religious instruction in the public confessional schools became fixed very quickly at the end of the nineteenth century and continued through a good deal of the twentieth. It rested on the most minimal consensus possible among the denominations.

Respecting denominational diversity favoured a moralistic approach to Scripture. Teachers thus avoided risking interpretations to which parents might object. As those responsible for drafting the program fleshed out their pedagogical instructions and the philosophy of education that was to prevail in the Protestant school system, this moralistic concern constantly crops up. In 1915, the pedagogical directions for the first three levels urge teachers to narrate the Bible as a story, stressing the good: "The stories should be so constructed and presented that the good, and not the evil, will be emphasized. Make the right so pleasing that the child will feel impelled to imitate it."[28] These instructions would be in force until 1956.

After 1923, the term "Scripture" gave way to "Moral and Religious Instruction," and, as was also the case on the Catholic side in the same period, stress was laid on the genuine feeling that was to support this material. In discussing the obligatory nature of the Opening Exercises, it is pointed out that "it were better to omit the exercises altogether than to conduct them in a hasty, perfunctory manner."[29] The fundamental objective of the school was to shape children's character, making them into responsible and honest citizens, more than making them specialists in religious subject matter. On the primary level, education was to take first place. In 1940, with the stress place on the pedagogical reforms, the official teachers' guides detailed the objectives of the Protestant Committee:

Changing ideas of the child's place in the process have led to a fresh definition of the purpose of education. This may now be regarded as the development of the entire personality of the child by activities of many kinds in accordance with his interests and abilities, so that he may become a good citizen, ready to make his contribution to a wholesome social life and capable of sharing in the varied cultural heritage of the race.[30]

This idea of cultural heritage was expressed in the disciplines that were taught in school. The order in which they were presented in the text is an indication of the modernity of the Protestant system. The world was not interpreted on the basis of religion. Instead, the child's body was the departure point, thus biology, then the physical sciences and mathematics, followed by the social sciences like history, geography, and civics. Morals are not mentioned until after literature and the arts, and Christianity is not specifically mentioned at all: "No education is complete which disregards the spiritual legacy of the ages. This consists of the great body of thought and aspiration which is comprised in morality and religion."[31] The explication that follows deals with the forming of moral persons who will be ready to involve themselves as citizens in the betterment of their country. "The objectives of education will be attained if children are so trained that they become healthy, moral, cultured, efficient, self-supporting, and co-operative citizens." This is the conclusion of the chapter entitled "The Educational Philosophy Underlying Our School System and Course of Study." Though the school might contribute to an education founded on morality, these instructions do not, however, specify Christian fundamentals.

Three years later, an expanded edition of this guide takes into account the crucial issues of the Second World War. The same chapter is revised to include training in democracy: "The process of democratic education must begin in the school and the constitution of the modern school makes this a simple process. For democracy is learned by the practice of co-operation with a common goal in view, rather than through the enunciation of democratic principles by the teacher."[32] For the Catholic system, the word "democracy" could have been replaced by the word "religion." The Protestant Committee felt the need to specify the foundation of a moral education: "As the Bible is the recognized foundation of our civilization, it has found a place in our school curriculum in grades I to XI."[33] A five-page subsection added under the title "Democracy and Education" defines democracy through references to the US, French, and English experiences, citing the Declaration of the Rights of Man in support. This would have been an unthinkable approach for the Catholic system, referring as it does to the heritage of the Enlightenment and the revolutions it inspired.

The Quebec Protestant school system did not particularly stand out in its assertion of its religious affiliations as compared with the Ontario public schools, which, though they were not denominational, nevertheless did not exclude any references to Christianity. Gidney and Millar have shown that up until the mid-1960s "a shared Christian heritage"[34] carried an enhanced value in Ontario textbooks, which could be seen in the exercises and in the literature. They point to the Drew regulations of 1944, "introduced during wartime by a new Conservative government as a response to both the perception of moral decline in a time of national crisis and of the desire to augment religious teaching in the schools, their main innovation was to make religious instruction compulsory in the elementary schools during the school day."[35] There was a double message, nevertheless. On the one hand, Nazism with its value system in open and active opposition to Christian morality was rejected, but at the same time non-Christians, Jews in particular, were shut out. In Quebec, where the English Protestants were pressing the claims of democracy, the Protestant School Board in Outremont closed its doors to Jewish children, citing budgetary reasons.[36] Still, Protestant parents opposed this decision; the mothers organized tea parties with the immigrants, in order to integrate them into their new environment.[37] The affirmation of general Christian values that seemed more tolerant than Catholicism was no automatic guarantee that a generous openness would be extended to other religions. After retaining the chapter on democracy through several later editions, the Protestant Committee dropped it in 1957. In that presentation of the curriculum, an explicit reference is made to the place of religion in the development of children: "Religious instruction is an essential part of the programme of our Protestant schools, and the school shares with the home and the church the responsibility for fostering the growth of a spiritual interpretation of life by means of an understanding and appreciation of our religious heritage."[38] For the first time in all the Protestant course programs, there is a mention of a connection to the church and the Christian faith. The community is stressed and the new course objectives go beyond the simple moralistic reading of the Bible:

1 To give the pupils a general knowledge of the Bible as a book which forms the basis of Christian Faith, Worship and Conduct.
2 To foster the growth of a moral and spiritual interpretation of life by means of an understanding and appreciation of the Christian Religion.[39]

This wording, more modulated than on the Catholic side, reveals a certain anxiety regarding a religious dimension that was no longer manifest. Religious exercises had been relegated to the background as the teachers relied on Sunday school for the religious education of their charges. After the Second World War, however, families sent their children less regularly to Sunday school.[40] To defend Christian values, the Protestant Committee restored the memorization of Bible texts to a prominent place.

Denominationalism in the Protestant public sector could not, however, be placed at the centre of the system because freedom of conscience, guaranteed by law, forbade any unitary system of the kind. The other courses increased in autonomy for that reason. Matters of faith were left to the denominations, which could pursue a fundamentalist orientation for themselves. In the Catholic sector, things worked quite differently; the education was Christian, not to say Catholic, and everything taught contributed to that end.

Unlike in the Catholic sector, Protestant religious instruction did not gather to itself various subtopics in the course programs. Sacred history was dominant in fact, and a table showing the distribution of courses in 1888 was even content merely to mention simply history at every level from elementary to high school. At the first level, oral lessons taught the pupils about the principal events in the life of Christ as well as the Lord's Prayer, which they had to know by heart. At the second level, oral lessons dealt with Old Testament history up to the death of Moses. The Ten Commandments were memorized. At the third and fourth levels, oral lessons continued with the Old Testament and the study of Canadian and British history was begun.[41] Morals came under the heading "Object Lessons or Useful Knowledge": "At least once a week, there should be a reading or a short discussion on morality, truth, honour, respect for others, good manners, temperance, and kindness to animals."[42]

The regulations that the Protestant Committee approved in 1899 and published the same year contained modifications and details. The history course was different from the previous one and would thereafter be connected with geography. In the first four years of elementary school, the first half-hour of the day was devoted to Scripture Knowledge. Bible reading, hymns, prayers, and lessons in Scripture and morals made up religious instruction in the Protestant schools for the entire period of interest to us. The moral teaching, it should be noted, came from a study plan written by Elson Irving Rexford and was based on piety, honesty, respect for others, good manners, temperance, health, and benevolence toward animals.[43]

All in all, the broad outlines of this religious instruction were laid down by the end of the nineteenth century. The regulations as amended in 1938, however, reduced devotional exercises and religious and moral instruction to twenty minutes a day. In the twentieth century, most discussion on the Protestant Committee concerned what optional textbooks might or might not be authorized for use. The *Jamaica Catechism* remained on the list of approved optional works from 1905 to 1915. Previously, G.F. Maclear's *Biblical Histories* had been allowed. After 1915, the Protestant Committee went back to only the Bible once again. About fifteen years later, a complete revision of the curriculum retained a selection of Bible extracts as published in *Bible Readings for Schools*. As had always been the case, the

Bible was used to implant good moral conduct in the pupils. But rather than presenting a vengeful God, swift to punish evil deeds, now stress was placed on the trust that children should develop so that they might contribute to the building of a better world as desired by a God who saw the best in human beings. This curriculum remained in force until 1957. Debates arose regularly over whether the Bible should be reduced to the teaching of good conduct. In the 1920s, complaints were heard about a reading of Scripture that was simply descriptive and too literal.[44] In the Protestant curricula, the choice of text did not vary a great deal. The revisions at the elementary level largely dealt with rearranging the content and reorganizing its presentation from one year to another.

CONCLUSION

The two confessional systems express anthropological models that run through the divisions between them. Catholics and Protestants did not share the same way of belonging to the world and to society. In order to accommodate students from diverse religious and ethnic backgrounds, the Protestant Committee had to rely on the least common denominator: the fundamental text, the Bible, access to which was open to all. We can see why the Committee felt much less obliged to lay out the details of teaching religion in the schools. But the characteristics of the anglophone population of Quebec encouraged the reinforcement of citizenship education, and the development of training in community life, as the diversity of Protestant denominations required the cultivation of tolerance and respect for difference.

The Catholic system, in its relations with society and its institutions, had more trouble making a place for outsiders. Religious instruction occupied a large place in the school day. The wide-reaching, encompassing vision of Catholic confessionalism, which could barely differentiate between religious affiliation and citizenship, left a clear mark on the functioning of the public school. This view could not open itself to pluralism and found itself on the defensive regarding the advance of modernity in Quebec society. The absence of reference to large world upheavals is significant. Even though the Catholic curricula might react to social change, they did not enunciate them. They were presented as absolute, disconnected from historical contingencies. The instructions to Protestant teachers, on the other hand, encouraged them to take reality into account and work with it.

Nevertheless, the texts of both Committees give evidence of secularizing impulses, and at times their responses resemble one another, as in the 1950s; a stiffening of authority appears in both sectors before major reforms. In the

Protestant system, we can detect fears that secularization and diversified school populations will result in a decline of religious teaching in the schools.

This parallel and autonomous development of the Catholic and Protestant schools over decades did not foster the establishment of a common social vision. The churches had a large stake in education, particularly the Catholic Church. As their control dwindled, the question of a substitute vision arose. A telling symptom is the call to develop a sense of citizenship, so as to focus the establishment of the social bond in the school.

NOTES

This study was supported by grants from FCAR and SSHRCC.

1 Quoted by Jean-Pierre Gaillard in *Un siècle d'école républicaine* (Paris, Seuil: 2000): 13–14.
2 British-North American Act 1867, article 93.
3 Jean-Pierre Charland, chapitre 2, "L'école, une institution de l'État libéral," *L'entreprise éducative au Québec, 1840–1900* (Quebec: PUL 2000): 53–89.
4 Much of the documentation used in this study is available at the Centre d'informations multimédias de la direction des communications du ministère de l'Éducation and in the archives of the Minister of Education and the ministry's many avatars in the Quebec National Archives. On the Catholic side, researchers can rely upon a research report by Jean-Pierre Duval, Clermont Gauthier and Maurice Tardif, dealing with *L'Évolution des programmes d'enseignement religieux de 1861 à nos jours* (Université Laval, *Les Cahiers du Labraps*, Série Études et documents, 17, 1994). This study forms a part of a much larger examination of all subjects, and applies a systematic analysis of all school programs. The programs in Catholic schools have been the subject of a critical study by Michel Allard and Bernard Lefebvre, *Les programmes d'études catholiques francophones du Québec. Des origines à aujourd'hui* (Montreal: Les Éditions LOGIQUES, 1998).
5 ANQ, E13/85-04-003, art. 75, loc. 1A14-3101B, "Sous-comité chargé de l'examen du programme d'études," 19 May 1891, np.
6 The work of Jeannine Gauthier and of Mélanie Lanouette indicates that those in charge of teaching catechism were troubled by the poor results obtained by pupils who had been made to learn a rather indigestible catechism by heart. The Christian Brothers, like the Assumption Sisters with Sr Saint Ladislas, regretted the lack of religious knowledge this kind of teaching incurred. They hoped to correct this problem by providing children with new methods and exercise books. Jeannine Gauthier, "Une production catéchistique pour le Québec des années 1930–1950.

Marguerite Gauthier (sœur Saint-Ladislas, a.s.v.)," (Doctoral thesis, University of Laval, 1996). Mélanie Lanouette, *Faire vivre ou faire connaître. Les défis de l'enseignement religieux en contexte de renouveau pédagogique, 1936–1946* (Sainte-Foy: Les Presses de l'Université Laval, 2002).

7 Hence the difficulties that Bill 118 presented in Quebec as the Catholic Church was not ready to again take over the responsibility for catechesis, which it had handed over to the schools.

8 Jacques Audinet, "Fonction et fonctionnements de l'enseignement religieux," Raymond Brodeur and Gilles Routhier, eds, in collaboration with Brigitte Caulier, *L'enseignement religieux: questions actuelles* (Ottawa, Paris, Bruxelles: Novalis, Le Cerf, Lumen Vitae, 1996): 93–100.

9 Raymond Brodeur, "De la confession de foi au système d'éducation: Le catéchisme de première communion," *Faiths and Education: Historical and Comparative Perspectives. Paedagogica historica*, Supplementary series, v, Gent, CSHP, 1999, 226.

10 *Règlements du Comité catholique du Conseil de l'Instruction de la Province de Québec*, (Quebec: Government Printing Office,1922), Appendice A: Programme d'études pour les écoles primaires élémentaires catholiques, Section 1: Organisation pédagogique des écoles, 1. Instruction morale et religieuse, 55. Significantly, all the regulatory documents begin with this point.

11 Ibid., 40.

12 Ibid., 60.

13 Brigitte Caulier, "Catechism and Pedagogy: The Influence of the Emerging School System on the Teaching of Religion in Quebec, 1888–1924," *Religious Education in History. Confessional and Inter-Confessional Experiences* (Umea, Sweden: Kulturens frontlinjer. Skrifter fran forskningsprogrammet Kulturgräns norr, 2003): 53–71.

14 ANQ, E-13, art. 1416, # 800-18, loc. IA 27–3403A, "Mémoire de Mgr Ross sur l'enseignement élémentaire adressé au Surintendant," 18 December 1918, 4.

15 *Programme d'études des écoles primaires élémentaires 1948*, Approved by the Catholic Committee of Public Instruction, 7 May 1948, 27.

16 *Programme d'études des écoles secondaires 1963*, Approved by the Catholic Committee of the Council of Public Instruction, 11.

17 *Code de l'Instruction publique, 1888, 29.*

18 *Anciens programmes d'études des écoles catholiques de langue française de la Province de Québec*, 3ᵉ partie 1927–1947, s.l. n.d., 60.

19 Ibid.

20 Ibid.

21 Ibid., 58.

22 "Programme d'études des Écoles primaires élémentaires et primaires complémentaires 1937," Michel Allard and Bernard Lefebvre, eds, *Les programmes d'études*

catholiques francophones du Québec. Des origines à aujourd'hui (Montreal: Les Éditions LOGIQUES, 1998): 582.

23 Province of Quebec, *Course of Studies for the Elementary Grades (I-VII) English Language Catholic Schools...*, Revised Edition, 1959, 7.

24 Serge Gagnon, *De l'oralité à l'écriture: le manuel de français à l'école primaire (1830–1900)* (Sainte-Foy: PUL, 1999).

25 *Code de l'instruction publique de la province de Québec*, compiled by Paul De Cazes Secretary of the Department de Public Instruction (Quebec: J.O. Filteau et frères, libraires-éditeurs, 1888): 44, article 159.

26 Ibid., 44, article 159.

27 Compiled by G.W. Parmalee, *The School Law of the Province of Quebec*, Quebec Daily Telegraph Job Print, 1899, Regulations of the Protestant Committee of the Council of Public Instruction, 56, article 139.

28 *Memoranda of Instructions for Teachers, Protestant Elementary Schools of the Province of Quebec for the Use of Teachers, Inspectors, and School Officials* (Quebec: Department of Public Instruction, 1916): 6.

29 *Manual Respecting the Course of Study in the Protestant Elementary Schools of the Province of Quebec for the Use of Teachers, Inspectors, and School Officials* (Quebec: Department of Public Instruction, 1923): 13.

30 *Memoranda for the Guidance of Teachers in the Protestant Schools of the Province of Quebec* (Quebec: Department of Education, 1940): 5–6.

31 Ibid., 9.

32 *Handbook for Teachers in the Protestant Schools of the Province of Quebec* (Quebec: Department of Education, 1943): 8.

33 Ibid., 9.

34 R.D. Gidney and W.P.J. Millar, The Christian Recessional in Ontario's Public Schools," in *Religion and Public Life in Canada: Historical and Comparative Perspectives*, Marguerite Van Die, ed. (Toronto, Buffalo, London: University of Toronto Press, 2001): 279.

35 Ibid., 280.

36 Arlette Corcos provides an excellent account of this episode in *Montréal, les Juifs et l'école* (Sillery: Septentrion, 1997): 113–21.

37 Roderick MacLeod, "Tea, Cookies, and Multiculturalism: Fostering World Citizenship through the Home and School Movement in Quebec, 1945–1964," Session held at the twelfth biannual Conference of the Canadian History of Education Association (ACHE/CHEA), 24–27 October 2003.

38 *Handbook for Teachers in the Protestant Schools of the Province of Quebec* (Quebec: Department of Education, 1957): 9.

39 Ibid., 129.

40 Margaret Assels, "Changing Attitudes of Catholic and Protestant Christians to the State as Reflected in the History of the Educational System of Quebec," Master's thesis (McGill University, 1972): 64.

41 *Code de l'instruction publique*, 1888, 20–1.

42 Ibid.

43 Parmalee, 33. Rexford was a teacher at the Montreal High School and an influential member of the Protestant Committee from 1882 to 1891.

44 Nathan H. Mair, *Recherche de la qualité à l'école publique protestante du Québec*, trans. from the English (Quebec: Conseil supérieur de l'éducation, Comité protestant, 1980).

6

The Saint Vincent de Paul Society and the Catholic Charitable System in Quebec (1846–1921)

JEAN-MARIE FECTEAU AND ÉRIC VAILLANCOURT

"Je sens que le passé tombe, que les bases du vieil édifice sont ébranlées et qu'une secousse terrible a changé la face de la terre. Mais que doit-il sortir de ces ruines?"[1]

"Where progress trumpeted the inevitable Kingdom, preoccupation with the souls of the poor became less. Religious leaders turned their attention more and more to social adjustment – to make the community more like the imagined Kingdom. And the churches themselves, where they met the poor, exerted greater energy in nonreligious programs to attract and aid the poor."[2]

"Nous nous refusons ... à aborder l'histoire de la religion au XIXe siècle par les biais, pourtant si communs, des notions de sécularisation et de renouveau institutionnel. Loin de voir des survivances ou des réveils, c'est-à-dire quelques nouveaux rameaux qui réussissent à pousser sur un vieux tronc apparemment desséché mais qui continue quand même à meubler le paysage et parfois à produire quelques rejets, nous voulons tenter de cerner la nouvelle économie religieuse selon les figures qui lui sont propres."[3]

Regardless of the era in which we examine its activity, the Catholic Church has always played an important role by providing assistance and, more broadly, by assuming responsibility for those social problems that strain the community of the faithful. Taking care of the poor and the ailing was, after all, part and parcel of the business of an institution that was supposed to guide its flock past earthly evil toward ultimate salvation. Providing help and assistance would thus seem consubstantial with the established faith in a kind of achrony in which Church time merges with that of the perpetual misfortunes of men and women on Earth. Both the forms of poverty and how it is dealt with have each undergone profound changes over time. Still more, how poverty is viewed as a social problem depends on the general structuring of a given social development. To put it another way, Catholic charity is a religious virtue open to indexing itself in various ways depending on the deeper structure of the societies in which it is in play. The transition of modern societies in the direction of the free market and democracy constitutes one of those moments in which the place of religion and of the institution that gives it form are called into profound question. This is not to say that the responses to the challenge of "modernization" offered by the religious authorities and the faithful have been always identical in every country. But the questions are the same: how to reconcile belief in a single supreme authority with the democratic freedom to act and think; how to accommodate a community of faith to the borders of a citizenship that might be located either within or without this community; how to harmonize the charitable impulse among fellow members of the religion with the solidarity owed to the community as a whole? The brief study that follows plans to tackle this question, first by interrogating the way in which, in a particular space (Quebec), these questions have been (partially) resolved, then by considering, as case study and as example, how assistance was provided by a religious organization such as the Saint Vincent de Paul Society.

THE QUEBEC CHURCH IN THE SOCIAL FIELD: IMPLICATIONS

In the last few years the historiography of the Church in Quebec has made major advances, especially regarding the difficult analysis of Catholic adaptation to "modernity." Several works have questioned making a simplistic equivalence between the Church and social conservatism, emphasizing the various tendencies within conservatism, the complexity of the responses to the challenges of democratization and the liberalization of the market, and the ambiguity at the heart of the mid-nineteenth-century religious revival. In particular, the work of Rousseau, Ferretti, Hudon, and Hubert allows us to go beyond the sort of approach the French historian Denis Pelletier recently complained of: "To simplify it to the extreme, social history theses may be said to approach the religious fact in an opening part devoted to a social tableau, as one component among others of this tableau, generally retrogressive and on the road to marginalization, and that thereafter they limit its role to acting as a brake on the dynamic of economic and social transformations that is at the heart of what the thesis is about."[4] But stressing the profoundly "modern" character of the responses to the challenges to religion in the course of the transition to capitalism[5] also requires us to assess carefully what was at stake for an institution like the Catholic Church. These issues were of two sorts: to redefine the Church's political place and to reconsider the modalities of its integration into the social fabric.

The Democratic Challenge, Liberal Politics, and the Quebec Church

The political history of the Church in contemporary Quebec remains to be written. Beyond vague ultramontane theocratic yearnings and aside from the (mis)adventures of their supporters in the political arena (see the saga of the "Catholic program" a document produced by Bishop Bourget and a number of his supporters to ensure the election of candidates faithful to an extreme ultramontanist agenda), once the many collusions and the multiple concessions made between the bishops and the state are related once more, we are struck with how little is known about the exact modes by which the religious dimension was incorporated into the political field.[6]

The advent of modern democracies created a political space that wanted to outclass and sublimate the old modes of identity-grouping that relied on rank, ethnic status, or religion. The public space that democratic power opened gave the citizenry only national boundaries as a horizon. Within this space, other types of allegiance could be expressed in total liberty, on the condition that they in no way threatened the integrity of that political collective, the nation, under the supreme authority of the state institution. In this context, the organic union between the Church and the old monarchies had become virtually impossible. State and religious allegiances cannot intersect exactly in a society that includes a number of religious affiliations insofar as the state cannot adhere to a particular faith without encroaching on the freedom of others.[7] It is not merely that faith has become free. It is that it has ceased to be a criterion for membership in the national collective; moreover, this liberty brings about competition among religions while displacing them in the depth of civil society. Thus, the transition to democracy brings about, in the deepest sense of the term, a profound depoliticization of religion.

Here we see all the ambiguity implicit in ultramontanism, often portrayed as the theocratic will endeavouring to subjugate the state to the interests of the "true religion," despite the fact that the whole possibility for this discourse rests on a liberation of the religious organization from state interference as was the case in former modes of regulation.[8] The renewed strength of the nineteenth-century Church, after all, came out of freeing the Church from the state. If this liberation reverberated only slightly on Canadian soil, it was because, in the religiopolitical context established by the Conquest, the Church had already lost, in fact if not in intention, its privileged connection to royal power. But the bishops, still imbued with Gallican traditions, had difficulty with the post-Conquest liberation of Catholicism, experiencing it less as a new freedom than as an exclusion.[9] The dynamism proper to an institution cast out from the lap of a civil society in full democratic development did not ensue. Even the freedom of action permitted by this marginalization from political power expressed itself only in de facto toleration in a context that made it impossible for the colonial state to do other than to permit it to exist.

This is why in Canada the crucial moment when Church and State parted ways was not aimed at the Catholic Church but at its Anglican equivalent. Wrapped up in the democratic reforms that culminated in England's conceding ministerial responsibility to the Canadian colony, the democratic powers had nothing more pressing than to decree freedom of religion in Canada and did so through a law addressing Anglican Church privilege:

Whereas the recognition of equality in the eyes of the law of all Religious Denominations is the admitted principle of Colonial Legislation and whereas in the state and condition of this province, where it is peculiarly applicable, it is desired that this same should receive the sanction of direct Legislative Assembly recognizing and declaring that the same is the fundamental principle of our civil policy; Be it be declared and enacted … That the free exercise and enjoyment of Religious Profession and Worship, without discrimination or preference, but so as the same be not made as an excuse for acts of licentiousness, or a justification for practices inconsistent with the peace and safety of the Province is by the Constitution and Laws of the Province allowed to all Her Majesty's subjects within the same.[10]

This recognition of the principle of religious freedom would make it impossible hereafter for religious and political spaces to coincide exactly. It would confirm the distinction between political community and religious affiliation, dismissing the latter to the rank of a demonstration of the liberties inscribed within civil society. Of course, once this fundamental principle was recognized, all kinds of useful arrangements remained possible, according to the dynamic appropriate to the various kinds of democratic social formations that had developed in the West. Thus, the strict religious neutrality of the state, even the radical separation of Church and State such as was established in the United States, was but one of the extreme manifestations of this breach. If the area of governmental activity expanded and the responsibilities of the state to regulate in capitalist societies became greater, this did not in any way imply the exclusion of the religious component. Nor is this merely because religion remained at the centre of modern morals.[11] On behalf of this moral religious necessity, the various established faiths had to find a new legitimacy as the guarantor of ethical conditions en route to the future. This is why it is hardly surprising that, in certain cases, religious authorities found themselves entrusted by the state with certain essential responsibilities. Such was the case in Quebec, where the Church succeeded in retaining important public functions, like maintaining the civil registers, let alone exercising a decision-making power in certain areas of public administration, like education and welfare.[12]

But this in no way questions the fundamental character of the breach, as long as the state retained the right to recommit to the areas of public intervention within its jurisdiction, let alone to open new ones.[13] Thus the 1851 law did not ascribe specific powers to the Church. The law was neither reducible to a passive recognition of the already established power of the Churches.[14] It simply sanctioned the fundamental parameters within which the presence of religious beliefs might prevail in Canadian society. From this time forward, a Church, whichever one, could only represent the civil institution that gave organized shape to a particular group of believers.[15] In a democratic context that recognized religious liberty, the issue was not one simply of assuring to every citizen freedom to practice a religion without granting particular privileges to an established religion (or, conversely, constraining it excessively); it also consisted just as much of restoring an institution that structured a given belief to the rank of an association in civil society. The lot reserved for the Catholic Church in the democratic era is thus similar to that which Westfall describes for the Protestant Churches: "The Anglican Church was now a private institution, cut off from its former ally, the colonial state. It continued, however, to define itself in public terms, holding on tenaciously to the dogma that its teachings and practices should play a major role in Canadian society."[16] But integrating the Church into a logical structure of control that restored it to the rank of an institution in civil society had a final fundamental effect. For the first time in Canada, it established a context of free competition among the various confessions.[17] The principle of rivalry among beliefs in the free market of personal conviction opened the door to all manner of proselytizing. The Protestant missionary societies to Lower Canada developed in just this context.[18] This competitive dynamic could only intensify the need on the part of the Church to consolidate its position in the societies of Lower Canada and Quebec. It is hardly accidental that the recognition of freedom of religion as a guiding principle of government in Canada coincided closely with the crystallization of Canadian confessional division. There are, after all, several modes of living out religious freedom in a liberal democratic society. It is possible simply to ensure that the faithful may have optimum conditions in which to exercise their religion freely while providing them the means by which to perpetuate the institution that structures their particular set of beliefs. This is the primary route chosen by the various Protestant sects, which were quick to claim civil incorporation for this purpose.

But the Catholic Church could not be satisfied with this expedient. The scope of its presence in Quebec and Canadian society, its claim to represent the one "true" faith, its desire not just to control the primary dimensions of the moral existence of its flock but to keep an eye on their various modes of social interaction – all these factors meant that, within a system of liberal control, the presence of the Church could extend far beyond that of an organization for the performance of religious rituals. The logic of liberalism left the Church free to work inside civil society and to occupy all the space that free citizens were pleased to allow to it. In this context, it was not merely a matter of insuring that souls were faithful but of securing a willing support and of constructing a wish to live together. Freedom for this Church could also be the occasion for a new social pattern, for a more systematic investment in the area of social relations within civil society. If we wish to understand the basis for the immense power wielded by the Catholic Church in Quebec society and its ability to affect government, we must comprehend this new logic of social and political control of belief at the centre of liberalism. This power could no longer flow from a privileged legal status or a peerage system with the power like that of the Ancien Régime. Hereafter it would rest on the confessional divide that would succeed in fracturing civil society, a divide that would extended all the way to those areas at the heart of civic solidarity, like education and assistance to the poor. The ability of the Church to interfere in these areas depended on this confessional faultline that developed rapidly after 1840. This would not grant the Church any "privilege" in itself but simply constituted the institutional condition that allowed the Church, on terms equal to the Protestants, to operate among a part of the population. The power of the Church would never coincide absolutely with the civil community taken as a whole, though this might make ultramontane partisans of a state religion unhappy.

In fact, the confessional logic, when it led to a specific structuring of civil society, constituted a wholly characteristic contradiction within a mode of liberal control. On the one hand, it resulted from the very dynamic of civil society, which structured itself according to the will of those who composed it. On the other hand, however, this very specific desire to associate with those of like beliefs runs the risk of fixing certain partial "identities" in an unhealthy way, identities attached to race, religion, and language, for example, which the logic of democracy would like to subsume under the identity of citizen.[19]

In this sense, there is nothing more revealing than the debate that took place in the United Canada Legislative Assembly in 1852. In that year, the government of the time proposed a bill that would enable the incorporation of different charitable and educational associations.[20] The motive was simple enough – the Assembly was being submerged in a flood of requests for individual incorporations of this sort of group, requests that had been multiplying since the end of the 1840s.[21] Most of these institutions were formed on a strictly confessional basis. It was this precise point that caused the bill to be attacked ferociously by George Brown, the member from York, who used it to launch a virulent attack against Catholic charitable institutions, which he saw as relics of a bygone era, when religious monopoly had quashed citizen unity. "Upper Canada, it is true, was not covered with institutions to relieve her people from the duties of consanguinity or friendship, and of neighbourhood – thank God that she was not! It is not by the cold, heartless intervention of legal corporations – but by the hand of private benevolence, by the genial warmth of personal kindness in the domestic abode, that distress and poverty ought to be relieved."[22]

The threat that Brown was conjuring up resided in the ability of the old corporate bodies to stifle liberty because of their monopoly. True liberty required breaking with these old allegiances.[23] But, on the other hand, what could be said when the energy properly belonging to civil society was revealing itself in these many associations that were bringing into being the host of projects that were the product of a free citizenry? John Rolph, former participant in the Upper Canada Rebellion and Member of the Legislative Assembly, very quickly spotted the contradiction underlying Brown's speech. If freedom is primary, then the implications cannot be avoided – association is not an obstacle but the favoured vehicle of expression of freedom of action in a liberal society. The result was a declaration that could serve as a charter of freedom of association whether in religious or other matters:

Let there be the same liberty for Christians and their associations as for lawyers and for doctors, for merchants and for painters and their respective associations ... It is the want of generality which is objectionable; the refusing to religious classes the civil rights of the lay people; the assumption that a religious association, because it is such, must not have the full measure of equal civil rights; the attempts, by indirect means, to impose disabilities on such associations and exclude them from legitimate fields of Christian exercise and usefulness; the erection of a Parliamentary standard about religious classes, instead of leaving them to the moral laws of Providence and the judgment of a Christian people ... The less we interfere with those moral laws which have been framed with striking adaptation to the physical condition of man, the better. Even if some religious associations make a headway, in opposition to our wishes and opinions, we are not to legislate them down. If one church, under equal civil and religious rights, attains a pre-eminence over others, the case must be met, not by the arm of power, but by a Christian spirit of emulation in increased and better directed moral efforts to decide the contest ... The most progressive countries are decentralizing, and the less we interfere with these benevolent institutions and leave them free under free laws, the more diffused will be their usefulness.[24]

Two years later, as requests for incorporations by confessional groups were constantly increasing, the legal recognition of this form of religious freedom began to give rise to fear in certain members:

The Honourable Mr Alleyn: Charity should be general and not bounded by sectarian feelings, but, if these gentlemen choose to put their hands into their own pockets and ask an act of incorporation, shall we refuse it? It would be desirable to have general institutions, but we must take people as we find them.

The Honourable Mr Brown: It is not what people ask us, but what we ought to do that is the question. It is on us that the responsibility rests, if we grant improper things! Do we not help directly to excite and keep alive those sectarian feelings by encouraging such institutions, and voting away the public money to sustain them? The moment they get their charter, the promoters of these schemes come to us for a grant out of the public chest ... Where two of three general institutions would be sufficient, by this system we have to support ten or twenty out of the public purse. The evil is increasing year by year, and will be perfectly ruinous before long.

The Honourable Mr Mackenzie: We meet here, Protestants and Catholics, on common ground, we transact business together without ever thinking of asking whether the man we deal with is a Protestant of a Catholic. But the moment a man gets sick, the first question must be, what is his religion, and if he did not happen to have any, what was the religion of his father or his mother ... We have a penitentiary, where the diseased in mind if not in body go. But we do not require a Catholic penitentiary and a Protestant penitentiary. Why, then, should you have sectarian hospitals and other institutions to divide the people into great classes hating each other for the love of God?[25]

This startling and premonitory vision of what might become of the Quebec charitable scene is a good demonstration of how the logic of liberalism constituted the grounds for an increased Church presence in social matters, but this was at the cost of a fundamental diversion of the civil dimension at the centre of that logic. It would be exaggerating only a little to observe that the power acquired by the Church in Quebec society at this point was a real misappropriation of freedom.

Inventing an Alternative Mode of Group Living

Catholic "occupation" of the social field by means of a dense thicket of educational and charitable institutions was certainly not a phenomenon that occurred only in Quebec. It was one of the principal manifestations of the nineteenth-century Catholic "renaissance" in the West.[26] But this investment in the social realm unfolded with a size and a tempo that varied depending on which social formations were involved. What strikes the observer in the case of Quebec is both the depth and the long-lived quality of this investment. Here the Church did not merely establish a remarkable network of institutions; it was successful in furnishing this network with a virtual monopoly on charitable aid, in insuring that the Church would manage it and in reducing governmental involvement in this area to a minimum. A remarkable achievement, especially since it was able to endure despite the growth of the role of the state and well into the twentieth century. This phenomenon that saw the network of social and health services become absolutely identified with particular denominations with minimal state involvement is extremely unusual among the Western nations. It can be put down to two closely interconnected and complementary factors.

First, there was the remarkable weakness of the provincial government arising from the compromises leading to Confederation in 1867. Confederation divided the Canadian social arena in two complementary ways: vertically, by concentrating the principal economic levers at the federal level and by passing the responsibility for social problems, especially justice, education, and social assistance, back to the provinces; horizontally, by cutting up the national space into a number of provincial territories, especially where there were established former colonial borders, at least insofar as the two principal provinces, Ontario and Quebec, were concerned. On the provincial level, the governments established were diminished by their weak powers of taxation and susceptible to the direct influence, even the partial supremacy, of institutions and identity groups that had organized the civil society under their jurisdiction. To put it another way, Confederation provided an extraordinary opportunity for the Church to consolidate its hold on a social arena that had already been cut up along denominational lines, insofar as it had already shown for at least two decades its ability and willingness to occupy this terrain. The Quebec government was only too happy to peddle its responsibilities in matters of social regulation by entrusting the tasks (and a good share of the costs) of welfare, not to speak of education, to the ecclesiastical powers.[27]

It was already clear by the end of the nineteenth century, even to unconditional supporters of private charity, that this exclusive hold the Church had over the field of social assistance was causing problems. One of these problems was the absence of any public institution able to receive "heavy" cases.[28] This was what Francis McLean, the general secretary of the Montreal Charity Organization, was complaining of in 1901:

Subtract the almshouse, subtract any form of public institution or aid for dependants or for defectives excepting the insane and a small fraction of the idiotic, and you have the conditions existing in Montreal ... In other words, neither the city nor province, either by the maintenance of public institutions or by reasonable grants to private institutions, assumes or pretends to assume any responsibility beyond the care of all delinquents, the care of the insane among the defectives and orphaned children among the dependants ... To begin with, the absence from the tax rates of compulsory benevolence has not in any way increased the generosity of the community at large with reference to charities organized into societies or institutions. In Montreal, as elsewhere, the supporters of one society are generally the supporters of a dozen others; and no institution can boast of a genuinely popular support ... The absence of governmental responsibility has even prevented the placing of any effective settlement laws on the statute books of the province. This has added even more to the unjust burdens borne by the city institutions ... Thus the simple absence of governmental responsibility works toward an unjust squandering of private charitable resources.[29]

This diagnosis was confirmed a few years later by Dr Georges Villeneuve, the most prominent psychiatric specialist in the province:

I mean by the term "public assistance" a type of action by which public powers, whether city or state, either directly or through the intervention of appointed or representative bodies, may provide for the relief of human suffering and infirmity in every guise, when accompanied by poverty. In this regard, there is actually no public aid in the Province of Quebec for poor mental patients ... All the other kinds of charity ... were founded and are maintained by religious congregations or philanthropic societies ... As admirable as this religious or private charity may be, it cannot extend to ease human suffering in all its aspects, because its initiatives are primarily addressed to new facilities that are more urgent, like hospitals or more indispensable, like orphanages, or more desirable, like institutions for the deaf and dumb and the blind, etc. The result is that cases that do not fall into these categories remain outside their sphere of activity, or rather, presenting as they do a specific feature or a difficult character, have not received from individual societies a solution which is incumbent on the government.[30]

The powerful resistance the Church offered to governmental gestures in the direction of intervening in social matters could of course seem like the vibrant strains of ultramontanism. But this resistance to the state was couched in terms that the most radical of liberals could not repudiate. Indeed, liberal discourse, which demanded that aid to the poorest be reserved to private initiatives, coincided perfectly with Catholic social projects. Furthermore, the ability of the Church to maintain its "no trespassing" signs around the areas of welfare and education would perpetuate this strict liberal logic in Quebec, deferring necessary reforms until the explosion of the Quiet Revolution.

But this hold the Church had did not depend solely on the weakness of the state. There was another intervening factor: the desire of the ecclesiastical institution to create an alternate identity within the space that was open to civil society, to construct an alternative community as a substitute for citizenship that would overtake and dominate that national Canadian identity that, due to the force of circumstances, French Canadian Catholics had to share with other religious denominations and other ethnic groups. We cannot comprehend why religious institutions occupied the Quebec social arena with such intensity if we do not take into account this appeal to a Catholic identity that at once sought to compete with and transcend the boundaries of political citizenship defined by the nascent Canadian state. This construction of a parallel identity, though it depended on members of religious orders and was soon to be overtaken by the cause of preserving the language at the beginning of the twentieth century, had to be firmly fixed in the concrete forms of social interaction of modern societies. This could only have been accomplished at the cost of an immense effort to duplicate the institutions of that modernity, an effort that became increasingly exhausting and utopian as the twentieth century wore on.[31] The weakness, not to say compliance, of Quebec governments with this development only makes it the more remarkable. It is within this context that we can understand the adoption of the broadest social legislation by the Quebec government before the Quiet Revolution, the Public Assistance Act of 1921, a law that dedicated public funds to charitable institutions but simultaneously perpetuated an ecclesiastical control (and the confessional division it established) over them that would last for another half century.

The control exercised by the Church over the welfare complex would have a series of effects. Despite the multiplicity of the institutions that were founded and the impressive number of nuns and priests involved in the effort, the network, with a significant dependence on charitable donations, would develop very unevenly both regionally and over time and would not be able to respond coherently to every need, as the comments of Villeneuve and McLean (cited earlier) indicate. It was a minimal service, then, claiming to be able to do without the substantial resources of the government for the sake of maintaining the grip of the Church.

It was a heavily institutional system as well, essentially based on facilities that were closed and locked. Indeed, the personnel, essentially members of religious communities, were much more comfortable running establishments that could often also act as their mother houses. The walled institution both witnessed to the enduring quality of the work and permitted a greater control over its inmates in a system of "moral" training that lay always at the heart of the charitable work of the religious orders. Fieldwork, among families, posed quite different challenges.

As a buttress for the institutionally heavy network of closed establishments for the destitute there emerged a more complex kind of activity, closely involved in the community's daily parish life. The social mesh is also strongly revealed at this level, one studied rather less often.[32] In this connection, then, the Montreal Saint Vincent de Paul Society will provide us with a kind of overview of the size and limitations of the Church's presence in the charitable field.

THE MONTREAL SAINT VINCENT DE PAUL SOCIETY

Challenges to the Church's presence in social affairs primarily arose in an urban setting. In Quebec, in the period under study here, it was Montreal that contained the most important population pool. Studying the Saint Vincent de Paul Society (SVDPS) in Montreal also involves a consideration of Church involvement in a field of activity that was family-centred, that is, in aid in the home. We shall first briefly establish the origins of the svdps, then see why it was that the Montreal religious authorities awarded so special a place to a lay charity like the svdps within a Catholic system of aid that was overwhelmingly dominated by the presence of the Church. Finally, we shall explain the consequences of this situation on the development of the svdps and on its members.

The Origins of the svdps

The svdps arose as part of the post-revolutionary renewal movement in French Catholicism.[33] In 1833 a group of young Catholic men, including Frédéric Ozanam, joined with one another to demonstrate the vitality of their faith through charitable work. The first general rule of the Society stipulated that "the Saint Vincent de Paul Society is open to all young Christian men who desire to unite in a communion of prayers and a participation in the same works of charity, in whatever country they may be found."[34] Clearly, the aim of the group was to achieve sanctity through a very specific type of charitable work: visiting the poor in their homes.

Although they hoped to revive pious confraternities and "the charitable observance launched during the Counter Reformation,"[35] the founders were clearly aware that they were dealing with a "new" poor. Indeed, according to Giovanna Procacci, poverty became one of the great public questions in the early nineteenth century and "ended by occupying a real and symbolic place in the general consciousness as representing the chances of the new social order and the obsession with its failure."[36] Indeed, though the svdps was in fact related to the devotional confraternity through the piety that it radiated and through the familiar kind of charity that it carried out, the intervention in the home no longer was characterized in the same way. The visit was less undertaken personally and individually but rather for an organization and within a framework that was much closer to an exchange or an exercise of a social duty: "The most philanthropic citizen ordinarily limits himself to giving when he is asked to give. The men of the Saint Vincent de Paul Society thought of the religious orders, the brothers of charity, and the intimate and gentle way in which they carried out their devotion by entering homes, observing poverty, and looking for the kind of help that would best serve the particular case they had before them."[37]

Another fundamental aspect must be stressed. Although the svdps may have been thinking about the religious orders, it was no less ferociously determined to preserve the lay character of the charitable work in which it was involved. In short, the svdps represented a kind of lay army that the renewed Catholicism of the nineteenth century wanted to call into being to counter both the radical supporters of the Revolution and the liberal philanthropists who were the chief apologists for the emerging bourgeois society. It was an army that was supposed to mark the moment when this Church would finally reach the mass of the poor that had been produced by the new social order. Thus one of its founders, Frédéric Ozanam, called for "going over to the Barbarians."[38]

For a variety of reasons, the svdps took root in Quebec in 1846.[39] In fact, in June 1846 the general council of the group, now well-established in Paris, sent a letter to the ecclesiastical authorities in Quebec and Montreal.[40] The council looked for support from the ecclesiastical authorities while extolling the benefits of this sort of charitable work: "You will observe that we, as a lay Society, desire above all else to remain obedient to the Church, wishing to improve our members through their practical charitable activities, by visiting the poor in their homes and by all the pious works connected thereto."[41]

The message seems to have worked, at least well enough that the Society established itself and expanded in both Montreal and Quebec within the next two years.[42] In fact, the need was considerable, and it appeared that the svdps would win the unanimous support of the Quebec clergy.[43]

The svdps first appeared in Quebec City in 1846.[44] Here, in addition to the support of the ecclesiastical authorities, the Society benefited from the enthusiasm of a former member of one of the Paris conferences, Dr Louis-Joseph Painchaud. As for Montreal, because there was no explicit lay initiative, it was up to the diocesan bishop, Mgr Ignace Bourget, to promote the establishment of the svdps in March 1848 and to encourage its continued growth,[45] though at the same time retaining its character as an organization of laymen.

A Unique Place within Montreal Catholic Charities

The fact that he could not count on the support of a layman, unlike in Quebec City, reveals Mgr Bourget's great determination to found a svdps in Montreal. It was here that he truly earned his reputation as a "pioneer in social affairs."[46] Beyond the question of the survival of French Canadian Catholicism, the profound changes society was undergoing would alter the social order so that, if the increasing needs of the population were to be met, it would be necessary to be closer to it. One way to help this happen was to develop a service of home assistance.[47]

It may seem surprising that Mgr Bourget might turn to a wholly lay charity at a time when various religious communities were actively developing a broad range of charitable institutions or that he came to believe that the SVDPS was called to play a role that was essentially complementary to the complex of charitable institutions established by the religious communities.[48] On the contrary, the bishop encouraged setting up the SVDPS in order to get around the limits imposed on the functioning of the Catholic charity system, in which the operations were almost wholly in the hands of the clergy. Immediately, it was clear that the Society should play a singular and vitally important role within the confessional system and would do so for three reasons: the flexibility of its institutional management, its "reassuring" lay presence, and the broader idea of the family that emanated from its charitable activity.

Institutional Flexibility   From the point of view of the ecclesiastical authorities, the Church was administering a charitable enterprise with a well-defined management; most prominent, as previously noted, were the religious communities (especially women's communities) who ran the majority of the charitable institutions. Moreover, even where the religious communities made home visits, they still remained attached to a particular and distinct institution (a shelter, a hospital, an asylum, and the like).

Thus an association that existed within the parish setting was in a better position to intervene in family life as well as in the other forms of ordinary social interaction that took place in that milieu. Operating from the parish base by means of a primary grouping called the conference,[49] the SVDPS was actually closer to the people. During the period under study, that is, from 1848 to 1921, a conference was established in almost every parish, to the point where at the end of the 1920s close to 2,500 active members were busily at work in 114 conferences.[50] Different levels of organizational structure were only added as needed as conferences were founded. The underlying intention was not to achieve hierarchical control but rather to ensure the best possible coordination in order to produce the most effective charitable work in the home.

The "Reassuring" Lay Presence   Difficulties had arisen as soon as Mgr Bourget asked the Sisters of Providence and the Grey Nuns to undertake domestic visits. Among other things, mixing too intimately with the population, sometimes even with friends and relations, sometimes resulted in a greater likelihood of a sister leaving the order. Moreover, the religious communities performed their visits in a strongly religious way, punctuating them with heavy and pressing moral exhortations. For example, while visiting the poor, the Grey Nuns were supposed to: "urge them to confess regularly and take the sacrament and speak to the parents to make sure that each child has his own bed, since promiscuity is deemed morally unhealthy. Regarding concerns of a moral order, admonitions should be added relative to 'evil speech' and 'harmful companions.'"[51]

This kind of approach would do little to promote a dialogue between poor and rich, the recipient and the alms-giver. It held tight to the old relationship of guardian and ward, in which the nun relayed the moral power of the Church. In contrast, the members of the svdps did not make their domestic visits on the same terms. There was, of course, always an underlying religious dimension, but the visitor tried hard to establish a connection with the visited families based on a commitment of self, endeavouring to counter the isolation and individualism of the poverty-stricken: "In order for alms to become charity, something of the self must be added, of time, trouble, advice, and it is precisely in this way that the member adds a moral value to material aid and thus a social value ... Devotion to others, that is, giving charity, is indeed a duty and a service to society."[52]

While a proper respect for the clergy was maintained, the operation of the Society remained in lay hands in both its organizational structure and in its activity, contrary to its cousin, the devotional confraternity.[53] Despite certain attempts to interfere in the internal operation of the group on the part of religious authorities, the Montreal members, with the support of the Paris General Council, were successful in preserving the original and lay character of the svdps.

The most flagrant case of interference came from Mgr Bourget. It was his task to organize Catholic charity so as to provide a counterweight to the Protestant institutions. At the same time, he was moved to try to reform the way the Montreal svdps was operating. On 25 October 1863, the Bishop of Montreal called a special meeting to this end at his residence, over which he presided. In essence, the bishop expressed the opinion that "Catholics should have a well-organized office to collect all the city's charitable donations and distribute them to the poor in due course."[54] The plan was for the svdps to forward whatever donations they collected to two religious communities, the Grey Nuns and the Sisters of Providence. Better still, the svdps should appoint the Superior of the Saint Sulpice Seminary as its director.

The president of the Particular Council, Raphaël Bellemare, was not slow in consulting the members of the Montreal svdps. The chief stumbling block was remitting the donations to the religious communities. Bellemare respectfully pointed out to the bishop that:

In passing over to the two houses of refuge under the direction of the Sisters of Charity the distribution of alms that the conference has usually themselves given to the poor whom they visit, certainly the poor would lose nothing, but what of the ardour of the visitors?

As you know, the principal aim of the Saint Vincent de Paul Society is the personal sanctification of its members through good works, and the most essential good work, the one on which the founders of the Society and those who direct it today insist most strongly as the condition on which the conferences live or die, is visiting the poor in their homes. It is from this point of view of the distinctive character of our Society that we must take under consideration the plan you have offered us. Do you feel that the members will continue their residential visits to the poor with the same assiduousness and the same charity when all they can offer is moral consolation and the promise of a recommendation for admission to a house of refuge?[55]

At its meeting on 9 November, the highest officials of the Montreal svdps adopted a resolution, the diplomatic wording of which only thinly disguised its firm refusal of Bourget's proposal:

Whereas the Particular Council receives with much gratitude the suggestions of His Excellency, the Bishop of Montreal, to provide more effective aid to the poor of this City, with which he has honoured the Society, as well as the expression of great interest that His Excellency has taken in general in all the works of the Saint Vincent de Paul Society;

Although the conferences do not feel themselves at present in a condition to undertake the fine works recommended by His Excellency, they will not lose sight of this admirable plan that will be preserved in the minutes of the Council and they will consider themselves fortunate if later they have the means to contribute to setting it in motion.[56]

The Bishop heard the message and did not return to the issue. From then on he would observe this firm wish to preserve the fundamentally lay quality of the svdps as integral to its charitable activity. For the rest of the period, his successors would adopt essentially the same attitude, not wishing to harm the operation of so effective a work.[57]

A Flexible Notion of Families in Need of Aid In addition to this great effectiveness, the svdps maintained that, compared to the Church, it had a more flexible conception of what constituted a family in need of help. A family did not simply come down to a French Canadian married couple with baptized children.[58] The svdp s did not hesitate to help a family in which the partners were cohabiting, although it did have a limited tolerance for such a situation, especially when it was not corrected within a reasonable time.

At first glance, the families supported by the svdp s had to satisfy certain material, moral, and religious conditions without necessarily being Catholics. For example, if, after an inquiry, an atheistic or Protestant family was proved to be decent, it might well find itself on the list of those to be helped because: "It is important to repeat and to show through our acts that our Society aids the poor because they are poor and without any conditions or ulterior motives; that it assists them of course with a Christian intention and in the hope of making them more Christian, but it does not demand of any of them in any way a sacrifice of their convictions and certainly not the superficial practice of religion."[59]

In addition, the svdp s accepted subscribers and benefactors who might come from various religious backgrounds. Finally, unlike the religious communities for whom the household visit was to be accomplished quickly while avoiding "hanging about the houses or talking about trifling matters in order to preserve a certain air of reverence,"[60] the visitor from the svdp s was supposed to take whatever time was necessary to develop a long-term relationship with each member of the family.

A BELATED AND TRUNCATED DEVELOPMENT

The Church was well aware that, in order to be closer to the population, it was most appropriate to call up a lay charity whose organizational structure made it a more effective means of providing aid to the homes of a large number of families. For its part, the Montreal svdp s understood that there were limits it must not breach. Although the members had been able to preserve the original lay character of the Montreal svdp s, the close control exercised by the religious communities and the bishop over the network of charitable institutions meant that the involvement of the svdp s in areas other than domestic visits would be very tentative.

Child Protection

The best example of this situation is in the area of child protection.[61] Shortly after the birth of the svdp s in Paris, it undertook a guardian service for children, specifically for schoolchildren and apprentices. In the first instance, this involved an approach that completed the family visit with the Vincentian making an attempt to either improve or procure a moral and religious education for children of the age of First Communion. As for apprentices, the aim was to place these children in apprenticeships in order to develop them into workers imbued with moral and Christian virtues. The Montreal svdps in both these instances ignored the directives of the General Council for several decades. Only in the 1880s did concern begin to develop.

From the very beginnings of the Society in Montreal, as a result of family visits and sometimes at the family's request, members had identified and supported certain children who were no longer attending school or who were on the verge of dropping out. They supplied money and material assistance, but they also arranged requests for entrance into various schools. From the earliest days of this work, the Paris General Council had tried to get the Montreal Particular Council to provide a more defined framework for this informal aid to schoolchildren. At last, in the Montreal Council's annual report for 1881 to the Superior Council of Canada, Raphaël Bellemare, the president, wrote: "Up until now, we have believed that our city, being exceptionally well endowed with established Catholic schools in every centre that, thanks to the generosity of the Sulpician Fathers, are open to poor and rich alike, had less need than elsewhere for such a service to youth. Upon consultation, however, and having asked the opinion of the Superior of the Seminary, it is admitted that this work could be extremely useful, and I hope that during this coming year it will be organized on a regular basis."[62]

It was only after they had received an official endorsement from the ecclesiastical authorities that the Council decided to forge ahead. In 1883, the Particular Council resolved that the conferences would henceforth designate certain of their members: "and entrust them with the special duty of searching out children in their areas who were abandoned or neglected by their parents. They are to report to the assembly and when they have found a number of these little ones, take steps to procure their admission into the nearest schools and provide them with what they need to attend."[63] It is noteworthy that the first concern of the French svdps regarding pupils, namely moral and religious education, is absent here.

Some ten years later, the scenario remained much the same when it came to establishing a facility for apprentices and orphans[64] between the ages of fourteen and eighteen: the patronage of the svdps. Once again, although the General Council in Paris wanted such a service to be established rapidly in Montreal, it would not be until 1892, that is, more than forty years after the svdps was founded in the region, that those orders would finally be carried out. As well – since initiating the service was the task of the chaplain of one of the conferences, another Sulpician priest, Onésime

Hébert – it appears that the wishes of the General Council still required the agreement of religious personnel if they were to be realized.

What is more, the internal authority and the moral and spiritual direction of the Patronage was under the jurisdiction of another religious order, this time the Brothers of Saint Gabriel. The svdps did, however, administer what were called its "temporal" affairs through a special management committee.[65] We should also point out the cooperation of benefactresses, who primarily saw to the orphans' clothing, and of the Sulpician Seminary, which provided the necessary buildings. The finances came for the most part from fees paid by boarders. At the beginning, harmony reigned. Respecting the aims of the General Council, the apprentices spent the major part of their time at work.[66]

After a few months, the enterprise was so successful that it had to move, entailing a higher level of indebtedness, which became even more a problem as a number of apprentices paid no fees at all. Moreover, the Brothers of Saint Gabriel seemed to be having more and more difficulty dealing with lay persons in authority. In 1895, after some negotiation,[67] using as a pretext recent money troubles,[68] the Sulpician Seminary succeeded in excluding members of the svdps from directorial positions in favour of the Brothers of Saint Gabriel. At the very most, the svdps would retain connections to the facility through an oversight committee and occasional financial support.

If it were to confine its energies strictly to household visits, the Society nevertheless was often party to negotiations regarding the opening of one or another institution. In this way, it served as an important liaison between the bishop, the religious communities, and the local community.[69] It also acted as an important intercessor between the population and the charitable institutions.[70]

The Inescapable Home Visit

The presence of a weighty network of charitable institutions that were under the close control of the religious communities and overseen by the bishop was a context that severely limited the initiatives open to the svdps. Beyond its occasional role as local intermediary, it would concentrate its work on its initial activities – that is, the home visits – strengthening the central presence of laymen on the local level if not at that of institutional charity taken as a whole.

In the first place, we must remember, visiting the poor was obligatory for all active Vincentians, whether or not they were conference officers or members of the highest leadership circle: "Visiting the poor must remain the basis of our Society everywhere, in the sense that as long as there is someone poor or ill to see, a home visit must be made."[71] Aside from some periods of adjustment, the Montreal members appeared to respect this incontrovertible principle.[72]

But, beyond respect for a principle, we have also to remember the two objectives that underlay all SVdP activity, the desire for personal salvation and aid to the poor. Thus, in Montreal, the missionary ambitions of members regarding visits to the poor were never of first importance. Here again, if members attended to their own salvation, they would discharge a large part of their spiritual obligation to the poor and take care of the moral and spiritual dimension of the visit: "As for the spiritual needs of the poor, we have the consolation of knowing that the clergy and the charitable sisters can be much more effective in that regard than can we. Nevertheless, our conferences do not neglect this duty when the occasion arises and requires it."[73] Still, the domestic visits of the SVdP seem to have been based on the same wish to adapt to the new challenges presented by urban poverty and the same desire to establish genuine dialogue with the poor, in accordance to the rules laid down.

The families on the list of those to be visited and helped had first to be to accepted. This required a process that began with a recommendation by members of the Society or the clergy but also might come from the family itself or its friends and relations. Most of the time, the recommendation was brought directly to the conference. Then came in all cases a strict evaluation of the needs of the family.[74]

The investigative visit allowed a check to see if the family fulfilled certain material, moral, or religious conditions. It is interesting to note that the SVdP placed more importance on worthiness than on being Catholic. These careful investigations had been undertaken in Montreal from the earliest days of the SVdP. An inquiry report, usually presented orally during a conference meeting, provided the basis for discussion concerning whether or not the family would be taken on. When approved, the family would be assigned two visitors, chosen specifically for the ability to establish real communication during their weekly visits, which would also provide the opportunity to win confidence and respect. At the end of the day, according to Alain Faure, "this extreme attention to the poor that was dictated by the evangelical culture and the faith of these men permitted them ... to see certain qualities and certain working-class behaviours that escaped the notice of most other observers."[75]

In the specific case of the Montreal SVdP, since it was difficult for laymen to take an active role in the development of charitable institutions, they could devote an enormous amount of energy to the home visit as much of their duty to moralize was taken over by religious personnel. The ability to detect the "real needs"[76] of families was amplified enormously. If they were able to secure adequate material aid for families, the members of the Society found themselves in a position to play the role of trusted intermediaries between the families and the numerous charitable institutions.

CONCLUSION

Modern poverty demanded new responses to the challenges it posed. In urban working-class districts especially, want and destitution bore witness to the continuing uncertainties of life. It was here that the modern presence of the Church in the world would become developed. In certain countries, this presence would extend to the control of the essential elements of the system overseeing poverty. Such was eminently the case in Quebec. Here we have a fascinating area in which to observe a particularly successful way that institutional religion involved itself in the social fabric. Of course, this involvement depended on an interconnected complex of institutional shelters able to serve as a resource and a last resort for poor families. But the parish, basic unit of a Catholic social interaction that was under construction, was *also* a site where mutual aid and, ultimately, philanthropy could express themselves. The Saint Vincent de Paul Society was, in this sense, the particular embodiment of a dynamic of aid that, through charity, strengthened the social bond that could serve as an alternative to the democratic solidarity that was increasingly being expressed through the intervention of the state.

NOTES

1 "I feel that the past has fallen, that the bases of the old edifice have been weakened and that a terrible jolt has changed the face of the earth. But what must emerge from these ruins?" Frédéric Ozanam, *Lettres de F. Ozanam* (Paris: Bloud et Gay, 1860): 1, 33–4.

2 Nathan Irvin Huggins, *Protestants against Poverty: Boston's Charities 1870–1900* (Westport, CT: Greenwood, 1971): 51.

3 "We refuse to approach the history of religion in the 19th century by means of the notions, however common, of secularization and institutional renewal. Far from seeing survivals or stirrings, that is, a few new twigs that succeed in sprouting on an old, apparently dried-out trunk, but one which nevertheless continues to occupy the landscape and occasionally produce the odd shoot, we wish to try to view the new

religious economy according to its own features." Michel Despland, *Les hiérarchies sont ébranlées. Politiques et théologies au XIXᵉ siècle* (Montrea: Fides, 1998): 17.

4 Denis Pelletier, "Les pratiques charitables française entre 'histoire sociale' et 'histoire religieuse.' Essai d'historiographie critique," Isabelle Bueltzingsloewen and Denis Pelletier, *La charité en pratique. Chrétiens français et allemands sur le terrain social: XIXᵉ-XXᵉ siècles* (Strasbourg: Presses universitaires de Strasbourg, 1999): 37.

5 "The Christian initiatives that began in community form at the beginning of the 19th century were informed by resolutely new principles that resided in the displacement of a society of rank by a bourgeois society and used the new possibilities offered by the development of social structures," Jochen-Christoph Kaiser, "Le rôle du facteur religieux dans le travail social aux XIXᵉ et XXᵉ siècles en Allemagne. Bilan de la recherche," Bueltzingsloewen and Pelletier, 26.

6 Even the important question of the relationship between the Church and the law does not seem to have interested either jurists or historians for more than half a century. See, however, two fascinating case studies: Lise Rodrigue, "L'exemption fiscale des communautés religieuses," *Les Cahiers de droit*, 37, 4 (December 1996): 1109–40, and Dominique Gobay and Claire O'Neill, "L'adoption, l'Église et l'État: les origines tumultueuses d'une institution légale," Renée Joyal, ed. *Entre surveillance et compassion: l'évolution de la protection de l'enfance au Québec, des origines à nos jours* (Sainte-Foy: PUQ, 2000): 97–130.

7 "Even if some are unconvinced by the arguments for freedom, and look either backward or forward to a day when men shall be organised in society on a basis of religious unity, it must be plain that we do not live in such an age; that there is nothing to be gained by pretending that we do; that whatever unity of opinion may underlie or come to underlie any probable polity, it will not be that body of doctrine we know as the Catholic Creeds … All we can claim, all we can hope for, is freedom for ourselves as one society among many," John Neville Figgis, *Churches in the Modern State* (London: Longmans Green, 1913): 119–20.

8 Roberto Perin has observed the deeper meaning of ultramontane discourse relevant to the state: "Ultramontanism was used to advance the church's claim of autonomy from the provincial state. Instead of reading this discourse literally as a bid for theocratic control, historians should see it as an argument in favour of a French-Canadian public space free from the influence of political parties." Roberto Perin, "Elaborating a Public Culture: The Catholic Church in Nineteenth-Century Quebec," in Marguerite van Die, ed., *Religion and Public Life in Historical and Comparative Perspective* (Toronto: University of Toronto Press, 2001): 92.

9 See the old debate on this issue between Marcel Trudel, "La servitude de l'Église catholique du Canada français sous le régime anglais," *La société historique du Canada*, 1963–64, 42–62, and Hilda Neatby, "Servitude de l'Église catholique: A Reconsideration," *Canadian Catholic Historical Association. Study Sessions*, 36 (1969): 9–26.

10 "An Act to Repeal so much of the Act of the Parliament of Great Britain passed in the 31st year of the Reign of King George III, c. 31, as relates to Rectories and to the Presentation of Incumbents of the same and for other Purposes connected with such Rectories," 14–15 Vict. (1851), c. 175. That this freedom implied a principal separation between Church and State was confirmed three years later in the preamble to the law that abolished the Anglican Clergy Reserves. "And whereas it is desirable to remove all semblance of a union between Church and the State and to effect a certain and final disposition of all matters, claims and interests arising out of the Clergy Reserves by so speedy a distribution of their proceeds as may be" ("An Act to make better provision for the appropriation of moneys arising from the Lands heretofore known as Clergy Reserves by rendering them available for Municipal purposes"), 18 Vict. (1854) c. 2, art. 3.

11 "Despotism may govern without faith, but liberty cannot. Religion is much more necessary in the republic which they set forth in glowing colors than in the monarchy which they attack; it is more needed in democratic republics than in any others. How is it possible that society should escape destruction if the moral tie is not strengthened in proportion as the political tie is relaxed? And what can be done with a people who are their own masters if they are not submissive to the Deity?" Alexis de Toqueville, *Democracy in America*, chapter 17, trans. Henry Reeve, 1839.

12 Lalonde states that "if a rigorous idea of the principle of separation of church and state and of the freedom and equality of religion is adopted, then it is appropriate to wonder whether these principles in Quebec do not entail so many exceptions that they hardly deserve their being called 'the fundamental principle of our civil policy,' as did one legislator in 1852," Marc Lalonde, "Les relations juridiques Église-État au Québec," Marcel Rioux, ed., *L'Église et le Québec* (Montreal: Éditions du Jour, 1961): 99–100.

13 This was the process that was abruptly at work during the Quiet Revolution of the 1960s.

14 This is Ferretti's hypothesis, who briefly mentions that this law contained nothing "to frighten the Catholic episcopacy, who understood the difference between organizational freedom for religions and a regime that separated Church and State. The 1851 act established nothing of the sort." Lucia Ferretti, *Brève histoire de l'Église catholique au Québec* (Montreal: Boréal, 1999): 83. Beyond the fact that the freedom instituted by the 1851 law was not in itself "organizational," it sanctioned an autonomous sphere for the Church about which it would not only have difficulty taking fright but which would also constitute the very condition for its future power. The history of the developing presence of the Church as an *institution* in the political realm continues to be restricted by a perspective that is exclusively centred on the fate of this institution. It is a perspective that prevents a systematic interrogation of the actual logic of the political area established by the democratic

transformation. So true is this that the question of the political status of the Church and of religious liberties after 1840 is seldom posed in religious historiography. Thus, the principal summary of the history of the Church in Quebec – Philippe Sylvain and Nive Voisine, *Histoire du catholicisme québécois. Vol 2: Réveil et consolidation (1840–1898)* (Montreal: Boréal, 1991) – makes no mention of the law of 1851.

15 Giroux has analysed the legal implications of the 1851 law: the Churches became voluntary associations enjoying independence from the state in the eyes of the law within a framework of public law. Georges-Michel Giroux, "La situation juridique de l'Église catholique dans la province de Québec," *Revue du Notariat* 48 (1945–46): 139–41.

16 William Westfall, "Constructing Public Religions at Private Sites: The Anglican Church in the Shadow of Disestablishment," in van Die, 24. This historian poses in remarkably succinct fashion the fundamental question underlying this essay: "How do you construct a public religion at a private site?"

17 This competitive principle was far from insignificant. It constituted yet another fundamental aspect of the new presence of the religious factor in democratic societies, a presence that, now freed from politics, became subjected to being tested in the marketplace of religions. "The different sects would all be placed on the same level in their competition with one another ... The relative standing and respectability of the different Churches would thus depend – not upon extrinsic or adventitious circumstances – but solely upon their comparative worth and usefulness, ascertained by public opinion – unfettered by prejudice – uninfluenced by political party." *Montreal Society for the Attainment of Religious Liberty and Equality in British North America*, 1837, 27–8.

18 See especially Dominique Vogt-Raguy, "Québec, terre de mission. Le début du prosélytisme protestant francophone (1834–1840)," *Études canadiennes*, 21, 1 (1986): 115–25.

19 This "competition of identities" at stake in nineteenth-century democracies is not a Quebec specificity. It took on particularly important dimensions in countries that were being settled by large numbers of immigrants, where ethnic, linguistic, or religious affiliations provided islands of protection for fragile immigrant populations. This was the case especially in the United States. See, for example, Mike Davis, "Why the United States Working Class Is Different," *New Left Review*, 123 (1980): 3–44.

20 A Bill to provide for the Incorporation of Societies formed for Charitable and Educational Purposes. *Journals of the Legislative Assembly of Canada*, 1852–53.

21 More than thirty-five charitable and religious associations had made such requests since 1840, fourteen of them since 1849. See Jean-Marie Fecteau, "État et associationnisme au 19ᵉ siècle québécoise. Éléments pour une problématique des rapports

État/société dans la transition au capitalisme." in Alan Greer and Ian Radforth, eds., *Colonial Leviathan: State Formation in Mid-Nineteenth-Century Canada* (Toronto: University of Toronto Press, 1992): 134–62.

22 *Debates of the Legislative Assembly of United Canada*, 9 (1852–53), 1723.

23 We see once more this Rousseauian critique of guilds and monopolies in the revolutionary measures passed against them at the end of the eighteenth century (the Le Chapelier law). See Jean-Marie Fecteau, "Le pouvoir du nombre: l'idée d'association et la transition à la démocratie au Québec au 19ᵉ siècle," Association française des historiens des idées politiques, *L'État, la Révolution française et l'Italie*, (Aix-en-Provence: Presses de l'Université d'Aix-Marseille, 1990): 91–107.

24 *Debates of the Legislative Assembly of United Canada*, 1476. Not everyone, of course, shared the enthusiasm of the ex-rebel. The legal recognition implied by incorporation could not be extended indiscriminately, as the Conservative member Sicotte pointed out: "The Mormons might have their Holy Temple, the Fourierists their phalansteries, just as the Turks may have their mosques. There is a great difference between tolerating the sects and giving them a legal existence by recognizing them as institutions. Society cannot go against facts in legislating on such matters, but it should anticipate eventualities and not sanction in advance every possible belief by means of a legislative measure that is too general" (ibid., 1985).

25 *Debates of the Legislative Assembly of United Canada*, 12 (1854–55), 3191.

26 The phenomenon has been well documented for France. For Germany, see the excellent collection edited by Isabelle Bueltzingsloewen, *La charité en pratique*.

27 This radical retreat is even perceptible on the municipal level, normally the favoured area for public action in matters of aid in the West in the nineteenth century; see Jacques-Guy Petit and Yannick Marec, eds, *Le social dans la ville en France et en Europe, 1750–1914* (Paris: Les éditions de l'Atelier, 1996). The role played by the cities in the area of welfare was remarkably slight in Quebec, even up until the beginning of the twentieth century. See Jean-Marie Fecteau, "Un cas de force majeure: le développement des mesures d'assistance publique à Montréal au tournant du siècle," *Lien social et Politiques/RIAC*, 33 (Spring 1995): 105–12.

28 It must be understood that despite liberals' long list of criticisms complaining about the involvement of government throughout the entire nineteenth century, most Western nations had given the most serious cases of poverty and dependency over to the state – the social budgets of the German Länder, public assistance in France, and the Poor Laws in England and the United States (not to speak of the important share of social services dispensed by the municipalities) in fact formed a backdrop of public financing against which private assistance, often directed toward cases that were easier or cheaper in terms of personnel or the capital required, might be deployed.

29 Francis H. McLean, "Effects Upon Private Charity of the Absence of All Public Relief," *Transactions of the 28th National Conference of Charities and Corrections*, 28 (1901): 140–1.

30 Georges Villeneuve, "Les lacunes de l'assistance publique dans la province de Québec." *Union médicale du Canada*, 33 (1904): 425.

31 In this sense, the social doctrine arising out of *Rerum Novarum* (1891) appeared as though it were a systematic presentation of the ultramontane appeal to the "perfect" society of the Church – the social wing of the Church was constructed out of it.

32 See, however, the pioneering work by Lucia Ferretti, *Entre voisins. La paroissiale en milieu urbain: Saint-Pierre-Apôtre de Montréal, 1848–1940* (Montreal: Boréal, 1992).

33 Locally, the Saint Vincent de Paul Society has been studied but surprisingly, after almost 175 years of international activity, a global history has yet to be published.

34 *Manuel de la Société de Saint-Vincent-de-Paul.* (Paris: Angers et Frère, 1937; twenty-first edition): 42.

35 Bruno Dumons, "De l'œuvre charitable à l'institution d'assistance: la société de Saint-Vincent-de-Paul en France sous la Troisième République," *Revue d'histoire ecclésiastique*, 93, 1–2 (January-June 1998): 50.

36 Giovanna Procacci, *Gouverner misère, La question sociale en France. 1789–1848.* (Paris: Seuil, 1993): 13.

37 Speech given by the Sulpician Fr Lemire on the 75th anniversary of the first Montreal conference. Undated letter. Archives of the Saint Vincent de Paul Society of Montreal (ASVPSM), file "Causeries, conférences, sermons sur la Société de Saint-Vincent-de-Paul," 4 May 1924 to 17 February 1957, P63/16.

38 "To go over to the Barbarians, that is to go from the king's side, the government's side in 1815, to go to the people. And when I speak of going over to the barbarians, I am asking that we do the same, that we concern ourselves with those people who have too many wants and not enough rights, who rightly demand to have a more complete share in public affairs, and guarantees of work and against poverty, who have bad leaders for want of finding good ones, and who cannot be held responsible for the History of the Girondins, which they have not read, nor for the banquets they have not eaten. We may not be able to convert Attila and Gaiseric, but with God's help, we may run out of Huns and Vandals." Ozanam to Foisset, February 1848, quoted in Jean-Baptiste Duroselle, *Les débuts du catholicisme social, 1822–1870* (Paris: Presses universitaires de France, 1951): 296.

39 At that time, there were thousands of members in many countries such as Austria, Belgium, England, France, Ireland, Mexico, Scotland, and the United States.

40 The same letter was sent to the Toronto diocese. For the SVDPS in Toronto, see Brian P. Clarke, "Poverty and Piety: The Saint Vincent de Paul Society's Mission to Irish Catholics in Toronto, 1850–1890," in *Canadian Protestant and Catholic Missions,*

1820s–1960s: Historical Essays in Honour of John Webster Grant, John S. Moir and C.T. McIntire, eds (New York: Peter Lang, 1988): 75–102.

41 Letter from Jules Gossin, general president of the svdps, co-signed by Adolphe Baudon, vice secretary-general, June 1846, Archives of the Council-General of the Saint Vincent de Paul Society (Paris), correspondence file 789, 150, 2 and 3.

42 The Society set up in Toronto in 1850.

43 In his history of the Society, Robert Rumilly notes that the charity "through its service to the poor, realized the sacred union of Catholics." *Le plus riche aumône. Histoire de la Société de Saint Vincent-de-Paul au Canada* (Montreal: Éditions de l'Arbre, 1946): 91.

44 One theory suggests that there was an informal svdps in Quebec in 1844.

45 At the first general assembly of the Montreal council in December 1848, the svdps had 381 active members, i.e., those who made home visits. On the eve of Mgr Bourget's retirement in 1876, there were 1037 members.

46 Huguette Lapointe-Roy, "L'engagement social de Mgr Ignace Bourget," *Bulletin de la Société canadienne d'histoire de l'Église catholique* 51 (1984): 52.

47 In the early 1840s, Mgr Bourget had hoped to see a growth of this sort of charitable work. The Sisters of Providence and the Grey Nuns, among others, were called upon to work in the southern and northern parts of the city in, respectively, 1843 and 1846.

48 Huguette Lapointe-Roy views the arrival of the svdps in this manner. See *Histoire sociale de Montréal, 1831–1871: l'assistance aux pauvres*. PhD thesis (history), Université Laval, 1985, 89.

49 Even though, over the years, other types emerged, like juvenile conferences in the schools, the parish conference remained the most important.

50 There were 104 French Canadian conferences, nine Irish, and one Italian. For a more detailed analysis, see Éric Vaillancourt, *La société de Saint-Vincent-de-Paul de Montréal: Reflet du dynamisme du laïcat catholique en matière d'assistance aux pauvres (1848–1933)*, PhD Thesis (history), Université du Québec à Montréal, 2005.

51 Huguette Lapointe-Roy, *Charité bien ordonnée. Le premier réseau de lutte contre la pauvreté à Montreal au 19e siècle* (Montreal: Boréal, 1987): 238.

52 From a speech given by the president of the Particular Council of Le Havre in April 1910, "La Société, type de l'œuvre sociale," *Bulletin de la Société de Saint-Vincent-de-Paul* 62, no. 739 (July 1910): 94.

53 See Brigitte Caulier, *Les confréries de dévotion à Montréal du 17e au 19e siècle*. PhD thesis (history), Université de Montreal, 1986, 586.

54 ASVPSM, minutes of the special meeting of 25 October 1863 of the Particular Council, 22 February 1863 to 3 November 1877, 30 (P61/1).

55 Ibid., 31 (P61/1).

56 ASVPSM, minutes of the special meeting of 9 November 1863 of the Particular
Council, 22 February 1863 to 3 November 1877, 29–32 (P61/1).

57 The case of the SVdPS allows us to qualify the long-dominant historiographic
scenario depicting French Canadian lay Catholics from 1830 until the Quiet
Revolution, indeed even until today, as appearing to be those who just carried out
the will of the clergy. See Pierre Hurtubise et al., *Le laïc dans l'Église canadienne-
française de 1830 à nos jours* (Montreal: Fidès, 1972), and, more recently, Guy
Lagacé, *La gestion participative dans l'Église locale de Rimouski. L'inconfort des
laïcs dans le processus décisionne*, PhD thesis (theology), Université de Montreal,
1998. This distorted view is found elsewhere: "In Quebec, a highly religious and
predominantly Catholic society, it was the priest who represented the full flowering
of humanity, and who was, therefore, a leading part of the authoritative mixture.
Generally speaking, the clergy received the ultimate honour of being deferred to and
obeyed. For the rest of the population, the lesser degrees of honour of good
reputation were accorded in proportion as the individual embodied the religious
virtues most perfectly represented by the priest; just as in a militaristic society a man
is honoured for displaying the virtues of a soldier [...] A man's good name in a
religious society depends ultimately on the judgment of the religious authority,"
Ranier Knopf, "Quebec's 'Holy War' as 'Regime' Politics: Reflections on the
Guibord Case," *Revue canadienne de science politique* 12, 2 (June 1979): 324.

58 English Catholics, the majority of them Irish, must not be forgotten.

59 "De la visite des pauvres," *Bulletin de la Société de Saint-Vincent-de-Paul*, 11, 121
(January 1859): 7.

60 Lapointe-Roy, *Charité bien ordonnée*, 239–40.

61 For a more extensive treatment of the question, see Éric Vaillancourt. "L'enfant et le
réseau charitable catholique montrealaise: le cas de la Société de Saint-Vincent-
de-Paul, 1848–1930," *Le temps de l'histoire*, 5 (September 2003): 173–89.

62 ASVPSM, minutes of the monthly meeting of the Particular Council of 13 February
1882, 8 December 1877 to 13 December 1885, 177–89 (P 61/3).

63 ASVPSM, minutes of the General Assembly of the Particular Council, 11 February
1883, 8 December 1877 to 13 December 1885, 328–45 (P 61/3).

64 We should point out that 20 percent of these boys were not orphans but simply the
sons of poor families. For a more extensive examination, see Stéphane Divay, *Le
Patronage Saint-Vincent-de-Paul de Montreal, 1892–1913*, MA thesis (history),
Université d'Angers, 1999.

65 It is worth pointing out that the work with apprentices in Paris was likewise a similar collaboration, this time between the SVdPS and the Christian Brothers.

66 The training program was supplemented with classes in hygiene and religion.

67 Briefly, it was a matter of entrusting the internal administration to the Grey Nuns.

68 The Vincentians had meanwhile succeeded in clearing up the finances.

69 The SVDPS also was an essential liaison during the negotiations that preceded the opening of the first Quebec reform schools. See Jean-Marie Fecteau, Sylvie Ménard, Véronique Strimelle and Jean Trépanier, "Une politique de l'enfance délinquante et en danger: la mise en place des écoles de réforme et d'industrie au Québec (1840–73)," *Crime, Histoire et Société*, 2, 1 (1988): 75–110.

70 The minutes of the meeting of 6 December 1908 of the Notre Dame conference is especially forthcoming on this subject. Thanks to the members' involvement, a mother and her two children were taken in by the Grey Nuns. A girl was placed in the Incurables Hospital, and another in the Saint Joseph Hospice; while one boy was sent to the Montreal Reform School, two others went to the Saint Vincent de Paul Patronage, and two more to the Saint Arsène Orphanage. ASVPSM, 29 April 1900 to 3 March 1912, 2 (P6 4/28).

71 "Conférences sans pauvres à visiter," *Bulletin de la Société de Saint-Vincent-de-Paul*, 64, 760 (April 1912): 99.

72 The Society considered that it was generally respected to the ratio of one family visit per active member. For example, for the Notre Dame conference from 1880s to the 1920s, there was an average of twenty-two active members for twenty families visited.

73 ASVPSM, minutes of the monthly meeting of the Particular Council of 13 February 1882, 8 December 1877 to 13 December 1885, 177–89 (P 61/3).

74 In this regard, the SVDPS earned the praise of Protestant supporters of "scientific charity": "Upon the Catholic side the world-wide traditions of the St. Vincent de Paul society have effectually prevented its degenerating along the line of officialism even under the pressure of local conditions. The steady, sure methods of personal visitation before relief, of ability to order relief at any time, of secrecy so far as the applications are concerned, excepting at the conference meetings, are followed in Montreal, as elsewhere." (McLean, 143–4).

75 Alain Faure, "L'intelligence des pauvres," *Démocratie et pauvreté. Du quatrième ordre au quart monde*. (Paris: Quart Monde/Albin Michel, 1991): 224.

76 Procacci, 232.

7

Factories and Foreigners: Church Life in Working-Class Neighbourhoods in Hamilton and Montreal, 1890–1930

MICHAEL GAUVREAU

Just before Christmas 1896, the Board of Trustees of Montreal's Point St Charles Congregational Church, located in an expanding neighbourhood near the Grand Trunk Railway shops, was rocked by conflict. A church with a predominantly working-class membership, Point St Charles's lay management comprised nine members, three of whom were middle class (a lawyer, a manager of a paper warehouse, and a miller) and six from the working class (a driver, a steamfitter, two storemen, a railway fireman, and a general weighman, the latter four all employed by the Grand Trunk Railway). One board member, Mr Cushing, the middle-class founder of the church and a prominent lawyer who resided "above the hill"[1] on the prosperous McGill College Street, called a full meeting to take up the matter of a letter that he had written to his fellow trustee, J.C. Richardson, a Grand Trunk storeman who doubled as director of the Gymnasium Institute attached to the church, "protesting against the boxing class (so called) in the room at the rear of the Congregational House" and implicitly accusing him of misleading church members as to the nature of the athletic exercises carried on there. At Cushing's insistence, the board passed a resolution, by a vote of five to three,[2] withdrawing permission for classes in boxing and single stick, "in view of the conscientious objection of members and adherents of the Church." Significantly, those voting to banish boxing from the church precincts included all the middle-class members of the board, while defenders of the sport were all working class. While the motion exonerated Richardson and the institute members from the charge of misleading the board, the gymnasium director immediately took the floor and resigned, charging that the proceedings amounted to a vote of censure "and also, that, indirectly, he was accused of acting in an underhanded way," as some members of the board claimed that "he did not mention boxing when he asked for the room."[3]

However, Richardson did not go quietly. His resignation was a signal for a general protest by most of the working-class members of the board. Mr Downie, a Grand Trunk fireman, joined the disgraced athletic director, resigning because Richardson had, in his view, been unfairly pilloried since he had clearly stated the purpose of his request for the room. Seeing the direction of events, Mr Symons, the church secretary, a Grand Trunk general weighman who, as chair of the meeting, had not voted, attempted to avert further controversy by proposing that the matter lie over until the next meeting, but he found no seconder, whereupon he, too, threw in his lot with the pro-boxing faction, declining to act any further and effectively resigning his position on the board. In a vain attempt to salvage the unity of the board, Cushing and his allies attempted to rescind their own motion regarding the use of the institute room, but they were pre-empted by the resignation of Mr Carmichael, a skilled steamfitter holding the key position of envelope steward, who staunchly backed Richardson. There the meeting adjourned, although it can be assumed that during the ensuing week, there was much acrimonious discussion among board members and the congregation over the place of athletics and boxing in the life of the church. By 26 December, the board had found a face-saving compromise, essentially allowing boxing to continue in the gymnasium but removing the institute from direct management by the congregation's board of trustees, essentially according it the status of an independent voluntary association affiliated with the church. By the end of January 1897, harmony appeared to have been restored within the board itself, with both Carmichael and Richardson resuming their positions as trustees.[4]

What meaning should we attach to this dispute within the Point St Charles congregation over the relationship between evangelical Christianity and "rough" male sports like boxing? Was the occupational divisions within the Board of Trustees another signal that churches and religious institutions had become focal points in a hardening of class lines, a process similar to what was occurring in the 1880s in the Protestant churches of smaller industrial towns of Ontario? There, religious institutions had apparently become sites of class conflict, as the churches increasingly reflected the cultural norms and practices of their middle-class leaders. This social "hegemony," based upon new, class-based definitions of what constituted a proper Christian, aroused the antagonism and "alienation" of working-class men and women whose religious practices and expectations clashed with the dominant middle-class norms of church attendance and "respectable" conduct. Workers, according to this account, were subtly but powerfully discouraged from involvement in churches and increasingly opted for religious indifference, or were drawn to populist, sectarian forms of Christianity that split from mainstream Protestantism, or joined labour organizations or secular voluntary associations, some of which articulated "counter-discourses" of Christianity that critiqued the apparent materialism and hypocrisy of the conventional middle-class dominated church institutions.[5]

However accurate this description may have been of the religious life in late-nineteenth-century small towns, it did not exactly mirror the social relations characteristic of Point St Charles Congregational Church during the first two decades of the twentieth century. Far from signalling greater class polarization, middle-class social hegemony, or working-class alienation, the boxing controversy remained an isolated incident because the compromise hammered out in 1897, in which boxing was permitted on church premises but managed by a voluntary association distinct from the Board of Trustees, in fact firmly indicated a growing pattern of control by working-class elements over the institutional life of the congregation. Far from non-involvement in the church, hostility to its message, or a bleeding away into sectarian religion, working-class Congregationalists of Point St Charles evinced a strong identification both with the liberal evangelical style of this church and its associated voluntary organizations and clubs. Although Mr Cushing, the prominent lawyer, continued to be honoured as a financial benefactor of the congregation, and in 1906 arranged for a loan of $7,500 to enable the Board of Trustees to acquire a new site to build a larger church at the corner of Hibernia and Wellington Streets, by 1902 he had been shunted aside from the active management of the congregation, no longer a member of the Board of Trustees.[6] Indeed, two-thirds of the members of this Congregational Church were drawn from the ranks of the working class,[7] and, of the slate of trustees elected for 1902, 57 percent were drawn from the ranks of skilled workers, while in 1895, only 50 percent of the trustees had been workers.[8] In addition, the workers of Point St Charles were actively asserting their office-holding presence in church-based voluntary associations and clubs. Indeed, the impulse for belonging to organizations may have been particularly well developed in this Montreal neighbourhood, where railway employees were particularly numerous. These workers formed one of the most highly unionized segments of the Canadian working class at the turn of the century, and their commitment to institutions may well have acted as a more general social imperative to active engagement in an associational life that centred on local church congregations. It seems that, in this particular urban environment, labour unions and religious organizations were not considered mutually exclusive alternatives but rather reinforced one another, contributing to a particularly vibrant working-class culture characterized not by a tendency towards withdrawal, privacy, and consolation but oriented towards public activity and traversed by particularly rich seams of religious associational networks that put a premium on accessibility.[9]

Evidence of working-class religious self-management in churches like Point St Charles Congregational adds an element of greater complexity to the way in which religion and class intersected in Canada's industrial revolution. Churches located in preponderantly working-class neighbourhoods of large urban centres like Montreal, Hamilton, Toronto, and Winnipeg, and whose congregations and voluntary organizations relied heavily on this social group for their leadership and support, cannot be easily fitted into a one-dimensional oppositional paradigm that defines the still-dominant trajectory in the social history of religion, equating the church institution with the middle classes and ascribing "alienation" to the working classes.[10] The central premise of this paper is that such churches, with their relatively homogenous congregations, were specific to Canada's early-twentieth-century industrial centres and differed markedly in leadership, organizational structure, and religious style from those socially diverse congregations dominated by middle-class elements that were typical of Ontario small towns minutely examined by Lynne Marks. Central to their working-class character was not only an inclusive, enthusiastic "evangelical" religious style and outward-looking missionary imperative but also a panoply of associated voluntary organizations and clubs that aggressively sought to expand the religious identity of their members beyond mere church attendance.

Two churches have been selected for this study: Barton Street Methodist Church, in the burgeoning industrial east end of Hamilton, and the aforementioned Point St Charles Congregational, near the sprawling Grand Trunk railway shops of Montreal. These working-class churches were a particular feature of an early-twentieth-century modernizing imperative among Canada's Protestant denominations, whose middle-class leaders sought to forge a broader notion of Christianity by redefining "evangelism" in order to reach diverse social constituencies through specialized religious messages, more centralized and "efficient" church machinery, and rationalized methods of management.[11] While this might be read as simply more effective middle-class control over the religious expression of Canadian workers, denominational centralization contained a key paradox: it effectively opened a space where, through increased financial assistance from central church bodies, ordinary working-class Protestants could in fact establish self-governing congregations whose daily management was in the hands of working-class people and responsive to their particular religious imperatives. In this sense, the "modern" church machinery typical of a period of capitalist expansion and consolidation enabled the people of the new working-class neighbourhoods of early-twentieth-century Canadian cities the opportunity to reinvigorate and reassert an older idea of "ecclesiastical republicanism,"[12] a kind of religious democratic localism typical of the plebeian evangelical Protestantism characteristic of an earlier stage of industrialism in late-eighteenth-century Britain.

RETHINKING THE CONVENTIONAL DICHOTOMY OF MIDDLE-CLASS CHURCHES/ALIENATED WORKERS

Since the early 1960s, a considerable body of historical writing has developed around the relationship between religion and the industrial working classes. The main, but often unstated, assumption that guides this historiography is a teleology of social and cultural change that dictates that "religion" and "working class" either are or are destined to become quite distinct, if not mutually hostile, historical entities. In any given society, while workers may, particularly in the early stages of industrialization, evince considerable religious belief and commitment, such values and practices are considered "traditional,"[13] and in the mature stage of industrialism the typical working-class response is one of a radical disconnection or alienation from religion, characterized either by indifference or a politicized, aggressively secularist hostility. The main trajectory that developed from this central underlying premise was concerned to measure the ways in which the linked processes of urbanization and the emergence of class distinctions either accelerated or retarded secularization in various national and local settings. Such historical treatments usually took the form of attempting to evaluate the nature and level of religious commitment, beliefs, and institutions among working-class people, pointing to the conclusion that, sometime between 1850 and 1900, religious belief and religious organizations entered into an irreversible decline, a central causal element being the inability of the churches to forge viable connections with the industrial working classes.

K.S. Inglis's classic *The Churches and the Working Classes in Victorian England*, published in 1963, stands as the historiographical fountainhead of the dichotomy. His study, strongly influenced by the impress of the "orthodox" theory of secularization that asserted a causal link between urbanization, modernization, the class differentiation attendant upon industrialization, and religious decline,[14] advanced an interpretation that established working-class alienation from the churches as an underlying given of the social and cultural life of nineteenth-century cities. Two key elements were compelling about Inglis's account: first, the statement that popular absence from worship – non-attendance at church – was an "inherited custom" among the British working classes that predated the nineteenth century; second, the overt link that he asserted between the urban environment and the absence of religious belief.[15] Thus, the massive efforts on the part of Victorian churches to reach working-class people, both through discursive strategies and organizational initiatives, could be written off as simply predestined to fail, as the urban environment, containing people uprooted from other settings, and its pattern of class-segregated neighbourhoods from the outset fostered an unpropitious climate for religious activism. As well, the cultural values and social practices of working-class people themselves imposed an innate barrier to religious involvement. Thus, not surprisingly, working-class people by and large remained beyond the purview of religion, and that indifference to the churches "was normal, moral and political hostility to them was common." Of equal significance, it was Inglis who most overtly asserted, as historical truism, that the churches were, by and large, middle-class institutions; in relation to religion, working people are "other"; and religion is a system of middle-class values and practices that holds little resonance for the experience of working-class people, whose only authentic response to religion is a consistent alienation. Thus, those workers who did participate in religious institutions could be largely written off as those "who were prepared to adapt themselves to middle-class ways"[16] – a euphemism for class traitors. Inglis's interpretation was influential because it posited the relationship between church institutions and working people in terms of an irrevocable class polarization; in terms of historical method, it elevated working-class church attendance as the principal gauge of popular religious values and practices, a direction that influenced the social history of religion for the better part of three decades.

During the 1960s, his work was buttressed by that of British Marxist historians like E.J. Hobsbawm and E.P. Thompson, whose concern was to elucidate the origins of British radicalism. Both Hobsbawm and Thompson in fact devoted considerable attention to popular religion in their historical writing and contended that religious ideologies and movements had, in some instances, articulated a set of oppositional languages and identities for plebeian Britons that influenced some of the radical movements in the early stages of the industrial revolution.[17] However, their argument rested upon the assumption that such movements were characterized by what Hobsbawm termed "the marks of archaism"[18] – the notion that religion was a characteristic of "traditional" communities destined to disappear under the blows of modernization. According to Callum Brown, their assumption was that working-class religiosity was a temporary phenomenon of the period 1770–1830, an aberration from the master dynamic of the exclusion of working people from the churches, or a total schism between a churched minority of skilled workers and the unchurched "authentic" majority of working-class people.[19] In Thompson's case, the quintessential forms of "popular" religion were the sectarian, the prophetic, and the heterodox; those, like Methodism, that stood closer to "mainstream" forms of Protestantism, while certainly appealing to working-class people, were judged to be part of a machinery of repression and political stabilization, crafted by designing social elites, which in many cases hampered the effectiveness of working-class political protest. Indeed, it was Thompson who first articulated the historiographical paradigm that churches and religious institutions functioned as "compensatory" mechanisms providing a refuge for those working-class people whose hopes for political action had been crushed.[20] The concerns of Thompson and Hobsbawm did have a wider impact on studies of working-class religion, contributing to ongoing attempts by historians to posit a relationship, either positive or negative, between the religious values of working-class people and the emergence of class-conscious forms of action.

Given the close links asserted between the emergence of the working class and the rise of secularization, it was not surprising that, since 1980, as revisionist interpretations began to question both the chronology and nature of the "orthodox" model of secularization, there would be new approaches to the study of working-class religion. Summarizing the standard view, the British historian Hugh McLeod indicated that the postulate of working-class alienation from religion involved three interrelated assumptions: the failure of churches to meet working-class religious needs; a focus on working-class living conditions and culture that might have limited workers' involvement in religious institutions; and the declining religious commitment of workers was related to growing class-consciousness and political organization.[21] Although McLeod largely accepted the Thompsonian view that periods of intense class conflict were marked by widespread alienation from the established churches and by the growth of sectarianism and/or secularism, he also argued that the central pillars of the "alienation" thesis suffered from excessive rigidity and that the extent of religious disaffection varied widely not only in national contexts but even between localities,[22] thereby reducing the universal validity of simply equating "working class" and "religious alienation." Indeed, as Callum Brown has recently observed, while most writing on the social history of religion has concluded that the key differentiating factor in church attendance was class, it should also be remembered that in Britain the working classes comprised the majority of churchgoers in every denomination from 1800 to the 1960s, with church involvement especially characteristic of skilled artisans and tradesmen.[23]

What decisively altered the direction of historical debate was the erosion of the ineluctable link between the movement of people into large urban centres and working-class religious disaffection. The main critique was formulated by Callum Brown, who argued that the presumed irreligion of the urban lower classes was, first and foremost, a construct of middle-class clergy and intellectuals who, in the late eighteenth century, sought to galvanize churches into greater missionary action. Indeed, in Brown's estimation, particularly in Britain, there was no radical discontinuity in the period 1780–1880 between the religion of the countryside and the religion of the city: the social and cultural pluralism of urban environments and, indeed, the emergence of conflictual class relations itself afforded greater religious vitality and for all classes and more, not fewer, opportunities for religious adherence and participation.[24] Building on the work of Jeffrey Cox, Brown urged historians to shift the chronology of religious decline forward, away from the emergence of industrial class society in the 1840s and 1850s to the turn of the twentieth century, giving greater weight to a more complex dynamic of organizational change within a religious culture experiencing a "crisis of voluntarism" rather than simply class polarization.[25]

The result of this new historiographic direction has been to shift the focus away from "alienation" to emphasize the ways in which working-class people participated in religious culture, ranging from formal, active church membership, to occasional attendance, to participation in "rites of passage" like baptism, marriage, and death rituals, to engagement in networks of church-centred voluntary associations and clubs. Encapsulating the newer direction of international historiography, Lucien Hölscher has observed of the religious situation in Germany, a society that contained a far more aggressively anti-religious socialist movement than did Britain or North America, that only a small minority of 10-20 percent of workers "was so estranged from the church that it took no part at all in church life, and also no longer kept up any of the familiar traditions of private piety."[26] In a recent synthetic treatment of secularization in the industrial societies of Western Europe, Hugh McLeod suggests that, while historians must acknowledge the fact of overall decline in church attendance, the great majority of the population attended Sunday school or catechism classes as children, claimed at least a nominal church membership as adults, married in church, and had their children baptized and, "above all, the moral influence of the churches remained great."[27] A new starting point for research should be Mark Smith's dictum that historians have placed too large an emphasis on the people who did not participate in the activities of organized religion and that the challenge is to study those who did enter into the culture and practices of the churches.[28]

Here, the key revisionist element has been a methodological one: shifting historical attention away from formal church attendance and membership as the primary tests of the religiosity of working people. In a key study of late-nineteenth- and early-twentieth-century religious life in West Yorkshire, S.J.D. Green bluntly stated that "[r]eligious commitment – total, partial, negligible – was not a function of social class" and that age profile and gender were more influential variables in determining an individual's level of religious adherence.[29] One does not have to go as far as Callum Brown, in arguing that statistics on church attendance and membership were elements of a middle-class discourse that served to exclude much of what constituted working-class religiosity by privileging the measurable, the rational, and the formal,[30] to realize that there existed a much broader terrain of religious "participation" among the industrial working classes. As Hugh McLeod suggested, it is important to consider that non-churchgoing working-class people were not less religious than middle-class churchgoers but were religious in different ways. While many remained uncommitted to church institutions, they were not wholly secular, and many would have claimed that they were more religious than those who displayed the more conventional attributes of piety.[31]

It can be argued that, given the revisionist tendencies of the social history of religion over the past two decades, it is difficult to sustain the older dichotomy of "middle-class church"/"alienated workers" that rested on the twinned assumptions that there was a direct causal link between industrialization and urbanization and the decline in churchgoing. As Hugh McLeod has recently reminded historians, taking formal participation as the key index of devotion or alienation contains many pitfalls, as these cannot measure actual levels of belief or ways in which people actually expressed their religious identities,[32] particularly in light of new findings that the discursive, the private, and the extra-institutional were more characteristic of working-class religion than the more overt, formal church involvement. From being the central actors in the great drama of religious decline, the working people of the industrializing societies of Western Europe and North America now occupy a far more complicated and ambivalent role. A second major contribution of the revisionist social history of religion, with its more "culturalist" turn, has been to undermine the "compensatory" hypothesis advanced by the radical labour history of the 1960s: that involvement of working-class people in religion was synonymous with the disappointments of political activism. Working-class religion might better be understood not in relation to radical politics but according to its own cultural structure and logic, as a primarily *religious* phenomenon.

However, one difficulty of emphasizing these cultural characteristics of popular religion in isolation from formal institutions is the implicit assumption that they are more "authentically" working-class practices than participation in church institutions. Indeed, to focus too exclusively on these characteristics perpetuates, under another guise, the view that, in terms of institutional religion, working-class people were marginal or alienated "others." These characteristics are particularly problematic when applied to North American urban industrial settings, where it cannot simply be assumed as a given that church congregations functioned like those in Britain, where most religious institutions and associations were structures provided *for* the working classes but managed by urban religious elites, rather than self-managing bodies operated and led *by* working-class people in reference to and expressive *of* their own religious needs.[33] And this caveat applies not only to those more "populist," sectarian brands of Protestant Christianity like the Salvation Army, which several generations of Canadian historians have elevated as an authentic working-class religious movement, but to more mainstream churches that evolved congregational machinery that expressed working-class religious priorities.[34] In such church congregations, formal institutional involvement cannot be assumed *a priori* to reflect middle-class social leadership or emulation of middle-class religious norms. Added to this, the discursive realm that constituted the religious experience of many working-class people was not a disembodied, merely private culture: sermons, publications, and religious tracts were produced by particular religious organizations that, in terms of the late nineteenth and early twentieth centuries, were the most widely accessible and non-exclusivist in the urban life of the period[35] and were understood by men and women who, in the vast majority, at some point in their life cycle experienced some active involvement or connection with specific religious institutions. The central assumption that guides this paper is the need to establish a continuous connection between the way in which people experienced the discursive and the way in which they lived their religious lives within the context of churches and associated religious societies and organizations, in order to give proper historical weight to the elements of the private and the civic that formed working-class religious life in the turn-of-the-century Canadian city.

CREATING AND SUSTAINING WORKING-CLASS CONGREGATIONS

One of the new departures in late-nineteenth-century religious life and organization in Canada was the effort by Protestant mainstream denominations to respond to the social and spatial segregation of life in the industrial city by providing churches in new working-class neighbourhoods. Smaller towns, such as those examined by Lynne Marks, would usually contain only one congregation of each denomination, and such churches heterogeneously mixed middle-class and working-class people, most frequently under the leadership of middle-class elites. However, in larger urban centres like Hamilton and Montreal, multiple congregations of each denomination allowed for the emergence of a different type of social relations within the institutional framework of religion, as a degree of neighbourhood specialization and greater class homogeneity within the local church in fact offered greater opportunities for working-class self-management and congregational leadership. Despite the relative poverty of these working-class Protestants, the new churches, because they belonged to more centralized religious bodies, could frequently depend upon the support of outside funds until they became self-sustaining congregations. This interface between the institutional churches and the working classes, including the existence of a wider space for working-class religious initiative that emerged in Canadian cities between 1890 and 1910, runs counter to what is the conventional wisdom about the relationship between religion and social class in this period.

In both British and Canadian historical writing, the dominant tendency has been to cast organized Protestantism as experiencing a social and cultural "crisis" because of its overall inability to cope with the conditions of city life and with the emergence of an industrial working class at the end of the nineteenth century. One of the most influential interpretations was advanced almost thirty years ago by Stephen Yeo, who argued that, in the years after 1890, the Victorian culture of voluntarism that had informed the churches experienced a crisis and decline due to changes in urban capitalist organization. As small, family firms whose identity was local and whose owners led and sustained a rich associational life were increasingly reorganized into larger, more bureaucratized corporations, middle-class people withdrew from the localist, voluntary enterprise, whose institutions had sought to include working-class people, throwing church organizations into disarray, driving the classes further apart, thus creating the preconditions for the emergence of a mass-based political socialism and an activist state in the areas of welfare and cultural provision.[36] For social historians of religion in Canada, there has been a tendency to place mainstream Protestantism and the working classes in a dynamic of progressive mutual incomprehension and estrangement. In the still-dominant historical orthodoxy, the churches after 1880 were by and large expressions of middle-class interests and increasingly run like business corporations; consequently, they failed to reach out to working-class people. Because of this organizational failure, the Canadian working classes, historians maintain, were drawn increasingly towards cultural "separateness": if not attracted to secular socialist alternatives or towards religious apathy, working people were drawn to enthusiastic, premillenial breakaway religious sects that noisily proclaimed hostility to the corporatist rationality – read spiritual barrenness – of modern ecclesiastical organization.[37]

One of the central difficulties with this line of interpretation is the assumption that, in the religious sphere, the emergence of new, managerial capitalist forms of organization was indicative of religious crisis and decline. An influential strand of interpretation holds that, by the early twentieth century, mainstream denominations appeared to devalue older forms of localism, associational life, and "traditional," more enthusiastic religious practices, replacing them with rather anodyne forms of religious identity empty of spiritual vitality and with a fixation on orderly forms of worship and behaviour. The latter were products of and served the cultural imperatives of middle-class elites,[38] driving working-class people away, thus rendering the churches less inclusive and weakening their social authority. However, the easy equation of middle-class church and working-class alienation is challenged by the fact that much of the energy evinced by these mainstream Protestant working-class churches depended upon an extremely active panoply of voluntary societies and clubs attached to urban churches. This accords well with the observation made by Bryan Palmer concerning working-class culture in early-twentieth-century Hamilton. There, in his estimation, the institutional churches displayed considerable vitality and enjoyed a good deal of social prestige because of their ability to integrate British workers into the town's social structure,[39] something that could not have been accomplished without cultural and institutional strategies that directly addressed and expressed the religious needs of working people. Within the major Protestant denominations, the early twentieth century did witness a centralization of power in the national church offices and a growing emphasis upon efficiency, business methods, and rationality, but they continued to seek, through a variety of organizations and practices, to accommodate working-class religious priorities. Thus, the centralization and bureaucratization of Canadian Protestantism was but one side of a coin, the other being the revitalization of "popular" and enthusiastic forms of spirituality, familiar to and desired by working-class people,[40] and, of equal importance, institutions like voluntary societies and clubs. The new working-class churches, financed, organized, and led by working-class Protestants, provided the institutional framework in which ordinary people could give voice to and manage their own social and cultural priorities. Here was a more complex religious reality, one that defies the conventional descriptions of withdrawal or splintering, the expression of a culture in which power was becoming at once *more* centralized and uniform and *more* diffuse and locally diverse.

Most typically, working-class congregations originated as "missions" or Sunday schools, founded by middle-class members of older, more financially viable and better-established churches who felt a continuing responsibility for less affluent co-religionists living in new industrial suburbs like the vicinity of the Grand Trunk railway yards in Montreal, or Hamilton's rapidly growing industrial east and north ends.[41] There is a tendency among British historians in particular to denigrate these "mission" churches as part of a middle-class strategy of social exclusivism, segregating those of a different class who might have been tempted to worship in the same space as the dominant urban groups.[42] However, this ignores two key considerations affecting church attendance by both working people and the middle classes: first, the desire for proximity and accessibility of religious facilities, particularly given the fact that the late-nineteenth-century city was still a walking city; second, the fact that, although middle-class people might have wanted to maintain "mission" churches in a kind of client status, the missionaries who served these churches had their own ambitions, ultimately desiring that their congregations become independent.[43] Thus, from the perspective of a working-class religious clientele, the building of a new church in the neighbourhood would not have been seen as synonymous with class exclusivism but as a positive convenience and, in many cases, an opportunity to exercise some initiative and control over church management and voluntary organizations. In this context, it should be noted that older, established congregations, while seemingly heterogeneous, more diverse, and less "exclusive" in their class composition, often containing substantial numbers of working-class members, presented relatively few opportunities for direct working-class management or leadership, as most church offices tended to fall into the hands of middle-class men.[44]

Point St Charles Congregational, for example, began in 1891 as a Sunday school founded by Charles Cushing, a member of Calvary Congregational Church, whom we have already encountered as the wealthy middle-class antagonist of the church boxing club. Point St Charles, located across the Lachine Canal from central Montreal, grew up in the 1870s and 1880s around the Grand Trunk Railway shops and was settled by primarily English and Scottish skilled workers.[45] By 1895, reflecting the relatively stable employment provided by the railway, the members were able to become a self-sustaining church, initially funded by pew rents, and were able to acquire, as a permanent home, the old St Matthew's Presbyterian Church, parts of which were rented to the Council of Arts and Manufactures, providing an additional source of income for the fledgling congregation.[46] In a similar manner, Barton St Methodist traced its beginnings to the efforts of Wesley Church, located in Hamilton's downtown, which in 1889 established a Sabbath school in Barton St Public School, with thirty-five scholars and seven teachers. As the neighbourhood's population expanded, the schoolroom became overcrowded; a lot was purchased and a building erected to house the "Star Mission." However, unlike Point St Charles Congregational, Barton St Methodist was from the first "conducted on the voluntary plan, no charge being permitted for anything,"[47] a choice that reflected not only a desire to make the church accessible to working-class people but the sense among the church's promoters that the local congregation could, in fact, depend upon the support of a prosperous national denomination. Symbolizing the importance of this development to the Methodist presence in Hamilton, the celebrated revivalist Rev. H.T. Crossley conducted the opening services at the mission. In 1894, the Methodist Conference appointed a regular pastor, launching the congregation "on the Ecclesiastical Sea" as Barton St Methodist Church.[48] For the first two decades of its existence, the church was staffed by a series of energetic ministers, all of them graduates of Victoria College; one Rev. Sanford Marshall who was at Barton from 1896 to 1904, even had a degree from Yale University.[49]

Between the mid-1890s and the First World War, the growth of both churches was extremely rapid, that of Barton St Methodist being particularly impressive. In this respect, the decision to locate the church near the corner of Barton and Sanford Streets was especially prescient, as major metallurgical industries began to locate in the East End, shifting Hamilton's economic axis. Significantly, Barton Methodist was in close proximity to Canadian Westinghouse, one of the city's leading firms, which in 1913 employed 3,250 men, a number that had increased to 4,500 in 1929.[50] For example, in 1901, just before a significant period of growth, the church reported 220 members, and, scarcely five years later, membership had more than doubled to 445. In the ensuing decade, especially under the pastorate of Rev. H.G. Livingstone, total numbers grew to 803 in 1911, and topped one thousand by May 1914, prompting plans for a new church building at the corner of Barton and Sanford Streets. It was only in 1916, during the upheavals caused by the First World War, that Barton St Methodist reported an actual decrease in membership. The church membership rebounded to 1112 in 1921 and thereafter stabilized, and the construction of a new church was finally begun during the early 1920s at the corner of Stirton and Huron, named after Rev. Livingstone in recognition of his leadership in building the congregation.[51] The growth rates at Point St Charles Congregational, although somewhat less impressive, were certainly steady, particularly under the pastorate of Rev. A.W. Main, who served the congregation from 1906 until his death in 1914. In 1905, the church reported 239 members, an increase of seventy-nine over the previous year, prompting the decision to build a new church on a new site at the corner of Hibernia and Wellington Streets, costing $25,000 with a seating capacity of eight hundred. By 1907, there were 271 church members; that total had grown to 426 by 1912.[52]

While it is possible to chart the bare numerical totals of growth through the annual statements reported by the management bodies of both churches, what does this reveal about the social composition of these two churches? Nominal membership lists are extremely sketchy, and, lacking access to the manuscript census beyond 1901, it is impossible to offer a sustained statistical analysis. In the case of Barton St Methodist, circuit registers do not survive beyond 1901,[53] and, for Point St Charles Congregational, the only way in which a list of members can be reconstructed is from a 1909 list of signatories approving the sale of the old church property prior to the construction of a larger church on a new site.[54] Despite these limitations, it is possible to establish the solidly working-class character of both congregations. At Barton St, 220 names in the 1901 circuit register were identified; of these, fifty-seven were men, 163 women. The names of forty-six male members of the congregation were then located in the 1901 census, from an analysis of occupations, it appears that the social composition of the congregation was 14.5 percent middle class and 82.6 percent working class, the latter category broken down into 47.8 percent skilled, 23.9 percent semi-skilled, and 10.9 percent unskilled.[55] More significantly, the lay management of the church remained predominantly working class into the 1920s. From a 1922–23 list of sixty-eight men who held offices in Barton St Methodist, forty-six were identified in the Hamilton City Directory. Of these, 39.1 percent were middle class, and 60.9 percent working class, with a strong core of skilled workers (45.6 percent) still active in church management. Of the middle-class total, 21.7 percent were commercial, again, largely men in clerical occupations.[56] At Point St Charles Congregational, 205 members signed the deed of sale in 1909; of these, ninety-two were men, and 113 women. Seventy-nine of ninety-two men were located in the Montreal City Directory: 32.9 percent held middle-class occupations, 67.2 percent were working class, broken down into 41.8 percent skilled, 8.9 percent semi-skilled, and 16.5 percent unskilled.

Two major differences between the social composition of these two churches call for some further analysis. First, in terms of male/female composition, Barton St Methodist in 1901 displayed a very high gender inflection, as only 25.9 percent of its membership was male, 74.1 percent female. Point St Charles Congregational, on the other hand, was characterized by greater gender balance, 44.8 percent of members being male, 55.2 percent being female. Second, for a working-class church, Point St Charles had a much higher proportion of middle-class members. This apparent anomaly was due to the fact that most of those listed as "middle class" fell under the rubric "commercial," 26.6 percent of the total membership, and 80.7 percent of the total middle-class category. The vast majority of these men were clerks or bookkeepers, confirming Lloyd Reynold's observation that skilled workers tended to direct their offspring into white-collar occupations, rather than having them follow as apprentices in their skilled trades.[57] Bearing this in mind, it can be safely affirmed that most of the "middle-class" members of Point St Charles Congregational had strong family links to the dominant working-class elements in the church.

On the numerical preponderance of women in the congregation, neither of these two congregations was unusual, as historians, in studying religion in a variety of local settings in both North America and Europe, have consistently demonstrated that women were always more likely to display "formal" adherence to the church.[58] According to Hugh McLeod, a number of general factors also affected the gender balance of churches. First, sectarian religions, rather than "established" churches, were characterized by a more even male/female ratio, as both sexes made lifelong commitments to the church. Second, the gender gap was more evident among the working class, as there was greater emphasis on family unity in religion and leisure activities in middle-class homes. A third variable was how "clericalized" a religious denomination happened to be: among Anglicans and Roman Catholics in particular, male membership tended to be markedly lower because the more dominant position of the clergy provoked a corresponding anticlericalism. Finally, those denominations that most sharply separated male and female roles had a marked preponderance of women in their congregations.[59]

Point St Charles Congregational, with its relatively strong element of male members, seems to most closely fit McLeod's model of a denomination in which there was a balance of power between clergy and laity in terms of congregational decision-making. Barton St Methodist's significant divergence from the British "sectarian" pattern, in which Methodists and Congregationalists had a roughly similar gender balance, can be explained by a number of social factors more particular to Hamilton and Canada. First, reflecting the far-reaching restructuring of the metal industries during the period after 1890 so well described by Craig Heron,[60] employment for working-class men in East End Hamilton, even for skilled workers, was far less stable than in Point St Charles, which was dominated by the railway trades, a factor that certainly would have affected an individual's decision whether or not to formally join a church. Second, in viewing itself as a "national" denomination and not a sectarian church, Methodism in Canada differed significantly from its British counterpart: compared to the Congregationalist church polity, in which power was highly localized and zealously guarded by the laity, Canadian Methodism at the turn of the century had a highly centralized church polity dominated by a professional clergy, a structure that might well have appeared "clericalized" and thus less congenial to working-class men. It should be remembered, however, that these statistics were taken from a relatively early period of Barton St Methodist's existence, *before* its dynamic period of growth, and there is no way of accurately assessing whether this extremely pronounced male/female imbalance continued to characterize the social composition of the church over the next two decades.

However, the exhaustive statistical analysis of the social composition of these two congregations does not illuminate questions of more vital moment to exploring the intersection of religious institutions and working-class life. Here, we need to adopt the more "culturalist" turn promoted by the more revisionist social history of religion and be specially attentive to the fact that much of the religious life of working people occurred outside formal indices of church membership. The questions thus become: how did working-class people perceive organizations connected to the church as relevant to their lives, and how did local church leaders adapt religious practices to cultivate a working-class clientele? For instance, if the underlying impulse in working-class life was towards withdrawal and separation from organizations dominated by the middle classes, why did these workers in Point St Charles and Hamilton's East End choose to adhere to large, well-established, mainstream Protestant denominations? Why not instead seek a stronger affirmation of religious control and independence in one of the "sectarian," more enthusiastic varieties of Protestantism, whose aggressive evangelism frequently struck a more populist, democratic, and accessible note? And what particular advantages did workers derive from their participation in the more standardized institutions of Canadian Protestantism? Did church societies and voluntary organizations reflect the special priorities of working-class neighbourhoods in which they were established? Did these organizations simply provide the means by which workers could emulate, and thus integrate into, a culture of order defined according to the norms of middle-class church leaders, or did these mainstream congregations successfully preserve and even enhance certain populist emphases that would have clearly resonated with working-class religious beliefs? Finally, historians need to understand that the process of creating and sustaining working-class congregations was not fixed or frozen in time. At what point and for what reasons can historians adduce an alteration in the social dynamic that produced the extremely energetic growth of working-class churches?

To put the matter bluntly, one of the major reasons for working-class people to adhere to a congregation belonging to a major national denomination was the sheer cost of building a church and sustaining a congregation financially. As observed by S.J.D. Green concerning religious life in late-nineteenth-century British towns, most new churches built during this period had high levels of debt, which was often far beyond the resources of the local congregation itself to initially incur, thus necessitating the support of wealthier congregations of the same denomination or of supra-local church bodies, at least in the early stages of congregational life.[61] For example, in 1895, when the Quarterly Board of Barton St Methodist discussed the possibility of rebuilding and expanding the original Star Mission, "it was thought best before going any further to ask permission of the Wesley Qut. Board and should it meet their approval to cooperate with us financially to carry out this scheme."[62] In a similar manner, when the workers of Point St Charles decided, in 1906, to acquire a larger property and expand the church, not only were they able to count upon Mr Cushing, the original middle-class benefactor, for a loan enabling them to acquire the land but they were also able "to lay our claims for a new church before the members of the Montreal Council of Congregational Churches which was done and received approval by them as a body they in turn suggested that each Congregational Church be asked to appoint a delegate to act as advisory committee with us."[63] The implication here was that, although this might have appeared to limit local management and authority, consultation with other churches would bring the advantage of financial assistance towards the cost of building the new, larger church. A similar procedure was adopted by Barton St Methodist, which in 1904 recommended inviting representatives of the official boards of the various Methodist churches in Hamilton "that they might lend us their sympathy & council us in bringing about satisfactory preliminary arrangements looking towards the better accommodation for the largely increased population of this End of the City."[64] In this case, dependence upon a centralized denomination enabled this Methodist congregation to purchase four city lots for $2,715.00 at 5 percent and to undertake the building of a new church costing $30,000.[65]

Another factor driving this dependence on central church bodies was a wider tendency apparent among all religious denominations in the early twentieth century to abandon pew rents, one of the most reliable sources of church income during the nineteenth century, and to move entirely to voluntary self-assessment. The shift away from pew rents was, at one level, ostensibly because church leaders had come to regard these in rather negative terms, as creating a social hierarchy within the church space that appeared to marginalize poorer people. As we have seen, Barton St Methodist very aggressively reflected this new priority, as it was explicitly established on the voluntary plan, while Point St Charles had pew rents at its inception in the early 1890s. By 1906 it had moved entirely to a system of envelopes and voluntary contributions.[66] However, the loss of the pew rent meant greater financial uncertainty, particularly during a period of intense denominational expansion and competition for resources, a situation compounded by the more unstable employment typical of working-class experience. For example, at Point St Charles Congregational in 1906, out of 205 church members, only sixty-one, or 29.7 percent, gave through the envelope system, while as late as 1922 at Barton St Methodist, out of more than 1,100 members, only 255 people, or 22.9 percent gave "fairly regularly" through the envelope system, with more than one hundred never using them at all.[67]

This entailed further consequences for the way in which church leaders came to regard participation. One key consideration that drove the new emphasis in the Canadian churches on "inclusivity" was the organizational pressure for a reliable source of financing from the widest number of people possible. There was a heightened emphasis upon creating a welter of voluntary organizations, each adopting a variety of expedients to collect money, a theme to which we will return, and an emphasis by clergy and lay church leaders upon a discourse of democratic, more intense church involvement. At Barton St Methodist, with a larger and rapidly growing population base, the rhetoric of financial contribution was more muted. However, church leaders there clearly felt the financial uncertainty caused by the economic depression of 1913 and sent letters to all church members urging them to contribute to the weekly envelopes. As well, during straitened times, the Official Board at Barton St adopted the expedient of seeking to drastically restrict outside benevolent organizations from using the church precincts to appeal for funds,[68] which would have further reduced the pool of money available for local church purposes.

With a smaller congregation and the decision to incur the major debt of a massive new church, the link between money and regular church membership was far more overt at Point St Charles. Significantly, just at the juncture when discussions concerning relocating and expanding the church had reached a critical point, the managers of this Congregational church suddenly gave voice to a concern regarding church attendance. "Our services on Sunday during the past year have been very well attended, notably the evening service," they observed, "but the attendance at the morning service could be improved very much ... if some members out of each family would only endeavour during the current year and attend regularly every Sunday morning what an inspiration it would foster in all to see the empty pews in the minority."[69] Although the popularity of the evening service versus the morning service was a well-established trope in working-class religious life,[70] local financial imperatives in this instance dictated its redefinition as a "problem," one that church leaders scrambled to solve through a variety of strategies. One expedient was to widen the basis of lay responsibility in the church, with the Trustees Board of Point St Charles Congregational Church seeking to devolve some of its authority, requesting the Church "to consider the advisability of electing a Church Council from the Male Members of the Church, for the discussion of Church matters and other matters concerning the welfare of the Church at large." Second, church leaders launched an aggressive program of visitation of families by church elders in order to induce more people to participate in the quarterly communion services, considered a time of heightened spiritual commitment whose imperatives could be easily translated into increased monetary contributions. Despite an increase in membership from 233 to 271 during 1907, the percentage of those taking communion ranged from a high of 37.2 percent (101) of church members in January 1907 to a low of 24.7 percent (sixty-seven) in April.[71] Third, although appearing counterproductive to the link between inclusivity and financial stability, the lay managers of the church attempted to purge irregular attendees from the membership rolls. "Experience," declared the Church Secretary's Report in 1907, "has taught us to be very careful not to press a large number to come forward as several of those who did join during the previous years were satisfied as long as they were received into the Fellowship to stay away since joining, which trait among Protestants is very deplorable and those who become members should take Pattern as to faithfulness to the services & obligations to the Church from the Catholics by making an effort to come once on Sunday to the services at least by so doing they place themselves in a position to derive some good besides being an inspiration to the Pastor and Officers of the Church."[72] Clearly being articulated here was the notion that the spiritual fellowship and other services offered by the church came at a price much higher than nominal membership: attendance and regular contribution to the church finances were now regarded as the reciprocal currency for the benefits that this working-class church provided.

The monetary implications of sustaining an urban church congregation leads, in turn, to another question central to the link between working-class people and mainstream religious institutions. Would not the incessant and at times heavy-handed appeals for money to service debts and expenditure not, in and of themselves, simply alienate people whose own economic circumstances were far from certain?[73] Why did these churches not only survive in the new urban, industrial environment but were so successful at expanding and recruiting new members between 1890 and 1920? Simply stated, these religious institutions were effective because they were, as a number of historians have pointed out, effective at providing for the social and cultural needs of waves of new British immigrants and at generally integrating groups of migrants to the city into the life of new neighbourhoods by fostering a culture of associational participation.[74] In this context, it is important to consider that large, well-established national churches were more effective in this respect than independent, "sectarian" churches, because their size and stability enabled them to offer migrants to the city a far wider range of networks and connections.[75]

However, from the perspective of working-class people, it is important to realize that there were tangible economic benefits to be derived from belonging to, and participating in, organized religion. In the first place, the large urban church could, in a very real sense, provide access to a job. One of the major reasons why Barton St Methodist's membership expanded so rapidly after 1904 was due to a series of measures adopted towards British immigrants by Rev. Livingston, the new pastor, which could only have been implemented through the organizational connections available to a large national denomination. From an early stage, Livingstone established relationships with the Methodist immigration chaplains at New York, Montreal, and Halifax, and "received cards almost every day naming the Methodists who intended locating in Hamilton." It was Livingston's practice to visit them in their homes or boarding houses, assuring them of a warm welcome at Barton St Church. More significantly, Livingston also had personal connections with the managers and employers at the large East End factories like Canadian Westinghouse and International Harvester and, through these arrangements, was able to secure "employment for thousands of men and made them feel at home and happy."[76] A 1913 article publicizing Barton Methodist clearly expressed that a key element in the church congregation's self-presentation as "accessible" involved an elision between regular church commitment and access to material benefits. For working men, it was clear that part of the appeal of membership in Barton St was a job, given the fact that the church also served as a referral agency for the city's "Labor Bureau,"[77] which would place British immigrant workers in Hamilton factories:

The church office is open continually throughout the week. No need to go in with fear and trembling. Remember, the person you will meet – either the pastor or his assistant – will soon make the fact known that a brother is meeting with brother so that you can "Talk it Over." In addition to helpful conversation – and, be it known ... there are troubles more depressing than lack of employment – in all probability a position may be found for those out of work.

The Labor Bureau has proved a valuable auxiliary in connection with the church, and times without number the pastor has witnessed benefits arising from his thoughtfulness in instituting the same.[78]

Here, the language of Christian fellowship and "brotherhood" carried a direct appeal to identify with the congregation and the pastor's leadership as a way affirming male status through gaining a secure job. Although the records of Point St Charles Congregational are silent on the clergy's direct attempts to secure jobs for prospective members of the church, it can be safely assumed that access to jobs through the church occurred on a more informal level, simply because church membership – a badge of respectability and reliability – provided a network of contacts, especially in the rather closed world of Montreal railway shops, in which preferential hiring was given to British immigrants and where the word of better-established workers could carry a great deal of weight in determining a newcomer's employment.

In addition, for working-class families living on a rather precarious margin, church membership and contacts also provided access to occasional charity in time of need. Again, the records of both churches on this subject are rather sketchy, although the minutes of Barton St Methodist did record a "Poor Fund" in 1899, whose treasurer, Brother Argent, was a blacksmith.[79] In 1894, at the inception of the Ladies' Aid Society, the members decided to allocate five cents per month each to provide funds to relieve the needy and appointed a subcommittee of two ladies "who's [sic] duty it would be to visit the poor and afflicted & report any sickness or poverty in the vicinity of the church."[80] To raise more money to assist the needy, the ladies of Barton St Methodist in 1899 put on a fancy dress "Poverty Social," in which those members whose costumes were deemed excessive by the "detectives" and the "judge" would have to pay a fine, paid into the association's poor fund.[81] During times of more acute economic distress, such as during the 1913–14 depression, larger efforts to collect food and second-hand clothing for the "unemployed and needy" were officially launched by the church managers.[82] Indeed, it was during a 1920 debate on the launch of a sick benefit society at Barton St Methodist Church that it was revealed that the Men's Bible Class had had an "emergency fund" of $170 to provide for its members in times of need,[83] a direct illustration that participation in the church and its organizations did provide a tangible social safety net for working-class men. In an era when, in Hamilton, any charity beyond the strictly familial was completely in the hands of churches and ethnic clubs, given the failed experiment in the 1890s with "secular" involvement by the municipal government or a federated association,[84] working-class people whose lives were frequently on the brink of poverty would most certainly feel a powerful additional material incentive drawing them to participate regularly in their local church. Because charity remained in the hands of local churches and voluntary organizations, which actually expanded their sphere of influence through extension into working-class neighbourhoods, Canadian Protestantism followed a trajectory opposite to that of Britain, where a number of historians have cited the assumption of welfare by government agencies after 1880 as a major factor in accounting for religious "decline."[85]

However, the employment and charitable networks that these urban churches provided would not, in and of themselves, have enlarged and sustained a primarily working-class congregation over the space of more than twenty years without some precise sense of affinity between the religious message and the spiritual needs and desires of working people. Indeed, for both givers and recipients, such material assistance would have been more broadly understood as "fellowship," or "practical Christian endeavour,"[86] terms that established a seamless connection with a specific type of inclusive, evangelistic spirituality that characterized these working-class churches. In recent years, social historians of religion have observed, in a variety of national contexts, that the "plebeian" Christianity usually expressed in urban settings was, by and large, more enthusiastic, less laden with doctrinal niceties, more insistent upon the validity of the individual experience, and thus more accessible and inclusive to ordinary worshippers than its middle-class counterpart.[87] While both Barton Methodist and Point St Charles Congregational exhibited the characteristics of this more plebeian spirituality, it was at Barton St that these were elevated as fundamental elements of the congregation's public identity, so effectively that by the outbreak of the First World War, this working-class congregation, which had originated as middle-class outreach, had established itself as the cutting edge of the evangelistic movement in Hamilton.

Significantly, far from stigmatizing it as a "poor" church in need of assistance, Barton Methodist's heritage of missionary outreach enabled it to affirm and refine the main elements of plebeian evangelism, both in larger venues and in more intimate, household settings. Indeed, the church's origins were reworked into a positive point of attraction, with emphasis on the facts that badges of social exclusion, such as pew rents, had never existed and that Barton St offered "AN OPEN DOOR" to all comers.[88] Beginning in 1895, the Quarterly Board consistently promoted special evangelistic services in the church, designed specially to reach people through popular approaches in which the invited preacher "told in a plain and touching way the story of his own life and conversion."[89] Enthusiasm and a more raucous, less restrained style of worship clearly appealed to this congregation, as during the 1890s the church managers held joint services with the local Salvation Army.[90] However, this occasional public evangelism only supplemented what was in effect an ongoing lay involvement in personal visitation and encouragement of individual devotional life. In 1895, the stewards and local lay preachers initiated a regular system of evening "Cottage Prayer Meetings" held in people's homes during the winter months.[91] Here was a technique directly imported from English industrial villages and particularly tailored to appeal to a growing wave of British immigrants to cities like Hamilton. As Mark Smith has observed of this brand of evangelism, weeknight cottage meetings were particularly effective at offering regular services in a more decentralized religious fellowship outside the church building and close to working-class homes, thus providing the ordinary faithful the consistency of religious participation that would enable them to sustain their commitment.[92] This willingness on the part of lay evangelists to make Christianity accessible to working people, at times and places convenient to them, it should be reiterated, was a key factor in the church's successful expansion and goes far to explaining why many working-class people opted to remain within the precincts of the Protestant mainstream, rather than opting to join sectarian congregations. Indeed, the success of large national religious institutions in attracting working-class people was due to the fact that working-class religious needs could be accommodated and expressed within the framework of the local church.

The deliberate cultivation of a more populist Christianity fostered not only the rapid expansion of the church itself but also a wider reputation for Barton St church within the Methodist denomination itself, in particular under Livingston's leadership. This clergyman was described as "a Gospel Preacher in the fullest meaning of the phrase," and accounts of his preaching style deliberately extolled those anti-theological elements that would attract working-class people. In a deliberate swipe at the "polite" Methodism of middle-class churches, Livingston was characterized as a man of plain, understandable sermons. "No abstruse passages of the Bible," declared the writer, "are dilated upon – no time lost in study or pulpit trying to explain higher criticism or theological tweedledum and tweedledee." Livingston also emphatically eschewed political discussion in the pulpit, preferring to remind his working-class audience about the great themes of a living Christian faith.[93] Barton St Methodist acquired the reputation for aggressive evangelism, the clear antithesis of other working-class congregations in the city whose approach was one of withdrawal into matters purely of concern to the local church itself.[94] In 1908, the church was specially designated by the Methodist Conference for "special mission work" among both English speaking and foreign immigrants. The outside funds contributed towards this endeavour enabled the church to hire two Deaconesses to carry out systematic visiting and kindergarten work among immigrants to the East End.[95] Indeed, Barton Methodist's initiatives made Christianity highly visible to working-class Hamiltonians in the first two decades of the twentieth century, as the church employed strategies ranging from gaudy billboards and posters to Rev. Livingston's organization of a band and the purchase of a "Gospel wagon" through private subscription. This horse-drawn vehicle, festooned with banners bearing Bible quotations or temperance slogans and bearing the preacher accompanied by his evangelistic band – a bevy of attractive young men and women – became a fixture of Hamilton's streetscape and was frequently loaned to pastors of other churches desiring to carry on their own evangelistic campaigns.[96]

Significantly, Barton Methodist's ongoing commitment to both an aggressively public and personal conversionist evangelism anchored this working-class congregation in a more conservative Protestant tendency that accentuated the primacy of individual conversion rather than an interest in the wider reform of relations of labour and capital or the systematic relief of poverty. The religiously and socially conservative character of the congregation was revealed with the arrival of Rev. Simon Edwards, a new minister appointed at the end of 1920. Edwards, unlike Livingston, was more typical of a new breed of Methodist clergy who, following the lead of progressive elites who now controlled the central offices of the church, sought to apply the tenets of "social evangelism," which aspired to harness the inclusive imperatives of populist evangelism to specific social reform measures,[97] thus creating a wider constituency for initiatives intended to harmonize the relations between labour and capital troubled by the postwar wave of working-class unrest and the formation of an Independent Labour Party that had made significant political gains in Hamilton in 1919. At one level, Barton Methodist seemed the perfect venue for Edwards's proposal of a mutual sick benefit scheme, cooperatively run on the congregational level. Such an experiment had already been put in place by Rev. Peter Bryce at Earlscourt Methodist Church in Toronto, like Barton a strongly working-class congregation in character that also contained a high concentration of British immigrants.[98]

Edwards sought to build popular support for the sick benefit scheme within the congregation by holding a public debate, with the lay leaders of the Quarterly Board taking opposing positions. Brothers Jamieson, a carpenter, and Frazer, both adherents of the minister's plan, argued that such benefit schemes were clearly supported in the Scriptures and that modern systems of widows' pensions and payments for unemployment were reformist measures that moved "in right direction." Frazer, in particular, lauded mutual benefits as an application of the brotherhood principle, which also safeguarded the idea of self-reliance, as the plan would be based upon "[s]mall fees within the limits of every home." More tellingly, he believed that the potential access to such benefits through the church would carry on initiatives like Rev. Livingston's Labor Bureau, which had successfully expanded the congregation by directly providing jobs to working men, in that its very existence would "[h]elp bring men into church service."[99] Speaking for the negative, Brother Moore, a plumber and steamfitter, argued that the church did not need a benefit scheme, as such relief was already carried out by existing congregational voluntary organizations, and, besides, he claimed that many of the beneficiaries "did not appreciate what was done for them," meaning that there was no direct link between receiving benefits and greater or more regular commitment to the church. However, it was Brother Walker, manager of a wire-fence company, who most clearly evoked the self-reliant individualism and the overt link between respectability and churchgoing that expressed the views of a relatively stable, successful group comprising both the working-class and middle-class elements that managed Barton St Church. This group was more interested in precisely identifying and policing the boundaries between themselves and less economically stable elements in the working class and cast the central social and cultural division in terms of the churchgoing and the non-churchgoing, rather than strictly in terms of economic class.[100] The debate also revealed that, although the working-class presence at Barton St remained dominant in the early 1920s, there had been a substantial intrusion of middle-class elements into positions of lay management. Walker stated flatly that "many people [were] too proud to accept charity. Sick Benefit had its weaknesses. Down and outs not generally church going people."[101]

The defeat of the sick benefit scheme by the congregation's lay leadership thus closed off Barton St's brief flirtation with social reform and returned it to its older emphasis on aggressive evangelism, which had brought so much success in the past. At the next Quarterly Meeting in February 1921, it was announced that the church would participate wholeheartedly in a city-wide campaign of simultaneous evangelism planned for the following month.[102] The fact that this working-class church proved so resistant to reform measures specifically designed to respond to the "labour question" illustrates, at the local level, one of the central divisions in early-twentieth-century Canadian religious culture. Social reform, as some historians have previously observed, was largely a preoccupation of middle-class church leaders and congregations, while those religious institutions serving the working-classes were far more oriented to a populist spirituality that stressed the experiential, the conversionist, and the appeal to the individual, rather than the political or social engineering that exerted greater influence in central church organizations.[103] In this respect, it must be reiterated that

Methodism at the end of the First World War provided the space for these more localist working-class imperatives to flourish and reassert control.

However, there was another resonance, also rooted in specifically local events, attached to the rather strident assertion of boundaries between the respectable churchgoing working class and the "down and outs." This flowed from a chain of divisive events that had occurred within the church after Rev. Livingston retired from ministerial duties due to ill health in 1916. He was replaced by Rev. Fred William Hollinrake, who appeared at first glance to be an ideal candidate, having previously served as the first minister to the newly created Barton Methodist between 1894 and 1898.[104] He also replicated Livingston's style of aggressive personal evangelism, a characteristic that was considered an asset in trying to reverse the contraction in both church membership and revenue after the onset of the First World War. Hollinrake pursued a combination of traditional and innovative methods: he extended invitations to professional evangelists like Chicago's N.H. Camp and Canadian Methodism's H.T. Crossley to "conduct meetings on Bible Evangelism" in the Barton St Church; and, in a manner evocative of the new management techniques evident in the neighbourhood factories, he instituted a system of church attendance cards for boys and girls that would be "punched at the door each Sunday and awards for attendance made ahead of year."[105] This clergyman also deployed the language of total war to both the organizational machinery of the church, forming a smaller "Cabinet" – a direct reference to Lloyd George's and Robert Borden's War Cabinets – from the Quarterly Board to conduct church business. He also sought to apply the more pungent language of trench warfare tactics to the cause of stimulating religious revival, outlining in 1917 what he termed a "Win One Campaign," using the morning service as a "get ready" event, with the "attack" and the winning of individual decisions carried out in the evening.[106] In the short run, Hollinrake's measures appeared successful, as he halted the decline in church memberships, in 1917 recording a gain of fifty members over the previous year. As well, the "Cabinet" was able to report increased revenues, average Sunday collections increasing to $75 from $54 in 1916. On the negative side, however, although Barton St confidently trumpeted the opening of a new Sunbeam Mission Building, a key to extending the missionary outreach of the congregation, they were forced to close their mission at Brightside, "on account of English speaking families moving out of district and foreigners taking their places."[107]

But it was Hollinrake's plan to expand church membership and outreach by tying a fundamentalist plebeian theological innovation, premillennialism, to a radical democratization of church finance that led to internal turmoil in 1919 and 1920. Although for reasons that differed from the later opposition to Rev. Simon Edwards's social reform initiatives, Hollinrake ran afoul of an economically stable working-class element that saw church finance and organizational control as its purview and maintained as a core of its religious commitment that regular monetary contribution implied recognition and authority. At first sight, Hollinrake's 1916 proposal to discontinue the passing of the offering plates at the regular church service and rely entirely upon the anonymity of an offering box placed at the church door[108] could be read as building upon the socially inclusivist foundation established early in the congregation's history. It should be reiterated that Barton Methodist's public identity involved firmly eschewing pew rents and a firm adherence to the voluntary, non-compulsory principle for participation in church activities. Envelopes, though less offensive because they did not foster the same social gradations within the church space could, like the pew rents of an earlier era, be seen as instituting a hierarchy discriminating between the committed "regular" participants, whose more stable jobs and circumstances enabled them to make a consistent monetary contribution – one that would certainly be known, recognized, and rewarded by the church leadership – and believers whose personal finances might not allow them to pay consistently and who might thus feel that they were consigned to a second-class religious status or, more negatively, be written off as "down and outs" unable to pay for religious services. More pragmatically, the fact that only a minority of people used the envelopes seemed to reinforce the urgency of Hollinrake's innovation. Despite these pressures, the church's managers balked at abolishing the envelopes, the board minutes referring only cryptically to a "further educative campaign on the subject." However, this decision was too much for two long-serving board members, C.P. McGregor, the head of the Quarterly Board in his capacity as recording steward, and Bro Wilds, a gardener who had been active at Barton St since the 1890s, who both protested their pastor's initiative by resigning.[109]

One suspects that at stake in this contest between the pastor and laity over church finance was that Hollinrake was attempting to rival the revered Livingston's success by drastically expanding the church membership by attracting an even more "plebeian" clientele. This impression was reinforced in 1919 with Hollinrake's overt espousal of an intellectualized, formalist dispensational premillennial theology, which some church members felt lacked emphasis on "hell fire and eternal punishment" characteristic of the spirituality of working-class Methodism. Challenged by P.F. Lalonde, the influential leader of the congregation's adult bible class, who withdrew and began a similar organization at another church, attracting a number of members away from Barton St,[110] Hollinrake was finally forced to resign his position. In his final statement to the Quarterly Board, he denied any heterodox beliefs on the subject of eternal punishment but charged that Methodism itself had become "unscriptural," "drifting away from the fundamentals of the Christian faith,"[111] obsessed with organizational machinery instead of spirituality and tending towards "worldliness" – an obvious swipe at his disagreement with the Quarterly Board over how to raise revenue. At the final meeting before his departure, Brother Widdows, an unskilled labourer who held the position of district visitor (a lay evangelist), expressed his sorrow at the pastor's departure but emphatically declared that "he would stick by the Methodist church" and hoped that "we would have a pure gospel."[112]

Significantly, Hollinrake pointed to less theological reasons for his resignation: an ambition frustrated by his sense that Barton Methodist's potential for expansion had come to an end, as the physical urban space in which the church existed was being squeezed out by "factories and foreigners." However, Hollinrake remained in Hamilton, serving a plebeian East End religious constituency operating first out of a nondenominational evangelical Ebenezer Tabernacle on Gage Street, and later, when differences of opinion over his preaching later compelled him to move, he founded Delta Tabernacle, which was inaugurated with great fanfare by the arch-conservative Chicago evangelist Paul Rader. Now a "confirmed funda-mentalist," Hollinrake was able to build a congregation that by December 1924 had more than six hundred members, based entirely on a purely voluntary plan, no collection plates passed and, what had been the centre of conflict at Barton St, a box for anonymous offerings located at the back of the church. "The church," he enjoined worshippers at Delta, "should come out and be separate from the world … our members are expected to dissociate themselves from worldly pleasures and amusements and have no fellowship with worldly societies or organizations."[113]

It would be too easy to conclude that this working-class congregation found Hollinrake's dispensational premillennialism ultimately unpalatable and divisive and that this was the major point at issue in the contest between the clergyman and the board. However, what split Hollinrake from men like Brother Widdows, an unskilled man who might have been expected to sympathize with the clergyman's more anonymous and less stigmatizing mode of church finance, was the place of church organizations in religious life. For men like Widdows, who had at times undoubtedly struggled to provide a regular financial contribution to the church coffers, well-established mainstream churches like Barton Methodist provided him with a public status and a church position that recognized his evangelical commitment. From his standpoint, Hollinrake's denunciation of organizational machinery as "worldly" flew in the face of what was the essence of Barton St and other working-class churches belonging to the Protestant mainstream: that is, the bond between local congregation and national church allowed working-class people access to a full panoply of voluntary organizations that catered to devotional life, youth sociability, leisure, and, most importantly, the social reproduction of church membership. In turn, participation in these associations served to demarcate what was in effect a religious and social space largely controlled by working people and, in turn, offering an accessible apprenticeship and access to a wider public culture of civic life, based on religious faith and a weekly involvement of time and modest financial contribution. In an era when holding political office was largely closed off by barriers of wealth and social prestige, and trade unions themselves were far less inclusive because of skill considerations, it was the voluntary associations affiliated with the churches that offered the widest opportunities for working-class social involvement and participation in institutions. To give but one example, Barton St Methodist in 1922–23 offered no fewer than 212 offices and executive positions on its various boards, lay preaching positions, and in its Sunday school and voluntary associations, an impressive 19 percent of a congregation of approximately 1,100 members.[114] Historians would be hard-pressed to find any early-twentieth-century organization, be it a labour union or a political party, that offered working-class people this type of opportunity for decision-making. By belonging to these organizations, working-class men and women learned collective values and practices (though not necessarily socially radical ones): how to conduct meetings, how to communicate through public speaking, how to manage an organization's finances. It is in these voluntary organizations, coupled with the populist, inclusive spirituality frequently evident in these neighbourhood churches, that the social historian of religion comes closest to discerning the meaning of the church for working-class people.

As urban churches, neither Barton Methodist nor Point St Charles Congregational were unusual in having a large spectrum of specialized voluntary associations attached to them. What drove this type of organizational model, which had evolved in both Catholic and Protestant churches after the 1840s, was the dynamic explained by Jeffrey Cox in his discussion of late-nineteenth-century London churches. Those local churches that emphasized public worship and nothing else were, in a competitive environment of religious pluralism, quite simply unsuccessful in attracting members. Those with the money and the energy to sponsor a range of activities and enroll a large number of participants succeeded in attracting more worshippers, even in working-class neighbourhoods.[115] Here again, the logic of belonging to a larger denomination that would assist local branch voluntary societies would certainly have attracted working-class members and adherents: the more well-connected the congregation to other groups and associations, the larger the range of voluntary organizations that could be created and funded and the more people could thus find interests and activities in which they could participate. It is important also to remember that the voluntary associations of these churches would have encompassed and involved people in organized religion who were not connected to the congregation through formal membership, especially adolescents and young men. In 1913, for example, Barton reported no less than twenty "auxiliary" associations linked to the church, ranging from the more traditional Sunday school, broken into several age-specific sections, to the national Methodist youth society, the Epworth League, a "Pocket Testament League" of three hundred members, a Ladies' Aid Association, a branch of the Methodist Women's Missionary Society, and a Men's Bible Class.[116]

Perhaps the most widely accepted and unproblematic voluntary association was the Sunday school, a ubiquitous fixture in all local churches. In the case of both Barton Methodist and Point St Charles Congregational, the enthusiasm for Sunday schools was dictated by the primary reason that both congregations traced their origins to this organization; to have such an institution in a flourishing condition was thus a mark not only of a healthy evangelical spirit but also proof of institutional maturity and independence as a church, the sense that one's own Sunday schools could serve as the embryos of new satellite congregations. Thus, in 1913, just at the apogee of Barton Methodist's period of dynamic growth, the Sunday school enrolled more people than the church itself, reporting 1,624 members, taught by sixty-five officers and teachers, and divided by age into departments and sections, four hundred young children registered on the Cradle Roll, 137 Primary, 485 Intermediate, 370 adults, and 160 in the Home Department.[117] For this working-class congregation that had begun as middle-class missionary outreach, it was a mark of particular pride that it was "now the largest S.S. in the city in our average attendance."[118] For the working people of Point St Charles, the Sunday school provided, in addition to Christian education, the opportunity for recreational summer outings for children and adolescents, a street railway ride around Montreal (in 1907) and an annual Christmas entertainment in which "each scholar received a present from the log cabin," which one year replaced the annual Christmas tree. But, more significantly, the Sunday school provided a link between the local congregation and the wider world of Montreal Protestantism, as the city's Sunday school Union held a Rally Day every New Year's. Point St Charles congratulated itself that for this particular occasion, it had far surpassed its average attendance, although in 1914 the church managers commented ruefully that "the usual bag of candy to each scholar was omitted, which was rather regrettable, however steps were taken in future this would be provided for at all Rallys."[119]

However, the main reason why the state of the Sunday school was monitored so closely was that it was the central institutional pillar for the social reproduction of the church congregation, the key to the religious socialization of children and adolescents into church membership, with both its spiritual and financial responsibilities. The latter aspect, in fact, was always commented upon in the congregations' annual reports, with the Sunday school sections always singled out for their monetary contributions to home and overseas missions. The combined giving of the children and adolescents who attended Barton Methodist's Sunday school in 1913 totalled no less than $1,460. This raises a further question: why would working-class parents, many of whom were in straitened circumstances, want to pay additional fees to have family members participate in religious voluntary organizations? In the first place, for those working-class people who were regular church attendees and contributors, the act of having children contribute small weekly sums to missions was regarded as a way of apprenticing, or initiating, young children into the obligations of regular church membership itself.[120] Second, sending one's children to the Sunday school was the preferred way, for working-class people who did not wish to make the formal commitment to church membership, to acquire an indirect link with a congregation and to offer one's children the possibility of acquiring a fixed religious identity. For many British immigrants in the early twentieth century, their entry into Canadian religious institutions was eased through first sending their offspring to the Sunday school.[121] In this respect, the position of the Sunday school as pre-eminent among voluntary associations linked to working-class churches reinforces K.D.M. Snell's recent insight that the Sunday school should not be regarded as the purveyor of a message of social control by one class to another but should be seen as an institutional strategy of denominational control in a competitive religious environment, as a way of forming a new adult church society. It was for this

reason that Point St Charles Congregational celebrated in 1907 the fact that
"[t]he most pleasing feature of our year's work is that we had 8 scholars
unite with the Church."[122]

However, despite the fact that voluntary societies were clearly the key to
sustaining an energetic, inclusive, and expansive congregation, the "fit"
between this type of lay endeavour and the church organization proper was
not always a smooth one. For example, at Point St Charles Congregational
in 1896, Mr Symons, one of the trustees (significantly a member of the
anti-boxing faction), objected to two musical numbers in the annual Foot
Ball Club concert, "claiming that there was too much Theatre Royal about
them, and that dancing is offensive to a large part of the Christian
community." In this case, although the Trustees had allowed boxing as an
expression of masculinity at the institute, they unanimously resolved that
dancing was against the rules, and they censored the concert.[123] Church
records from this period are filled with requests to boards of managers
from various church clubs asking for use of church facilities, such as that of
the Barton Methodist Young Men's Union wishing to use the church lot for
a skating rink during the winter.[124] This power of decision over the use of
church property, particularly with reference to the leisure activities of
voluntary organizations, was always jealously guarded and asserted, the
assumption being, particularly with musical entertainments, that such
activities "would not be of such a highly spiritual character."[125] Another
source of conflict was the ubiquitous issue of finance, which arose over the
issue of monetary or labour contribution to the church proper. The Barton
Methodist Ladies' Aid Association in 1899 recorded its objection to
funding and hosting two Tea Meetings, preferring to provide only one to
open the new church, with further social evenings organized by the
Married Men's and Married Women's groups. In 1901, the Quarterly
Board sought to devolve some of its financial responsibility for paying and
housing the pastor and requested the Ladies Aid Association to assume
responsibility for the rent of the parsonage, an obligation that they
reluctantly agreed to undertake on an ad hoc basis, with the proviso that
this would not set a precedent requiring their association to assume
compulsory payment of rent.[126]

It is apparent from these exchanges that the presence of an ever-expanding
panoply of lay voluntary associations attached to these early-twentieth-
century congregations instituted a constant tension between strictly devotional purposes and the potential that members of these associations could use
them for quite different ends. One of the most striking institutional

developments in religious life after the 1890s was the literal explosion of voluntary societies designed to socialize young people; by the early twentieth century, both these working-class churches listed boys' and girls' clubs, Young People's Christian Endeavour Societies, divided into male and female sections, the Methodist Epworth League, and Young Men's Clubs, all designed to bridge the transition from adolescence to full church membership. In some cases, despite the trepidations of adult lay managers who viewed some of these associations as lacking in overt spiritual commitment, activist clergy like Rev. A.W. Main of Point St Charles Congregational were instrumental in blurring the boundaries between religion and leisure in order to use youth-oriented voluntary societies to recruit church members. Speaking in 1912 of the need for an athletic club attached to the church, Main declaimed that

The Church has been looked upon as a place consecrated to the interests of the soul and the body must go some place else for improvement and exercise, God redeemed the body, as well as the soul and the church of today that is to have a place need be a power in the city of Montreal, must minister to the body as well as to the soul. I want to bring this part of Church work to your prayerful consideration, namely the exercise and development of the muscle and the proper care of the body. I hope that this may be provided for our young people as soon as possible. Those who have given the money for this building should not be obliged to pay a heavy tuition for bodily instruction in other institutions.[127]

What lay behind Rev. Main's not-so-veiled critique of the spiritual narrowness of his own board of trustees was not simply a new, more liberal view of Christian masculinity, in which the body was also viewed as a spiritual organism.[128] In this case, promotion of athletic facilities directly connected with the church was a way of ensuring that young men – the central targeted constituency to ensure the ongoing social reproduction of the congregation – were kept enlisted in an institution directly under church auspices, so that they would not seek out leisure activities in other clubs or associations and be lured away to join other churches or no church at all. Thus, the annual report of the Gymnastic Club expressed great satisfaction in 1914 that "we are bringing into contact with the Church, those who would be otherwise perhaps undesirably engaged on that particular evening."[129]

Church choirs were particularly monitored because, although a key part in enhancing worship and devotion, they were regarded as vehicles for heterosexual sociability: they enlisted both young men and women, and church leaders particularly feared that young people would seek to become members for other than religious reasons. Thus, in 1899, Barton Methodist's Quarterly Board found it necessary to issue a stern edict that "no person, shall be allowed to become, a regular member of the Church Choir, unless he or she is a member, in good standing, of some Protestant Evangelical denomination." Significantly, the rule was waived for those under sixteen years of age,[130] a strong indication that involvement in the choir particularly appealed to a late adolescent age bracket interested in the possibilities of courtship. The popularity of the choir with youth actually allowed church managers to enforce a quid pro quo in which they would have to become church members if they wished to join. However, the working people of Point St Charles fully subscribed to the logic that, if such sociability leading to courtship could be expressed within institutions connected with the church, the local congregation would be the principal beneficiary. For example, the Young Men's Society of this Montreal church, established in 1907 soon after Rev. Main's arrival, had the ostensible devotional purpose of visiting young men in their homes and inviting them to church. However, what was offered was a series of leisure activities oriented around male camaraderie and civic initiation: public speaking, mock city council elections, debates on subjects of current interest like the Naval Question, addresses by prominent local political figures like H.B. Ames, the urban reformer, dinners such as the popular Robert Burns night and the St Patrick's Banquet, where, in this largely English and Scottish congregation, people impersonating Irish navvies afforded a source of considerable amusement. The underlying intentions, however, were hardly homosocial: "Sociable Evenings" and the New Year's "last chance social" were held in tandem with the church's Young Ladies' Circle, outings such as sleigh rides around Mount Royal afforded further opportunities for courtship, and, if any other promptings were needed, Rev. Main's "inspiring and interesting" address to a mixed banquet of young men and women, significantly entitled "Don't die on the third base"[131] would have underscored the message that the purpose of masculine camaraderie was directed to meeting the young women of the church, courtship must issue in marriage, and marriage would establish young men in an adult status as contributing, regular members of the congregation. Participation in religious institutions for working-class men thus offered the twin advantages of stable marriage and access to the knowledge and skills that would initiate them into the values and practices of Canadian citizenship.

In September 1919, the minutes of Barton St Methodist recorded the decision to "sell the Gospel Wagon and devote the proceeds towards purchase of an Auto."[132] The replacement of the horse-drawn wagon, with its loud banners and crowd of singers and exhorters, with the sleek, more individualist anonymity of an automobile intended to transport only the parson on his rounds signalled the end of an era for this expansive, aggressively evangelistic working-class congregation. Although the 1920s did not witness a decline in church members, the days of unlimited expansion of the congregation were over. Spiritual life along the older pattern of revivals and cottage meetings continued, but the old dynamic, in which missions and Sunday schools had spun off into new working-class congregations, was halted in the East End, exactly according to Hollinrake's prediction, by the encroachment of factories and the establishment of neighbourhoods in which non-British immigrants predominated. In one sense, religious organizations in Canadian cities were affected by demographic change at the end of the 1920s, in particular, congregations like Barton faced the consequences of the slackening of the stream of British working-class immigrants in the late 1920s. This, in turn, stalled any impetus to continue to articulate a synthesis between an ebullient populist evangelism and the accommodation of working-class social needs through institutional innovation. However, the crucial question raised from institutional Protestantism's intersection with the industrial working class during the years between the 1890s and the Great Depression centres on the need to recast the questions social historians have asked. These have traditionally focused on what alienated the working classes from religion, or, if religion is acknowledged as a constituent element of working-class culture, it is usually to emphasize the private, anti-institutional, or sectarian nature of this involvement. What has been relatively neglected is a consideration of the factors that induced them to participate in a complex, multifaceted religious life defined by mainstream, highly institutionalized churches and networks of religious voluntary associations. Just as no labour historian would advance the argument that, because only a minority of workers joined trade unions, they were a priori alienated from these organizations, so social historians of religion should be wary of taking as their starting point the view that being working class meant alienation from church organizations. In this respect, given the sheer volume of institutional records left by working-class congregations, such research will enable historians of religion in Canada to re-engage creatively with revisionist international scholarship on secularization[133] and more accurately define and identify the nature and chronology of the complex and changing ways in which ordinary people have defined their relationship between religious belief and organizational involvement.

Table 7.1
Barton St Methodist, Occupational Status of Members, 1901

Occupational Status	%	Number
Manufacturing	6.5	3
Professional	1.5	1
Commercial	6.5	3
Skilled	47.8	22
Semi-Skilled	23.9	11
Unskilled	10.9	5
TOTAL NUMBER: 46		

Source: 1901 Census.

Table 7.2
Barton St Methodist, Church Office-holders, 1922–23

Occupational Status	%	Number
Manufacturing	10.9	5
Professional	6.5	3
Commercial	21.7	10
Skilled	45.6	21
Semi-Skilled	6.5	3
Unskilled	8.7	4
68 names, 46 identified		

Source: Quarterly Board Minutes, Hamilton City Directory.

Table 7.3
Point St Charles Congregational Members, 1909

Occupational Status	%	Number
Manufacturing	2.5	2
Professional	3.8	3
Commercial	26.6	21
Skilled	41.8	33
Semi-Skilled	8.9	7
Unskilled	16.5	13
92 male members, 79 names and occupations identified		

Source: Minutes of the Board of Trustees, Lovell's Montreal City Directory.

Table 7.4
Point St Charles Congregational Board of Trustees, 1895 and 1902

Occupational Status		%	Number
Manufacturing	1895	16.6	1
	1902	14.2	1
Professional	1895	16.6	1
	1902	0	0
Commercial	1895	16.6	1
	1902	28.5	2
Skilled	1895	33.3	2
	1902	57.1	4
Semi-Skilled	1895	16.6	1
	1902	0	0

Source: Minutes of the Board of Trustees, Lovell's Montreal City Directory.

NOTES

For their comments and reflections on this article, I would particularly thank Nancy Christie, Craig Heron, and Bryan Palmer. Carrie Dickenson provided invaluable research assistance linking church membership lists with the 1901 census.

1 For the well-known class segregation of Montreal's neighbourhoods into "above" and "below" the hill, see the classic account by Herbert Brown Ames, *The City below the Hill* (Toronto: University of Toronto Press, 1972; first edition, 1897), and the more recent analysis by Terry Copp, *The Anatomy of Poverty: The Condition of the Working Class in Montreal, 1897–1929* (Toronto: McClelland & Stewart, 1974).

2 Archives Nationales du Québec (Montreal), P603, S2, SS22, Main Memorial Church (Point St Charles), 1995-03–007/205, Minutes of the Board of Trustees, Point St Charles Congregational Church, 18 Dec. 1896. Cushing was backed by Mr Boyd (miller), Mr Eason (storeman), Mr Fox (proprietor, Williams Paper Warehouse), and Mr Sargeant (driver), and opposed by Mr Richardson (storeman), Mr Downie (fireman, Grand Trunk), and Mr Carmichael (steamfitter). For occupations of board members, see *Lovell's Montreal Directory*, 1896.

3 Ibid., Minutes of the Board of Trustees, Point St Charles Congregational Church, 18 December 1896.

4 Ibid., Minutes of the Board of Trustees, 26 December 1896; 30 January 1897.

5 With some qualifications imposed by gender and age, which affected church attendance among both working class and middle class, this is the overarching thesis proposed by Lynne Marks in what is to date the most comprehensive analytical

treatment of the relationship between the churches and the working class in Canada, *Revivals and Roller Rinks: Religion, Leisure, and Identity in Late-Nineteenth-Century Small-Town Ontario* (Toronto: University of Toronto Press, 1996): 3–21.

6 ANQM, Main Memorial Church, Minutes of the Board of Trustees, "Annual Report, 1905"; 2 Feb. 1902, "Board of Trustees, 1902," occupational status from *Lovell's Montreal Directory.*

7 See table 3.

8 See table 4.

9 For a pessimistic interpretation of working-class culture in the first two decades of the twentieth century, which emphasizes the emergence of a privatized "culture of consolation" oriented to consuming commercialized leisure, see W. Craig Heron, "Working-Class Hamilton, 1895–1930," PhD thesis, Dalhousie University, 1981, 725–7. In a stimulating analysis of the religious culture of late-Victorian Britain, S.J.D. Green has stressed that church voluntary organizations successfully combined both accessibility and ambition. See *Religion in the Age of Decline: Organisation and Experience in Industrial Yorkshire, 1870–1920* (Cambridge: Cambridge University Press, 1996): 24.

10 In this respect, this paper builds upon the suggestion offered by Craig Heron that the class relations and social experiences in working-class churches in large Canadian cities may have differed significantly from what characterized small-town Canada. See Heron, unpublished paper presented to panel discussion on Religious History and Social History, Canadian Historical Association, Annual Meeting, Dalhousie University, May 2003.

11 For this new "progressive" religious imperative among Canadian Protestants, see Nancy Christie and Michael Gauvreau, *A Full-Orbed Christianity: The Protestant Churches and Social Welfare in Canada, 1900–1940* (Montreal and Kingston: McGill-Queen's University Press, 1996), especially chapters 1 and 2.

12 For the concept of "ecclesiastical republics" as the quintessential expression of the popular Protestantism of late-eighteenth-century Britain, see Callum G. Brown, "The Mechanism of Religious Growth in Urban Societies: British Cities since the Eighteenth Century," in Hugh McLeod, ed., *European Religion in the Age of Great Cities, 1830–1930* (London: Routledge, 1995): 243. Brown argues that "The characteristic evangelical culture which emerged in the second half of the eighteenth century incorporated family piety, community chiliasm, individual aspiration and, above all, the claim to class independence through 'democratic' church government."

13 For a more complete analysis of this historiographical assumption, see Michael Gauvreau and Ollivier Hubert, "Introduction: The Problem of Institutional Churches in Canadian History."

14 For a more extended discussion, see Gauvreau and Hubert, "Introduction"; and for an effective brief statement of the "orthodox" theory of secularization, see Roy Wallis and Steve Bruce, "Secularization: The Orthodox Model," in Steve Bruce, ed., *Religion and Modernization: Sociologists and Historians Debate the Secularization Thesis* (Oxford: Clarendon Press, 1992).

15 K.S. Inglis, *Churches and the Working Classes in Victorian England* (London: Routledge & Kegan Paul, 1963): 1, 3, 323.

16 Ibid., 334.

17 See, in particular, E.P. Thompson's *The Making of the English Working Class* (New York: Vintage Books, 1966; first published 1963): 26–54.

18 E.J. Hobsbawm, "Religion and the Rise of Socialism," in E.J. Hobsbawm, *Worlds of Labour: Further Studies in the History of Labour* (London: Weidenfeld & Nicolson, 1984): 33.

19 Callum Brown, *The Death of Christian Britain: Understanding Secularisation, 1800–2000* (London and New York: Routledge, 2000): 28.

20 Thompson, *The Making of the English Working Class*, 349–400.

21 Hugh McLeod, *Piety and Poverty: Working-Class Religion in Berlin, London and New York, 1870–1914* (New York and London: Holmes & Meier, 1996): xxiii.

22 Ibid., 205, xxv.

23 Brown, *The Death of Christian Britain*, 149, 156.

24 Brown, "The Mechanism of Religious Growth in Urban Societies," 240–1, 250. For a similar view of urban religious vitality in the US religious context, see Robert Orsi, "Introduction," in Robert Orsi, ed., *Gods of the City: Religion and the American Urban Landscape* (Bloomington and Indianapolis: Indiana University Press, 1999): 1–78.

25 Ibid., 255–7; Jeffrey Cox, *The English Churches in a Secular Society: Lambeth, 1870–1930* (New York: Oxford University Press, 1982). Another key work that stresses an early-twentieth-century "crisis" in religious voluntary organizations is J.N. Morris, *Religion and Urban Change: Croydon 1840–1914* (Woodbridge, Suffolk: The Boydell Press, 1992).

26 Lucien Hölscher, "Secularization and Urbanization in the Nineteenth Century: An Interpretative Model," in McLeod, ed., *European Religion in the Age of Great Cities*, 282.

27 Hugh McLeod, *Secularisation in Western Europe, 1848–1914* (New York: St Martin's Press, 2000): 7.

28 Mark Smith, *Religion in Industrial Society: Oldham & Saddleworth, 1740–1865* (Oxford: Clarendon Press, 1994): 1994.

29 Green, *Religion in the Age of Decline*, 200, 209.

30 Brown, *The Death of Christian Britain*, 11.

31 McLeod, *Piety and Poverty*, 206.

32 McLeod, *Secularisation in Western Europe*, 172, 182.

33 According to Callum Brown, much of the post-1850 church extension movement
    in British industrial cities was a product of middle-class missionary enterprise to
    provide religious services for the working class. See *The Social History of Religion
    in Scotland since 1730* (New York: Methuen, 1987): 117.

34 There is a long-standing Canadian historiography, predating the "alienation" thesis
    of the international social history of religion that presupposes that in the 1880s, just
    as industrialization was affecting the culture and society of English Canada, main-
    stream Protestantism became the religious expression of the middle classes and lost
    its ability to connect with the emerging industrial working classes. Rather than ex-
    hibiting religious indifference, workers displayed another form of "alienation" from
    mainstream religion by being drawn to "populist," enthusiastic, and sectarian
    forms of religion like the Salvation Army, the Hornerites, and, in the twentieth cen-
    tury, various anti-intellectual fundamentalist movements. For the genesis of this his-
    toriography, see S.D. Clark, *Church and Sect in Canada* (Toronto: Ryerson Press,
    1948). Its outlines have, in large measure, been followed and given a Marxist gloss
    by Lynne Marks, *Revivals and Roller Rinks*.

35 Green, *Religion in the Age of Decline*, 22.

36 Stephen Yeo, *Religion and Voluntary Organisation in Crisis* (London: Croom Helm,
    1976). While aspects of Yeo's thesis have been challenged, neither his chronology nor
    broader themes have been seriously revised, as his study informs recent work on ur-
    ban religion by Jeffrey Cox, J.N. Morris, Callum Brown, and S.J.D. Green.

37 This was the historical dynamic first advanced by S.D. Clark in 1948 in *Church and
    Sect in Canada*. It has been largely taken up more recently by Lynne Marks, who iden-
    tifies the Salvation Army as a more authentically working-class religion, as opposed to
    the mainstream churches, which continued to be sites of class alienation. A more nu-
    anced treatment, which still views the religious identities of working-class people as
    constructed in opposition to institutional churches is provided by Kenneth L. Draper,
    "A People's Religion: P.W. Philpott and the Hamilton Christian Workers' Church,"
    Histoire Sociale/Social History, 35:71 (May 2003): 99–122 (special number, *Intersec-
    tions of Religon & Social History*, eds, Nancy Christie and Michael Gauvreau).

38 For a powerful evocation of this line of argument, see George Rawlyk, *Canadian
    Baptists and Christian Higher Education* (Montreal and Kingston: McGill-Queen's
    University Press, 1988); Phyllis Airhart, *Serving the Present Age: Revivalism,
    Progressivism and the Methodist Tradition in Canada* (Montreal and Kingston:
    McGill-Queen's University Press, 1992).

39 Bryan D. Palmer, *A Culture in Conflict: Skilled Workers and Industrial Capitalism
    in Hamilton, Ontario, 1860–1914* (Montreal: McGill-Queen's University Press,
    1979): 238–9.

40 For these tendencies in early-twentieth-century Canadian Protestantism, see Christie and Gauvreau, *A Full-Orbed Christianity*.

41 The creation of urban working-class congregations has only recently begun to be explored by Canadian historians. For two illuminating studies, see Rosalyn Trigger, "Protestant Restructuring in the Canadian City: Church and Mission in the Industrial Working-Class District of Griffintown, Montreal," *Urban History Review*, 31:1 (Fall 2002): 5–18; Edward Smith, "Working-Class Anglicans: Religion and Identity in Victorian and Edwardian Hamilton, Ontario," *Histoire sociale/Social History*, 35:71 (Spring 2003): 123–44.

42 Yeo, *Religion and Voluntary Organisations in Crisis*, 178.

43 On the latter point, see Green, *Religion in the Age of Decline*, 120.

44 Taking turn-of-the-century Methodism in Hamilton as an example, it should be observed that at Centenary Church, whose congregation contained a middle-class majority and some working-class people, the latter were totally unrepresented among the male lay leadership of the church. For an analysis of three Hamilton "middle-class" congregations in this period, see "Moral Order and the Influence of Social Christianity in an Industrial City, 1890–1899: A Social Profile of the Protestant Leaders of Three Hamilton Churches – Centenary Methodist, Central Presbyterian and Christ's Church Cathedral," MA thesis, McMaster University, 1984. On working-class desires for "control" of congregational life, see Smith, "Working-Class Anglicans," 128–30.

45 Lloyd G. Reynolds, *The British Immigrant: His Social and Economic Adjustment in Canada* (Toronto: Oxford University Press, 1935): 118–20.

46 ANQM, Main Memorial Church, Minutes of the Board of Trustees, 17 March 1893, 11 November 1893.

47 UCA, Barton St. Methodist Church Records, 2–7, "Official Board Minutes," 2 July 1894.

48 UCA, Barton St Methodist Church Records, 2–7, "Official Board Minutes," 2 July 1894; Hamilton Public Library, Department of Special Collections, Livingstone United Church Scrapbook, "The New Church of Barton Methodists," *Semi-Weekly Times*, 21 February 1899.

49 For the clergy at Barton St Methodist, see UCA, Biographical Files, "Rev. F.W. Hollinrake," "Rev. Sanford E. Marshall," "Rev. Henry Gilbert Livingstone." All were described as young, energetic graduates of Victoria College and as very effective evangelistic preachers.

50 Heron, "Working-Class Hamilton, 1895–1930," 9–10.

51 For church membership statistics at Barton, see UCA, 1999.083L, Barton St Methodist Church, Box 2–2, "Circuit Register, 1900–01"; "Minutes of Quarterly Board: Annual Report, 1906"; ibid., Annual Report, 1911; ibid., Annual Report, 1914; ibid., Annual Report, 1916; ibid., Annual Report, 1921.

52 ANQ, Main Memorial Church, "Church Secretary's Report, 1907"; ibid., 1912; "First Annual Report of the Forward Movement Committee, 1906."

53 UCA, 1999.083L, Barton St Methodist, Box 2–2, "Circuit Register."

54 ANQ, Main Memorial Church Fonds, "Re Selling of Old Church Property," 9 May 1909.

55 See table 1.

56 See table 2.

57 Reynolds, *The British Immigrant*, 99.

58 For the British context, see Green, *Religion in the Age of Decline*; Brown, *The Death of Christian Britain*, 129–32. For the international comparative perspective, see McLeod, *Piety and Poverty*, who notes that this was also characteristic of working-class religion in London, Berlin, and New York. For Canadian studies that have uncovered a similar phenomenon in a variety of chronological and local settings, see Hannah Lane, "'Wife, Mother, Sister, Friend': Methodist Women in St Stephen, New Brunswick, 1861–1881," in Janet Guildford and Suzanne Morton, eds, *Separate Spheres: Women's Worlds in the 19th Century Maritimes* (Fredericton: Acadiensis Press, 1994); Marks, *Revivals and Roller Rinks*; Lucia Ferretti, *Entre voisins: La société paroissiale en milieu urbain: Saint-Pierre-Apôtre de Montréal, 1848–1930* (Montreal: Boréal, 1992).

59 McLeod, *Piety and Poverty*, 160–1.

60 On the technological and managerial innovations in the Hamilton metal trades, which seriously destabilized the position of skilled artisans, see Craig Heron, "The Crisis of the Craftsman: Hamilton's Metal Workers in the Early Twentieth Century," in Michael Piva, ed., *A History of Ontario: Selected Readings* (Toronto: Copp Clark Pitman, 1988): 109–43.

61 Green, *Religion in the Age of Decline*, 129.

62 UCA, Barton St Methodist, Quarterly Board Minutes, 22 February 1895.

63 ANQ, Main Memorial Church, "Annual Report of Deacons Board, 1906."

64 UCA, Barton St Methodist, "Minutes of Quarterly Board," 21 November 1904.

65 Ibid., 4 May 1905.

66 ANQ, Main Memorial Church, "Envelope Steward's Report, 1906." For the increased clerical rhetoric opposing pew rents in the late nineteenth century, see Green, *Religion in the Age of Decline*, 152–3. In the British context, Green has observed that the abandonment of pew rents in fact did not have the intended social effects: there was no massive movement on the part of the poor to become regular church members, prompting him to note that arguments against pew rents were, in fact, largely partisan, a critique levelled by clergy seeking more control at the expense of local lay vestries and managers of congregations.

67 UCA, Barton St Methodist, "Quarterly Board Minutes," 22 March 1922; ANQ, Main Memorial Church, "Envelope Steward's Report, 1906."

68 UCA, Barton St Methodist, "Quarterly Board Minutes," 11 November 1913, 9 February 1914.

69 ANQ, Main Memorial Church, "Church Secretary's Report," 1906.

70 On the reasons for lower working-class church attendance at Sunday morning services, see Brown, *The Death of Christian Britain*, 134.

71 ANQ, Main Memorial Church, Annual Report of Deacons Board, 1908; ibid., "Church Secretary's Report, 1906."

72 ANQ, Main Memorial Church, "Church Secretary's Report," 1907.

73 This is the thesis advanced by Lynne Marks, who argues that, during the 1880s, increasing levels of church debt as a result of building projects marginalized poorer members of the congregation and shifted the balance of power in the church in favour of middle-class elements. See *Revivals and Roller Rinks*, 61–4.

74 There is at present very little historiography on this question central to the social experience of early-twentieth-century Canadians. Despite the substantial historical literature on the centrality of Catholicism to the definition and enhancement of Irish identity, there has not been a comparable effort undertaken for Protestants. One of the more stimulating but little-known studies that centres explicitly on urban working-class experience is Lucia Ferretti, *Entre voisins: La société paroissiale en milieu urbain: Saint-Pierre-Apôtre de Montréal, 1848–1930* (Montreal: Boréal, 1992). See, however, the earlier articles by Ross McCormack, "Cloth Caps and Jobs: The Ethnicity of English Immigrants in Canada, 1900–1914," in J.M. Bumsted, ed., *Interpreting Canada's Past: Volume 2, After Confederation* (Toronto: Oxford University Press, 1986): 183–4, which argues for the centrality of churches and church-based voluntary associations as badges of "English" identity in Canada. For Hamilton, see Jane Synge, "Immigrant Communities – British and Continental European – in Early-20th-Century Hamilton, Canada," *Oral History*, 4:2 (Autumn 1976): 38–51.

75 Running counter to the current dominant tendency in Canadian religious historiography, the US sociologist Kevin Christiano has argued that mainstream denominations were able to prosper in the urban context simply by being the largest church in any local environment and being recognized as having the largest networks of personal ties and organizational resources. See *Religious Diversity and Social Change: American Cities, 1890–1906* (Cambridge: Cambridge University Press, 1987): 148–9.

76 UCA, Biographical Files, "Henry Gilbert Livingston (1859–1925)," Extract from Methodist Church Hamilton Conference Minutes, 1925.

77 For the Hamilton Labor Bureau, a central placement agency that constituted the only amalgamated charitable association in the city, see Hanlon, "Moral Order and the Influence of Social Christianity," 130–5.

78 "Barton Street Methodist Church," *Hamilton Herald*, 14 March 1913.

79 UCA, Barton St Methodist, Quarterly Board Minutes, 7 February 1899.

80 Ibid., Box 3–1, "Minutes of Ladies' Aid Committee, 1895–1902," 29 October 1894.

81 Ibid., 5 October 1899, 12 October 1899.

82 UCA, Barton St Methodist, Quarterly Board Minutes, 8 September 1914, 5 March 1908.

83 See, for this debate, UCA, Barton St Methodist, Quarterly Board Minutes, 3 January 1921.

84 See Hanlon, "Moral Order and the Influence of Social Christianity," 130–5. It should be noted in this context that, in Hamilton, local church congregations and benevolent societies consistently opposed a central fund or organization, on the grounds that they were best-equipped to deal with the needs of their own members.

85 Both Cox, *English Churches in a Secular Society*, and Morris, *Religion and Urban Change*, build their dynamic of secularization and loss of religious influence around a perceived decline in voluntarism, particularly in the area of public welfare.

86 See Christie and Gauvreau, "'The World of the Common Man Is Filled with Religious Fervour,'" 343, for the association between the community work of charity and associational life and the "old-time gospel of personal evangelism" in the working-class neighbourhoods of north Winnipeg.

87 See, for both British and Canadian contexts, Christie, "'On the threshold of manhood,'" and for aspects of working-class religion in Winnipeg during the First World War, Nancy Christie and Michael Gauvreau, "'The World of the Common Man Is Filled with Religious Fervour.'" For turn-of-the-century Britain, Jeffrey Cox has observed that, in the "plebeian chapels" of Lambeth, there was a marked contempt for certain forms of middle-class respectability, an almost compulsive informality, and an insistence upon the need for conversion. See *The English Churches in a Secular Society*, 140.

88 "Barton St Methodist Church," *Hamilton Herald*, 14 March 1913.

89 "Revival at Barton Methodist," *Semi-Weekly Times*, 7 November 1899; UCA, Barton St Methodist, Quarterly Board Minutes, 25 September 1895, 7 October 1895.

90 Ibid., 11 January 1896, 18 March 1896.

91 Ibid., 16 May 1895, 9 November 1897.

92 Smith, *Religion in Industrial Society*, 149.

93 "Barton St Methodist Church," *Hamilton Herald*, 14 March 1913. Livingston's reputation as a highly successful evangelist earned him an invitation in 1914 to leave Barton St and serve as the Conference Evangelist for the Nova Scotia Methodist Conference. See UCA, Barton St Methodist, Quarterly Board Minutes, 21 June 1914.

94 For this working-class religious strategy, see Smith, "Working-Class Anglicans," 144.

95 UCA, Barton St Methodist, Quarterly Board Minutes, 15 March 1908, 12 May 1910.

96 Ibid., 19 March 1909, 21 June 1914, 8 November 1920; UCA, Biographical Files, "Henry Gilbert Livingston."

97 For the prominence of this religious "progressivism" in the central offices of mainstream Protestantism by the end of the First World War, see Christie and Gauvreau, *A Full-Orbed Christianity*, chapter 3. Significantly, the year 1920 marked the high point of the Methodist Church's interest in labour questions.

98 UCA, Barton St Methodist, Quarterly Board Minutes, 20 December 1920. For Rev. Peter Bryce and his reformism at Earlscourt, which he then translated into the chairmanship of the Ontario Mothers' Allowance Commission, see Nancy Christie, *Engendering the State: Family, Work, and Welfare in Canada* (Toronto: University of Toronto Press, 2000): 357n50.

99 UCA, Barton St Methodist, Quarterly Board Minutes, 3 January 1921.

100 Based on the oral evidence of early-twentieth-century British immigrants in Hamilton, Jane Synge has noted that they often tended to point to a lack of class feeling, preferring to describe themselves as "'Just the ordinary class. The people that went to church.'" See "Immigrant Communities – British and Continental European – in Early-20th-Century Hamilton, Canada," 45. For the working-class evangelical perception that the central social divide was a cultural one based upon religion, see Christie, "'On the threshold of manhood.'"

101 Ibid., 3 January 1921.

102 Ibid., 8 February 1921.

103 While much further local research needs to be pursued on this theme, see, for a preliminary statement, Christie and Gauvreau, "'The World of the Common Man Is Filled with Religious Fervour,'" for an analysis of the polarized labour climate of Winnipeg during and after the 1919 General Strike.

104 UCA, Biographical Files, "Fred William Hollinrake."

105 UCA, Barton St Methodist, 2–7, Quarterly Board Minutes, 1916–17.

106 UCA, Barton St Methodist, Quarterly Board Minutes, 3 September 1918, 5 December 1917, 7 November 1916.

107 Ibid., 8 May 1917, 12 November 1917.

108 Ibid., "Minutes of Quarterly Board, 1916–17."

109 Ibid., "Minutes of Quarterly Board, 1916–17."

110 Hamilton Public Library, Department of Special Collections, Scrapbooks, "Livingston United Church," "Disagree with Their Pastor," *Hamilton Spectator*, 14 April 1919.

111 Hamilton Public Library, Department of Special Collections, "Delta Tabernacle Scrapbook," "Rev. Hollinrake Draws some Fire," *Hamilton Spectator*, 1 March 1920.

112 UCA, Barton St Methodist, "Quarterly Board Minutes," 13 April 1919, 4 May 1920.

113 Hamilton Public Library, "Delta Tabernacle Scrapbook," "First Services held Yesterday at Tabernacle," *Hamilton Spectator*, 16 February 1925.

114 UCA, Barton St Methodist, "Official Board 1922–23."

115 Cox, *The English Churches in a Secular Society*, 40–3. It is interesting in this context to speculate that the small-town churches examined by Lynne Marks may have been limited in the organizational possibilities they offered working-class people, and as a result attendance from that social category may have suffered.

116 "Barton St Methodist Church," *Hamilton Herald*, 14 March 1913.

117 UCA, Barton St Methodist, "Quarterly Board Minutes," 7 May 1913.

118 Ibid., 7 May 1913.

119 ANQ, Main Memorial Church, "Annual Report of Sunday School," December 1914; ibid., "Sunday School Report, 1907."

120 According to Smith, "Working-Class Anglicans," Sunday school donations "represented the initiation of the young into the Victorian and Edwardian financial world …" ("Working-Class Anglicans," 132).

121 Reynolds, *The British Immigrant*, 222, observed that Sunday school attendance by children was frequently the key to church attendance by parents.

122 ANQ, Main Memorial Church, "Sunday School Report, 1907." For the idea of "denominational control," a description that could be applied to other religious voluntary associations, see K.D.M. Snell and Paul S. Ell, *Rival Jerusalems: The Geography of Victorian Religion* (Cambridge: Cambridge University Press, 2000): 288.

123 ANQ, Main Memorial Church, Board of Trustees Minutes, 8 February 1896.

124 UCA, Barton St Methodist, "Quarterly Board Minutes," 21 November 1907.

125 UCA, Barton St Methodist, "Quarterly Board Minutes," 1 March 1929; ibid., 24 November 1919, 11 January 1896.

126 UCA, Barton St Methodist, 3–1, "Minutes of Ladies' Aid Committee, 1895–1905," 4 October 1901, ibid., "Minutes of Quarterly Board," 21 January 1899.

127 ANQ, Main Memorial Church, "Pastor's Report for 1912."

128 For the "body as temple" theology, which enjoyed a considerable vogue in Britain and North America between 1880 and the Great Depression, see Clifford Putney, *Muscular Christianity: Manhood and Sports in Protestant Christianity, 1880–1920* (Harvard: Harvard University Press, 2001).

129 Ibid., "Annual Report of the Gymnastic Club," 31 December 1914.

130 UCA, Barton St Methodist, "Quarterly Board Minutes," 21 January 1899.

131 ANQ, Main Memorial Church, "Report of the Young Men's Club for the Year Ending Dec. 1912"; ibid., "Secretary's Report of the Young Men's Club, 1908"; ibid., "Annual Report of the Young Ladies' Circle," 1912.

132 UCA, Barton St Methodist, Quarterly Board Minutes, 16 September 1919.

133 One fruitful trajectory, suggested by the evidence in this paper, is to seriously engage with S.J.D. Green's model of religious change, which urges more serious attention to the ways in which people have defined their relationship to religious

institutions, rather than the content of theological belief itself. According to Green, religious "decline" may be explained not by a crisis of belief that then led to a withdrawal from religious organizations but by a withdrawal from organizations that then impelled a loss of faith. See *Religion in the Age of Decline*, 389–90.

8

The Churches and Immigrant Integration in Toronto, 1947–65

ROBERTO PERIN

The role played by the Churches and in particular local places of worship in the integration of immigrants in Canada has not attracted much academic interest. The pioneering works on immigration influenced by the new social history represented integration as an essentially socioeconomic process in which immigrants as protagonists used their own networks to secure such immediate needs as housing and employment.[1] In studies in which integration was instead defined in cultural terms, the receiving society became the prime agent of acculturation, imposing its language, behaviour, and values on newcomers. In this instance the focus was largely on the school in shaping the integration particularly of immigrants' offspring.[2] While a few works in this second category have analyzed the strategies of churches in promoting the Canadianization of first-generation immigrants, like most institutional studies they provide the view from the head office. Little insight is gained into how such strategies worked at the local level or how immigrants responded to them.[3] More recent publications have had greater success in integrating religion and religious institutions in the immigrant story; but, with a few notable exceptions, the focus still is not on integration.[4]

The historiographical school first mentioned above unquestionably offers a much finer understanding of how the process of immigration changes those involved in it. While newcomers may retain their language, continue to frequent their kin and country folk, and keep ancestral folkways and traditions, still the changed environment subtly but persistently alters their speech patterns, ways of thought, and behaviour. The new land indelibly marks their psyche. Even as they continue in their daily lives to speak what sounds to outsiders as their native tongue, the new context changes the structure and content of that language.[5] While the current investigation is guided by this view of integration, at the same time it aspires to go beyond the labour market and neighbourhood within which most studies in this school have confined their analysis.

Examined here are three themes relating to the topic of this paper: the institutional churches' involvement in selecting and receiving postwar immigrants generally; the function local churches fulfilled in helping particular immigrant groups through the initial phase of settlement; the use that newcomers themselves made of places of worship to reach their overall objectives. The second and third themes focus attention on a number of churches of varied denominational affiliation catering to immigrants from Central and Eastern Europe and situated in the west end of the old city of Toronto, the main reception area for new arrivals. Ethnic and denominational diversity was not a critical factor in their carrying out what was in fact a common mission. If anything, the size of a congregation, more than its beliefs or polity, determined the range and number of activities provided. Immigrants considered these churches to be vital community institutions whose activities transcended the purely spiritual and moral, encompassing practical ones such as immigrant advocacy, language training, childcare, leisure, and financial assistance. These places of worship not only facilitated the integration of immigrants, but also were institutions in which immigrants themselves took a leading part in accordance with the very gendered expectations of the postwar era.

Immigration after the Second World War had a considerable impact on Toronto, the Canadian city that received the largest number of immigrants. By 1971, 40 percent of its population was born abroad, the highest level in a century. Toronto was on the verge of displacing Montreal as Canada's most populous urban centre and had already become its economic metropolis. Although not solely responsible for these transformations, immigration certainly did alter Toronto's religious and ethnic makeup. The Belfast of the New World was still solidly Protestant in 1941. Fully two-thirds of its population belonged to the Anglican, United, and Presbyterian Churches, while Catholics made up a meagre 15 percent. By 1971 the tables had turned as Catholicism became the city's leading denomination, claiming 40 percent of the city's inhabitants. While in 1941 people of British origin comprised four out of five Torontonians, thirty years later they were slightly less than one in two, their share of the population having in fact fallen to 46 percent.

After the war, Canadian Churches were forceful lobbyists and intermediaries in the crisis involving millions of displaced persons confined or not to special camps in Central Europe. They were well positioned to play this role because of their heavy involvement in refugee relief work as well as their access to international funds and networks. For more than a decade the Canadian government gave them a privileged position in identifying, assembling, and presenting prospective newcomers to immigration officials in accordance with the department's criteria, and even in transporting them to Canada. This work was done either through strictly denominational agencies such as Canadian Lutheran World Relief or the Catholic Immigrant Aid Society (and later the Rural Settlement Society of Canada), through temporary coalitions of religious and other private-sector organizations such as the Canadian Christian Council for the Resettlement of Refugees, or through interdenominational bodies such as the Canadian Council of Churches established in 1951 by the major Protestant denominations.[6] Since only particular international relief agencies were authorized to operate in German territory under Allied control, Canadian denominational groups had to work through their authorized US counterparts. This explains the prominence that Canadian Lutherans affiliated with the conservative US Missouri Synod came to have over other Lutheran groups in refugee relief, migration, and settlement.[7]

Shortly after the end of hostilities, some Toronto churches responded to the government's announced intention to resume immigration based on family reunification and contract labour. A few such as St John's Evangelical Lutheran, an English-speaking congregation affiliated to the Missouri Synod, became conduits informing their congregants about government programs and endorsing individual applications for domestic or farm labour. Through Lutheran contacts in Europe, St John's also received letters from refugees asking for assistance with immigration matters. Donald Ortner, the recently ordained assistant pastor who was born and educated in the United States, spent much of his time responding to requests from prospective Baltic immigrants regarding such questions as accommodation, employment, and schooling for their children. He was in constant contact with the Department of Labour's National Employment Service, the personnel offices of large companies, and the Canadian Overseas Garment Commission, in order to arrange for work and for their other immediate needs.[8]

Involved in providing relief to Russian orphans and refugees in the camps during the war, Christ the Saviour Russian Orthodox church helped to sponsor a number of families in 1948. At St Wolodymyr Ukrainian Orthodox church, the St Olha Branch of the Ukrainian Women's Association of Canada supported relief work in European camps providing shelter to Ukrainian refugees. St Patrick's, a bilingual Catholic parish run by the

Redemptorists serving German speakers since 1929, welcomed the first relatives of sponsoring members in 1948. Most refugees were *Volksdeutsche* and therefore ineligible for assistance by International Refugee Organization. They had been able to leave war-ravaged Europe through denominational agencies such as the Catholic Immigrant Aid Society. The following year the pastor, Daniel Ehman, made personal and written representations urging the government to relax the rules limiting immigration to first-degree kin and threatening to bring the full weight of the Canadian Redemptorist order to bear unless this issue were favourably resolved.[9]

When they arrived in Toronto, immigrants were met at the train station by family members and not infrequently by representatives of the local church, which offered them help in securing jobs and housing. Some congregants even made loans available for the purchase of a first home. English-language classes were also organized in church facilities.[10] The pastor of Christ the Saviour Russian Orthodox church, John Diachina, and his wife, Mary, offered a few newcomers temporary shelter in the rectory. They organized the distribution of clothing to needy families. Jobs were found by exploiting contacts both inside and outside the parish, particularly among wealthy Anglicans who had befriended prominent parishioners. At times immigrants were accompanied to their jobs by the pastor or his wife. Mary Diachina recalled: "In some cases I had to be an interpreter and show them (young immigrant women) how to operate the machines for some weeks. Some bosses took the new immigrants on condition that I would be with the girls at the factory for some time and I did it."[11] Finally the parish helped refugees who wished to sponsor their relatives with the necessary paperwork and intervened on their behalf with immigration officials.

As chief coordinator of the Lutheran Labour Scheme in Toronto, Donald Ortner enjoyed the trust of the city's employers. He wrote letters of reference on behalf of recently arrived refugees who had no standing in the community, attesting to their personal, moral, and civic qualities. In the case of a Latvian immigrant who had broken his farm labour contract, the clergyman even obtained legal advice to halt deportation proceedings against him. The situation of domestics received his particular attention. He worked closely with the YWCA to provide them with an appropriately structured environment. Reflecting fears about the spread of communism pervasive in the Cold War era, both Ortner and the YWCA counselled them "about the Communist Party in Canada and redirect[ed] their interests into church and traditional social activities."[12] The agency supplied Ortner with lists of young women of Lutheran background with whom they had been in contact and kept him informed about the language and civics classes that they were offering specifically to domestics. For its part, St John's established similar classes for domestics and their spouses, who as couples were ineligible for YWCA courses.

The arrival of these newcomers had a powerful impact on the immigrant groups already settled in Toronto. The case of the five thousand Lithuanian refugees who totally overwhelmed their previously established compatriots, numbering no more than a thousand, represents perhaps one of the more extreme examples of this reality. According to historian Milda Danys they "quickly constituted a majority whose interests and aims superseded the traditions of the older community."[13] Even among Hungarians, Poles, and Ukrainians, there were at least as many new arrivals as earlier settlers. The scale of this change at the parish level can be grasped by comparing the combined totals of baptisms and weddings performed in peak years during the interwar and postwar periods at St Patrick's: 111 in 1933 against 673 in 1959.[14] But the impact was not only demographic, it was also political. In this new immigrant cohort, there were large numbers of articulate professionals whose nationalist sentiments had been heightened by the foreign occupation of their homeland and by their stay in the camps. They impatiently claimed leadership positions in their communities, dismissing their prewar predecessors as ignorant, unpatriotic, and pro-communist. Their profound anti-Soviet views were enthusiastically welcomed by supporters of the Cold War in Canada. But these newcomers often caused discord within their immigrant group and between it and a growing segment of Canadian opinion sympathetic to the cause of world peace and disarmament.[15]

Created for the most part in the interwar era, the parishes and congregations that received these immigrants had experienced varying degrees of instability. While boasting a number of organizations and services that were both religious and cultural, they had trouble retaining their clergy, meeting their financial obligations, or finding a suitable place of worship. The parishioners of Christ the Saviour Russian Orthodox, St Wolodymyr Ukrainian Orthodox, St Elizabeth of Hungary Catholic, Sts Cyril and Methodius Slovak Catholic, and St Paul Slovak Lutheran churches moved several times after their foundation. In the late 1930s both St Elizabeth and St John the Baptist Lithuanian Catholic were assigned English Canadian pastors in an effort to resolve their financial and pastoral difficulties. While St Patrick's had none of these problems because it was under the care of the Redemptorist order, the war did severely constrain parish life. The pastor noted that only three hundred of Toronto's 1,500 German-speaking Catholics were attending the church and that even baptisms and weddings were failing to attract the faithful.[16] By contrast, some parishes and congregations acquired permanent facilities in this difficult period. This was the case with St Wolodymyr (1935), First Hungarian Presbyterian (1937), Ukrainian Presbyterian (1941), Sts Cyril and Methodius (1941), Hungarian Baptist (1943), Russian-Ukrainian Pentecostal (1943), and St Elizabeth (1944).

Postwar immigrants breathed new life into these churches. As a result of their expanding numbers, parishioners at St John the Baptist Lithuanian and St Elizabeth of Hungary finally obtained pastors from their countries of origin. St Elizabeth's pastoral needs were firmly secured when Jesuits who left Hungary after the Communists came to power in 1947 took charge of the parish. The influx of newcomers made Toronto into the seat of four new dioceses: Ukrainian Catholic (1948), Ukrainian Orthodox (1951), Russian Orthodox (1953), and Polish National Catholic (1968). As a result, St Josaphat, St Wolodymyr, Christ the Saviour, and St John were all raised to the status of cathedrals. St John's was moved in 1954 from a commercial-residential structure to a solid-brick church erected by Methodists in 1886 and previously occupied by the Nazarenes. St Wolodymyr's membership continued to rise in the 1950s and early 60s, reaching a peak of one thousand families and requiring the appointment of a second priest in 1965. At Christ the Saviour, it was becoming ever more difficult to accommodate parishioners in the existing structure. As a result, the cathedral was relocated in 1966 after St Cyprian's Anglican church was bought and renovated. At St Patrick's, growth in membership led in 1951 to the enlargement of the church carried out through the money and labour donated by four hundred parishioners. By 1957 Sunday masses for German speakers had risen from one to three. Annual events and festivities suppressed during the war, such as passion plays, pilgrimages to Midland, and *Katholikentagen* (literally, Catholic Days), which brought together German Catholics from southwestern Ontario around a particular religious theme, were restored.[17]

Within a few short years, immigrants also founded thirty new parishes and congregations in the west end of Toronto, many of them led by postwar or refugee clergy. The size of these congregations ranged widely.[18] In general, the largest were Catholic parishes containing hundreds and even thousands of families. The smallest tended to be evangelical or Pentecostal congregations with a few dozen families.[19] Building new churches or buying old ones to accommodate these new congregations entailed significant collective indebtedness at a time when immigrant families were trying to get themselves established. For example, in the 1950s Lithuanians raised $300,000, largely through individual interest-free loans, in order to construct the parish building that would house their church. The faithful at St Wolodymyr borrowed $80,000 in 1947 to erect a harmoniously proportioned church in the

Cossack Baroque style on land purchased a decade earlier. In the next few years they spent $11,000 to buy a rectory, $42,000 to paint and decorate the church, and $19,000 on a building addition. Even the relatively small Ukrainian Pentecostal congregation was able to pay $82,000 in 1957 to buy a charming edifice, recently a synagogue but originally a Church of Christ church. In the same year, their Baptist compatriots spent $60,000 to purchase and repair Memorial Baptist church, erected in 1897. The new Croatian church, built in 1965 at a cost of $240,000, replaced an older structure originally a Seventh-Day Adventist place of worship destroyed in all likelihood by politically motivated arsonists three years earlier.[20]

Often for political motives, immigrants created parishes and congregations even when establishments already existed to serve their particular group. Appalled by the leftist sympathies that apparently found expression at St John the Baptist Lithuanian, postwar immigrants wasted no time in forming Resurrection parish in 1953 under Lithuanian Franciscans from the United States. Holy Trinity Russian Orthodox church was created in 1949 by refugees who viewed the existing parish, Christ the Saviour, as both too Russian and not Russian enough. Compatriots from the earlier wave of immigration were seen as too anglicized in their speech and spirituality, while the parish's support for the Soviet Union's war effort was equated with collaboration with Stalinism. As a result, the faithful at Holy Trinity associated their church with the European-based Orthodox Church Abroad created a few years after the Russian Revolution. Meanwhile Ukrainian Pentecostals and Baptists who had joined mixed Russian-Ukrainian congregations when they arrived after the war established ethnically exclusive congregations in 1953.[21]

Analogous jurisdictional divisions occurred even among postwar immigrant groups. In 1952 Belarusans were split over support for the government-in-exile, judged by some to be too close to the Vatican and the Polish government-in-exile. As a result two rival parishes, St Euphrasinia and St Cyril of Turov, joined to separate Orthodox synods, were founded within blocks of each other. Similarly in 1962 a rift between the Belgrade Patriarchate and its North American diocese led to the creation on this continent of the Free Serbian Church, prompting its fiercely anti-communist supporters in Toronto to leave St Sava church in order to establish St Michael the Archangel parish. Among Baltic Lutherans, competition between the conservative Missouri Synod and the Canada Synod led to the creation of separate parishes.[22]

In some cases the influx of postwar immigrants provided the critical mass that allowed previously existing but tiny congregations that rented space in older churches to strike out on their own. Because of its central location and dwindling membership early in the twentieth century, Beverley Street Baptist was made responsible for outreach to non-English-speaking immigrants. Missions to various groups were instituted and resulted in the interwar years in the founding of recognized congregations all housed under its roof. Eventually Poles (1962), Estonians (1963), Russians (1969), and Czechs (1976) moved into their own facilities.[23] For the same reasons, in 1928 the United Church of Canada turned Queen Street United into the Church of All Nations. While its Czech and Ukrainian congregations disbanded after the war because of shrinking membership, the Hungarians took over the entire building in 1971, renaming it the Hungarian Free Reformed church.[24] St Paul Slovak Lutheran had a resident pastor after 1940, but remained a mission of Trinity German Lutheran until it acquired its own facilities ten years later.[25]

Whether in previously established or newly created parishes and congregations, immigrants eagerly joined associations, often taking over existing ones or founding new ones to reflect their specific interests. These groups fulfilled a primary need for social interaction. Faithful to traditionally conceived gender roles, women were the backbone of social life in every place of worship. They organized bazaars and banquets to raise funds for the church and wider immigrant group, as well as to bring parishioners or congregants together. In many instances they arranged exhibitions, lectures, and concerts highlighting the folk culture of their land of origin. These events often entailed the formation of choirs, lyric and theatrical groups, and musical ensembles connected with the church. In many Catholic and Orthodox churches women were also the mainstay of devotional associations that were structured according to gender and age. At St Elizabeth, first the Catholic Youth Organization and later, as the age profile of the parish rose, the Married Couples Club hosted dances every Sunday evening usually featuring the music of a Gypsy ensemble. After its establishment at St Patrick's in 1955, the Kolping Society, a mutual aid society set up to help skilled workers and tradesmen integrate into Canadian life, sponsored picnics in the summer season, as well as a series of seasonal festivities, such as carnival and winefest, that frequently ended with dances. These activities would have been unthinkable without the unpaid and perhaps unacknowledged labour of women.

Men, too, satisfied prevailing gender roles, for example, by creating in many Catholic parishes sports clubs that at times played to broader audiences. They also established political lobby groups associated with the church. St Wolodymyr's could have been described as the Ukrainian Self-Reliance League at prayer in light of its close connection with the liberal nationalist movement that called for Ukrainian independence in the interwar years.[26] Although under wartime exigencies the Canadian government had pressured the League to amalgamate with other groups to form a broad non-communist umbrella organization, the Ukrainian Canadian Committee, with its female and youth wings, survived intact. After the war, new nationalist organizations sprang up at the church. Created in 1952, a local branch of the Ukrainian National Democratic League aspired to organize the diaspora into an effective political alternative to the representative institutions in the Communist homeland. A Volhynia regional club was founded to disseminate and publish material because "contemporary works about Ukraine, printed under Soviet control, are falsified by Communist doctrinaires." At St Patrick, Danube Swabians, German-speaking immigrants from the region of Vojvodina in present-day Serbia, formed the St Michaelswerk Verband in 1949, a lobby group seeking compensation from the West German government for the confiscation of their properties. Meanwhile the Lutheran Church encouraged the formation of the Latvian Democratic Party, which lobbied for the restoration of democracy in that country.[27]

At a time in Canada when married women were entering the paid workforce in unprecedented numbers, the assortment of childcare programs provided by churches was of great help to working parents. Not only did such programs provide the religious and cultural setting that parents were seeking for their offspring, it facilitated the achievement of their economic objectives as well. Childcare services run by female religious communities were available at St Patrick's, Resurrection, and Our Lady Help of Christians.[28] A kindergarten was in operation for a dozen years at St Wolodymyr before the more stringent provisions of the new Nurseries Act closed it down in 1964. Eight years later, however, the parish offered limited childcare to parents on Saturday mornings.[29]

Schools of heritage culture were a common feature of most parishes. Operating on Saturdays or on weekday afternoons or evenings, they offered young people a range of courses in language, history, geography, and culture at the primary and at times secondary levels. Some schools, such as the ones at St Patrick's and St John the Baptist, were revived after being closed down during the war. The latter hired a Lithuanian refugee who had taught in the camps before coming to Canada. Others were established soon after the immigrants' arrival. For example, Estonians, Latvians, the Russians of Holy Trinity, and Slovenians opened theirs between 1949 and 1953.[30] Ukrainian Catholics differentiated themselves from other groups by creating regular day schools, run by a Ukrainian order, the Sisters Servants of

Mary Immaculate, under the Metropolitan Toronto Separate School Board.[31] Often staffed by teachers who were themselves postwar immigrants, these institutions all capitalized on rapidly expanding enrolments in the 1950s and 1960s, a reflection of the demographic weight of young immigrant parents and their contribution to the baby boom. For example, the number of students at the Taras Shevchenko Ukrainian School at St Wolodymyr's peaked at 255 in 1964, rising steadily from eighty-four in 1953. Meanwhile the parish's Sunday school, which imparted religious instruction, boasted 430 enrolments in the mid-1960s.[32]

The larger churches offered young people facilities that encouraged them to spend their leisure time there. The parish hall at St Patrick's staged films, dances, plays by its own theatrical troupes, and musical events by its choirs and bands. It was also equipped for table tennis, billiards, and bowling. In the winter months, boys played hockey on church grounds. St Elizabeth of Hungary's hall had card tables and a swimming pool. The parish's Catholic Youth Organization (CYO) organized sporting activities, including volleyball, fencing, boxing, and gymnastics, which in the 1940s usually ended with dances featuring big-band music. In Slavic churches youth tended to be involved in folk dancing and music groups, as well as in plays and literary recitals with folk or national themes. Before television and other forms of mass entertainment captured the immigrant generation's attention, such events drew large and enthusiastic crowds. Many parishes also had Boy Scout and Girl Guide troops.[33]

In the 1950s a number of churches purchased land in the countryside around Toronto and established camps that gave working parents the opportunity to place their children in a structured environment during part of the summer holidays. Once again leisure was associated with the inculcation of particular religious and cultural values. With the help of the Missouri Synod, Estonians rented a farm on the Nottawasaga River for inner-city children. Latvians bought a three-hundred-acre site in the Hockley Hills, while Lithuanians acquired twenty-five acres of land on Georgian Bay at New Wasaga. Hungarian Catholics purchased property near Streetsville, later called Mindszenty Park (after the Primate of Hungary, who was imprisoned by the Communist government), where the nearby riverbed was excavated to create a safe swimming area for children. Slovenians bought eight acres of land between Alliston and Bolton, where they built a camping ground for family use that included cottages, a pool, and a pavilion. This property was then sold to the Vincentians, the order of priests in charge of Our Lady Help of Christians, who expanded its size and facilities. The Russians of Holy Trinity established a summer colony at Jackson's Point near Lake Simcoe. For its part, St Wolodymyr acquired a one-hundred-acre farm near Oakville, called Camp Kiev, where in time a swimming pool, dining hall, kitchen, and sewage system were installed for a total cost of $81,000. Parents could send their children there for up to one month, and in some years as many as three hundred were enrolled. Finally, during the war, St Patrick's bought land in Richmond Hill where later "a lodge, swimming pool, dance pavilion, tennis-court and baseball diamond were constructed in order to ensure that outings by young people were still contained within the parish and they (sic) would not be 'lost to Communist clubs and to inter-marriage with non-Catholics.'"[34]

Credit unions were another parish-based service facilitating the integration of immigrants. Almost all of these financial institutions were founded after the war, and their growth was exponential, reflecting both the rapid insertion of most immigrants into the workforce at a time of sustained economic expansion and their need to obtain credit in order to consolidate their settlement in Toronto.[35] Because of their recent arrival, newcomers found it virtually impossible to obtain loans from commercial banks. Trust built on personal contact was more easily secured within immigrant-based institutions. In contrast to the rigid operating hours of banks, credit unions adjusted to the busy schedules of working immigrant parents by being open evenings and weekends, even Sundays. Such institutions also provided a culturally and linguistically familiar environment. Within a decade membership swelled from a few dozen or less to several hundred or more. In 1959 the largest parish-based credit unions, St Stanislaus–St Casimir, So-use (St Wolodymyr), and St Mary's, all had thousands of members.[36] Founded later than its Ukrainian counterparts, Our Lady Help of Christians (Slovenian) reached two thousand members in 1968, while in the same year the Czechoslovak credit union counted 1,300 shareholders.[37] In 1965 one third of Toronto's Ukrainians were members of credit unions, compared to a little more than one tenth of Ontario's population.[38] This figure is even more significant in light of the fact that native-born urban Canadians, who had greater access to commercial banks than rural dwellers, were less inclined to join credit unions.

Fragmentary evidence suggests that immigrants borrowed twice as much per capita from credit unions than their native-born counterparts and Ukrainians three times more than did native-born Canadians.[39] Immigrants also made different use of this money. In contrast to the short-term personal loans taken out by most native-born members, those by immigrants were more likely to be longer term, with the aim of buying or renovating a home, purchasing a car, or setting up a business. In 1957 seven parish- and

non-parish-based Ukrainian credit unions in Toronto released figures showing that 71 percent of their loans were made for the purchase or payment of
a home, 14 percent for the building or buying of a new home, 5 percent for
home repairs, and 5 percent for buying a car. Ten years later, mortgage
loans still accounted for 80 percent of the total advanced by ten Ukrainian
credit unions in Toronto.[40] These institutions treated borrowers differently
than did the banks. A review conducted in 1965 by an independent audit-
ing firm noted that credit unions were slow in pursuing members who were
behind or delinquent in their payments, some of which had been made on
terms different from those explicitly stated in official loan documents. Another firm observed that, in 1967, 23 percent of personal loans were delinquent at Our Lady Help of Christians.[41]

CONCLUSION

Although not the only or even the main organizations involved in the re-
cruitment, settlement, and adaptation of postwar immigrants, some
churches did have a special role to play in the process. Allied governments
assigned to them a distinctive place in the selection of refugees in the war
camps of Europe. In Canada, public servants at various levels, voluntary
agencies, and employers collaborated closely with churchmen and church-
women in helping immigrants to achieve their immediate targets of shelter,
work, and security. At the same time, while not all newcomers were religious or churchgoing, a majority of them clearly did establish a close relationship with the church. In part they were reflecting what the historian of
religion John Webster Grant termed a yearning for normalcy, which sustained a significant rise in church attendance among Canadian families as a
whole in the 1950s.[42] More especially, however, they were expressing their
own need to create a familiar environment in an unfamiliar land of adoption. More than a place of worship, the church became a focus of community life and an instrument to help immigrants re-establish a collective sense
of social ease and self-confidence.

The church served a number of their needs, most notably social interaction.
While worship was undoubtedly what bound congregations together, and devotional associations and practices helped to strengthen such bonds, before
the era of mass consumption entertainment, churches were also important vehicles of social interaction and integration. Dances, picnics, seasonal festivities, sports competitions, theatrical, dance, and musical performances, and
meetings of secular and religious organizations took place on church premises

and under their auspices. Since for most working immigrant parents Saturday was devoted to gender-specific domestic tasks, Sunday was their only day of rest. Their need for leisure, however, was at odds with Ontario's blue laws, whose popularity was still strong if the local plebiscites of the 1950s are any indication.[43] The church was therefore able to provide a sanction for pastimes stigmatized by both the law and the wider community.

Places of worship also offered immigrants a set of specific services that helped them fulfill their economic goals by allowing them fully to exploit the postwar boom. In households where both parents frequently had paid employment outside the home, there was a pressing need for childcare. The larger churches established a range of services and activities that might include kindergartens, after-school and weekend classes in heritage language and culture, summer camps, choral, dance, and theatrical groups, scout and guide troupes, and sports teams. While not immune from the all-pervasive influence of the English language and Canadian culture, such activities helped to reinforce the language of the home. They also promoted moral, social, political, and religious values that working parents often felt they could not inculcate in their children on their own. Parental concerns over the generation gap were thereby lessened.

One normally does not think of immigrant churches as helping to promote integration. On the contrary, whether one adheres to a melting-pot or multicultural model, one tends to see them, either positively or negatively, as helping to retain and transmit the language of origin, as well as perpetuate old-world traditions, causes, and identities. Certainly the host society has perceived them as bulwarks ensuring the survival of the culture of origin. Such a view, however, ignores the North American context in which congregants and especially their children lived their lives. Most Central and Eastern European immigrants grew up in the interwar period under authoritarian regimes whose tolerance of civil society was at best very limited. The ability of men and women to join or organize a wide range of associations, take up leadership positions in them, and discuss issues publicly was a significant departure from their culture of origin. They and their children participated in leisure activities with a decidedly North American content: picnics, dances where North American and European music mixed, and sporting events including baseball, hockey, and bowling. Parish-based services such as childcare and credit unions facilitated their achievement of the dreams that they shared with all postwar Canadians: the ownership of a single-family dwelling and a car, as well as the education of their offspring.

The very language, identity, and traditions that churches were striving to perpetuate were subtly changing in contact with the North American environment. Old-world languages were forced to integrate English words and expressions to convey the new realities of work, home, community, consumption, and leisure. Traditions acquired different meanings in the climate of pluralism. Identities became hybrid. Within one short generation, immigrant churches were confronted with a harsh choice: respond to change or face rapid decline. The children of immigrants demanded greater use of English in church life, clergymen with a North American mentality, and religious practices more in tune with North American cultural norms. The irony is that immigrant churches had become victims of their own success.

NOTES

I would like to acknowledge the generous financial assistance of the Department of Canadian Heritage through its multiculturalism research program. I would also like to thank the following research assistants for their invaluable work: Eileen Doucet, Jeet Heer, Julia Lütsch, Lori Pucar, Audrey Pyée, Todd Stubbs, Judith Szapor, Krista Taves, and Todd Webb.

1 See for example Pierre Anctil and Bruno Ramirez eds, *If One Were to Write a History: Selected Writings of Robert F. Harney* (Toronto: Multicultural History Society of Ontario, 1991); Bruno Ramirez, *Les premiers Italiens de Montréal: l'origine de la Petite Italie du Québec* (Montreal: Boréal Express, 1984); Franc Sturino, *Forging the Chain: Italian Migration to North America 1880–1930* (Toronto: Multicultural History Society of Ontario, 1990); Donald Avery, *'Dangerous Foreigners': European Immigrant Workers and Labour Radicalism in Canada, 1896–1932* (Toronto: McClelland & Stewart, 1979).

2 See M.L. Kovacs ed., *Ethnic Canadians and Education* (Regina: Canadian Plains Research, 1978); Manoly Lupul, "Ukrainian-Language Education in Canada's Public Schools," *A Heritage in Transition: Essays in the History of Ukrainians in Canada* (Toronto: McClelland & Stewart, 1982). Some studies in this category have emphasized the role of immigrants as protagonists. See David Cheunyan Lai, "The Issue of Discrimination in Victoria, 1901–1923," *Canadian Ethnic Studies*, 19, 3 (1987); Luigi Pennacchio, "The Defence of Identity: Ida Siegel and the Jews of Toronto versus the Assimilation Attempts of the Public School and Its Allies, 1900–1920," *Canadian Jewish Historical Society Journal* (Spring 1985).

3 See for example P. Gruneir, "The Hebrew-Christian Mission in Toronto," *Canadian Ethnic Studies*, 9, 1 (1977). For an excellent analysis of immigrant response to Protestant proselytism, see Enrico Cumbo, "Impediments to the Harvest: The Limitations of Methodist Proselytization of Toronto's Italian Immigrants,

1905–1925," in Mark McGowan and Brian Clarke, eds, *Catholics at the "Gathering Place": Historical Essays on the Archdiocese of Toronto 1841–1991* (Toronto: Canadian Catholic Historical Association, 1993).

4 One notable exception is the impressive study by Marlene Epp, *Women Without Men: Mennonite Refugees of the Second World War* (Toronto: University of Toronto Press, 2000), which deals explicitly with the period after the Second World War. The other exceptions concern nineteenth-century Irish Catholic immigrants. See Brian Clarke, *Piety and Nationalism: Lay Voluntary Associations and the Creation of an Irish-Catholic Community in Toronto, 1850–1895* (Montreal: McGill-Queen's University Press, 1993); Mark McGowan, *The Waning of the Green: Catholics, the Irish and Identity in Toronto, 1887–1992* (Montreal: McGill-Queen's University Press, 1999); Michael Cottrell, "St Patrick's Day Parades in Nineteenth-Century Toronto: A Study of Immigrant Adjustment and Elite Control," in Franca Iacovetta et al., eds, *A Nation of Immigrants: Women, Wokers, and Communities in Canadian History, 1840s-1960s* (Toronto: University of Toronto Press, 1998).

5 For linguistic changes, see Marcel Danesi, "Ethnic Languages and Acculturation: The Case of Italo-Canadians," *Canadian Ethnic Studies*, 17 (1985): 98–103.

6 Freda Hawkins, *Canada and Immigration: Public Policy and Public Concern* (Montreal: McGill-Queen's Press, 1988): 304–8; Gerald Dirks, *Canada's Refugee Policy: Indifference or Opportunism?* (Montreal: McGill-Queen's University Press, 1977): chapters 6–7; Ninette Kelley and Michael Trebilcock, *The Making of the Mosaic: A History of Canadian Immigration Policy* (Toronto: University of Toronto Press, 1998): 337–9; Epp, *Women Without Men*, chapter 2; Howard Margolian, *Unauthorized Entry: The Truth about Nazi War Criminals in Canada, 1946–1956* (Toronto: University of Toronto Press, 2000), chapters 4–5; Angelika Sauer, "Christian Charity, Government Policy and German Immigration to Canada and Australia, 1947–1952," *Canadian Issues/Thèmes canadiens*, Special Issue on Immigration and Ethnicity in Canada, 18, (1996): 159–80.

7 Dirks, 136–7.

8 Peter Wukasch, "Baltic Immigrants in Canada, 1947–1955," *Concordia Historical Institute*, 50 (Spring 1977): 4–22.

9 Archives of Ontario (AO), Russian Canadian Papers, MFN 108, Mary Diachina Papers, Notice of the White Russian Red Cross Group, 24 July 1940; Multicultural History Society of Ontario (MHSO), Rus-0337–DJA, Interview with Mary Diachina, 9 May 1977. She was the wife of the parish priest who served in Toronto from 1942 to 1976; Ivan Dubylko ed., *Fiftieth Anniversary of St Vladimir's Ukrainian Greek Orthodox Cathedral in Toronto, 1926–1976* (Toronto: n.p., 1979), 355; Karl J. Schindler, *Aussaat und Ernte: Jahrbuch zum fünfzigjährigen Jubiläum der deutschsprachigen katholischen Gemeinde in Toronto* (Toronto: n.p., n.d.): 51.

10 Wukasch, 13; Schindler, 60, 68; Milda Danys, "Lithuanian Parishes in Toronto," *Polyphony* 6, 1 Special Issue on Toronto's People (Spring 1984): 104–9.

11 AO, Russian Canadian Papers, Mary Diachina interview. In the same collection, see the interview with Stephen Cocherva-Curtis, September 1977, on the subject of a prominent parishioner: "Madame Gideonoff also had very good connections with a lot of important people in Canada and with the assistance of an Anglican women's group, she secured a great number of jobs."

12 Wukasch, 9–13.

13 Danys, 105.

14 Schindler, 2.

15 See Franca Iacovetta, "Making Model Citizens: Gender, Corrupted Democracy, and Immigrant and Refugee Reception Work in Cold War Canada," in Gary Kinsman, D.K. Buse, and Mercedes Steedman, eds, *Whose National Security? Canadian State Surveillance and the Creation of Enemies* (Toronto: Between the Lines, 2000), 154–67.

16 Dubylko, 336–7; *50 Ev/Years Szent Erzsebet Egyhazkozseg/St Elizabeth of Hungary Church, Toronto, 1928–1978* (Toronto: n.p., 1978); Joseph Kirschbaum, *Slovaks in Canada* (Toronto: n.p., 1967); Danys, 104; Schindler, 42–5.

17 Danys, 106; *50 Ev/Years Szent Erzsebet Egyhazkozseg/St Elizabeth of Hungary Church*; Interview with Bishop Yurij, 10 October 2000; Dubylko, 341; interview Cocherva-Curtis who put the mortgage on the new church at $140,000 and renovations at $50,000; Schindler, 57–86.

18 Their denominational breakdown is as follows: eight Catholic, six Lutheran, five Orthodox, four Baptist, three Pentecostal, two Evangelical, one United, and one Seventh-Day Adventist. Their ethnic composition is as follows: seven Ukrainian, five German, three Polish, two each for Belarusans, Slovaks, and Lithuanians, one each for Russians, Latvians, Czechs, Hungarians, Slovenians, Croats, and Serbs, as well as two mixed congregations: Ukrainian-Russian and Polish-Slovak.

19 Figures, although partial, still give an idea of the range in size. Resurrection Lithuanian had 1266 families in 1963; see Danys, 109. Our Lady Help of Christians Slovenian had 660 families (2,675 parishioners) in 1961; see AO, MFN 109–1/2, Tone Zrnec Papers, parish report to the Archdiocese of Toronto, 1961. St John's Latvian Evangelical Lutheran had two thousand members in 1954, while Redeemer Lithuanian Lutheran had one hundred families in 1953; see Wukasch, 17–18. Our Lady Queen of Croatia had one thousand parishioners in 1963; see *Globe and Mail*, 3 January 1963. The Ukrainian Baptists had two to three members in the 1960s; see interview with William Dawidiuk. In 1970 the *Evangelische Gemeinde* had some sixty members, that is, congregants who had received baptism as adults; see interview with Hermann Mayer, 28 November 2000.

20 Danys, 108; Dubylko, 338–40; interview Kolesnichenko; Canadian Baptist Archives (CBA), Minutes of the Home Mission Board, 1 October 1957; Archives of the

Roman Catholic Archdiocese of Toronto (ARCAT), parish files, Our Lady Queen of Croatia, Hrvatska Zupa Toronto, 27 September 1964. The pastor, Charles Kamber, a US citizen, blamed Communists for the attack. For his part, the archbishop, Cardinal McGuigan, had received a letter from the Canadian-Yugoslav Association, protesting against celebrations marking the anniversary of the wartime proclamation of the Croatian puppet state, held at our Lady Queen of Croatia. See ARCAT, Branko Mihic and Leo Fister to McGuigan, 7 April 1961.

21 Danys, 106; MHSO, Rus-0734 Mal, interview with Vladimir Malchenko, 6 October 1977; interview with Ludmilla Kolesnichenko, 24 August 2001, and with William Dawidiuk, 11 October 2000.

22 V.J. Kaye, "Canadians of Byelorussian Origin," *Revue de l'Université d'Ottawa* 30, 3 (July-September 1960): 300–14; Sofija Skoric and George Vid Tomashevich, eds, *Serbs in Ontario: A Socio-Cultural Description* (Toronto, 1988), 86–98; Wukasch, 13–19.

23 CBA, Minutes of the Home Mission Board, 6 November 1962; Annual Report of the Home Mission Board, *Baptist Yearbook*, 1963; Joan Oliphant to F. Elnitski, 10 September 1973; Minutes of the Department Canadian Missions, 13–15 May 1976.

24 United Church Archives (UCA), 83.050C, box 26, file 411, Memorandum, re: visit to the Church of All Nations, Toronto, 10 March 1944.

25 Kirschbaum, 271–2.

26 See Oleh Gerus, "Consolidating the Community: the Ukrainian Self-Reliance League," in Lubomyr Luciuk and Stella Hryniuk eds, *Canada's Ukrainians: Negotiating an Identity* (Toronto: University of Toronto Press, 1991); Dubylko. 353–4.

27 Dubylko, 363, Hildegard Martens, "The German Community of St Patrick's Parish, 1929 to the Present," *Polyphony* (Spring-Summer 1984): 98–100.

28 Schindler, 32, speaks of Felician Sisters taking over the parish kindergarten in 1938; Danys, 109, identifies the Lithuanian Sisters of the Immaculate Conception as running a day-care centre; AO, MFN 109–Reel 2, Tone Zrnec Papers, the New Year's 1961 issue of *Bilten*, the parish bulletin at Our Lady Help of Christians, refers to childcare for children between the ages of two and five.

29 Dubylko, 348.

30 Wukasch, 14, 17; Malchenko interview 1977; Peter Urbanc and Eleanor Tourtel, *Slovenians in Canada* (Hamilton: n.p., 1985), 116.

31 *Globe and Mail*, "Immigrant Faith and Culture," 23 November 1968.

32 Schindler, 54–74; Danys, 106; Dubylko, 347–8; Vladimir Handera, "The Russian Orthodox Church in Toronto," *Polyphony* (Spring-Summer 1984): 83.

33 Hildegard Martens, "The German Community of St Patrick's Parish, 1929 to the Present," in *Polyphony* (Spring-Summer 1984): 98–100; *50 Ev/Years Szent Erzsebet Egyhazkozseg/St Elizabeth of Hungary Church*; Dubylko, 349; Urbanc and Tourtel, 125–55; interview with John Barczek, 29 September 2000, Vladimir Malchenko 1977; Handera, 83.

34 Martens, 99; Wukasch, 15–17; Danys, 108; *50 Ev/Years Szent Erzsebet Egyhazkoz-
seg/St Elizabeth of Hungary Church*; Urbanc and Tourtel, 203; Dubylko, 340–1,
349.

35 There is some disagreement on the founding date of St Mary's Ukrainian Catholic
credit union. Myron Stasiw states that it was during the depression. See interview
Myron Stasiw, 29 September 2000. However, Plawiuk gives the date as 1950. See
Mykola Plawiuk, "Ukrainian Credit Unions in Canada," *Slavs in Canada*, II (Toronto: n.p., 1968): 146–53. St Wolodymyr established a Savings Aid Fund (*Shchad-
nycha* Kasa) in 1936 that was later incorporated into the So-Use Credit Union.
Perhaps St Mary's followed a similar pattern in which a financial organization was
set up in the 1930s and only later was formally recognized as a credit union. The
following are the founding dates of other parish-based credit unions: St Patrick,
1939; St Stanislaus, 1945; So-Use (St Wolodymyr), 1950; St Josaphat, 1950; Czechoslovak, 1953; Resurrection, 1953; St Elizabeth of Hungary, 1956; St Nicholas,
1957; Our Lady Help of Christians, 1957; St Casimir, 1958. See Rudolf Cujes,
"The Involvement of Canadian Slavs in the Co-operative Movement in Canada,"
in Cornelius Jaenen ed., *Slavs in Canada* III (Toronto: n.p., 1968), 151–70. Non-
parish based credit unions were established by Belarusans in 1953, as well as by
Estonians in the same year and Latvians in 1954. It has not been possible to ascer-
tain the founding date of the Croatian Credit Union that is still situated one block
away from Our Lady Queen of Croatia church.

36 Plawiuk, 151.

37 Cujes, 159.

38 By overestimating the number of Ukrainians living in Toronto (65,000 as opposed
to 46,650 listed in the 1961 census for the metropolitan area), Plawiuk, 147, provided a lower percentage. His membership figures are drawn from the reports of
seven Ukrainian credit unions in Toronto.

39 Plawiuk, 147; Cujes, 159–60, cited figures from a survey of twenty-two Slavic
credit unions in Toronto that he conducted in 1969.

40 Cujes, 161. See as well, Milos Greif, "Kampelicka (Czechoslovak Credit Union)
History," www.kampelicka.com/english.html. Greif is the chair of the Board of Di-
rectors of Kampelicka.

41 AO, Peter Markes papers, MU 9772 MSR 4868, F1405-75. Markes was president of
Our Lady Help of Christians Credit Union.

42 John Webster Grant, *The Church in the Canadian Era* (Burlington: Welch Publishing, 1988; revised edition): 160–5.

43 Ibid., 166.

9

Governance of the Catholic Church in Quebec: An Expression of the Distinct Society?

GILLES ROUTHIER

Being interested in the future of post-Council Catholicism in Quebec, I was drawn to look at different aspects of Catholic modernization[1] – in particular governance structures at the diocesan level – and, as I centre this research on the concept of "reception," understood not just as the impact of Vatican II on Quebec, but rather as the assimilation and appropriation of its teachings in a given culture and society, I was led to situate the modernization of Church forms, institutions, and modes of governance within the social history of Quebec and, in this instance, within the framework of the Quiet Revolution.

VATICAN II REVEALING TWO DISTINCT CANADIAN CATHOLICISMS

Vatican II offers virtually inexhaustible opportunities for those interested in comparative history. It in fact permits us to compare various Catholicisms.[2] The frequent meetings of the international team of scholars who are producing the history of Vatican II, though lacking a comparative intention, allow us easily to draw conclusions of this sort. Vatican II comprises Catholicisms in the plural, and this is probably one of the finest fruits of the Council, as it has allowed the Catholic Church to attain a new understanding of itself, not merely as a Latin Church or Roman Church but as a "World Church."[3] These various Catholicisms do not speak with a single voice and are far from homogeneous. I have made this point in dealing with the debates over religious freedom and about the constitution of the Church in the modern world.[4] Furthermore, the various national presses often represented the Council in quite different fashions. Until now, however, there have been rather few studies available that would permit us to situate Quebec Catholicism on the conciliar scene,[5] and, more importantly, we lack studies comparing francophone and anglophone Catholicisms during the course of the Council. We already know, of course, that there were important differences. An analysis of the *vota* of the Canadian bishops makes this difference plain.[6] We also know that the consultations with lay people, priests, and religious prior to the Council were a distinctly francophone phenomenon.[7] In addition, in the conciliar phase, the interventions on the part of francophone bishops appear to have been much more important than were those of their anglophone counterparts. We can also observe that the two groups used the media differently.[8] The two groups of bishops functioned fairly independently in Rome,[9] so that men who were living in different places had relatively little contact or shared work. Only a few individuals bridged the gap between the two groups. Though there are many points of comparison, to date nothing systematic has appeared.

Otherwise, in looking at the reactions of the francophone press in Canada to Pope John XXIII's announcement of his intention to call an ecumenical council (25 January 1959), it seemed to me quite clear that, in the liberal press, the stories that provided a glimpse into the running of the Council were useful to the reformist faction that, backed by an "ideological visa," made the Quebec episcopate aware of the reforms it was putting forward.[10] From that moment, the idea of movement and change implied by John XXIII in his use of the notion of *aggiornamento* found an atmosphere of particular expectation in Quebec, linked to the social situation. An MA student now working on representations of Vatican II in the Quebec press has identified a vocabulary of description quite similar to that used in writing about the Quiet Revolution. Such comparative studies are worth pursuing in English Canada,[11] but I have to say at this point that I am better informed about how the Council appeared in the foreign press[12] than in the English Canadian press, for which not enough studies exist.

Following Vatican II, things have developed independently in several areas. Such is the case with liturgical reform,[13] for example, which, despite being coordinated at the beginning, later followed separate, parallel roads. Indeed, in December 1964, the Canadian bishops published a joint pastoral letter, an ordinance, containing directives regarding liturgical music and practical instructions for the introduction of the vernacular into the liturgy (21 December 1964). The action was coordinated and orchestrated. Later on, however, we observe parallel paths differentiating francophone and anglophone Canada. The creation of distinct bodies devoted to similar movements – the Sécretariat national de pastorale liturgique, created by the episcopate in 1962[14] and afterwards replaced by the Office national de liturgie, would be addressed to the entire francophone sector. It had its counterpart in the National Liturgical Office, which was established as a permanent body in the late 1960s. The episcopate also launched a monthly review, the *Bulletin national de liturgie*, which promoted liturgical revival in francophone Canada and had its English-language equivalent in the *National Bulletin on Liturgy*, which began publication in 1965. Furthermore, on the international level, the two sectors were affiliated with markedly different cultural spaces – the international linguistic commissions in charge of the translation and adaption of different rituals – ICEL for anglophones, dominated by the United States, and CIFT for the francophones, with its predominant European base. If we take a careful look at the debates within the different bodies dealing with orientation, formation, and communication, it is possible to see whether these developments were symmetrical or if they followed parallel, not to say different, lines. In particular it should be observed whether the debate over language represented a determinant issue, as was the case in the Spanish Basque country,[15] at a time when the debate over official languages was going on in Canada.

Similar conclusions could have been arrived at by following the Canadian reception of the Decree on Ecumenism during the years immediately after the Council. Even in the phase of the Council immediately prior to the preparatory stage, the gap between the perceptions of anglophone and francophone bishops regarding "separated brethren" was considerable, as M. Fahey has shown in his work on the *vota* of the Canadian anglophone bishops. This asymmetry certainly persisted into the post-conciliar period.[16]

After the Council ended, there had been a general wish in Canada to coordinate the implementation of the Council's intentions on the national level. In October and November 1965, the Canadian bishops in Rome initiated a discernment that went in this direction. In a letter in November 1965, Mgr Sanschagrin reported that "The Canadian episcopate ... has decided to work collegially toward the application of the Council's decisions and directions in Canada. A joint communique will shortly inform the Canadian people of the plans drawn up toward this end and how the bishops wish to work along with their priests, their religious, and their faithful." (letter 41). In fact, the Canadian episcopate had already met and had had lengthy exchanges on the subject. The desire was to work in a coordinated fashion, as had been the case previously in 1964, when liturgical reform was first being floated.

There exists in the archives of the Episcopal Conference of Canada a document that was produced by its secretary-general, Mgr Charles Mathieu, entitled "Lendemain de concile en terre canadienne"[17] ("The Aftermath of the Council in Canada"). It contains several practical proposals regarding the reception of the Council in Canada, one of which is "immediately and officially to take actual leadership in the matter of post-conciliar adaptations in Canada."[18] Thus the episcopate could retain the initiative rather than leaving itself open to uncontrolled change. A brief common declaration would have the advantage of "bringing together those individuals who might have considered some of the actions or declarations too far out of the mainstream or too daring; it would focus all their energy toward certain *precise objectives*, according to set dates and *reasonable stages* ..."[19] Beyond this idea of a common declaration, the secretary-general made further concrete proposals: a systematic program to study the conciliar documents, the reorganization of the Episcopal Conference so as to make it "the body capable par excellence of placing and maintaining the Canadian Church in a CONCILIAR STATE"[20] and the holding of a plenary council in Canada in ten years.

This dialogue paper seems to have been well received: about a month later, following several requests coming from both francophone and anglophone sectors of the CCC (Canadian Council of Catholic Bishops), Mgr Louis Lévesque, the sitting president, asked the secretary-general of the CCC to consult the bishops on the question of such coordinated activity and about establishing the "broad outlines of an eventual post-conciliar program"[21] in Canada. From 17 to 22 November, the secretary-general of the bishops' conference did consult all the Canadian bishops on this matter.[22] A very strong majority (fifty-seven of the sixty responding) supported in principle the idea that the Canadian bishops should develop the outlines of a ten-year post-conciliar program for the country. Another large majority was in favour of a proposed plan for the bishops, on their return to Canada, to communicate with the faithful so as to make them aware of this plan and "ensure a future for the Council in a collegial and methodical way"[23] in Canada. Finally, as the point of departure for this post-conciliar undertaking, a huge program of systematic study of the Council documents was proposed that was to culminate in the holding of a plenary council in Canada in 1975, ten years after the end of Vatican II concluded its deliberations. This last proposal, however, received somewhat less support – only fifty-two respondents were in favour of such an initiative.

What happened thereafter? It is difficult to say, but all of this lovely unanimity didn't last long. We do know that a project called "Declaration and Greetings from the Catholic Bishops of Canada on their return to the country following the fourth and last session of the Council" was drawn up.[24] This text was not, however, published.[25] Furthermore, this text packed very little punch. It talked vaguely about a plan to be developed and all references to calling a plenary council have disappeared.[26] In a letter to the Canadian bishops dated 24 February 1966, C.E. Mathieu informed them that "After a long discussion of the question of a 'Post-Conciliar Program' ... the Most Reverend members of the Council have taken the following decisions ... The Council believes that this is no longer an opportune time to promulgate the Declaration 'on the occasion of the Bishops' return to the country' that was projected in Rome. And every other sort of declaration would seem premature! ... The Council deems it too soon to formulate broad outline of a post-conciliar program, as endorsed by the CCC."[27]

The Canadian episcopate did not present a united front upon their return to Canada after the Council. It is thus necessary to collect the bishops' various scattered initiatives. Initially, a few of the proposals caught on, but independently of any coordinated effort by the Conference. Among the most important accomplishments were the April 1966 publication of a French translation of sixteen conciliar documents in a single volume[28] and the holding of the International Theological Congress in Toronto in 1967,[29] which had been provided for in the pilot study of October 1965. Apparently, the first test of collegial action on the national level was a failure; not altogether, however, since it was agreed that the Secretariat of the CCC would provide "an inter-diocesan communications service allowing all the Bishops Ordinary to keep each other mutually informed about their diocesan projects and the fruits of their respective experiences."[30] Despite conciliar recognition of episcopal collegiality and the encouragement that was given to national episcopal conferences, the Canadian bishops were not successful in establishing a common front at a time when the Catholic Church was reviewing its institutional features and its presence in society. In the period following the Vatican II, Canadian Catholicism tended to become increasingly regionalized, with the creation of four regions within the Episcopal Conference and, ultimately, to form two blocs, despite all the pressures that had been pressing it since the beginning of the century to come together in a coherent sort of way.[31] All of this is evidence that comparative studies regarding Vatican II are well worth pursuing.

Following Vatican II, the Quebec Catholic Church, in addition to undertaking a thoroughgoing reconsideration of its position in Quebec society, was also developing certain organizational features and, on the level of governance, putting forward quite original institutions, policies, and ecclesial operations. These can easily be related to the political culture of their period and, more generally, to the culture animating the large governmental public services then under construction in Quebec. I shall look principally at one aspect, consultation procedures, although the inquiry could readily be extended to administrative or even judicial functioning.

As I indicated earlier, the tradition of consultation in the Quebec Church went back to the period before the Council, and it continued to undergo frequent new developments. I shall take up four areas: pre-conciliar consultation, the *Grandes Missions*, the Dumont Commission, and the councils and synods.

Pre-conciliar consultations

Toward the end of 1961, but especially in 1962, a number of Quebec bishops launched extensive pre-conciliar consultations with priests and religious and lay persons in their dioceses. According to our research, priests in at least eleven of twenty-two dioceses then situated in whole or in part in the civil Province of Quebec were consulted. These sessions took place in the dioceses of Montreal (November 1961), Joliette, St Jean de Québec and Quebec (February 1962), Rimouski (March 1962), Sherbrooke, Amos and St Jerome (May 1962), Ottawa (August 1962), Nicolet, and Gaspé. As we have already said, this phenomenon is peculiar to the Quebec dioceses.

Consultations with the laity were also very numerous. To date we have come across them in eleven dioceses: Montreal (29 October 1961), Joliette (early 1962), St Jean de Québec (28 January 1962), Quebec (25 march 1962), Saint Anne de la Pocatière (29 April 1962), St Jerome (5 May 1962), Amos (May 1962) Sherbrooke (10 June 1962), Rimouski (June 1962), Nicolet (9 September 1962), and Ottawa (15 September 1962). To these dioceses, we should add those of St Boniface (5 May 1962) and Moncton (24 September 1962), though the consultation held at St Boniface did not have the same breadth.

In terms of the history of Vatican II, we are dealing here with a peculiarity, with an uncompromising fact that is found nowhere else, at least not to the

Figure 1
Chronology of consultations

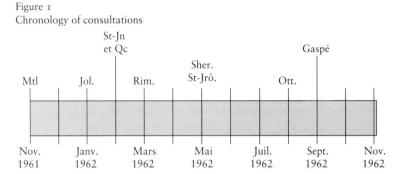

same degree. Though there were opinion surveys conducted by European reviews and newspapers, we do not find consultations as extensive and as systematic among Church members.[32] We do run across a few attempts of this kind in other places, but they remain isolated and not part of any unified movement. Thus, between March and May 1961, Mgr Willem Bekkers (Saint Hertogenbosch) arranged talks between the clergy and particular laymen. This seems to have been the earliest diocesan consultation with the laity relating to preparation for the Council. It was, however, far less extensive than the ones that took place in Quebec. Each parish consulted (there were four) was supposed to delegate four lay Catholics, two of whom were to be members of their business councils. This was also true for Paris, where the *Semaine religieuse de Paris* on 13 January 1962 reported the results of a survey taken in two parishes (St Jacques de Haut Pas and St Paul at Ivry) on 19 November 1961. Here again, this was a very limited undertaking. In 1962, a few other dioceses proceeded with their consultations: Namur and Malines-Bruxelles; Grenoble, Pamiers, Poitiers, and St Brieuc; Munich, Northampton, and Florence. Yet again, these represented scattered initiatives, not a concerted movement.

There were also consultations with specific groups. Thus, toward the end of 1961, Bavarian Catholic Action undertook an inquiry into lay expectations of the Council. In December 1961 in Paris, a survey was taken among students in the university chaplaincy. This was primarily to see if the students were aware that there was to be a Council and to find out if they had any opinions about it. Again, these consultations were nothing like those undertaken in Quebec. These were not bishops who were consulting their flocks before attending the Council so as to convey what was on the minds of their people.

What was happening in the province of Quebec was truly original, and it never reached the anglophone dioceses of Canada. José de Broucker, a journalist writing for the *Informations Catholiques Internationales* talked about the "Québec Awakening" or the "Québec thaw."[33] These pre-conciliar consultations or dialogues caused considerable surprise, moreover, to those observing the Catholic scene, whether Canadian or foreign. As one example, I will cite an editorial in an Abitibi weekly:

Has anyone ever heard of a popular consultation being undertaken by a Catholic bishop among his flock in order to learn their views and suggestions about what the Church should do in their area?

This, nevertheless, is what is going on right now in the Amos diocese ...

Under the enlightened leadership of his Holiness Pope John XXIII, the Church wishes to use this meeting (the Vatican Council) to try to adapt its strictures to modern times by softening them, should that be called for. At the same time, it hopes to clear the way for the unification of the Christian world under a single authority and for the conversion of those peoples who are still heathen.

No one is surprised to see Catholic spiritual leaders harbouring such magnificent designs, but everyone, especially the simple faithful, remains astounded that their feeble insight is being called upon to help carry them out. A more dazzling proof of the pains the Church takes to facilitate to the utmost degree the work of salvation could not be found.[34]

It is not a matter of linking this consultation movement to the event of the Council itself, as it had not yet taken off. The commissions in Rome were getting ready for a council that would ratify the teachings of Pius XII and confirm all the condemnations that had been issued since Vatican I. Despite all hopes and expectations, by the end of 1961 and during the first half of 1962, *aggiornamento* had not yet prevailed. Holding these consultations can of course be directly linked to the Catholic Action movements that were calling for them. But this demand would never have had the effect it had if Quebec society had not been ready for such a dawn and such a spring. The movement corresponded with the ferment that was bubbling up in Quebec society and can be directly connected to the social and political thaw that followed the election of the government of Jean Lesage.

The Grandes Missions and Regionalization

Even before Vatican II, another mode by which the faithful could participate in the life of the Church and its governance was in place: the *Grandes Missions*. Saint Jerome diocese initiated its *Grande Mission* in 1958, run by Yves Martin and Fernand Dumont, two sociologists from the University of

Laval, an institution that had played a considerable part in the training of the group that would soon be running the Quebec Government. The method they then developed and that they described in their work *L'analyse des structures sociales régionales*[35] is the foundation for three large areas of work: first, in the ecclesial field, the *Grandes Missions* – those in Montreal and Saint Jean de Québec (Longueuil) in 1960, in Saint Anne de la Pocatière and Chicoutimi in 1962, and finally in Quebec City, which began in 1963 and continuing until 1970; next, in the public arena, the large studies undertaken by the Planning Office; finally, students from the University of Laval sociology department would participate in a variety of field studies following the same model of investigation and analysis, with particular application to the regionalization of secondary education, which would eventuate in the establishment of the province's comprehensive secondary schools. What we see then, in the course of the conciliar period and the years that followed, is a series of interactions between the process of regionalization that the Government of Quebec was engaged in and the reorganization of the dioceses on the basis of the creation of pastoral regions. It is important to take things one at a time if we are to fully understand the reciprocal and intersecting influences of these various phenomena that appeared at the same time.

Though their name might suggest that they drew their inspiration from the earlier parochial missions, the *Grandes Missions* at the turn of the 1960s operated according to a different logic. They were different not merely because of their duration (the one in Quebec City went on for seven years) but especially because their geographic base was no longer the parish but a homogenous sociological region and because of the new and important means by which they operated. A *Grand Mission* had the expressed aim of developing a unified pastoral plan or of establishing a pastoral unity.

The studies undertaken by Y. Martin, F. Dumont, M. Matte, J.-G. Bissonnette, L. Bovy, and R. Doyon, some of whom were formed by the school of F. Boulard and others by the Chicago School, described in detail the socioreligious milieu and drew up general outlines of the Church's situation in this specific milieu (institutions, personnel, questions of faith troubling Church members, and so on). They included a section as well that looked to the future, formulating suggestions and pastoral priorities. To construct these dossiers, different sorts of group animation were used; priests and lay people of a whole region were brought together in order to record what they were thinking. Afterwards, the results of these investigations were announced at sociological evenings attended by those in charge of the sociopastoral life of a region. Inquiry, participation, and social animation were the key words of this experiment.

It is important to note that this movement was absolutely contemporary with the first economic planning and regionalization experiments set in motion by the Lesage Government in 1961, following the adoption of the bill regarding the Quebec Council of Economic Orientation, whose particular mission was to draw up an economic development plan for Quebec.[36] Though this body and those that replaced it may have dealt with economic sectors (like electricity or the steel industry), they were primarily concerned with the regions (the Lower Saint Lawrence, the Saguenay, Lac Saint Jean, northwestern Quebec, etc.).[37] The intention was to improve both the regions and the province as a whole. The most advanced planning project was that which took place in Eastern Quebec. Its history is bound up with that of the BAEQ, the Bureau d'aménagement de l'Est du Québec (Eastern Quebec Planning Board), the body that in 1963 was charged with developing a plan for regional development.[38]

The *Grandes Missions* thus corresponded precisely with the heady days of regional economic councils and regional development councils. The extensive regional animation activities that these bodies set in motion have been described in terms very much like those used about the regional *Grandes Missions* of the same period:

From 1963 to 1966, a number of stages of investigation and participation took place which led to the submission of a draft plan in 1965, then to the submission of a definitive plan in 1966. During this time, a permanent team, assisted in the summer by again as many students, led the enquiry and prepared the study documents. The permanent team included biological and physical scientists, but mostly sociologists, economists and social animators ... In this regard, the work of the social animators was typical – the operated within local committees, in close to two hundred villages in order to assist the citizens in formulating the objectives they recommended ... [39]

An analysis of these documents (research and papers), which led to the establishment of a pastoral ministry (*"pastorale d'ensemble"*) in the Quebec diocese between 1963 and 1966, turns up the same features as those found in the documents produced by the regional development councils of the same period. The terms "pastoral plan" (*"pastorale d'ensemble"*)[40] and "coordination"[41] appear and correspond to "regional development plan," "overall plan," and so on. Just as with the state apparatus, the central institutions involved in coordinating "all the live forces of the Church" were put in place.[42] The *Grande Mission* would call upon "the *whole* of the apostolic forces to work in a socially homogenous geographic *whole* in order to reach the *whole* range of life ... and to contact the *whole* man ... in his religious, family, professional life, his pastimes, etc."[43] The modes of operation that were adopted were the same as those in the organizations created by the government: huge enquiries leading to the production of voluminous reports,[44] an intense round of meetings in the pastoral regions, and the use of the social sciences and new communication techniques.[45] In short, the *pastorale d'ensemble* was right at home with the new administrative culture of government planning. After all, it identified itself as the "coordination of every diocesan Church effort – coordination both on the active level and on the management level. That is, on the one hand, to plan all the enterprises undertaken by each of the large pastoral sectors ... and, on the other hand, to integrate all these initiatives into a plan laid out by a management committee."[46]

As might have been foreseen, this general planning and coordination of all activities was only achieved at the price of a certain degree of centralization. This appeared primarily in two ways: those large pastoral areas that were not controlled by a diocesan office (catechesis, sacramental ministry) now became attached to a diocesan office, and thereafter a diocesan administration took charge of all pastoral areas (ecumenism, social ministries, family ministry, and the like); as well, central bodies intervened more pronouncedly in the pastoral life of the parishes, regions, groups, associations, and movements. We see a genuine vertical integration of pastoral activity.

It was not only in the area of reconfiguring central governance institutions that the Quebec Church echoed public administration. The same phenomenon of regionalization can be seen in both institutions. The movement toward regionalization in the Quebec diocese, for example, began at the very time that the public administration was itself seized with a passion for regionalization. This was the period that saw the creation of the regional school boards with the launch of Operation 55 in 1964 and the establishment of regional health and social services boards (CRSSS), soon to be followed by the regional municipalities. On 29 March 1966, an order in council divided Quebec into ten administrative regions, established seven regional municipalities, and instituted eighteen subregional centres.[47] It was a fertile period for regional economic centres, soon to be taken over by the regional development councils. The most advanced regionalization experiment was certainly that undertaken in Eastern Quebec, the pilot project, in 1963.

On the diocesan level, the same movement appears. The central pastoral body dealing with planning and coordination was responsible for setting up regional structures and the curial offices needed by the *pastorale d'ensemble*. "In regard to the sectorial commissions ... the role of the CDP is to *found* them, *set them to work*, and *coordinate* them. As for the regions, the CDP will have to set them up while zoning the diocese and organize what is going on within each and coordinate them with one another."[48]

These phenomena that appear in both the Quebec Church and the Quebec state are not only exactly concomitant, but the two reforms proceed according to the same logic – they were piloted by experts trained in the same schools, led to the same outcomes, and belong to the same administrative culture that relied upon the same methods and the same experts. Indeed, this comes as no surprise when we consider the interchange of personnel between the governmental administration and the ecclesiastical administration, especially in the Department of Education, which represented the epitome of the new public service philosophy of centralization and social engineering. The Quebec Catholic Church, because of the confessional character of the public schools and school boards, was by no means wholly removed from the public schools. The numerically significant number of priests and religious in education opened the Church to the influence of this new administrative culture.[49] A fair number of persons hired by the new diocesan organizations starting in 1965 had had previous experience in organizations under the jurisdiction of the Quebec Government and brought into the Church the culture of the public service. A prosopography of those active in the renewal of Church institutions during this period would illuminate the interaction between church and state in Quebec at a period when wide-ranging institutional reforms were taking place in the two institutions that encompassed Quebec society.

The diocese of Quebec was thus engaged in institutional reforms of great breadth, adopted the *pastorale d'ensemble* model, redefined its central governance organizations, established a regionalization plan and went on to a reform of its administrative procedures, all this at a time when the Quebec Government was renewing its central administrative bodies, going forward with regional planning and development, and modernizing its administrative procedures. This is not simply a matter of synchrony but of symmetrical development. We observe the same logic of action, similar institutions, closely related procedures and methods of work, and even the same administrative jargon In short, the influence of the state bureaucracy went far beyond its proper sphere of activity, as James I. Gow concludes:

its development [of the public administration] obliged institutions and groups who dealt with the administration likewise to bureaucratize themselves ... Decentralized public services were by shaken up their contacts with the provincial bureaucracy. This bureaucratization appeared as well at the intermediary level which had to restructure itself due to exchanges with the administration. This pattern appears very clearly – they sent representatives to the consultative bodies, and these direct contacts had to be preceded by studies and research that took the place normally occupied by reports or other documents of the kind.[50]

The Laity Commission and the Church: The Dumont Commission

Commissions of Inquiry are a characteristic tool of Canadian political institutions. Rising above partisan political and linguistic divides, they are thought to represent an effective means of reaching a consensus among the various elements of society and the country. Presided over by the highly respected, sheltered from the contradictory and partisan debates of parliamentary existence, they are believed to represent a means of arriving at a fundamental consideration of thorny problems. As genuine forums of opinion, they permit various constituent groups to express their views. A commission of inquiry is, in the first instance, a listening post where a range of points of view may be both expressed and heard. As a symposium where different biases, experiences, and ideas find expression, it fills the role of the *agora*, a site for exchange and discussion. It becomes a place where opinions are formed and consensus is gradually achieved.

Though the tradition of the commission of inquiry had been building since the nineteenth century,[51] James Ian Gow notes that in the 1960s in Quebec "we observe ... the creation of a record number of commissions of inquiry and study committees as well as the proliferation of study groups and consultative bodies in the administration."[52] He even remarks that "the proliferation of committees and consultative councils was such that no one knew in 1970, or even today, exactly how many there were."[53]

The Quebec Church did not remain untouched by this specifically Canadian and Quebec political tradition. Not only did the Church take part in this movement by presenting papers to the various committees set in motion, but it also contributed through the presence of the ecclesiastics who sat as commissioners.[54] During the 1960s, the Church itself adopted this style. The most famous Church commission remains the one on the laity and the Church, created by the Quebec bishops in 1968.[55] This would be the first in a series, as the Church would later return more than once to the procedure.[56] In short order, however, this commission, which was initially supposed to deal with all of Canada, limited its mandate to Quebec, a limitation that contributed to creating a gap between francophone Catholics in Quebec and those in the rest of Canada; thus, helped by the debate concerning the national question and the assimilation of francophones outside of Quebec, the development of the Quebec Catholic Church would be more and more linked to the evolution of Quebec.

The link between the political culture of Quebec and this ecclesial practice cannot be overlooked. The Quebec Church adopted institutional features that reflected the political ethos characteristic of where it was, thus freeing itself from the forms put forward by the ecclesial legislation.

The Disqualification of the Councils and Synods

In the context of a virtual *vacatio legis*,[57] all sorts of parallel organizations and divergent paths were created locally in the effervescent atmosphere of the post-Council years, so that institutions that were recommended by the Church and in due time prescribed by law would have trouble establishing themselves and reaching maturity. The presbyterial councils went through regular bursts of growth, and the pastoral councils sometimes fell into insignificance. Indeed, it was as if they were unnecessary. No one quite knew what to do with them. Most of all, they were an annoyance. There were good reasons to deal with the newer bodies that had developed parallel to the official structures and that were draining them of their substance.

Thus we see that, even before the conciliar studies had come to fruition, institutional renewal was well under way in the majority of Catholic dioceses in Quebec. As for the institutional development specifically anticipated by Vatican II, this would not be in place until the late 1960s or after. In Quebec, for example, the Presbyterial Council was created in 1967 and the Diocesan Pastoral Council would not really be baptized until 1971. The early years of the Presbyterial Council were not without crises,[58] and it would continue to bear the marks of the confusions that marked its birth. As for the second body, it never got off the ground.[59] Historically, these organizations that were called for by Vatican II came late, the restructuring of these institutions having been begun in 1960, and they would always bear the marks of the decisive influence of the reforms in Quebec governmental institutions undertaken in the same period. One could almost say that they look like tacked-on additions, lacking consistency with the other elements of the renewed Curia, following the model of the Quebec public service and unaware of conciliar developments. In 1969, just when the decisions of Vatican II were supposed to be implemented, the central pastoral coordinating body was dissolved. This consisted of a team of senior administrators, and it gathered to itself every task, such as advising the bishop, supporting the *pastorale d'ensemble*, and coordinating all the pastoral organizations in the diocese.[60] When it was dissolved in 1969, all of its prerogatives, functions, and activities were, for all practical purposes, taken over by the Pastoral Service, including proceeding "every year, after consultation, to develop an annual pastoral plan for the whole of the diocese."[61] The vertical and horizontal integration of pastoral institutions (diocesan bodies and pastoral regions) remained intact. It could be said that what distinguishes the councils coming out of Vatican II from those set up at the beginning of the 1960s is largely that they proceeded from different waves of reform, that they operated according to different kinds of logic, and conveyed distinct administrative cultures. Two institutional cultures are superimposed on one another and have a parallel existence in the diocesan organizations – one culture inspired by the modernization of the Quebec public service, the other by Vatican II.

CONCLUSION

In addition to using Vatican II as a reference point by which to understand the evolution of diocesan institutions, this study, by drawing attention to the influence of the Quiet Revolution on the Catholic Church in Quebec, situates the Quebec dioceses within a larger whole, that of Quebec society, its political culture, and the construction of its governmental structures. The Catholic Church in Quebec did not only live in the wake of Vatican II and adopt the administrative culture of the Church as a whole, it also was deeply involved in a place that would determine its evolution. It is here at the intersection of these different determinants that new features appear in the central governing institutions of the dioceses. These do not simply replicate locally the norms decreed by Roman Catholic canon law in the Latin tradition, a law worked out in Rome and with claims to universal application, but are original constructions, constantly changing, and heavily dependent on the cultural changes sweeping over Quebec. This gives rise to the reflection that the connections between the evolution of Quebec Catholicism and the Quiet Revolution are more complex than might have been first thought.

From the comparative standpoint, the innovations in the Quebec Church during the conciliar and post-conciliar periods are of interest not just to historians concerned with interregional but also with interconfessional comparison. Ecumenical dialogues, all of which broach the question of the exercise of authority in the different Christian churches, often adopt a comparative approach. But different governance systems are compared on paper and, as Jean Baubérot insists, "if, in our famous self-discussion (reformed), everything works for the best in a democratic exemplarity, the scholar can record a mixture of interesting functions and dysfunctions."[62] The interconfessional comparative analysis of how authority indeed functions can release us from that pleasant saint's tale in which Reform is the mother of democracy, Anglicanism chose the system of synodical government following the model of the British Parliament, Orthodoxy is distinguished by the reign of *sobornost*-conciliation, while Catholicism inherited an authoritarian and centralized system. Paul Harrison's discussion of how authority is wielded in the Free Baptist tradition shows that, despite the saint's tale, these churches are not decentralized and communitarian but just as centralized as the Catholic Church.[63]

For their part, the interregional comparative analyses brought out the cultural data present in the emergence of Church institutional features. It is clear that, as far as Quebec went in the second half of the twentieth century, the Catholic Church adopted a mode of functioning similar to a mode of governance common in public administrations and large companies, i.e., "administrative consultation."[64] This is the way of operating that the public administration in Quebec adopted in the early 1960s and that since has since been refined and extended to large companies.[65] This institutional mode is characterized by the fact that it is the administration itself that defines the consultative group and establishes its rules. In the process, the administration plays a key role, not only by defining who shall be consulted and how the consultation will work but also by determining the issues and even the vocabulary with which the questions submitted for consultation are posed. Thus, those consulted end up internalizing the administrations' mode of thought. In this way, the administration increases its power, rather than giving it up, succeeding in enlisting consultative practices into the service of its own ends. The instrumentalization of consultative practices ultimately deflected these institutional reforms from their original more democratic potential by nullifying the counter-power they might have possessed.

In conclusion, I would like to underline the link between the culture of a specific place and the mode of Church governance therein. This can be shown in the particular case of Quebec but also in other historical examples.[66] More specifically, a connection exists between forms of ecclesial government and the terms of political reference belonging to a given society.

Some years ago, James H. Provost noted that two concurrent models appear to be operative in the Catholic Church – one a European type, the other North American.[67] In his view, the organization and functioning of the diocesan apparatus in the United States belongs to a particular type that he terms "business oriented." He notes that this development is in broad contrast to legislative proposals that tend to follow a European model or the "governmental policy" model. What exactly do we have in Quebec? The first model corresponds quite well to what we have seen in Quebec, even if this one seems inspired more by the large public services. Does this mean that, in terms of Catholic administrative structure, Quebec possesses what is in fact an expression of a distinct society within North America?

NOTES

1 On the subject of Vatican II as the occasion of Catholic modernization, see P. Hünermann, ed., *Das II Vatikanium – christlicher Glaube im Horizont globaler Modernisierung* (Paderborn: Schöningh, 1998).

2 The reactions to third-period conciliar work in twelve different countries has been analysed, for example. See *Paolo VI e I Problemi eclesiologici al Concilio, Brescia*, 431–560, where a number of analyses of press coverage and public opinion during the third period in Belgium, the Netherlands, Chili, France, Germany, Great Britain, Italy, Poland, Spain, Switzerland, the United States, and the USSR may be found.

3 See K. Rahner, "Theologische Grundinterpretationen des II. Vatikanischen Konzil," *Schriften zur Theologie*, 14 (1980): 73–195.

4 G. Routhier, "Portare a termine l'opera iniziata: la faticosa esperienza del quarto periodo," in G. Alberigo, ed., *Storia del Concilio Vaticano II*, vol. 5, *Concilio di transizione settembre-dicembre 1965*, Peeters/Il Mulion, 2001, 73–195.

5 See Jan Grootaers, "Le catholicisme du Québec et son insertion dans le milieu conciliare," in G. Routhier, ed., *Vatican II en Canada* (Montreal: Fides, 2001), 447–76.

6 Comparisons may be made between the responses of the Québec bishops and those in the rest of Canada. See G. Routhier, "Les *vota* des évêques du Québec," 25–60; M.A. Fahey, "A Vatican Request for Agenda Items Prior to Vatican II: Responses by Canadian Bishops," 61–72; and "A Vatican Request for Agenda Items Prior to Vatican II: Responses from Canadian Faculties of Theology," in G. Routhier, ed., *L'Église canadienne et Vatican II* (Montreal: Fides, 1997).

7 On these pre-conciliar consultations, see P. Lafontaine, "La consultation préconciliare de l'archidiocèse de Montréal auprès du clergé: portrait d'une Église," 81–98; P. Allaire, "La consultation du clergé de Québec," 99–112; S. Serré, "Les consultations préconciliaires des laïcs au Québec entre 1959 et 1962," 113–41, in G. Routhier, ed., *L'Église canadienne et Vatican II*. See as well P. Allaire, "La consultation du clergé des diocèses de Rimouski, Saint-Jean-de-Québec, Saint-Jérôme et Sherbrooke," in G. Routhier, ed., *Évêques du Québec (1962–1965): Entre Révolution*

tranquille et aggiornamento conciliaire (Québec: CIEQ, 2002): 4–11; and the MA theses by S. Serré, *Les consultations préconciliaires au Québec* (Université Laval, 1998) and Raymond Martel, *Un évêque à Vatican II, Mgr Albert Sanschagrin* (Université Laval, 2000).

8 For an initial survey, see my article, "Assurer la couverture du concile Vatican II au Canada: Les initiatives de l'épiscopat canadien," *Études d'histoire religieuse*, 68 (2002): 57–72.

9 The Canadian bishops held weekly meetings in Rome, in order to form an opinion about the matters being discussed in Council. The francophones met together while the anglophones formed another group. Only a few bishops worked in both groups, which operated quite independently.

10 See G. Routhier, "L'annonce et la préparation de Vatican II: réception et horizon d'attente au Québec," *Études d'histoire religieuse*, 63 (1997): 25–44.

11 Studies of the Québec press are already quite far along. In addition to the MA thesis by Charles-Étienne Guillemette now under way, also available is the MA thesis by Y. Therrien (Université Laval, 1997), *La couverture de presse de Vatican II dans les quotidiens francophones du Canada*, part of which appears as well in Y. Therrien, "La couverture de Vatican II dans les quotidiens francophones du Canada (1959–1962)," in *L'église canadienne et Vatican II*, 145–64. See also the MA thesis by R. Martel that deals with coverage in the weekly press of a region (Abitibi), as well as J.-P. Proulx, "Le quotidien *Le Devoir* et l'aggiornamento conciliaire: (1960–1970)," *Études d'histoire religieuse* (1997): 45–57; R. Plamondon, "Le service d'information de la CCC à Vatican II" et P. Hurtubise, "Vatican II: propos d'un témoin engagé in *L'Église canadienne...*, respectively: 209–22 and 223–34. Coverage in reviews and magazines may also be added. For these see J.-C. Dupuis, "La revue 'Relations' et le Concile Vatican II," *Les Cahiers d'histoire du Québec au XXᵉ siècle*, 6 (Autumn 1996): 33–50; G. Baillargeon, "Les intellectuels québécois et Vatican II: de l'annonce du concile à son ouverture (1959–1962)," in *L'Église canadienne et Vatican II*, 189–208, and "'De la cathédrale au chantier!': Les intellectuels québécois et Vatican II (1963–1966)," in G. Routhier, ed., *Vatican II au Canada: enracinement et réception* (Montreal: Fides, 2001): 273–93.

12 In addition to the studies of press coverage in various countries already mentioned, there are also the more detailed work by D. Beloeil, *La réception du concile oecuménique Vatican II dans les médias: l'exemple du diocèse de Nantes (1959–1965)* (University of Nantes, 1998); D. Beloeil et M. Lagrée, "Le catholicisme breton devant le concile," in É. Fouilloux,, ed. *Vatican II commence... Approches Francophones* (Leuven: Bibliotheek van Faculteit der Godgeleerdheid, 1993): 262–74.

13 See G. Routhier, "Hopes for the Preparatory Period of Vatican II," *Celebrate*, 42, 3 (2003): 10–15; "The Liturgical Renewal of Vatican II in Canada, *Celebrate*, 42, 2 (2003): 8–13.

14 It organized training sessions on 15–17 October 1963 at Maison Montmorency (Quebec), 19–22 January 1965 in Ville LaSalle (Montreal), and 19–21 October 1965 at Châteauguay Station (Montreal).

15 On this question, see the article by Angel Unzuetta (in press), in G. Routhier, ed., *La réception de Vatican II: méthodes et approches* (Leuven: Biblioteek van Faculteit der Godgerleerdheid).

16 Ecumenism developed exceptionally in Montreal in this period, while this concern remained in the background in the rest of Canada, except in Manitoba. See G. Routhier et R. Burigana, "La conversion œcuménique d'un évêque et d'une Église: Le parcours œcuménique du cardinal Léger et de l'Église de Montréal au moment de Vatican II. – I. Les premiers ébranlements. II. L'engagement résolu," *Science et Esprit*, 52, 2 (2000): 171–92, and 52, 3 (2000): 293–319.

17 The fifteen-page document was produced in Rome and dated 29 October.

18 Ibid., 5.

19 Ibid.

20 Ibid.

21 CCC, "Lendemain au concile," 17 November 1965, ref. 99.

22 The results of this consultation are compiled in CCC, "Lendemain au concile," 17 November 1965, ref. 99, 11 pages. In addition to supplying the results of the consultation, the document provides three appendices and five pages of commentary.

23 CCC, "Lendemain au concile," 17 November 1965, ref. 99.

24 This was a very brief text of one page. We found it in both an English and a French version in the archives of the CCC.

25 Moreover, there is no collective pastoral letter of the Canadian bishops in the Centro Francescano collection, "Lettere pastorali 1964–1965. Il Concilio ecumenico Vaticano II," Edizioni Esca Vicenza.

26 Only Mgr Caza, in a pastoral letter to his priests for the end of the Council, raised the possibility of a Canadian council in ten years. No other bishop mentioned it publicly. This does, however, suggest that in mid-December, the idea was still around. It was later that the plan was abandoned.

27 CCC, "Programme postconciliare," 8 February 1966, ref. 121, 2 pages.

28 *Vatican II. Les seize documents conciliares* (Montreal: Fides, 1966).

29 The proceedings of this colloquium have been published in L.K. Shook and G.M. Bertrand, eds, *La théologie du renouveau*, 2 vols (Paris: Cerf, 1968).

30 CCC, "Les diocèses et leurs activités postconciliaires," 24 February 1966, ref. 139, 3 pages.

31 See my article, "Les défis de l'Église," in S. Courville and R. Caron, eds, *Québec ville et capitale*, coll. Atlas historique du Québec (Quebec: PUL, 2001): 280–91.

32 On 12 February 1961, the Catholic review *Témoignage chrétien* published a survey undertaken in the daily papers *Le Monde*, *Ouest-France*, and *Le Nouveau-Rhin*

Français. It wished to find out what questions were most of interest to the laity on the eve of the Council. A few European Catholic reviews, *Tygodnik powszechny* (Poland), *Katolsk Uglebad* (Denmark), and *L'Anneau d'Or* and *Chronique Sociale* (France), also held consultations with the laity. In a different vein, there was a survey organized by the French Institute of Public Opinion concerning the aims of the Council. It merely wanted to know if the French were aware that a council was about to take place.

33 José de Broucker, *Informations Catholiques Internationales*, 15 June 1962, 20.

34 Armand Beaudoin, "Nous sommes invités au concile," *L'Écho d'Amos*, 13, 20 (17 May 1962): 4.

35 PUL, 1963.

36 This was replaced in 1968 by two bodies, the Office de planification et de développement du Québec (OPDQ) and the Conseil de planification et de développement du Québec.

37 On planning in Quebec, see J. I. Gow, *Histoire de l'Administration publique québécoise, 1867–1970* (Montreal: Les Presses de l'Université de Montréal, 1986): 302–7; J. Benjamin, *Planification et politique au Québec* (Montreal: PUM, 1974); A. Baccigalupo, "Administrations publiques territoriales et planification régionale dans la province de Québec," *Revue administrative* 25 (1972): 61–5; J. Leblanc, "Le conseil d'orientation économique du Québec," *Relations industrielles* 18, 1 (1963): 110–20; M. Lord et G. Daoust, "Le gouvernement du Québec et la planification," *La Presse*, 13–15 March 1969; R. Parenteau, "L'expérience de la planification au Québec," *Actualité économique*, 24, 4 (1970): 679–96.

38 Such plans were also developed for the northwest, the Saguenay, and Lac Saint Jean. See Gow, *Histoire*, 304–10; see also Baccigalupo.

39 Gow, *Histoire*, 308.

40 See for example extracts from a text by Roland Doyon describing the objectives of the *Grande Mission*: it intended "to establish a pastoral ministry that would gather all the forces of the Charlevoix Church around the Bishop, coordinate them and orient them according to a evangelization plan." Later, he says, "Before operating in the field and establishing an evangelization plan, it was necessary to develop a synthesizing and explanatory view...of the socio-religious universe in question." R. Doyon, "La Grande Mission de Charlevoix," *La Semaine religieuse de Québec* 41 (11 June 1964): 654–8.

41 The word "coordination" or its derivatives appear nine times in two pages in a circular letter to the clergy announcing a new pastoral diocesan council. It fits very nicely with those other bewitching terms like "plan" and "consult" that accompany it in the same paragraph. In the first draft of the letter, it appeared four times in two pages. See "Projet de circulaire 1," 4–5; 2, 2–3, AAQ 1J. The term "coordination" is the one that appears most frequently in documents relative to the diocesan Pastoral

Council between 1963 and 1966. It occurs ten times in nine pages in the "Mémoire Doyon" and six times in three pages in an article by Claude Bélanger.

42 In 1962, a General Pastoral Commission was struck, from which derived the *Grande Mission* Secretariat and the Diocesan Catholic Action Committee; in 1963 came the Diocesan Pastoral Council; in 1968, the Secretariat of the *pastoral d'ensemble*; in 1969, the creation of the Pastoral Service; and, in 1970, the Organizations Committee and the Regions Committee.

43 R. Doyon, "La Grande Mission de Charlevoix," 17 April 1963, 2, AAQ, Grande Mission, 1S.

44 The final Diocesan Pastoral Council was assigned the tasks of "reflection ... study ... inviting specialists ... calling upon informed persons ... submitting reports ... to determine future objectives and distance them from the pastoral and arrange them into a overall plan." C. Bélanger, "Le Conseil diocésan de pastorale," *L'Église de Québec*, 15 (14 April 1966). It was nothing other than a mandate that could have come from a Planning Board.

45 A broadcasting techniques office was opened in the diocese of Québec in 1962. The *Grande Mission* would be the first diocesan operation to utilize a new communication tactic in the diocese. The second circular announcing the creation of the Diocesan Pastoral Council referred to the use of these new sciences and techniques: "Just as precious an aid for the Church as the progress of the human sciences such as sociology, psychology, pedagogy, etc, science that can provide much help in understanding man and lighting the Church's path ... The Church takes advantage of all of these. Moreover, it is now able even to use means like the press and film, radio and television, to holy ends." "Circulaire, projet 2." The government likewise established a Quebec office to deal with information and publicity, which reorganized the old provincial publicity office, giving it a new mandate.

46 C. Bélanger, "Le conseil diocésain de pastorale." This passage may be compared to this passage from "Mémoire Doyon" (March 1965): "Setting up a *pastorale d'ensemble* is to *work for the cure of souls in a planned and communal fashion*. What best characterizes the *pastorale d'ensemble* is ... the organization that it proposes to establish ..." (AAQ 21J).

47 This was order 524. This revision of the administrative map began in 1961 in the Department of Industry and Commerce with the creation of fourteen industrial development territories. See Baccigalupo, "Administrations publiques," 61–5; see also J.I. Gow, *Administration publique québécoise* (Montreal: Beauchemin, 1970): 241–53.

48 "Mémoire Doyon," 4. See also " Conseil diocésain de pastorale. Rapport global de ses activités depuis ses débuts" (AAQ, 1J).

49 This presence made itself felt as well in the colleges and universities and in school administration itself as much on the regional level as on the administrative level of the Department of Education. The presence of representatives of the Church on the

Board's consultative bodies as well as on the Superior Council on Education and the Catholic Committee is important. A more complete study of the links between the Quebec Catholic Church and the public administration remains to be done.

50 J.I. Gow, *Histoire*, 364.

51 Shortly after Confederation, there was a Royal Commission of Inquiry on the relation between capital and labour (1886–89). Later, in the first third of the twentieth century, the commission on the civil rights of women distinguished itself by its work. Since then, commissions of inquiry have multiplied. To get some idea of their popularity, see the list of Commissions of Inquiry held in the postwar period provided by R. Boily in *Québec 1940–1969: bibliographie* (Montreal: Presses de l'Université de Montréal, 1971): 160–9. Additionally, see A. Bazinet, *Les Commissions d'enquête du Québec (1960 à 1966) comme organisme d'étude et de consultation*, MA thesis (Université de Montréal, 1976).

52 J.I. Gow, *Histoire*, 297. See previous remarks on Commissions of Inquiry. In addition to the bibliography already noted, see A. Bazinet, *Les Commissions d'enquête du Québec (l960 à l966) comme organisme d'étude et de consultation*, MA thesis (Université de Montréal, 1976).

53 Gow, *Histoire*, 301. See the table provided on page 498. Gélinas counts 43. However, in addition to the announced bodies, there are all those whose existence is unknown.

54 Very famous were Mgr Alphonse-Marie Parent, the Vicar General of the Quebec diocese, who presided over a Royal Commission on Education from 1961 to 1964, Fr Paul Lacoste, who participated in the Commission on Bilingualism and Biculturalism, and Fr Georges-Henri Lévesque, co-chair of the Royal Commission on National Development in the Arts, Letters, and Sciences.

55 This Commission published five documents in addition to its report. See particularly *L'Église du Québec, un héritage et un projet* (Montreal: Fides, 1971).

56 For example, in the 1980s, after the revised code of canon law came into force, the diocese of Quebec would launch three commissions of inquiry: in 1984, the "Justice and Faith" commission; again in 1985, when it came to discussing pastoral reorganization, the Presbyteral Council could make no better recommendation to the Archbishop than to convene a diocesan study commission; finally, in 1986, when a Study Commission was also charged with reporting on the liturgical situation of the diocese, twenty-five years after *Sacrosanctum Concilium*. The same situation obtained in other dioceses.

57 It was evident that, following Vatican II, a good number of the legal prescriptions of the Latin Rite of the Roman Catholic Church that were promulgated in 1917 could no longer be applied. It was, however, necessary to wait until 1983 before a new code of Canon Law would be promulgated. In the interval, a situation of *vacatio legis* virtually reigned, and special laws had no trouble developing.

58 The bylaws of the Presbyterial Council were revised in January 1969 and April 1970. Relaunched in 1971 after a number of constitutional drafts, it sputtered along and never completely recovered from the crisis it had passed through from 1968 to 1971.

59 The first Diocesan Pastoral Council (CDP) was dissolved in the autumn of 1968, "leaving to a special committee the task of working out a new constitution. After seven or eight successive drafts, the constitution of the 'second' CDP was achieved, adopted in January 1969 and completed by two revisions by the Presbyterial Council in January 1969 and April 1970." See, "Le Conseil diocésan de pastorale," 26 May 1971, vol. 9–6. The new CDP was in fact a federation of four councils: religious, laity, regions, and organizations. "This federation has power of its own. Instead, it is only a place for exchanges...." (ibid.) "In June 1970, a new proposal structured the CDP more specifically ... This proposal was rejected by the general assembly of the CDP in February 1971..." ("Le conseil diocésain de pastorale," 26 May 1971, vol. 9–6), which struck a provisional committee to restructure a new CDP. A new constitution was presented on 31 May, approved on 8 June 1971, ratified the same day by Cardinal Roy, and printed on page 16 of *Pastorale-Québec* 12, 24 June 1971. It was later amended on 10 August 1972 and 11 June 1975.

60 See C. Béanger, "Le Conseil diocésan," 209.

61 "Conseil diocésan de pastorale. Rapport global," 2.

62 Jean Baubérot, "Protestantisme et démocratie," in J. Famerée, ed., *Démocratie dans les Églises* (Bruxelles: Lumen Vitae, 1999): 94.

63 Paul Harrison, *Authority and Power in the Free Church Tradition. A Social Study of the American Baptist Convention* (Princeton: Princeton University Press, 1959).

64 For a good idea of this, see Y. Weber, *L'administration consultative* (Paris: LGDJ, 1968).

65 For its application in the public sector in Québec, see A. Baccigalupo, "L'administration consultative au Québec," *Revue administrative*, 178 (1977), 409–20; Léon Dion, "Politique consultative et système politique," *Revue canadienne de science politique*, 2 (June 1969): 226–44; A. Gélinas, *Organismes autonomes et centraux*, 103–9 and 144–55.

66 See especially R. Campiche, F. Baatard, G. Vincent et J.-P. Willaime, *L'exercice du pouvoir dans le protestantisme, les conseillers de paroisse de France et de Suisse* (Genève: Labor et Fides, 1990).

67 See "Diocesan Administration: Reflections on Recent Developments," *The Jurist* 41 (1981): 83, 93–6, 103. The author explains this type of development by reason of the US experience of the separation of church and state (83) or by "the commercialist mood of the Country itself" (95). We have identified another type of influence in Quebec that has produced effects quite similar to those that Provost describes.

About the Authors

BRIGITTE CAULIER is professor, Department of History, Université Laval, and director of the Centre interuniversitaire des études québécoises. Her interests have ranged extensively in the field of Quebec religion and culture, from major studies of popular devotions to her current research on nineteenth- and twentieth-century religious education.

NANCY CHRISTIE is a research associate, Frost Centre for Canadian and Native Studies, Trent University, Peterborough, and the award-winning author of *A Full-Orbed Christianity: The Protestant Churches and Social Welfare in Canada* and *Engendering the State: Family, Work, and Welfare in Canada*. Her current research centres on the history of gender and the family in Canada, 1760–1900.

KENNETH DRAPER is senior vice-president (Academics) and professor of history, Alliance University College, Calgary. His research has centred on the changing structure of Protestant religious discourse in late-nineteenth-century Canadian urban communities.

JEAN-MARIE FECTEAU is professor, Département d'histoire, Université du Québec à Montréal, and director of the Centre d'histoire des regulations sociales. He is the author of major studies of the changing modes of regulating crime and poverty in Quebec, most notably *Un nouvel ordre des choses: la pauvreté, le crime, l'État au Québec, de la fin du XVIIIᵉ siècle à 1840* and *La liberté du pauvre: sur la régulation du crime et de la pauvreté au XIXᵉ siècle québécois*.

MICHAEL GAUVREAU is professor, Department of History, McMaster University, and author of numerous works in the history of religion, including *The Evangelical Century: College and Creed in English Canada from the Great Revival to the Great Depression*, *A Full-Orbed Christianity: The Protestant Churches and Social Welfare in Canada*, and *The Catholic Origins of Quebec's Quiet Revolution, 1931–1970*.

OLLIVIER HUBERT is associate professor, Département d'histoire, Université de Montréal, and author of the award-winning *Sur la terre comme au ciel: la gestion des rites par l'Église catholique du Québec (fin XVIIe siècle – mi-XIXe siècle)*. His research has ranged widely in the religious and cultural history of Quebec, exploring the themes of the representation of gender, honour, and power from the late eighteenth to the early nineteenth centuries.

CHRISTINE HUDON is associate professor, Département d'histoire et de sciences politiques, Université de Sherbrooke. Author of the award-winning *Prêtres et fidèles dans le Diocèse de Saint-Hyacinthe, 1820–1870*, her current research centres on the construction of gender identities in Quebec's Catholic educational system in the nineteenth and twentieth centuries.

HANNAH LANE is a member of the Department of History, University of New Brunswick. Her numerous publications centre on the intersection of gender and religious identity in the Maritimes.

ROBERTO PERIN is associate professor, Department of History, York University. His publications include *Rome in Canada: The Vatican and Canadian Affairs in The Late-Victorian Age* and *A Concise History of Christianity in Canada*, as well as numerous studies exploring the intersection between religion, immigration, and ethnic identity in Canada.

GILLES ROUTHIER is professor, Faculté de théologie, Université Laval, and is a leading specialist on the comparative international Catholic response to the Second Vatican Council. His interests have ranged widely in the field of religious history, from the development of theological education to the transformation of the Quebec Catholic Church in the period after the Second World War.

ÉRIC VAILLANCOURT is currently a member of the Département d'histoire, Université du Québec à Montréal, and has recently completed a thesis exploring the Catholic charitable impulse in nineteenth- and early-twentieth-century Quebec.